Glencoe Science From Bacteria to Plants
Contents in Brief

Teacher Wraparound Edition

Student Edition

D1716192

SAFETY SYMBOLS

SAFETY SYMBOLS	HAZARD	EXAMPLES	PRECAUTION	REMEDY
DISPOSAL	Special disposal procedures need to be followed.	certain chemicals, living organisms	Do not dispose of these materials in the sink or trash can.	Dispose of wastes as directed by your teacher.
BIOLOGICAL	Organisms or other biological materials that might be harmful to humans	bacteria, fungi, blood, unpreserved tissues, plant materials	Avoid skin contact with these materials. Wear mask or gloves.	Notify your teacher if you suspect contact with material. Wash hands thoroughly.
EXTREME TEMPERATURE	Objects that can burn skin by being too cold or too hot	boiling liquids, hot plates, dry ice, liquid nitrogen	Use proper protection when handling.	Go to your teacher for first aid.
SHARP OBJECT	Use of tools or glassware that can easily puncture or slice skin	razor blades, pins, scalpels, pointed tools, dissecting probes, broken glass	Practice common-sense behavior and follow guidelines for use of the tool.	Go to your teacher for first aid.
FUME	Possible danger to respiratory tract from fumes	ammonia, acetone, nail polish remover, heated sulfur, moth balls	Make sure there is good ventilation. Never smell fumes directly. Wear a mask.	Leave foul area and notify your teacher immediately.
ELECTRICAL	Possible danger from electrical shock or burn	improper grounding, liquid spills, short circuits, exposed wires	Double-check setup with teacher. Check condition of wires and apparatus.	Do not attempt to fix electrical problems. Notify your teacher immediately.
IRRITANT	Substances that can irritate the skin or mucous membranes of the respiratory tract	pollen, moth balls, steel wool, fiberglass, potassium permanganate	Wear dust mask and gloves. Practice extra care when handling these materials.	Go to your teacher for first aid.
CHEMICAL	Chemicals that can react with and destroy tissue and other materials	bleaches such as hydrogen peroxide; acids such as sulfuric acid, hydrochloric acid; bases such as ammonia, sodium hydroxide	Wear goggles, gloves, and an apron.	Immediately flush the affected area with water and notify your teacher.
TOXIC	Substance may be poisonous if touched, inhaled, or swallowed	mercury, many metal compounds, iodine, poinsettia plant parts	Follow your teacher's instructions.	Always wash hands thoroughly after use. Go to your teacher for first aid.
OPEN FLAME	Open flame may ignite flammable chemicals, loose clothing, or hair	alcohol, kerosene, potassium permanganate, hair, clothing	Tie back hair. Avoid wearing loose clothing. Avoid open flames when using flammable chemicals. Be aware of locations of fire safety equipment.	Notify your teacher immediately. Use fire safety equipment if applicable.

Eye Safety
Proper eye protection should be worn at all times by anyone performing or observing science activities.

Clothing Protection
This symbol appears when substances could stain or burn clothing.

Animal Safety
This symbol appears when safety of animals and students must be ensured.

Radioactivity
This symbol appears when radioactive materials are used.

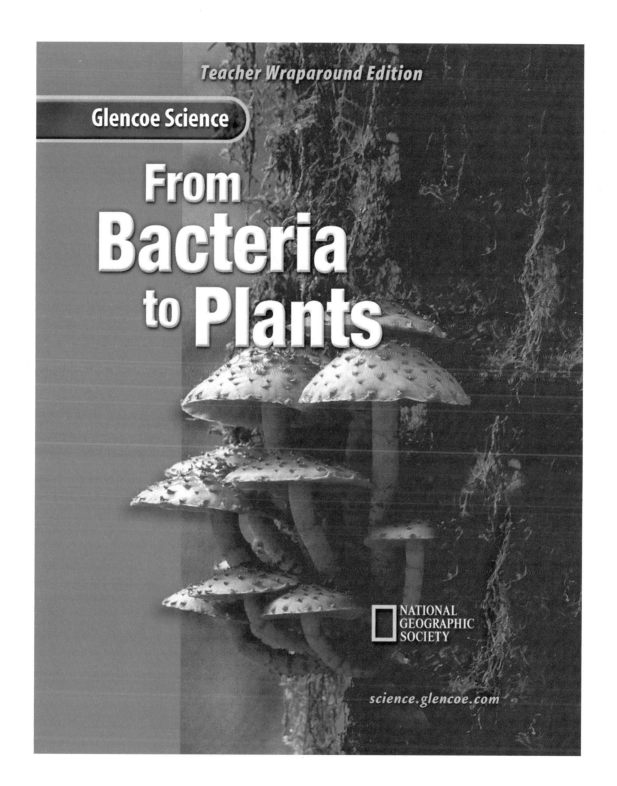

Teacher Wraparound Edition

Glencoe Science

From Bacteria to Plants

NATIONAL GEOGRAPHIC SOCIETY

science.glencoe.com

Glencoe McGraw-Hill

New York, New York   Columbus, Ohio   Woodland Hills, California   Peoria, Illinois

GLENCOE SCIENCE
From Bacteria to Plants

Student Edition
Teacher Wraparound Edition
Interactive Teacher Edition CD-ROM
Interactive Lesson Planner CD-ROM
Lesson Plans
Content Outline for Teaching
Directed Reading for Content Mastery
Foldables: Reading and Study Skills
Assessment
  Chapter Review
  Chapter Tests
  ExamView® Pro Test Bank Software
  Assessment Transparencies
  Performance Assessment in the Science Classroom
  The Princeton Review Test Practice Booklet
Directed Reading for Content Mastery in Spanish
Spanish Resources
English/Spanish Guided Reading Audio Program
Reinforcement
Enrichment

Activity Worksheets
Section Focus Transparencies
Teaching Transparencies
Laboratory Activities
Science Inquiry Labs
Critical Thinking/Problem Solving
Reading and Writing Skill Activities
Mathematics Skill Activities
Cultural Diversity
*Laboratory Management and Safety in the
  Science Classroom*
MindJogger Videoquizzes and Teacher Guide
Interactive CD-ROM with Presentation Builder
Vocabulary PuzzleMaker Software
Cooperative Learning
Environmental Issues in the Science Classroom
Home and Community Involvement
Using the Internet in the Science Classroom
Dinah Zike's Teaching Science with Foldables

THE PRINCETON REVIEW

"Test-Taking Tip," "Study Tip," and "Test Practice" features in this book were written by The Princeton Review, the nation's leader in test preparation. Through its association with McGraw-Hill, The Princeton Review offers the best way to help students excel on standardized assessments.

The Princeton Review is not affiliated with Princeton University or Educational Testing Service.

Glencoe/McGraw-Hill

A Division of The McGraw-Hill Companies

Send all inquiries to:

Glencoe/McGraw-Hill
8787 Orion Place
Columbus, OH 43240

ISBN 0-07-825561-9

Printed in the United States of America
2 3 4 5 6 7 8 9 10 027/043 10 09 08 07 06 05 04 03 02

Authors, Reviewers, and Consultants

for the *15-Book Series*

Authors

National Geographic Society
Education Division
Washington, D.C.

Alton Biggs
Biology Teacher
Allen High School
Allen, Texas

Lucy Daniel, PhD
Teacher/Consultant
Rutherford County Schools
Rutherfordton, North Carolina

Cathy Ezrailson
Science Department Head
Academy for Science and Health
Professions
Conroe, Texas

Ralph M. Feather Jr., PhD
Science Department Chair
Derry Area School District
Derry, Pennsylvania

Nicholas Hainen
Chemistry/Physics Teacher
Worthington City Schools
Worthington, Ohio

Patricia Horton
Mathematics/Science Teacher
Summit Intermediate School
Etiwanda, California

Norman G. Lederman, PhD
Professor of Science and Math
Education
Oregon State University
Corvallis, Oregon

Deborah Lillie
Math and Science Writer
Sudbury, Massachusetts

Thomas McCarthy, PhD
Science Department Chair
St. Edwards School
Vero Beach, Florida

Edward Ortleb
Science Consultant
St. Louis Public Schools
St. Louis, Missouri

Susan Leach Snyder
Earth Science Teacher,
Consultant
Jones Middle School
Upper Arlington, Ohio

Peter Rillero, PhD
Professor of Science Education
Arizona State University West
Phoenix, Arizona

Eric Werwa, PhD
Department of Physics and
Astronomy
Otterbein College
Westerville, Ohio

Dinah Zike
Educational Consultant
Dinah-Might Activities, Inc.
San Antonio, Texas

Margaret K. Zorn
Science Writer
Yorktown, Virginia

Reviewers

Sandra K. Enger, PhD
Coordinator
UAH Institute for Science Education
Huntsville, Alabama

Lee Meadows, PhD
Associate Professor of Science Education
University of Alabama
Birmingham, Alabama

Gilbert Naizer, PhD
Assistant Professor of Elementary Education
Texas A&M University
Commerce, Texas

Kimberly S. Roempler, PhD
Associate Director
Eisenhower National Clearinghouse
for Math and Science
The Ohio State University
Columbus, Ohio

Cultural Diversity Consultants

Nedaro Bellamy
Associate Director,
Rice Model Science Laboratory
Lanier Middle School, Houston ISD
Houston, Texas

Joyce Hilliard-Clark, PhD
Director, Imhotep Academy
North Carolina State University
Raleigh, North Carolina

Inclusion Strategies Consultant

Barry Barto
Special Education Teacher
John F. Kennedy Elementary School
Manistee, Michigan

Introducing the
Glencoe Science 15-Book Series

Teach science your way!

With the 15 Life, Earth, and Physical Science titles in our modular series, you can select the science topics you want to cover and customize your science curriculum in any way you choose.

The Glencoe 15-Book Series provides:

- Flexibility—you can easily meet your curriculum requirements.
- Convenience—the books are easy for students to carry and ideal for whenever locker space isn't available.
- A sense of accomplishment—as students complete each book, they can see the progress they're making.

A Life's Structure and Function

1 Exploring and Classifying Life
2 Cells
3 Cell Processes
4 Cell Reproduction
5 Heredity
6 Adaptations Over Time

B From Bacteria to Plants

1 Bacteria
2 Protists and Fungi
3 Plants
4 Plant Reproduction
5 Plant Processes

C Animal Diversity

1 Introduction to Animals
2 Mollusks, Worms, Arthropods, Echinoderms
3 Fish, Amphibians, and Reptiles
4 Birds and Mammals
5 Animal Behavior

D Human Body Systems

1 Structure and Support
2 Nutrients and Digestion
3 Circulation
4 Respiration and Excretion
5 Control and Coordination
6 Regulation and Reproduction
7 Immunity and Disease

E Ecology

1 Interactions of Life
2 The Nonliving Environment
3 Ecosystems
4 Conserving Resources
5 Conserving Life

Correlation to **Benchmarks**

The five **Life Science** books in the *15-Book Series* address many of the Benchmarks for Science Literacy. These benchmarks are presented in *Benchmarks for Science Literacy*, a publication of the American Association for the Advancement of Science.

A	Life's Structure and Function
B	From Bacteria to Plants
C	Animal Diversity
D	Human Body Systems
E	Ecology

Benchmark	Book and Chapter
4 **The Physical Setting**	
4B. The Earth	A6, C1, E2, E3
4C. Processes That Shape the Earth	A6, E2, E4
4D. Structure of Matter	A3, E2
4E. Energy Transformation	A3, B5, E1, E3
5 **The Living Environment**	
5A. Diversity of Life	A1, A2, A5, B1, B2, B3, B4, B5, C1, C2, C3, C4, E5
5B. Heredity	A4, A5, B4
5C. Cells	A2, A3, A4, B1, B2, C1, D7
5D. Interdependence of Life	B1, B2, B4, C1, C2, C4, C5
5E. Flow of Matter and Energy	A3, B1, B2, B5, E1, E2, E3, E4, E5
5F. Evolution of Life	A1, A4, A5, A6, B1, B2, B3, C1, C2, C3, C4, D7
6 **The Human Organism**	
6A. Human Identity	D1, D2, D3, D4, D5, D6, D7
6B. Human Development	D6
6C. Basic Functions	C5, D1, D2, D3, D4, D5, D6, D7
6D. Learning	C5, D5
6E. Physical Health	B1, B2, C1, D1, D2, D3, D4, D5, D6, D7
8 **The Designed World**	
8F. Health Technology	A2, A5, B1, B2, C1, D1, D2, D3, D4, D5, D6, D7
9 **The Mathematical World**	
9A. Numbers	All Math Skills and Problem-Solving Activities
9B. Symbolic Relationships	All Math Skills and Problem-Solving Activities
9C. Reasoning	All Math Skills and Problem-Solving Activities
10 **Historical Perspectives**	
10G. Explaining the Diversity of Life	A1, A4, A5, C1, C2, C3, C4
10I. Discovering Germs	A2, B1
12 **Habits of Mind**	
12A. Values and Attitudes	A1, All "Oops, Accidents in Science!," "Science and History," and "Science and Language Arts" features
12B. Computation and Estimation	Math Skills and Problem-Solving Activities
12D. Communication Skills	All Activities and Skill Builders

Correlation to National Science Education Standards

The following chart illustrates how the five **Life Science** books in the *15-Book Series* address the National Science Education Standards.

Content Standard	Book, Chapter, and Section
(UCP) Unifying Concepts and Processes	
1. Systems, order, and organization	A1-4, A2-1, A2-2, A3-3, B2-1, B2-2, B3-1, B5-1, B5-2, D1-1, D1-2, D1-3, D2-2, D3-1, D4-1, D4-2, D5-1, D5-2, D6-1, D6-2, D7-1, E1-1, E1-2, E1-3, E2-1, E2-2, E2-3, E3-1, E3-2, E3-3, E5-1, E5-2
2. Evidence, models, and explanation	A1-1, A1-2, A1-3, A3-1, A5-1, A5-2, A5-3, B1-2, D7-2, E4-1, E4-2, E4-3
3. Change, constancy, and measurement	A4-1, A4-2, A4-3, B4-1, C2-1, C2-2, C2-3, C2-4, C3-1, C3-2, C3-3, C3-4, C4-1, C4-2, C5-1, C5-2, D2-1, D6-2, E3-1
4. Evolution and equilibrium	A3-2, A4-2, A4-3, A6-1, A6-2, A6-3, D7-3, E5-1, E5-2
5. Form and function	A2-1, A2-3, B1-1, B2-1, B2-2, B3-2, B3-3, B4-2, B4-3, C1-1, C1-2, C1-3, D3-2, D3-3, D6-1, D6-3
(A) Science as Inquiry	
1. Abilities necessary to do scientific inquiry	A1-1, A1-4, A2-1, A2-2, A2-3, A3-1, A3-2, A3-3, A4-1, A4-3, A5-1, A5-2, A5-3, A6-1, A6-3, B1-1, B1-2, B2-1, B2-2, B3-2, B3-3, B4-1, B4-2, B4-3, B5-1, B5-2, C1-1, C1-2, C1-3, C2-3, C2-4, C3-1, C3-2, C3-3, C3-4, C4-1, C4-2, C5-1, C5-2, D1-1, D1-2, D1-3, D2-1, D2-2, D3-1, D3-2, D3-3, D4-1, D4-2, , D5-1, D5-2, D6-2, D6-3, D7-1, D7-2, D7-3, E1-1, E1-2, E1-3, E2-1, E2-2, E2-3, E3-2, E3-3, E4-1, E4-2, E4-3, E5-1, E5-2
2. Understandings about scientific inquiry	A1-1, A1-3, A1-4, A6-1, C5-2
(B) Physical Science	
1. Properties and changes of properties in matter	A1-1, A3-1, E2-2, E2-3
2. Motions and forces	D1-1, D1-2, E2-3
3. Transfer of energy	A3-3, E2-3
(C) Life Science	
1. Structure and function in living systems	A1-2, A1-3, A1-4, A2-1, A2-2, A2-3, A3-1, A3-2, A3-3, A4-1, A4-3, A6-1, A6-2, A6-3, B1-1, B2-1, B2-2, B3-1, B3-2, B3-3, B4-1, B4-2, B4-3, B5-1, B5-2, C1-1, C1-2, C1-3, C2-1, C2-2, C2-3, C2-4, C3-1, C3-2, C3-3, C3-4, C4-1, C4-2, D1-1, D1-2, D1-3, D2-1, D2-2, D3-1, D3-2, D3-3, D4-1, D4-2, D5-1, D5-2, D6-1, D6-2, D6-3, D7-1, D7-2, D7-3, E1-1, E1-2, E1-3, E2-1, E2-2, E2-3, E5-1, E5-2
2. Reproduction and heredity	A2-3, A4-2, A4-3, A5-1, A5-2, A5-3, A6-1, A6-2, A6-3, B1-1, B2-2, B4-1, B4-2, B4-3, C2-3, C3-2, C3-3, C3-4, C4-1, C4-2, C5-2, D6-2, D6-3
3. Regulation and behavior	A3-2, B1-1, B5-1, B5-2, C1-1, C1-2, C1-3, C2-4, C3-1, C3-2, C3-3, C3-4, C4-1, C4-2, C5-1, C5-2, D1-3, D2-2, D5-1, D5-2, D6-1, D6-2, D6-3, D7-1, D7-2, D7-3
4. Populations and ecosystems	A1-2, A3-3, B1-2, C1-2, C3-2, C3-3, C3-4, C4-2, E1-1, E1-2, E1-3, E2-1, E2-2, E2-3, E3-1, E3-2, E3-3, E5-1, E5-2
5. Diversity and adaptations of organisms	A6-1, A6-2, A6-3, B1-1, B2-1, B2-2, B3-1, B3-2, B3-3, B4-2, B4-3, C1-1, C1-2, C1-3, C2-1, C2-2, C2-3, C2-4, C3-1, C3-2, C3-3, C3-4, C4-1, C4-2, C5-1, C5-2, D7-1, D7-2, D7-3, E3-2, E3-3, E5-1, E5-2
(D) Earth and Space Science	
1. Structure of the Earth system	E2-1, E2-2, E2-3
2. Earth's history	A1-3, A6-1, A6-2
3. Earth in the solar system	E2-3
(E) Science and Technology	
1. Abilities of technological design	A5-3, D7-3
2. Understandings about science and technology	A2-3, A4-3, A5-3, B3-3, B4-3, D2-2, D7-3, E4-2, E4-3
(F) Science in Personal and Social Perspectives	
1. Personal Health	A2-3, A5-2, B1-2, C1-3, D1-2, D1-3, D2-1, D2-2, D3-2, D3-3, D4-1, D4-2, D6-2, D6-3, D7-1, D7-2, D7-3, E4-2
2. Populations, resources, and environments	C1-2, C2-1, C2-2, C2-4, C4-2, E2-1, E2-2, E2-3, E3-1, E3-2, E3-3, E4-1, E4-2, E4-3, E5-1, E5-2
3. Natural hazards	E3-1
4. Risks and benefits	B3-2, D7-3, E4-1, E4-2, E4-3
5. Science and technology in society	A1-4, A4-3, A5-3, B1-2, B2-2, B3-3, B4-3, C3-4, E1-3, E4-1, E4-2, E4-3, E5-1, E5-2
(G) History and Nature of Science	
1. Science as a human endeavor	A1-1, A3-3, A4-3, A5-3, A6-1, A6-3, B2-2, B5-2, C2-4, C4-2, C5-2, D5-2, D7-3, E1-3, E3-3, E4-3
2. Nature of science	A1-4, A6-2, A6-3, B1-2, B3-3, D1-3
3. History of science	A1-3, A1-4, A2-3, A5-1, A6-1, A6-2, A6-3, C1-3, C4-2, C5-2, D1-3, D3-3, D4-2, D7-2, E1-3

Technology Resources

Online Science

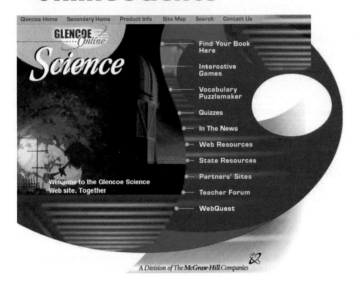

The Glencoe Science Web site **science.glencoe.com** is an invaluable resource for all teachers and students. You will find current information, Web links, chapter content, and Internet activities that allow students to connect to other students worldwide.

Teaching TODAY

Access *Teaching Today* at **teachingtoday.glencoe.com** for teaching tips, annotated Web resources, educational news, and more. New material is added each week to meet the diverse needs of secondary classroom teachers.

Interactive CD-ROM Program

This program provides students the opportunity to develop hypotheses, manipulate variables, build presentations, review content, and think critically.

ExamView Pro® Test Bank CD-ROM

Use this software to design and create your own test instruments in minutes. This versatile program allows you to create paper tests, tests for your school LAN system, or tests posted to a class Web site.

Interactive Lesson Planner

Here's the perfect solution for help in planning your lessons and organizing your resources. Every page of your Teacher Classroom Resources is available in this product at the click of a mouse.

MindJogger Videoquizzes

The interactive quiz-show format of this program, with three levels of difficulty, provides excitement for your students in reviewing key concepts for every chapter. It's a fun way to help you assess students' understanding of science content.

Guided Reading Audio Program
English/Spanish

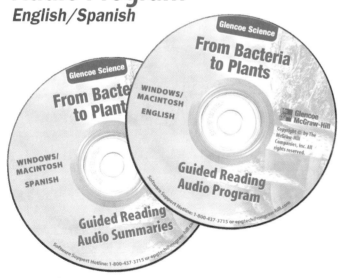

Students can listen to complete chapter texts read in English or listen to chapter summaries in Spanish. They're perfect for students who are auditory learners or for English Language Learners.

Vocabulary PuzzleMaker Software

This software program allows you to create crossword puzzles, jumble puzzles, or word searches in minutes to review chapter vocabulary. The puzzles can be printed or played on the computer screen.

Interactive Teacher Edition

You can view your entire *Teacher Wraparound Edition* and Teacher Classroom Resources on your computer screen. Export all worksheet masters to your own word processor for editing, if you choose.

Teacher Classroom Resources

Chapter Resources Booklets

We've organized all of the materials you need for each chapter into convenient chapter-based booklets! The Fast File system provides an easy way to stay organized.

Each **Chapter Resources** booklet contains:

Reproducible Student Pages

Assessment
- Chapter Review
- Chapter Test

Hands-On Activities
- Activity Worksheets for each activity in the *Student Edition*
- Two additional laboratory activities
- Foldables: Improving Reading and Study Skills

**Meeting Individual Needs
(Extension and Intervention)**
- Directed Reading for Content Mastery

- Directed Reading for Content Mastery *in Spanish*
- Reinforcement
- Enrichment
- Note-taking Worksheets

Transparency Activities
- Section Focus Activity
- Teaching Transparency Activity
- Assessment Transparency Activity

Teacher Support and Planning
- Content Outline for Teaching
- Spanish Resources
- Teacher Guide and Answers

Additional Resources

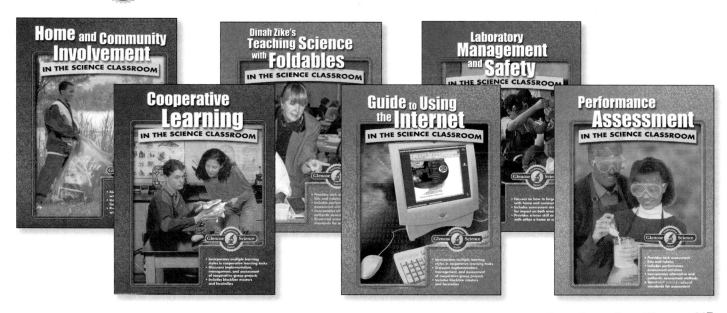

Glencoe Professional Series

Foldables: Improving Reading and Study Skills

Students love Foldables because they're fun. Teachers love them because they're effective.

What is a Foldable?

Foldables are three-dimensional, interactive graphic organizers. As students fold paper, cut tabs, write, and manipulate what they have made, they are kinesthetically involved in learning. These unique, hands-on tools for studying and reviewing were created exclusively for Glencoe Science by teaching specialist Dinah Zike.

FOLDABLES
Reading & Study Skills

Foldables are Useful!

Reading in the Content Area

Foldables help students develop ways of organizing information that are fun and creative. These useful activities help students practice basic writing skills, find and report main ideas, organize information, review key vocabulary terms, and much more!

Every chapter begins with a Foldable activity. Students make the physical structure of a Foldable that incorporates one of many prereading strategies. Then, as students read through the chapter and do the activities, students record information as they learn it in the appropriate part of the foldable. In the Chapter Study Guide, the After You Read feature gives students a strategy for using the fold they made to help them review the chapter concepts.

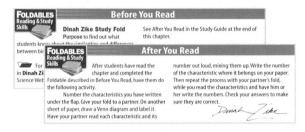

FOLDABLES
Reading & Study Skills

Before You Read

Dinah Zike Study Fold
Purpose to find out what students know about the similarities and differences between bir...

For ... in Dinah Zi... Science Web:

After You Read

After students have read the chapter and completed the Foldable described in Before You Read, have them do the following activity.

Number the characteristics you have written under the flap. Give your fold to a partner. On another sheet of paper, draw a Venn diagram and label it. Have your partner read each characteristic and its

number out loud, mixing them up. Write the number of the characteristic where it belongs on your paper. Then repeat the process with your partner's fold, while you read the characteristics and have him or her write the numbers. Check your answers to make sure they are correct.

Dinah Zike

Review One advantage of Foldables is that they result in an organized study guide. The Foldables then can be used not only while preparing for the chapter test, but they can also be used for reviewing for unit tests, end of course exams, and even standardized tests.

Assessment Foldables present an ideal opportunity for you to probe the depth of your students' knowledge. You'll get detailed feedback on exactly what they know and what misconceptions they may have.

Climate

polar
temperate
tropical
temperate
polar

Foldables are Easy!

Anyone who has paper, scissors, and maybe a stapler or some glue can implement Foldables in the classroom. Glencoe's Foldables have been tested with teachers and middle school students to make sure the directions are easy for both students and teachers. After doing a couple of them, your class will quickly become seasoned experts. Don't be surprised if you find them inventing their own for use in projects and reports in all of their classes!

A message from **the creator of Foldables,** Dinah Zike

You might not know my name or me, but I bet you have seen at least one of my graphic organizers or folds used in supplemental programs or teacher workshops. Today, my graphic organizers and manipulatives are used internationally. I present workshops and keynote presentations to over 50,000 teachers a year, sharing the manipulatives I began inventing, designing, and adapting over thirty years ago. Around the world, students of all ages are using them as daily work, note-taking activities, student-directed projects, forms of alternative assessment, science lab journals, quantitative and qualitative observation books, graphs, tables, and more. But through all my years of teaching, designing, and publishing, my materials had never been featured in a middle school textbook. When Glencoe/McGraw-Hill approached me to share some of my three-dimensional, manipulative graphic organizers with you in this new and innovative science series, I was thrilled.

Working with Glencoe, we all had the vision that Foldables should be an integral part of the curriculum, not simply tacked on. What we ended up with was a strategy that will help students read and learn science concepts. One of the advantages of using the same manipulative repeatedly is that students are immersed in what they are learning. It is not out of sight and out of mind. How long is your average student actively involved with a duplicated activity sheet? Ten minutes? Fifteen? Students will use the Foldable at the beginning of each chapter, before reading the chapter, during reading, and after reading. That's a lot of immersion!

Dinah Zike

Principles and Standards for School Mathematics

Students often make personal, educational, and career choices on their own that can influence the rest of their lives. Throughout their school years, they acquire skills that help them make these decisions. The development of keen mathematical skills can ensure that students have a wide variety of life options.

Principles and Standards for School Mathematics of the National Council of Teachers of Mathematics describes the foundation of mathematical concepts and applications that can provide students with the necessary mathematical skills to help achieve their life goals.

The ten categories of mathematical concepts and applications, as shown in the table below, allow students to increase their abilities to visualize, describe, and analyze situations in mathematical terms.

In the *Glencoe 15-Book Series*, each Math Skill Activity and Problem-Solving Activity provides students with the opportunity to practice and apply some of the mathematical concepts and applications described in the Standards. These activities serve to reinforce mathematical skills in real-life situations, thus preparing students to meet their needs in an ever-changing world.

A	Life's Structure and Function	C	Animal Diversity	E	Ecology
B	From Bacteria to Plants	D	Human Body Systems		

Correlation of Math Skills Activities and Problem Solving Activities in the **Life Science** books, *Glencoe 15-Book Series,* to **NCTM Standards Grades 6–8**

Standard	Book and Page
1. Number and Operations	D-11, A-13, E-15, C-25, D-40, A-46, C-52, A-74, D-78, E-80, C-82, D-104, A-109, B-112, E-114, E-129, A-133, D-133, C-147, D-147, D-185
2. Algebra	D-11, E-15, C-25, E-40, C-52, A-74, E-80, C-82, B-112, E-114, D-133, B-135, D-147
3. Geometry	D-11, A-46
4. Measurement	D-11, E-15, D-40, E-40, A-46, E-80, C-82, D-133
5. Data Analysis and Probability	A-13, D-78, E-114, C-117, E-129, A-133, B-135, C-147, D-185
6. Problem Solving	D-11, A-13, E-15, B-20, C-25, D-40, B-41, C-52, B-70, A-74, D-78, E-80, C-82, D-104, A-109, B-112, E-114, C-117, A-133, B-135, C-147, D-147, A-159, D-185
7. Reasoning and Proof	D-40, B-41
8. Communication	A-13, E-15, B-20, D-40, B-41, A-46, C-52, B-70, D-78, C-82, D-104, A-109, E-114, C-117, E-129, C-147, A-159, D-185
9. Connections	D-11, A-13, E-15, B-20, C-25, D-40, E-40, B-41, A-46, C-52, B-70, A-74, D-78, E-80, C-82, D-104, A-109, B-112, E-114, C-117, E-129, A-133, D-133, B-135, C-147, D-147, A-159, D-185
10. Representation	E-40, B-70, D-78, E-114, E-129, A-133

Materials List

It is assumed that goggles, laboratory aprons, tap water, textbooks, paper, calculators, pencils, and pens are available for all activities.

All laboratory activities have been thoroughly reviewed by a safety expert.

All full-length labs were bench tested by Science Kit to ensure quality and safety.

Materials support is provided by Science Kit® & Boreal® Laboratories. Call Science Kit at 1-800-828-7777 to get your activity materials folder. This folder makes it easy for you to order materials and equipment for the program.

Consumables

Item	EXPLORE ACTIVITY Page	Mini LAB Page	Activity Chapter and 1-page or 2-page
Aluminum foil	123		1-2, 5-2
Apple core			1-2
Banana peel			1-2
Branches, different kinds			3-1
Button		110	
Cheesecloth		69	
Construction paper, black		126	
Food coloring, red		75	
Food-bananas, green (2)		136	
Food-dried beans		16	
Food-grapes, two different kinds	93		
Food-green onion		75	
Food-lettuce			5-1
Food-mushroom(s)	31	47	
Food-salt			4-2
Hair styling gel	7		
Leaf			1-2
Magazines	61		
Marking pen			5-2
Newspaper			1-2
Paper bag(s)		136	
Paper towel(s)	93		5-2
Plastic bag, self-sealing	123		
Plastic candy wrapper			1-2
Plastic cups			4-2
Plastic knife	93		
Salt solution			5-1
Seeds			4-2, 5-2
Sphagnum moss		69	

Materials List

Consumables *continued*

Item	EXPLORE ACTIVITY Page	Mini LAB Page	ACTIVITY Chapter and 1-page or 2-page
String		9, 110	
Synthetic kitchen sponge	7		
Tape		126	1-2, 4-2, 5-2
Water	7	16, 69, 75, 95	
Yarn		9	

Non-Consumables

Item	EXPLORE ACTIVITY Page	Mini LAB Page	ACTIVITY Chapter and 1-page or 2-page
Art supplies			2-2
Beaker(s)	69	16	4-2
Collection jars			2-2
Container		69, 75, 95	
Coverslip			2-1, 2-2, 4-1, 5-1
Cup		95	
Dissecting needle			4-1
Dropper			2-1, 4-1
Forceps			4-1, 5-1
Glass, clear, 1 L			5-2
Graduated cylinder		69	4-2
Hand lens/Magnifying glass	31	40	2-2, 4-1
Jar(s)			1-2, 5-2
Meterstick	9		
Metric ruler		75	
Micrograph photo of *Nostoc*			1-1
Micrograph photo of *Oscillation*			1-1
Microscope			1-1, 2-1, 2-2, 4-1, 5-1
Microscope slide(s)			2-1, 2-2, 4-1, 5-1
Plant trays			4-2
Plate	7		
Prepared slide of *Anabaena*			1-1
Prepared slide of *Gloeocapsa*			1-1
Prepared slide of slime mold			2-1
Reference-field guide to club fungi			2-2
Reference-field guide to fungi			2-2
Scissors	7, 61	95, 126	

Non-Consumables *continued*

Item	EXPLORE ACTIVITY Page	Mini LAB Page	ACTIVITY Chapter and 1-page or 2-page
Soil		95	1-2, 4-2
Spring scale		69	
Thermometer(s)			4-2
Watering can			1-2

Live Organisms

Item	EXPLORE ACTIVITY Page	Mini LAB Page	ACTIVITY Chapter and 1-page or 2-page
Coleus		95	
Culture of *Amoeba*			2-1
Culture of *Euglena*			2-1
Culture of *Paramecium*			2-1
Culture of *Spirogyra*			2-1
Ferns with gametophytes			4-1
Ferns with sporophytes			4-1
Houseplant with leaves		95, 123, 126	
Live mosses			4-1
Liverworts			4-1
Physarum polycephaalum		40	
Seedling plants (in pots)	123		

Lab Safety

The activities in the *Glencoe 15-Book Series* have been tested in the laboratory and have been reviewed by safety consultants. Even so, there are no guarantees against accidents. For additional help, refer to the *Laboratory Management and Safety* booklet, which contains safety guidelines and masters to test students' lab and safety skills.

General Guidelines

- Post safety guidelines, fire escape routes, and a list of emergency procedures in the classroom. Make sure students understand these procedures. Remind them at the beginning of *every* lab session.

- Understand and make note of the Safety Symbols used in each activity.

- Have students fill out a safety contract. Students should pledge to follow the rules, to wear safety attire, and to conduct themselves in a responsible manner.

- Know where emergency equipment is stored and how to use it.

- Supervise students at all times. Check assembly of all setups.

- Perform all activities before you allow students to do so.

- Instruct students to follow directions carefully.

- Make sure that all students are wearing proper safety attire. They should secure long hair and loose clothing.

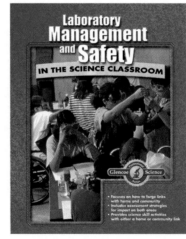

Handling Chemicals

- Always wear safety goggles, gloves, and an apron when handling chemicals. Treat all chemicals as potentially dangerous.

- Never ingest chemicals. Use proper techniques to smell solutions.

- Use a fume hood when handling chemicals that are poisonous or corrosive or that give off a vapor.

- *Always add acids to water, never the reverse.*

- Prepare solutions by adding the solid to a small amount of distilled water, then diluting with water to the volume listed. If you use a hydrate that is different from the one specified, adjust the amount of hydrate to obtain the correct concentration.

- Consider purchasing premixed solutions from a scientific supply house.

- Maintain appropriate MSDS (Materials Safety Data Sheets).

- Do not permit wearing contact lenses, even with safety glasses; splashing chemicals could infuse under a lens and cause eye damage.

Disclaimer

Glencoe/McGraw-Hill makes no claims to the completeness of this discussion of laboratory safety and chemical handling. The material presented is not all-inclusive, nor does it address all of the hazards associated with handling, storage, and disposal of chemicals, or with laboratory management.

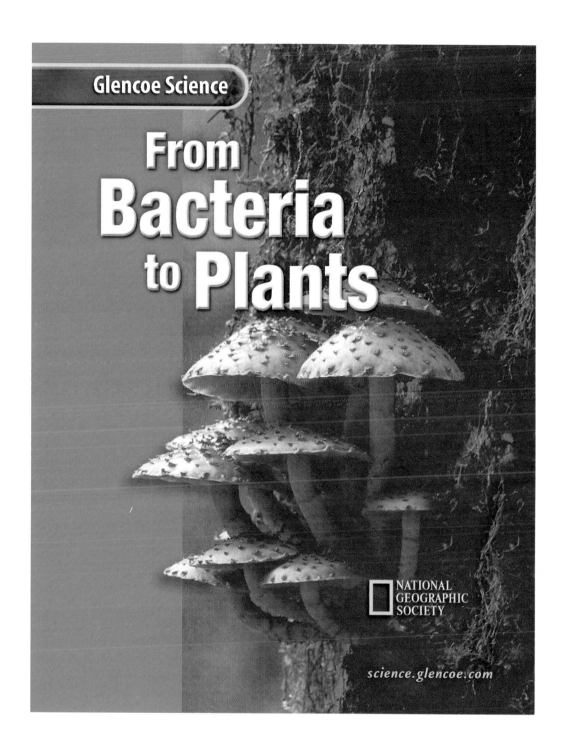

Glencoe Science

From Bacteria to Plants

NATIONAL GEOGRAPHIC SOCIETY

science.glencoe.com

Glencoe McGraw-Hill

New York, New York   Columbus, Ohio   Woodland Hills, California   Peoria, Illinois

Glencoe Science

From Bacteria to Plants

Student Edition
Teacher Wraparound Edition
Interactive Teacher Edition CD-ROM
Interactive Lesson Planner CD-ROM
Lesson Plans
Content Outline for Teaching
Dinah Zike's Teaching Science with Foldables
Directed Reading for Content Mastery
Foldables: Reading and Study Skills
Assessment
    Chapter Review
    Chapter Tests
    ExamView Pro Test Bank Software
    Assessment Transparencies
    Performance Assessment in the Science Classroom
    The Princeton Review Standardized Test Practice Booklet
Directed Reading for Content Mastery in Spanish
Spanish Resources
English/Spanish Guided Reading Audio Program
Reinforcement

Enrichment
Activity Worksheets
Section Focus Transparencies
Teaching Transparencies
Laboratory Activities
Science Inquiry Labs
Critical Thinking/Problem Solving
Reading and Writing Skill Activities
Mathematics Skill Activities
Cultural Diversity
Laboratory Management and Safety in the Science Classroom
MindJogger Videoquizzes and Teacher Guide
Interactive CD-ROM with Presentation Builder
Vocabulary PuzzleMaker Software
Cooperative Learning in the Science Classroom
Environmental Issues in the Science Classroom
Home and Community Involvement
Using the Internet in the Science Classroom

THE PRINCETON REVIEW

"Study Tip," "Test-Taking Tip," and the "Test Practice" features in this book were written by The Princeton Review, the nation's leader in test preparation. Through its association with McGraw-Hill, The Princeton Review offers the best way to help students excel on standardized assessments.

The Princeton Review is not affiliated with Princeton University or Educational Testing Service.

Glencoe/McGraw-Hill

A Division of The **McGraw·Hill** Companies

Send all inquiries to:
Glencoe/McGraw-Hill
8787 Orion Place
Columbus, OH 43240

ISBN 0-07-825560-0
Printed in the United States of America.
3 4 5 6 7 8 9 10 027/043 06 05 04 03 02

Authors

National Geographic Society
Education Division
Washington, D.C.

Alton Biggs
Biology Teacher
Allen High School
Allen, Texas

Dinah Zike
Educational Consultant
Dinah-Might Activities, Inc.
San Antonio, Texas

Consultants

Content

Betsy Wrobel-Boerner
Department of Microbiology
Ohio State University
Columbus, Ohio

Leanne Field, PhD
Lecturer Molecular Genetics and
Microbiology
University of Texas
Austin, Texas

Safety

Sandra West, PhD
Associate Professor of Biology
Southwest Texas State University
San Marcos, Texas

Reading

Elizabeth Babich
Special Education Teacher
Mashpee Public Schools
Mashpee, Massachusetts

Math

Teri Willard, EdD
Department of Mathematics
Montana State University
Belgrade, Montana

Reviewers

Maureen Barrett
Thomas E. Harrington Middle
School
Mt. Laurel, New Jersey

Cory Fish
Burkholder Middle School
Henderson, Nevada

Linda V. Forsyth
Merrill Middle School
Denver, Colorado

Amy Morgan
Berry Middle School
Hoover, Alabama

Michelle Punch
Northwood Middle School
Houston, Texas

Billye Robbins
Jackson Intermediate
Pasadena, Texas

Delores Stout
Bellefonte Middle School
Bellefonte, Pennsylvania

Darcy Vetro-Ravndal
Middleton Middle School of
Technology
Tampa, Florida

Series Activity Testers

José Luis Alvarez, PhD
Math/Science Mentor Teacher
El Paso, Texas

Nerma Coats Henderson
Teacher
Pickerington Jr. High School
Pickerington, Ohio

Mary Helen Mariscal-Cholka
Science Teacher
William D. Slider Middle School
El Paso, Texas

José Alberto Marquez
TEKS for Leaders Trainer
El Paso, Texas

Science Kit and Boreal Laboratories
Tonawanda, New York

CONTENTS

Interdisciplinary Connections/Activities

Feature Contents

Activities/Science Connections

Problem-Solving Activities

Math Skills Activities

Skill Builder Activities

Science

Math

Technology

Science INTEGRATION

SCIENCE Online

THE PRINCETON REVIEW

Feature Contents

The NATURE OF SCIENCE

Plant Communication

Introduction

This feature introduces students to scientific inquiry by capturing their interest and then guiding them through the steps scientists used to determine whether or not plants are able to communicate with each other. Scientists who are examining this question use the scientific method by

1. Asking the question "Is it possible for plants to communicate with each other?"
2. Gathering and using information to form hypotheses;
3. Testing hypotheses through experimentation;
4. Analyzing the results; and
5. Drawing conclusions about their data.

1 Motivate

Review with students their knowledge of plants. Have students make a list of what they know about plants. Areas could include plant structure and function, general biology, and reproduction. Point out that plants are complex organisms that are adapted to live in many environments. There is evidence of plant communication through the use of chemicals, including plant to plant communication as well as plant to animal communication.

Plant Communication

F or hundreds of years, scientists have been performing experiments to learn more about plants, such as how they function and respond to their environment. Early experiments were limited to just observations. Today, scientists experiment with plants in many ways to learn more about their biology. Recently, scientists have been investigating the idea of plant communication and asking questions like "Is it possible for plants to communicate with each other?"

Figure 1
Acacia trees communicate by emitting a gas that travels to surrounding trees. This communication helps protect them from predators.

Evidence of Communication

Observations of certain species of plants reacting to predators or disease have interested scientists conducting experiments in an attempt to understand the exact nature of plant communication. In 1990, researchers discovered evidence of plant communication. As part of their defense against predators, acacia (ah KAY shah) trees produce a toxin– a poisonous substance. In response to a predator, such as an antelope nibbling on its leaves, an acacia tree releases a gas that stimulates other acacia trees up to 50 m away to produce extra toxin within minutes. Although the toxin does not prevent the antelopes from eating the acacia leaves initially, if the antelopes consume enough of the toxin, it can kill them. Thus, the chemical warning system used by the acacias can help guard these trees against future attacks.

Figure 2
A tobacco plant produces methyl salicylate when infected with TMV.

2 ◆ B STUDENT RESOURCES

Science Journal

Importance of Plants Have students consider why scientists should continue to learn as much as possible about the biology of plants. Have them list in their science journals reasons why plants are so important to life on Earth.

Possible answers: Plants are a source of oxygen and they take up carbon dioxide. They are a source of food and the roots of plants help stop soil erosion in many areas. Different medicines, spices, and dyes can be derived from plants.
IS Linguistic

Another Warning System

Other evidence suggests that tobacco plants also might use a chemical warning system. One of the most common problems of tobacco and several vegetable and ornamental plants is the tobacco mosaic virus (TMV). TMV causes blisters on the tobacco plant, which disfigure its leaves and keep it from growing to its full size. Recently, scientists have discovered that TMV-infected tobacco plants produce a chemical that may warn nearby healthy tobacco plants of the presence of the virus and stimulate them to produce substances to help fight against the virus.

Researchers at a university tested some TMV-infected tobacco plants. They noted the presence of a gas called methyl salicylate (MEH thul • suh LIH suh late), also known as oil of wintergreen, in the air near TMV-infected plants. The researchers hypothesized that methyl salicylate is a chemical warning signal of a TMV infection.

Testing the Hypothesis

To test this hypothesis, they inoculated some healthy tobacco plants with TMV and monitored the air around them for methyl salicylate. They detected the gas above infected plants and found that the production of the gas increased as leaf damage progressed. The gas was not produced by healthy plants. The researchers allowed the gas to move through the air from infected to healthy plants. They found a connection between the presence of methyl salicylate and responses in healthy plants. As the levels of methyl salicylate increased, the healthy plants began to produce substances that could help them fight viruses. These results supported the hypothesis that methyl salicylate is a warning signal because it was produced by infected plants and was linked to resistance to the virus in healthy plants.

Figure 3
These tobacco mosaic viruses are magnified 34,000 times.

Figure 4
This tobacco leaf shows symptoms of a TMV infection.

THE NATURE OF SCIENCE   B ◆ 3

Quick Demo

Show students photos in a botany book that demonstrate the idea that plants can and do respond to their environment. Examples could include positive phototropism, where a plant's leaves grow toward light, thigmotropism, where a plant responds to contact with an object in its path of growth, and contact movements, such as the Venus's flytrap consuming a fly. Reinforce the idea that plants are not as passive as some people would assume. **LS Visual-Spatial**

Use Science Words

Word Meaning Have students look up and report on the meaning of the word *phytoalexin* in a dictionary. A phytoalexin is a chemical produced by plants to fight off infections from bacteria or fungus. The root *alexin* is derived from the Greek word *alexein,* meaning to "ward off or protect."

Teacher FYI

Response to predators is not the only situation in which plants use chemicals for protection. Competition for nutrients, water, or space from nearby plants can trigger the release of chemicals in some plants. The black walnut tree produces a chemical that damages other plants such as tomato plants or apple trees that are growing in the proximity of its roots.

The Study of Living Things

The study of all living things and their interaction with their environments is life science. In this book, you will learn about the characteristics of bacteria, protists, fungi, and plants.

Experimentation

Scientists try to find answers to their questions by performing experiments and recording the results. An experiment's procedure must be carefully planned before it is begun. First, scientists must identify a question to be answered or a problem to be solved. The proposed answer to the question or explanation of the problem is called a hypothesis. A hypothesis must be testable to be valid. Scientists design an experiment that will support or disprove their hypothesis. The scientists studying tobacco plants tested their hypothesis that methyl salicylate is a chemical warning signal produced by TMV-infected plants.

Figure 5
Scientists experiment with plants to learn more about their biology.

Sampling

If a hypothesis refers to a very large number of objects or members of a species, scientists cannot test every one of them. Instead, they use sampling—they test their hypothesis on a smaller, representative group. The university scientists were not able to test every tobacco plant. Instead, they used a group of plants that were grown in a greenhouse.

Variables and Controls in an Experiment

Scientists must make sure that only one factor affects the results of an experiment. The factor that the scientists change in the experiment is called the independent variable. The dependent variable is what the scientists measure or observe to obtain the results. A constant is any factor in an experiment that is always kept the same. The observations and measurements that scientists make are called data. A control is an additional experiment performed for comparison. A control has all factors of the original experiment except the variables.

Curriculum Connection

Health Have students research and report on examples of plants and the chemicals they produce being used for medicinal purposes. Examples include ginger to relieve nausea, Ginko biloba to improve memory, and aloe to help soothe burned skin. **LS Linguistic**

Inclusion Strategies

Gifted Have students design an experiment to test whether or not oil of wintergreen would be an effective pesticide. Possible answer: Have four groups of plants. Group 1: no treatment (control). Group 2: Not exposed, but sprayed. Group 3: Exposed to the virus but not sprayed with the oil. Group 4: Sprayed with the oil and exposed to the virus. **LS Logical-Mathematical**

Determining Variables

In the experiment on tobacco plants, the independent variable was the addition of the tobacco mosaic virus to the healthy plants. The dependent variable was the production of methyl salicylate gas. The effect of this gas on healthy tobacco plants provided evidence for its function as a signal. Factors that were constant included the growth conditions for the tobacco plants before and after some were infected. The control was the uninfected plants. Because the only difference in the treatment of the plants was inoculation with TMV, it can be said that the independent variable is the cause of the production of methyl salicylate, the dependent variable. If more than one factor is changed, however, the dependent variable's change can't be credited to only the independent variable. This makes the experiment's results less reliable.

Drawing a Conclusion

A conclusion is what has been learned as the result of an experiment. Conclusions should be based only on the data. They must be free of bias—anything that keeps researchers from making objective decisions. Using what they had learned from their experiments, the scientists studying tobacco mosaic virus concluded that their hypothesis was correct.

To be certain about their conclusions, scientists must have safeguards. One safeguard is to repeat an experiment, like the university scientists did. Hypotheses are not accepted until the experiments have been repeated several times and they produce the same results each time.

Because oil of wintergreen is not known to be dangerous to humans, using oil of wintergreen to prevent TMV infection may be practical as well as scientifically sound. Scientists are investigating how oil of wintergreen might be used as an alternative pesticide.

Figure 6
A scientist often uses a computer to record and analyze data.

Figure 7
Someday, spraying oil of wintergreen might prevent the spread of the tobacco mosaic virus.

Describe a procedure you would use to test this hypothesis: vaccine X protects plants from being infected by the deadly plant virus Z. What would be your independent and dependent variables? How could you establish controls in your experiment?

Extension

Have students consider the following questions and record their answers in their Science Journals.

How will scientists know that the oil is effective against viral infection? The oil is effective if the plants that are sprayed with the oil and subsequently exposed to the virus remain healthy, while the plants not sprayed became infected.

If the hypothetical experiment is successful, how will scientists determine what amount of the oil is the least amount that can be sprayed and still be effective? How can scientists determine at what point in the plant's life cycle the oil should be sprayed to be most effective? Will spraying have to take place more then once in the plant's lifetime? Possible answers: Student's answers will vary for the remaining questions but should involve descriptions of different experimental set-ups that can further test the most effective way to use the oil as a pesticide.

③ Assess

Use the question in You Do It to assess understanding. Answers should relate to ways of testing of the hypothesis and should be as specific as possible.

Lead students through this as a class to reinforce the steps in the scientific method. Emphasize that there are no right or wrong answers. Scientists may use many different methods to test a hypothesis. Scientists may also interpret data differently. Possible answers: The independent variables would be exposing the plants to the virus and giving them the vaccine. The dependent variable would be whether the plants become infected. Control: a group of healthy plants that continue to be grown under the same conditions. Experimental groups: one that is given the vaccine and not exposed to the virus (to make sure the vaccine does not cause problems to the plant), one group that is exposed to the virus and not given the vaccine, and a third group that is given the vaccine and then exposed to the virus.

Section/Objectives	Standards		Activities/Features
Chapter Opener	**National**	**State/Local**	**Explore Activity:** Model a bacterium's slime layer, p. 7 **Before You Read,** p. 7
	See p. 5T for a Key to Standards.		
Section 1 What are bacteria? 2 sessions 1 block 1. **Identify** the characteristics of bacteria cells. 2. **Compare and contrast** aerobic and anaerobic organisms.	National Content Standards: UCP5, A1, C1, C2, C3, C5		**MiniLAB:** Modeling Bacteria Size, p. 9 **Science Online,** p. 11 **Earth Science Integration,** p. 12 **Activity:** Observing Cyanobacteria, p. 14
Section 2 Bacteria in Your Life 3 sessions 1.5 blocks 1. **Identify** some ways bacteria are helpful. 2. **Determine** the importance of nitrogen-fixing bacteria. 3. **Explain** how some bacteria can cause human disease.	National Content Standards: UCP2, A1, C4, F1, F5, G2		**MiniLAB:** Observing Bacterial Growth, p. 16 **Visualizing Nitrogen Fixing Bacteria,** p. 17 **Chemistry Integration,** p. 18 **Science Online,** p. 19 **Problem-Solving Activity:** Controlling Bacterial Growth, p. 20 **Activity:** Composting, p. 22–23 **Science Stats:** Unusual Bacteria, p. 24–25

NATIONAL GEOGRAPHIC

Teacher's Corner

PRODUCTS AVAILABLE FROM GLENCOE
To order call 1-800-334-7344:
CD-ROM
NGS PictureShow: The Cell
Curriculum Kit
GeoKit: Cells and Microorganisms

Transparency Set
NGS PicturePack: The Cell
Videodisc
STV: The Cell

**PRODUCTS AVAILABLE FROM
NATIONAL GEOGRAPHIC SOCIETY**
To order call 1-800-368-2728:

Videos
Bacteria; Discovering the Cell

INDEX TO NATIONAL GEOGRAPHIC SOCIETY
The following articles may be used for research relating to this chapter:
"Body Beasts" by Richard Coniff,
December 1998.

Activity Materials	Reproducible Resources	Section Assessment	Technology
Explore Activity: synthetic kitchen sponge, water, hair-styling gel, plate, scissors	**Chapter Resources Booklet** Foldables Worksheet, p. 13 Directed Reading Overview, p. 15 Note-taking Worksheets, pp. 27–28	GLENCOE'S **ASSESSMENT** ADVANTAGE	
MiniLAB: meterstick, yarn or string **Activity:** prepared slides (or micrograph photos) of *Oscillatoria, Nostoc, Gloeocapsa,* and *Anabaena;* microscope	**Chapter Resources Booklet** Transparency Activity, p. 38 MiniLAB, p. 3 Enrichment, p. 25 Reinforcement, p. 23 Directed Reading, p. 16 Activity Worksheet, pp. 5–6 Lab Activity, pp. 9–10 Transparency Activity, pp. 41–43 **Home and Community Involvement,** p. 37 **Life Science Critical Thinking/ Problem Solving,** p. 1	Portfolio Science Journal, p. 11 Performance MiniLAB, p. 9 Skill Builder Activities, p. 13 Content Section Assessment, p. 13	♪ Section Focus Transparency ♪ Teaching Transparency ◉ Interactive CD-ROM ∩ Guided Reading Audio Program
MiniLAB: 2–3 dried beans, distilled water, glass beaker **Activity:** 4 or more wide-mouth clear glass jars, soil, water, watering can, banana peel, apple core, scrap of newspaper, leaf, plastic candy wrapper, scrap of aluminum foil *Need materials?* Contact Science Kit at 1-800-828-7777 or www.sciencekit.com on the Internet.	**Chapter Resources Booklet** Transparency Activity, p. 39 MiniLAB, p. 4 Enrichment, p. 26 Reinforcement, p. 24 Directed Reading, pp. 17, 18 Lab Activity, pp. 11–12 Activity Worksheet, pp. 7–8 **Mathematics Skill Activities,** p.19 **Reading and Writing Skill Activities,** p. 25 **Lab Management and Safety,** p. 58	Portfolio Cultural Diversity, p. 16 Science Journal, p. 20 Performance MiniLAB, p. 16 Problem Solving Activity, p. 20 Skill Builder Activities, p. 21 Content Section Assessment, p. 21	♪ Section Focus Transparency ◉ Interactive CD-ROM ∩ Guided Reading Audio Program

End of Chapter Assessment

GLENCOE'S **ASSESSMENT** ADVANTAGE

Blackline Masters	Technology	Professional Series
Chapter Resources Booklet Chapter Review, pp. 31–32 Chapter Tests, pp. 33–36 **Standardized Test Practice by The Princeton Review,** pp. 35–38	▭ MindJogger Videoquiz ◉ Interactive CD-ROM ◉ Vocabulary PuzzleMakers ◉ ExamView Pro Test Bank ◉ Interactive Lesson Planner ◉ Interactive Teacher Edition	Performance Assessment in the Science Classroom (PASC)

Transparencies

Section Focus

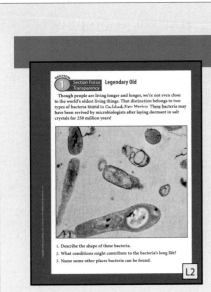

Section Focus Transparency — Legendary Old

Though people are living longer and longer, we're not even close to the world's oldest living things. That distinction belongs to two types of bacteria found in Carlsbad, New Mexico. These bacteria may have been revived by microbiologists after laying dormant in salt crystals for 250 million years!

1. Describe the shape of these bacteria.
2. What conditions might contribute to the bacteria's long life?
3. Name some other places bacteria can be found.

L2

Section Focus Transparency — Bacterial Invasion

On the left is a deer tick. These ticks are responsible for the transmission of Lyme disease, a bacterial infection that invades almost the entire human body. The spiral-shaped bacteria that causes this infection is shown in the other image.

1. Name some places bacteria can be found.
2. What are some ways to prevent infections caused by bacteria?
3. In what ways are some bacteria helpful?

L2

This is a representation of key blackline masters available in the Teacher Classroom Resources. See Resource Manager boxes within the chapter for additional information.

Assessment

Assessment Transparency — Bacteria

Directions: Carefully review the diagram and answer the following questions.

1. Which hypothesis is probably being tested by this experiment?
   A Beef broth is a good substance for growing bacteria.
   B A cotton stopper will prevent bacteria from getting inside the test tubes.
   C Bacteria need nutrients in order to grow.
   D The more chemical X added, the less bacteria will grow.
2. About how much more liquid does Test tube 4 contain than Test tube 1?
   F 10 mL   G 15 mL   H 20 mL   J 25 mL
3. In a properly designed experiment, a control is set up exactly like the other setups except that the control does not contain the variable. According to this definition, which is the control in this experiment?
   A Test tube 1   C Test tube 3
   B Test tube 2   D Test tube 4

L2

Teaching

Teaching Transparency — Bacteria Cell

L2

Key to Teaching Strategies

The following designations will help you decide which activities are appropriate for your students.

L1 Level 1 activities should be appropriate for students with learning difficulties.

L2 Level 2 activities should be within the ability range of all students.

L3 Level 3 activities are designed for above-average students.

ELL ELL activities should be within the ability range of English Language Learners.

COOP LEARN Cooperative Learning activities are designed for small group work.

LS Multiple Learning Styles logos are used throughout to indicate strategies that address different learning styles.

P These strategies represent student products that can be placed into a best-work portfolio.

Hands-on Activities

Activity Worksheets

Activity — Observing Cyanobacteria

Lab Preview

Directions: Answer these questions before you begin the Activity.

1. What safety symbols are associated with this activity?

2. Under what power of the microscope do you observe your slide?

You can obtain many species of cyanobacteria from ponds. When you look at these organisms under a microscope, you will find that they have many similarities and differences. In this activity, you will compare and contrast species of cyanobacteria.

What You'll Investigate
What do cyanobacteria look like!

Materials
micrograph photos of Oscillatoria and Nostoc
* prepared slides of Oscillatoria and Nostoc
prepared slides of Gloeocapsa and Anabaena
* micrograph photos of Anabaena and Gloeocapsa
microscope
* Alternate materials

Goals
• Observe several species of cyanobacteria.
• Describe the structure and function of cyanobacteria.

Safety Precautions

Procedure
1. Review the data table in the Data and Observations section. Record the presence or absence of each characteristic in the data table for each cyanobacterium you observe.
2. Observe prepared slides of Gloeocapsa and Anabaena under low and high power of the microscope. Notice the difference in the arrangement of the cells. Draw and label a few cells of each on a separate sheet of paper.
3. Observe photos of Nostoc and Oscillatoria. On a separate piece of paper, draw and label a few cells of each.

L2

Laboratory Activities

Laboratory Activity — Shapes of Bacteria

Thousands of different types of bacteria are known and have been observed, and there are possibly many more that have not yet been observed. How can a scientist tell these organisms apart when they are so small? One way is by their characteristic shapes, or patterns of joining together in groups.

Strategy
You will identify bacteria by using their shape and other characteristics in class. You will discover a process of elimination or "key" that will be used to help in the identification.

Materials
key (see the next page)

Procedure
1. Examine Figure 1 in the Data and Observations section, which shows bacteria magnified 2,000 times their natural size.
2. Use the key on the next page to identify each type of bacterium (singular for bacteria). Start at the top of the key. Following the directions, the key will allow you to identify each of the bacterium shown by name.

Each bacterium has a first name that describes its shape in scientific language, and a last name that may also describe some specific characteristic. The also join to pairs; threes the disease caused by the bacterium or type of food in which the bacterium may be found. Label each bacterium in the Data and Observations section.

Data and Observations
Figure 1

L2

Meeting Different Ability Levels

Content Outline

Reinforcement

Directed Reading

Assessment

Chapter Tests

Enrichment

Spanish Directed Reading

Test Practice Workbook

Chapter Review

Science Content Background

SECTION 1

What are bacteria?
Characteristics

The sizes of bacteria are genetically determined and are measured in microns—1 micron (mμ)=0.001 mm. Most bacteria range from 0.2mμ to 2mμ in width and from 2 mμ to 8mμ in length. Bacteria generally have a rigid cell wall that maintains the shape of the organism. Bacterial cell walls prevent cells from bursting in environments where the pressure in the cell is greater than the pressure in the surrounding medium or fluid. Bacterial cells usually die in environments where the external pressure is greater than the pressure in the cell. Bacteria have three basic shapes. Unlike the rod-shaped bacilli (singular, *bacillus*) and helical spirillia (singular, *spirillum*), the spherical cocci (singular, *coccus*) never possess flagella.

Eubacteria

Most named bacteria are members of Kingdom Eubacteria. The five major phylogenetic groups of eubacteria are based on comparisons of their ribosomal RNA.

Cyanobacteria, formerly called blue-green algae, are bacteria that contain chlorophyll, enabling them to make their own food. This process is different from photosynthesis in plants. These organisms probably produced most of the original free oxygen in the atmosphere about 2.5 billion years ago. Cyanobacteria may be unicellular or colonial. Most live in freshwater, but some are symbiotic with fungi to form lichens.

Reproduction

Most bacteria reproduce by a process of cell division known as binary fission. In binary fission, the one or more circular chromosomes of the bacterial cell are duplicated. The duplicated chromosomes attach to the cell membrane. Continued growth of the cell separates the chromosomes, and the cell membrane eventually pinches in two as a cell wall is deposited between the daughter cells.

Fun Fact

In the late 1970s and 1980s, Carl Woese studied bacteria classification by examining sequences of genetic mutations. He determined that archaebacteria are more closely related to animals, plants, and fungi than to other bacteria.

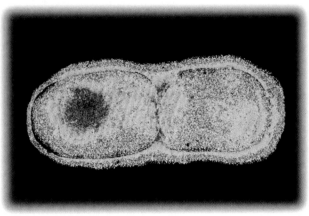

George Musil/Visuals Unlimited

SECTION 2

Bacteria in Your Life
Beneficial Bacteria

Prokaryotes have a large impact on ecology. They and fungi are the organisms primarily responsible for the decay and recycling of materials. Of these materials, carbon and nitrogen are essential.

Nitrogen gas can be used as a source of nitrogen only by some eubacteria, including cyanobacteria. These organisms not only remove nitrogen from the air for their own use, but also change the nitrogen into compounds other organisms can use. This is important, because nitrogen is necessary in order for plants and animals to make amino acids and nucleic acids. Because the nitrogen content of the environment varies considerably in quantity and kinds of nitrogen-containing compounds, it is not surprising that organisms have evolved the ability to utilize more than one nitrogen source.

Antibiotics and Vaccines

An antibiotic is a chemical that is able to kill or inhibit the growth of a microorganism. Thousands of antibiotics are known, but only a

Fun Fact

In 1939, Rene Dubos isolated the antibiotic tyrothricin from soil bacteria. This was the first antibiotic to be used successfully to treat a human disease.

few have practical uses. Many types of microorganisms including bacteria, protists, and fungi, produce antibiotics.

The action of an antibiotic is dependent on its chemical structure. Certain antibiotics affect cell wall synthesis or destroy cell membrane permeability. Others act by inhibiting protein synthesis by causing the wrong amino acid to be inserted into the growing polypeptide chain of proteins in ribosomes. Broad spectrum antibiotics act on many different kinds of organisms. Some antibiotics, such as penicillin, act only on prokaryotes. Other antibiotics, such as cycloheximide, are active against eukaryotes but not prokaryotes.

VCG/FPG International

Vaccines, on the other hand, are specific to certain bacteria or viruses. This is because a vaccine is made of damaged or killed bacterial cells or viruses. The white blood cells learn to recognize these pathogens and can respond quickly when they enter the body. It is important to note that antibiotics are taken after a bacterial pathogen enters the body, whereas a vaccine is a preventive measure.

Pasteurization

Pasteurization is achieved by passing milk continuously through a heat exchanger where its temperature quickly is raised to 71.6°C, held at that temperature for 15 s, and then quickly cooled. The process, named for Louis Pasteur, was first used to control spoilage of wine and saved the wine industry in France. Pasteuriza-

tion does not kill all the microbes present and should not be confused with sterilization, which uses high heat and pressure to kill all bacteria. Although pasteurization was originally used to kill organisms that cause tuberculosis, typhoid, and brucellosis, today it is used to increase the shelf life of milk.

SCIENCE Online

For additional content background on this topic, go to the Glencoe Science Web site at science.glencoe.com.

Chapter Vocabulary

What do you think?

Science Journal The photo shows bacteria on the surface of a protist. Bacteria live on surfaces or within the cells of organisms.

CHAPTER

1 Bacteria

I magine a world of such small scale that a powerful microscope is needed to see the organisms that live there. What effects do these small organisms, some of which are bacteria, have on living things including you? In this chapter you will find the answer to this question. You also will read about many of the ways humans use bacteria, such as for composting. In addition, you will learn how the unique characteristics of bacteria help them live in almost every environment.

What do you think?

Science Journal Look at the picture below with a classmate. Discuss what you think this might be or what is happening. Here's a hint: *Bacteria can live on the surface of other organisms.* Write your answer or best guess in your Science Journal.

6 ◆ B

Theme Connection

Systems and Interactions The role of bacteria in maintaining a homeostatic balance is discussed. In addition to homeostasis, the ecological importance of bacteria is illustrated by using examples of niches filled by these organisms.

EXPLORE ACTIVITY

Bacterial cells have a gelatinlike, protective coating on the outside of their cell walls. In some cases, the coating is thin and is referred to as a slime layer. A slime layer helps a bacterium attach to other surfaces. Dental plaque forms when bacteria with slime layers stick to teeth and multiply there. A slime layer also can reduce water loss from a bacterium. In this activity you will make a model of a bacterium's slime layer.

Model a bacterium's slime layer

1. Cut two 2-cm-wide strips from the long side of a synthetic kitchen sponge.

2. Soak both strips in water. Remove them from the water and squeeze out the excess water. Both strips should be damp.

3. Completely coat one strip with hair-styling gel. Do not coat the other strip.

4. Place both strips on a plate (not paper) and leave them overnight.

Observe

The next day, record your observations of the two sponge strips in your Science Journal. Infer how a slime layer protects a bacterial cell from drying out. What environmental conditions are best for survival of bacteria?

FOLDABLES
Reading & Study Skills

Before You Read

Making a Venn Diagram Study Fold Make the following Foldable to compare and contrast the characteristics of bacteria.

1. Place a sheet of paper in front of you so the long side is at the top. Fold the paper in half from top to bottom.

2. Fold both sides in. Unfold the paper so three sections show.

3. Through the top thickness of paper, cut along each of the fold lines to the topfold, forming three tabs. Label the tabs *Kingdom Archaebacteria, Both,* and *Kingdom Eubacteria.* Draw ovals on the front of the paper as shown.

4. As you read the chapter, list characteristics of each kingdom of bacteria under the tabs.

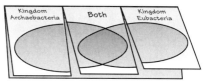

Kingdom Archaebacteria | Both | Kingdom Eubacteria

Purpose Use this Explore Activity to help students discover how the slime layer surrounding bacterial cells helps protect them from dehydration. L2

IS Kinesthetic

Preparation Collect kitchen sponges, plates, and hair styling gel. Locate areas where students can leave their sponges overnight.

Materials synthetic kitchen sponge; scissors; water; hair styling gel; plate

Teaching Strategy Have students do this activity the day before you introduce the topic of bacteria slime layers. Use the activity to demonstrate the properties of a slime layer.

Observe

Students should find that the gel-treated sponge is still damp and adheres to the plate. The untreated sponge will have dried out. A slime layer seals moisture inside the bacteria cell. Bacteria cells thrive in moist, damp environmental conditions.

✔ *Assessment*

Process Ask students to infer how Earth's nutrient cycles would be affected if bacteria cells did not have slime layers. Bacteria decompose dead and decaying materials into nutrients. Slime layers allow bacteria to lie dormant during drier conditions. Without slime layers, fewer bacteria would survive dry conditions, which would result in fewer nutrients being recycled. Use **PASC,** p. 89.

FOLDABLES
Reading & Study Skills

Before You Read

Dinah Zike Study Fold

Purpose Have students use a Foldable Venn diagram to determine what they know about bacteria in general and to record similarities and differences between the two kingdoms of bacteria.

For additional help, see Foldables Worksheet, p. 13 in **Chapter Resources Booklet,** or go to the Glencoe Science Web site at **science.glencoe.com.** See After You Read in the Study Guide at the end of this chapter.

SECTION

1

What are bacteria?

1 Motivate

Bellringer Transparency

Display the Section Focus Transparency for Section 1. Use the accompanying Transparency Activity Master. L2

ELL

Tie to Prior Knowledge

Review with students the characteristics of living things. Emphasize that bacterial cells have all of these characteristics, although they are smaller than the more familiar cells of plants and animals.

Caption Answer

Figure 1 sphere, rod, and spiral

Resource Manager

Chapter Resources Booklet

Transparency Activity, p. 38
MiniLAB, p. 3
Directed Reading, pp. 15, 16

SECTION

1 What are bacteria?

As You Read

What You'll Learn
- **Identify** the characteristics of bacterial cells.
- **Compare and contrast** aerobic and anaerobic organisms.

Vocabulary
flagella   aerobe
fission   anaerobe

Why It's Important
Bacteria are found in almost all environments and affect all living things.

Figure 1
A Coccus-, B bacillus-, and C spirillum-shaped bacteria can be found in almost any environment. *What common terms could be used to describe these cell shapes?*

Characteristics of Bacteria

For thousands of years people did not understand what caused disease. They did not understand the process of decomposition or what happened when food spoiled. It wasn't until the latter half of the seventeenth century that Antonie van Leeuwenhoek, a Dutch merchant, discovered the world of bacteria. Leeuwenhoek observed scrapings from his teeth using his simple microscope. Although he didn't know it at that time, some of the tiny swimming organisms he observed were bacteria. After Leeuwenhoek's discovery, it was another hundred years before bacteria were proven to be living cells that carry on all of the processes of life.

Where do bacteria live?   Bacteria are almost everywhere—in the air, in foods that you eat and drink, and on the surfaces of things you touch. They are even found thousands of meters underground and at great ocean depths. A shovelful of soil contains billions of them. Your skin has about 100,000 bacteria per square centimeter, and millions of other bacteria live in your body. Some types of bacteria live in extreme environments where few other organisms can survive. Some heat-loving bacteria live in hot springs or hydrothermal vents—places where water temperature exceeds 100°C. Others can live in cold water or soil at 0°C. Some bacteria live in very salty water, like that of the Dead Sea. One type of bacteria lives in water that drains from coal mines, which is extremely acidic at a pH of 1.

Magnification: 10,000×

Magnification: 4,400×

Magnification: 3,525×

8 ◆ B   CHAPTER 1 Bacteria

Section ✔*Assessment* Planner

PORTFOLIO
Science Journal, p. 11
PERFORMANCE ASSESSMENT
Try at Home MiniLAB, p. 9
Skill Builder Activities, p. 13
See page 28 for more options.

CONTENT ASSESSMENT
Section, p. 9
Challenge, p. 9
Chapter, pp. 28–29

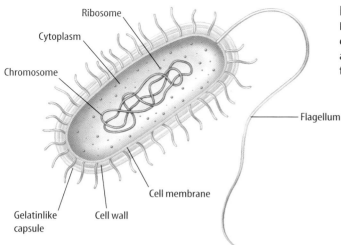

Ribosome
Cytoplasm
Chromosome

Flagellum

Cell membrane

Gelatinlike capsule
Cell wall

Figure 2
Bacterial cells are much smaller than eukaryotic cells. Most bacteria are about the size of some organelles found inside eukaryotic cells.

Structure of Bacterial Cells Bacteria normally have three basic shapes—spheres, rods, and spirals, as shown in **Figure 1.** Sphere-shaped bacteria are called cocci (KAH ki) (singular, *coccus*), rod-shaped bacteria are called bacilli (buh SIH li) (singular, *bacillus*), and spiral-shaped bacteria are called spirilla (spi RIH luh) (singular, *spirillum*). Bacteria are smaller than plant or animal cells. They are one-celled organisms that occur alone or in chains or groups.

A typical bacterial cell contains cytoplasm surrounded by a cell membrane and a cell wall, as shown in **Figure 2.** Bacterial cells are classified as prokaryotic because they do not contain a membrane-bound nucleus or other membrane-bound internal structures called organelles. Most of the genetic material of a bacterial cell is in its one circular chromosome found in the cytoplasm. Many bacteria also have a smaller circular piece of DNA called a plasmid. Ribosomes also are found in a bacterial cell's cytoplasm.

Special Features Some bacteria, like the type that causes pneumonia, have a thick, gelatinlike capsule around the cell wall. A capsule can help protect the bacterium from other cells that try to destroy it. The capsule, along with hairlike projections found on the surface of many bacteria, also can help them stick to surfaces. Some bacteria also have an outer coating called a slime layer. Like a capsule, a slime layer allows a bacterium to stick to surfaces and reduces water loss. Many bacteria that live in moist conditions also have whiplike tails called **flagella** to help them move.

✔ **Reading Check** *How do bacteria use flagella?*

TRY AT HOME
Mini LAB

Modeling Bacteria Size

1. One human hair is about 0.1 mm wide. Use a **meterstick** to measure a piece of **yarn or string** that is 10 m long. This yarn represents the width of your hair.
2. One type of bacteria is 2 micrometers long (1 micrometer = 0.000001 m). Measure another piece of yarn or string that is 20 cm long. This piece represents the length of the bacterium.
3. Find a large area where you can lay the two pieces of yarn or string next to each other and compare them.

Analysis
1. How much smaller is the bacterium than the width of your hair?
2. In your **Science Journal** describe why a model is helpful to understand how small bacteria are.

---

2 Teach

Characteristics of Bacteria

Visual Learning

Figure 1 Emphasize that bacteria have three-dimensional shapes. Ask students to name common objects that are similar in shape to bacteria. Balls are similar to cocci, lengths of thick wire are similar to bacilli, and wire spirals on notebooks are similar to spirilla. **Figure 2** Emphasize that bacterial cells are small. Compare the size of a bacterium to another object you have studied. Chloroplasts and mitochondria are about the same size as a bacterium.

TRY AT HOME
Mini LAB

Purpose to model the size of bacterial cells **IS** **Visual-Spatial**

Materials 11 m of yarn or string; meterstick

Teaching Strategy Have students compare the size of bacteria with viruses. The diameter of the average virus is 100 nm, or 0.0000001m, which is 10 times smaller than the average bacteria.

Analysis
1. 50 times smaller
2. Using models for size comparison allows one to understand the actual size of a bacterium.

Curriculum Connection

Math Ask students whether they would rather have $10 every 20 minutes for 13 hours or start with one penny and have their money doubled every 20 minutes for 13 hours. $400 by arithmetic growth or more than $5 trillion by exponential growth Point out that the growth rate of bacteria is like that of the penny. L2 **IS** **Logical-Mathematical**

✔ Assessment

Oral Explain how the size of bacteria contributes to the spread of infection. Their small size allows them to be transferred through the air when a person sneezes or coughs. Use **PASC**, p. 87.

✔ **Reading Check**

Answer to help them move

Fun Fact

Fission is also called binary fission. Binary fission is a quick and efficient means of producing many cells to utilize an energy resource.

Make a Model

Have students use objects from home to make a model of bacteria undergoing fission. For instance, two golf balls could be used to model fission in cocci. L1 IS Kinesthetic

Discussion

Have groups of students discuss the possible combinations of cocci, such as pairs (diplococci), strands (streptococci), and clusters (staphylococci). Explain that different species of bacteria assume all these shapes. L2 COOP LEARN IS Interpersonal

Magnification: 500×

Figure 3
Before dividing, these bacteria are exchanging DNA through the tubes that join them.

Figure 4
Observing where bacteria can grow in tubes of a nutrient mixture shows you how oxygen affects different types of bacteria.

Reproduction Bacteria usually reproduce by fission. **Fission** is a process that produces two new cells with genetic material identical to each other and that of the original cell. It is the simplest form of asexual reproduction.

Some bacteria exchange genetic material through a process similar to sexual reproduction, as shown in **Figure 3.** Two bacteria line up beside each other and exchange DNA through a fine tube. This results in cells with different combinations of genetic material than they had before the exchange. As a result, the bacteria may acquire variations that give them an advantage for survival.

How Bacteria Obtain Food and Energy Bacteria obtain food in a variety of ways. Some make their food and others get it from the environment. Bacteria that contain chlorophyll or other pigments make their own food using energy from the Sun. Other bacteria use energy from chemical reactions to make food. Bacteria and other organisms that can make their own food are called producers.

Most bacteria are consumers. They do not make their own food. Some break down dead organisms to obtain energy. Others live as parasites of living organisms and absorb nutrients from their host.

Most organisms use oxygen when they break down food and obtain energy through a process called respiration. An organism that uses oxygen for respiration is called an **aerobe** (AY rohb). You are an aerobic organism and so are most bacteria. In contrast, an organism that is adapted to live without oxygen is called an **anaerobe** (AN uh rohb). Several kinds of anaerobic bacteria live in the intestinal tract of humans. Some bacteria, like those in **Figure 4B,** cannot survive in areas with oxygen.

A Aerobic bacteria can grow only at the top of the tube where oxygen is present.

B Some anaerobic bacteria will grow only at the bottom of the tube where there is no oxygen.

C Other anaerobic bacteria can grow in areas with or without oxygen.

Inclusion Strategies

Learning Disabled Have pairs of students create flash cards that have the vocabulary for this chapter on one side and the definitions on the other. Allow students to practice using the vocabulary with their flash cards until they show proficiency with the terms. Students can also use flash cards to learn the names or structures of bacteria. L1 IS Linguistic

Teacher FYI

Leeuwenhoek was probably not the first person to observe bacteria, but he was the first to keep convincingly accurate records of his microscopic observations. He was also the first to show fission in cells.

Figure 5
Many different bacteria can live in the intestines of humans and other animals. They often are identified based on the foods they use and the wastes they produce.

Can they use lactose as a food?

No — Can they use citric acid as their only carbon source?

No → *Shigella* (Magnification: 3,500×)
Yes → *Salmonella* (Magnification: 6,000×)

Yes — Can they use citric acid as their only carbon source?

No → *Escherichia* (Magnification: 3,600×)
Yes → Do they produce acetoin as a waste?

No → *Citrobacter* (Magnification: 750×)
Yes → *Enterobacter* (Magnification: 4,000×)

Eubacteria

Bacteria are classified into two kingdoms—eubacteria (yew bak TIHR ee uh) and archaebacteria (ar kee bak TIHR ee uh). Eubacteria is the larger of the two kingdoms. The organisms in this kingdom are diverse, and scientists must study many characteristics in order to classify eubacteria into smaller groups. Most eubacteria are grouped according to their cell shape and structure, the way they obtain food, the type of food they eat, and the wastes they produce, as shown in **Figure 5.** Other characteristics used to group eubacteria include the method used for cell movement and whether the organism is an aerobe or anaerobe. New information about their genetic material is changing how scientists classify this kingdom.

Producer Eubacteria One important group of producer eubacteria is the cyanobacteria (si an oh bak TIHR ee uh). They make their own food using carbon dioxide, water, and energy from sunlight. They also produce oxygen as a waste. Cyanobacteria contain chlorophyll and another pigment that is blue. This pigment combination gives cyanobacteria their common name—blue-green bacteria. However, some cyanobacteria are yellow, black, or red. The Red Sea gets its name from red cyanobacteria.

 Reading Check *Why are cyanobacteria classified as producers?*

SCIENCE Online

Research Not all producer eubacteria use photosynthesis. Visit the Glencoe Science Web site at **science. glencoe.com** for more information about the ways that producer bacteria make food. Communicate to your class what you learn.

SECTION 1   What are bacteria?   **B ◆ 11**

Activity

Have students make a wet mount to observe *Oscillatoria*. Point out that swaying movements are made as the bacteria secrete a slimy substance from their cells. L2 IN **Visual-Spatial**

Earth Science
INTEGRATION

Ocean vents form where two of Earth's tectonic plates are splitting apart. The conditions are hypothesized to be similar to those on early Earth. Some organisms that live near ocean vents include tube worms, clams, mussels, and bacteria.

Caption Answer

Figure 7 thick if the cells are purple or thin if the cells are pink

Quick Demo

Demonstrate the classification of bacteria through staining by allowing students to view commercially prepared slides of gram-positive and gram-negative organisms. L2 IN **Visual-Spatial**

Magnification: 100×

Figure 6
These colonies of the cyanobacteria *Oscillatoria* can move by twisting like a screw.

Earth Science
INTEGRATION

Ocean vents are geysers on the floor of the ocean. Research and find out how ocean vents form and what conditions are like at an ocean vent. In your Science Journal, describe organisms that have been found living around ocean vents.

Figure 7
When stained with certain chemicals, bacteria with thin cell walls appear pink when viewed under a microscope. Those with thicker cell walls appear purple. *What type of cell walls do the coccus bacteria in this photo have?*

12 ◆ B   CHAPTER 1 Bacteria

Importance of Cyanobacteria Some cyanobacteria live together in long chains or filaments, as shown in **Figure 6.** Many are covered with a gelatinlike substance. This adaptation enables cyanobacteria to live in groups called colonies. They are an important source of food for some organisms in lakes, ponds, and oceans. The oxygen produced by cyanobacteria is used by all other aquatic organisms.

Cyanobacteria also can cause problems for aquatic life. Have you ever seen a pond covered with smelly, green, bubbly slime? When large amounts of nutrients enter a pond, cyanobacteria increase in number. Eventually the population grows so large that a bloom is produced. A bloom looks like a mat of bubbly green slime on the surface of the water. Available resources in the water are used up quickly and the cyanobacteria die. Other bacteria that are aerobic consumers feed on dead cyanobacteria and use up the oxygen in the water. As a result of the reduced oxygen in the water, fish and other organisms die.

Consumer Eubacteria Many of the consumer eubacteria are grouped by the type of cell wall produced—a thick cell wall or a thinner cell wall. This difference can be seen under a microscope after they are treated with certain chemicals that are called stains. As shown in **Figure 7,** thick-cell-walled bacteria stain a different color than thin-cell-walled bacteria.

The composition of the cell wall also can affect how a bacterium is affected by medicines given to treat an infection. Some medicines will be more effective against the type of bacteria with thicker cell walls than they will be against bacteria with thinner cell walls.

One group of eubacteria is unique because they do not produce cell walls. This allows them to change their shape. They are not described as coccus, bacillus, or spirillum. One type of bacteria in this group, *Mycoplasma pneumoniae*, causes a type of pneumonia in humans.

Magnification: 800×

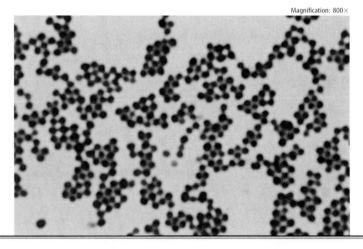

Inclusion Strategies

Learning Disabled If possible, bring in some pond water that has a mat of cyanobacteria on it. Place the mat in the light and ask what the bubbles are that appear in the mat. They are oxygen bubbles produced by photosynthesis. Then ask how large numbers of cyanobacteria can cause problems. When cyanobacteria die and decompose, oxygen levels drop. This can cause other organisms, such as fish, to die. L1
IN **Visual-Spatial**

✔ Active Reading

Buddy Interviews This strategy helps students understand and clarify the reading. Have students interview one another to find out what helps them to understand what they are reading, how they find answers, and how they assimilate new vocabulary terms. Have students use Buddy Interviews to help them master concepts about bacteria.

Archaebacteria

Kingdom Archaebacteria contains certain kinds of bacteria that often are found in extreme conditions, such as hot springs. The conditions in which some archaebacteria live today are similar to conditions found on Earth during its early history. Archaebacteria are divided into groups based on where they live or how they get energy.

Salt-, Heat-, and Acid-Lovers One group of archaebacteria lives in salty environments such as the Great Salt Lake in Utah and the Dead Sea. Some of them require a habitat ten times saltier than seawater to grow.

Other groups of archaebacteria include those that live in acidic or hot environments. Some of these bacteria live near deep ocean vents or in hot springs where the temperature of the water is above 100°C.

Methane Producers Bacteria in this group of archaebacteria are anaerobic. They live in muddy swamps, the intestines of cattle, and even in you. Methane producers, as shown in **Figure 8,** use carbon dioxide for energy and release methane gas as a waste. Sometimes methane produced by these bacteria bubbles up out of swamps and marshes. These archaebacteria also are used in the process of sewage treatment. In an oxygen-free tank, the bacteria are used to break down the waste material that has been filtered from sewage water.

Magnification: 4,200×

Figure 8
Some methane-producing bacteria live in the digestive tracts of cattle. They help digest the plants that cattle eat.

Section Assessment

1. What are the characteristics common to all bacteria?
2. How do aerobic organisms and anaerobic organisms differ?
3. How do most bacteria reproduce?
4. Who is given credit for first discovering bacteria?
5. **Think Critically** A pond is surrounded by recently fertilized farm fields. What effect would rainwater runoff from the fields have on the organisms in the pond?

Skill Builder Activities

6. **Classifying** A scientist recently found bacteria that grow in boiling water. In what kingdom is the bacteria most likely classified? Why? **For more help,** refer to the Science Skill Handbook.
7. **Solving One-Step Equations** Some bacteria reproduce every 20 min. Suppose that you have one bacterium. How long would it take for the number of bacteria to increase to more than 1 million? **For more help,** refer to the Math Skill Handbook.

Reteach

To demonstrate the role of bacteria as decomposers, bring a piece of decomposing fruit to class. Have students observe the process over a few days or a week. L2 **IS** **Visual-Spatial**

Challenge

Have students research the cells of prokaryotes and eukaryotes to determine differences. **How are flagella of bacteria different from flagella of other organisms, such as** *Euglena?* Flagella of bacteria are simpler and are not surrounded by a membrane. L2 **IS** **Linguistic**

✔Assessment

Performance To further assess students' abilities to observe cyanobacteria, set up a practical to have them identify organisms or answer questions about them. Use **Performance Assessment in the Science Classroom,** p. 89.

Answers to Section Assessment

1. one-celled; cytoplasm surrounded by cell membrane and cell wall; single circular chromosome; ribosomes in cytoplasm; plasmid; no membrane-bound organelles
2. Aerobic: require oxygen to live; anaerobic: can live without oxygen. Oxygen kills some anaerobes.
3. Fission; some bacteria also exchange

genetic material in a process similar to sexual reproduction.
4. Antonie van Leeuwenhoek
5. It could potentially kill the pond organisms as cyanobacteria flourish, die, and decompose.

6. Kingdom Archaebacteria; these organisms often live in harsh conditions.
7. 6 hours and 40 minutes (1,048,576 bacteria)

Resource Manager

Chapter Resources Booklet
Reinforcement, p. 23
Lab Activity, pp. 9–10

Activity
BENCH TESTED

Purpose to observe and record the characteristics of several cyanobacteria L2 ELL

LS Naturalist

Process Skills observing, classifying, interpreting data

Time Required 50 minutes

Alternate Materials In addition to the cyanobacteria listed, many others can be found in biological supply house catalogs.

Teaching Strategy Having prepared slides for use will be more interesting and visually stimulating for students than having them look at pictures.

Troubleshooting If students have trouble seeing the jellylike layer of the capsule, have them reduce the amount of light coming through the microscope's diaphragm.

Answers to Questions

1. You can infer that they are producers that carry on photosynthesis.
2. Cyanobacteria contain chlorophyll, which makes them photosynthetic eubacteria.

✔ Assessment

Performance Have students draw, label, and describe different cyanobacteria they observe. Use **Performance Assessment in the Science Classroom,** p. 127.

Activity
Observing Cyanobacteria

Y ou can obtain many species of cyanobacteria from ponds. When you look at these organisms under a microscope, you will find that they have similarities and differences. In this activity, compare and contrast species of cyanobacteria.

Cyanobacteria Observations

Structure	Anabaena	Gloeocapsa	Nostoc	Oscillatoria
Filament or Colony	filament	colony	filament	filament
Nucleus	no	no	no	no
Chlorophyll	yes	yes	yes	yes
Gel-Like Layer	yes	yes	yes	yes

What You'll Investigate
What do cyanobacteria look like?

Materials
micrograph photos of *Oscillatoria* and *Nostoc*
prepared slides of Oscillatoria *and* Nostoc
prepared slides of *Gloeocapsa* and *Anabaena*
micrograph photos of Anabaena *and* Gloeocapsa
microscope
Alternate materials

Goals
■ **Observe** several species of cyanobacteria.
■ **Describe** the structure and function of cyanobacteria.

Safety Precautions

Procedure

1. Copy the data table in your Science Journal. **Record** the presence or absence of each characteristic in the data table for each cyanobacterium you observe.

2. **Observe** prepared slides of *Gloeocapsa* and *Anabaena* under low and high power of the microscope. Notice the difference in the arrangement of the cells. In your Science Journal, draw and label a few cells of each.

3. **Observe** photos of *Nostoc* and *Oscillatoria.* In your Science Journal, draw and label a few cells of each.

Conclude and Apply

1. What can you infer from the color of each cyanobacterium?

2. How can you tell by observing that a cyanobacterium is a eubacterium?

Communicating
Your Data

Compare your data table with those of other students in your class. **For more help, refer to the** Science Skill Handbook.

Communicating
Your Data

Data tables should be the same for all students. Students who have differences should be prepared to explain them to others.

Resource Manager

Chapter Resources Booklet
Activity Worksheet, pp. 5–6

Bacteria in Your Life

Beneficial Bacteria

When most people hear the word *bacteria,* they probably associate it with sore throats or other illnesses. However, few bacteria cause illness. Most are important for other reasons. The benefits of most bacteria far outweigh the harmful effects of a few.

Bacteria That Help You Without bacteria, you would not be healthy for long. Bacteria, like those in **Figure 9,** are found inside your digestive system. These bacteria are found in particularly high numbers in your large intestine. Most are harmless to you, and they help you stay healthy. For example, the bacteria in your intestines are responsible for producing vitamin K, which is necessary for normal blood clot formation.

Some bacteria produce chemicals called **antibiotics** that limit the growth of other bacteria. For example, one type of bacteria that is commonly found living in soil produces the antibiotic streptomycin. Another kind of bacteria, *Bacillus,* produces the antibiotic found in many nonprescription antiseptic ointments. Many diseases in humans and animals can be treated with antibiotics.

As You Read

What You'll Learn
- **Identify** some ways bacteria are helpful.
- **Determine** the importance of nitrogen-fixing bacteria.
- **Explain** how some bacteria can cause human disease.

Vocabulary

antibiotic	toxin
saprophyte	endospore
nitrogen-fixing bacteria	vaccine
pathogen	

Why It's Important
Discovering the ways bacteria affect your life can help you understand biological processes.

Magnification: 250× — *Lactobacillus*

Magnification: 11,000× — *Klebsiella*

Magnification: 20,000× — *E. coli*

Proteus — Magnification: 1,000×

Fusobacterium — Magnification: 3,000×

Figure 9
Many types of bacteria live naturally in your large intestine. They help you digest food and produce vitamins that you need.

SECTION 2 Bacteria in Your Life **B ◆ 15**

SECTION

Bacteria in Your Life

1 Motivate

Bellringer Transparency
Display the Section Focus Transparency for Section 2. Use the accompanying Transparency Activity Master. [L2] ELL

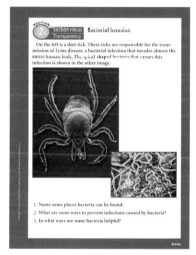

Tie to Prior Knowledge
Ask students if they have ever had a sore throat or eaten cheese. Explain that both of these experiences involve bacteria. In this section, they will learn about beneficial and harmful bacteria.

Section ✓Assessment Planner

PORTFOLIO
Cultural Diversity, p. 16
Science Journal, p. 20

PERFORMANCE ASSESSMENT
MiniLAB, p. 16
Skill Builder Activities, p. 21
See page 28 for more options.

CONTENT ASSESSMENT
Section, p. 21
Challenge, p. 21
Chapter, pp. 28–29

Beneficial Bacteria

Caption Answer
Figure 10 aerobes

✔ **Reading Check**

Answer an organism that uses dead material as a food and energy source

Mini LAB

Purpose to observe and infer the growth rate of bacteria L1
ELL COOP LEARN IS **Kinesthetic**
Materials dried beans, distilled water, glass beaker
Teaching Strategies

• You may want to soak the beans for 24 hours prior to doing the lab, as this makes it easier for students to break them apart.

• Point out that the water's cloudiness indicates bacterial growth.

Safety Precautions Tell students to wash their hands after handling the materials and not to eat any of them.

Troubleshooting To avoid odors, caution students not to leave the beans and water in the classroom for more than five days.

Analysis
1. It usually takes 3–4 days.
2. the beans

✔ Assessment

Process Have students hypothesize the doubling time of bacterial cells. Then have them design an experiment to test their hypothesis. Use **PASC,** p. 93.

Figure 10
Air is bubbled through the sewage in this aeration tank so that bacteria can break down much of the sewage wastes. *Are the bacteria that live in this tank aerobes or anaerobes?*

Mini LAB

Observing Bacterial Growth

Procedure 🔲 🔲 🔲
1. Obtain two or three **dried beans.**
2. Carefully break them into halves and place the halves into 10 mL of **distilled water** in a **glass beaker.**
3. Observe how many days it takes for the water to become cloudy and develop an unpleasant odor.

Analysis
1. How long did it take for the water to become cloudy?
2. What do you think the bacteria were using as a food source?

Bacteria and the Environment Without bacteria, there would be layers of dead material all over Earth deeper than you are tall. Consumer bacteria called saprophytes (SAP ruh fitz) help maintain nature's balance. A **saprophyte** is any organism that uses dead organisms as food and energy sources. Saprophytic bacteria help recycle nutrients. These nutrients become available for use by other organisms. As shown in **Figure 10,** most sewage-treatment plants use saprophytic aerobic bacteria to break down wastes into carbon dioxide and water.

✔ **Reading Check** *What is a saprophyte?*

Plants and animals must take in nitrogen to make needed proteins and nucleic acids. Animals can eat plants or other animals that contain nitrogen, but plants need to take nitrogen from the soil or air. Although air is about 78 percent nitrogen, neither animals nor plants can use it directly. **Nitrogen-fixing bacteria** change nitrogen from the air into forms that plants and animals can use. The roots of some plants such as peanuts and peas develop structures called nodules that contain nitrogen-fixing bacteria, as shown in **Figure 11.** It is estimated that nitrogen-fixing bacteria save U.S. farmers millions of dollars in fertilizer costs every year. Many of the cyanobacteria also can fix nitrogen and are important in providing nitrogen in usable forms to aquatic organisms.

Bioremediation Using organisms to help clean up or remove environmental pollutants is called bioremediation. One type of bioremediation uses bacteria to break down wastes and pollutants into simpler harmless compounds. Other bacteria use certain pollutants as a food source. Every year about five percent to ten percent of all wastes produced by industry, agriculture, and cities are treated by bioremediation. Sometimes bioremediation is used at the site where chemicals, such as oil, have been spilled. Research continues on ways to make bioremediation a faster process.

Teacher FYI

Bioremediation has been used on a wide variety of organic and toxic compounds. Cleanup of oil spills by bioremediation is likely to increase in the future.

Cultural Diversity

In a Pickle Pickling is a process of food preservation that depends on the chemical process of fermentation and the inhibition of bacterial growth in a highly acidic solution. It is found in the cuisine of many cultures. Have students research different pickling processes and prepare lists of how and what products are pickled in different cultures. L2 P

Figure 11

Although 78 percent of Earth's atmosphere is nitrogen gas (N_2), most living things are unable to use nitrogen in this form. Some bacteria, however, convert N_2 into the ammonium ion (NH_4^+) that organisms can use. This process is called nitrogen fixation. Nitrogen-fixing bacteria in soil can enter the roots of plants, such as beans, peanuts, alfalfa, and peas, as shown in the background photo. The bacteria and the plant form a relationship that benefits both of them.

Root hair

Bacterium

◀ Nitrogen-fixing bacteria typically enter a plant through root hairs—thin-walled cells on a root's outer surface.

Root hair

Beadlike nodules full of bacteria cover the roots of a pea plant.

Root cells containing nitrogen-fixing bacteria

Infection thread

▲ Once inside the root hair, the bacteria enlarge and cause the plant to produce a sort of tube called an infection thread. The bacteria move through the thread to reach cells deeper inside the root.

▲ The bacteria rapidly divide in the root cells, which in turn divide repeatedly to form tumorlike nodules on the roots. Once established, the bacteria (purple) fix nitrogen for use by the host plant. In return, the plant supplies the bacteria with sugars and other vital nutrients.

SECTION 2 Bacteria in Your Life **B ◆ 17**

Visualizing Nitrogen Fixing Bacteria

Have students examine the pictures and read the captions. Then ask the following questions.

What is the "cost" to a plant for having nitrogen-fixing bacteria in its root cells? The "cost" to the plant is that the carbohydrates it makes are used by the bacteria.

When pea plants are producing peas, the nitrogen fixation of the associated bacteria dips to a low level. What would be a logical explanation for this? When producing peas, the plant has little extra sugar for the bacteria to use, so nitrogen fixation slows.

Activity

Have students model the relationship between plants and nitrogen fixation. Designate each student as either a plant or a nitrogen-fixing bacterium. Plants should carry two index cards, one labeled "sugars" and one labeled "nutrients." Bacteria should carry two index cards, each labeled "NH_4^+." Explain that each student must have one sugar and nutrient card and one NH_4^+ card to survive. Have the students exchange cards to meet their needs. L1 IS **Interpersonal**

Extension

Direct interested students to examine the contents of different brands of garden and lawn fertilizer and infer why nitrogen is an ingredient in most of these products. Nitrogen is needed for plants to grow well. Nitrogen in the form provided by the fertilizers can be absorbed and used by plants.

Resource Manager

Chapter Resources Booklet
Transparency Activity, p. 39
MiniLAB, p. 4

Beneficial Bacteria,
continued

Chemistry
INTEGRATION

Answers will vary, but most bacteria require a slightly acidic pH.

A Mutualist Relationship

Have students explain in their Science Journals why "infection" of roots by nitrogen-fixing bacteria is beneficial for both plant and environment. Nitrogen gas in the atmosphere is unusable for most organisms. The bacteria fix nitrogen in a form that plants can use. After the plant dies, nitrogen is available for use by other organisms. L2 IS **Linguistic**

Visual Learning

Figure 12 Enhance the impact of the photo by having students taste cheese curds. You may also have students bring various cheeses from home to taste. Point out that these foods were prepared by using beneficial bacteria. Caution students who may have food allergies to avoid tasting the cheeses. L1 ELL IS **Kinesthetic**

✔ Reading Check

Answer methane

Chemistry
INTEGRATION

One condition that must be monitored in a bioreactor is pH, or how acidic the conditions are in the bioreactor. Research and find out what pH levels different bacteria require for growth. In your Science Journal, write a paragraph describing what you find out about bacteria and pH levels.

Figure 12
Ⓐ When bacteria such as *Streptococcus lactis* are added to milk, it causes the milk to separate into curds (solids) and whey (liquids). Ⓑ Other bacteria are added to the curds, which ripen into cheese. The type of cheese made depends on the bacterial species added to the curds.

Ⓐ

Bacteria and Food Have you had any bacteria for lunch lately? Even before people understood that bacteria were involved, they were used in the production of foods. One of the first uses of bacteria was for making yogurt, a milk-based food that has been made in Europe and Asia for hundreds of years. Bacteria break down substances in milk to make many dairy products. Cheeses and buttermilk also can be produced with the aid of bacteria. Cheese making is shown in **Figure 12.**

Other foods you might have eaten also are made using bacteria. Sauerkraut, for example, is made with cabbage and a bacterial culture. Vinegar, pickles, olives, and soy sauce also are produced with the help of bacteria.

Bacteria in Industry Many industries rely on bacteria to make many products. Bacteria are grown in large containers called bioreactors. Conditions inside bioreactors are carefully controlled and monitored to allow for the growth of the bacteria. Medicines, enzymes, cleansers, and adhesives are some of the products that are made using bacteria.

Methane gas that is released as a waste by certain bacteria can be used as a fuel for heating, cooking, and industry. In landfills, methane-producing bacteria break down plant and animal material. The quantity of methane gas released by these bacteria is so large that some cities collect and burn it, as shown in **Figure 13.** Using bacteria to digest wastes and then produce methane gas could supply large amounts of fuel worldwide.

✔ Reading Check
What waste gas produced by some bacteria can be used as a fuel?

Ⓑ

🔬 LAB DEMONSTRATION

Purpose to observe the activity of bacteria
Materials plastic wastebasket, soil, paper, grass clippings, leaves, small sticks, dried food, bacteria culture, water, thermometer
Preparation Provide materials for students to see. Have them write down their expectations for mixed materials.

Procedure Mix the materials, keeping the mixture as light as possible. Add small amounts of water. Take the temperature of the mixture every couple of days and stir the compost pile. You may want to continue adding materials.

Expected Outcome Students should observe the decay of organic materials.

✔ Assessment

Why does the temperature rise above room temperature? As bacteria respire, they release heat. **What happens to the paper and other organic material?** It decays to form compost.

Figure 13
Methane gas produced by bacteria in this landfill is burning at the top of these collection tubes.

Harmful Bacteria

As mentioned earlier, not all bacteria are beneficial. Some bacteria are known as pathogens. A **pathogen** is any organism that causes disease. If you have ever had strep throat, you have had firsthand experience with a bacterial pathogen. Other pathogenic bacteria cause anthrax in cattle, as well as diphtheria, tetanus, and whooping cough in humans.

How Pathogens Make You Sick Bacterial pathogens can cause illness and disease by several different methods. They can enter your body through a cut in the skin, you can inhale them, or they can enter in other ways. Once inside your body, they can multiply, damage normal cells, and cause illness and disease.

Some bacterial pathogens produce poisonous substances known as **toxins**. Botulism—a type of food poisoning that can result in paralysis and death—is caused by a toxin-producing bacterium. Botulism-causing bacteria are able to grow and produce toxins inside sealed cans of food. However, when growing conditions are unfavorable for their survival, some bacterial pathogens like those that cause botulism can produce thick-walled structures called **endospores**. Endospores, shown in **Figure 14,** can exist for hundreds of years before they resume growth. If the endospores of the botulism-causing bacteria are in canned food, they can grow and develop into regular bacterial cells and produce toxins again. Commercially canned foods undergo a process that uses steam under high pressure, which kills bacteria and most endospores.

> **SCIENCE Online**
>
> **Research** Visit the Glencoe Science Web site at **science.glencoe.com** for more information about pathogenic bacteria and antibiotics. Communicate to your class what you learn.

Figure 14
Bacterial endospores can survive harsh winters, dry conditions, and heat. *How can endospores be destroyed?*

Magnification: 47,500×

Harmful Bacteria

Quick Demo
Burn natural gas (methane) using a Bunsen burner to emphasize to students that the product of landfill bacteria can be useful. **IS Visual-Spatial**

Extension
Tuberculosis is caused by *Mycobacterium tuberculosis.* The number of cases of this disease is on the rise in the United States and worldwide. Have students research the reasons for this increase. Answers may include population growth, spread of HIV, immigration, and drug-resistant bacteria. L2

Caption Answer
Figure 14 with long term high-heat treatment

Discussion
Have students research various pathogens to find the species of bacteria that causes each of the following diseases: cholera, strep throat, tetanus, and salmonella food poisoning. *Vibrio cholerae, Streptococcus pyogenes, Clostridium tetani, Salmonella species* Discuss each disease's symptoms and cure. L2 **IS Linguistic**

Teacher FYI
Some pathogens produce exotoxins, which are proteins secreted by bacteria. Exotoxins cause symptoms even if the bacteria aren't present. Some diseases caused by exotoxins are botulism, tetanus, and cholera. Other bacteria cause endotoxins, which cause symptoms only when bacteria are present. Some diseases caused by endotoxins are typhoid and meningitis.

Resource Manager

Chapter Resources Booklet
Directed Reading for Content Mastery, pp. 17, 18
Enrichment, p. 26
Lab Activity, pp. 11–12

SCIENCE Online
Internet Addresses

_____
_____
_____

Explore the Glencoe Science Web site at **science.glencoe.com** to find out more about topics in this section.

Harmful Bacteria,
continued

Use an Analogy

Some antibiotics bind to fat-like molecules found in cell membranes. Just like detergents break up food and grease on dirty dishes, these antibiotics break up the fatlike molecules and destroy the cell membranes of harmful bacteria.

Science Journal

Battling TB Have students write one-page reports in their Science Journals explaining why the battle with tuberculosis and other pathogens is becoming increasingly difficult. L2

[S] **Linguistic** P

Problem-Solving Activity

National Math Standards

Correlation to Mathematics Objectives

6, 8

Answers

1. Students could place disks of paper soaked in different mouthwashes in petri dishes that have bacteria growing on them.
2. Paper disks soaked in distilled water could be placed into a dish as a control.
3. Alcohol is the antiseptic. Water, glycerin, preservatives, and dyes also are listed. The dyes are solely for appearance.

Figure 15
Pasteurization lowers the amount of bacteria in foods. Dairy products, such as ice cream and yogurt, are pasteurized.

Pasteurization Unless it has been sterilized, all food contains bacteria. But heating food to sterilizing temperatures can change its taste. Pasteurization is a process of heating food to a temperature that kills most harmful bacteria but causes little change to the taste of the food. You are probably most familiar with pasteurized milk, but some fruit juices and other foods, as shown in **Figure 15,** also are pasteurized.

Problem-Solving Activity

Controlling Bacterial Growth

Bacteria can be controlled by slowing or preventing their growth, or killing them. When trying to control bacteria that affect humans, it is often desirable just to slow their growth because substances that kill bacteria or prevent them from growing can harm humans. For example, bleach often is used to kill bacteria in bathrooms or on kitchen surfaces, but it is poisonous if swallowed. *Antiseptic* is the word used to describe substances that slow the growth of bacteria.

Identifying the Problem

Advertisers often claim that a substance kills bacteria, when in fact the substance only slows its growth. Many mouthwash advertisements make this claim. How could you test three mouthwashes to see which one is the best antiseptic?

Solving the Problem

1. Describe an experiment that you could do that would test which of three mouthwash products is the most effective antiseptic.
2. What control would you use in your experiment?
3. Read the ingredients label on a bottle of mouthwash. List the ingredients in the mouthwash. What ingredient do you think is the antiseptic? Explain.

20 ◆ B   CHAPTER 1 Bacteria

Curriculum Connection

Geography Have students show on a world map where each of the major diseases discussed in this section occurs with greatest incidence. L2

[S] **Visual-Spatial**

Resource Manager

Chapter Resources Booklet
   Reinforcement, p. 24
Mathematics Skill Activities, p. 19

Figure 16
Each of these paper disks contains a different antibiotic. Clear areas where no bacteria are growing can be seen around some disks.
Which one of these disks would you infer contains an antibiotic that is most effective against the bacteria growing on the plate?

Health
INTEGRATION

Treating Bacterial Diseases

Bacterial diseases in humans and animals usually are treated effectively with antibiotics. Penicillin, a well-known antibiotic, works by preventing bacteria from making cell walls. Without cell walls, certain bacteria cannot survive. **Figure 16** shows antibiotics at work.

Vaccines can prevent some bacterial diseases. A **vaccine** can be made from damaged particles taken from bacterial cell walls or from killed bacteria. Once the vaccine is injected, white blood cells in the blood recognize that type of bacteria. If the same type of bacteria enters the body at a later time, the white blood cells immediately attack them. Vaccines have been produced that are effective against many bacterial diseases.

Section 2 Assessment

1. Why are saprophytic bacteria helpful and necessary?
2. Why are nitrogen-fixing bacteria important?
3. List three uses of bacteria in food production and industry.
4. How do some bacteria cause disease?
5. **Think Critically** Why is botulism associated with canned foods and not fresh foods?

Skill Builder Activities

6. **Measuring in SI** Air can have more than 3,500 bacteria per cubic meter. How many bacteria might be in your classroom? **For more help, refer to the** Science Skill Handbook.
7. **Developing Multimedia Presentations** Prepare a presentation on how bacteria are used in industry to produce products you use. **For more help, refer to the** Technology Skill Handbook.

3 Assess

Reteach

Show students photographs of processes carried out by bacteria. Have students identify each process and its importance. L2
IS Visual-Spatial

Challenge

Have students demonstrate their understanding of the work of bacteria by bringing to class foods that are processed using bacteria or objects that show the effects of bacteria. L2

✔ Assessment

Process Assess students' understanding of vaccines by having them make a concept map outlining what happens when someone receives a vaccination for a disease, and later is infected with that disease. The individual receives a vaccine, which allows their white blood cells to recognize and develop a defense against a particular disease-causing organism. When the organism later enters the individual's bloodstream, it is immediately recognized and killed by the white blood cells. Use **Performance Assessment in the Science Classroom,** p. 161.

Answers to Section Assessment

1. They recycle nutrients.
2. They change atmospheric nitrogen into a form that can be used by plants or animals.
3. Bacteria are used in making yogurt, sauerkraut, and other food products. Biotechnology industries use bacteria to produce medicines and other products. Methane gas can be produced in landfills.
4. Some bacteria produce toxins; others multiply in the body, damaging normal cells and causing illness and disease.
5. The bacteria that cause botulism are anaerobes, which grow in an oxygen-free environment, such as that in canned foods.
6. To calculate the answer, measure the length, width, and height of the classroom in meters. Multiply these numbers to find the volume of air in the classroom. Multiply the volume by 3,500 to obtain the number of bacteria per cubic meter.
7. Check students' work for accuracy.

Activity

Recognize the Problem

Purpose

Students design an experiment to determine the types of materials that will decompose in a compost pile. L2 IS **Visual-Spatial**

Process Skills

comparing, contrasting, predicting, describing, making a data table, interpreting data

Time Required

One 45-minute class period; three or four 20-minute observation periods over a period of four weeks

Form a Hypothesis

Possible Hypotheses

Most student hypotheses will reflect the knowledge that food items will decay most rapidly, but many students will not be able to identify all the biodegradable items in their experiments.

Test Your Hypothesis

Possible Procedure

Establish several compost piles in wide-mouthed jars or flat baking pans by burying food scraps, grass clippings, and leaf litter under 10 cm of soil. Water, turn, and add layers of soil to the containers regularly. After the compost is established, place test items flat on the compost and bury them under 10 cm of soil. Examine the items once a week for signs of decomposition.

Activity

Composting

Over time, landfills fill up and new places to dump trash become more difficult to find. One way to reduce the amount of trash that must be dumped in a landfill is to recycle. Composting is a form of recycling that changes plant wastes into reusable, nutrient-rich compost. How do plant wastes become compost? What types of organisms can assist in the process?

Recognize the Problem

What types of items can be composted and what types cannot?

Form a Hypothesis

Based on readings or prior knowledge, form a hypothesis about what types of items will decompose in a compost pile and which will not.

Safety Precautions

Be sure to wash your hands every time after handling the compost material.

Goals

■ **Predict** which of several items will decompose in a compost pile and which will not.

■ **Demonstrate** the decomposition, or lack thereof, of several items.

■ **Compare** and **contrast** the speed at which various items break down.

Possible Materials

widemouthed, clear glass jars (at least 4)
soil
water
watering can
banana peel
apple core
scrap of newspaper
leaf
plastic candy wrapper
scrap of aluminum foil

22 ◆ B

Teaching Strategies:

• Encourage students to use common items such as polystyrene cups, aluminum cans, notebook paper, glossy magazine paper, and articles of clothing made of both natural and artificial fibers as well as biodegradable food items.

• Encourage students to bring garden gloves to school to use when unearthing their items.

Test Your Hypothesis

Plan

1. **Decide** what items you are going to test. Choose some items that you think will decompose and some that you think will not.

2. **Predict** which of the items you chose will or will not decompose. Of the items that will, which do you think will decompose fastest? Slowest?

3. **Decide** how you will test whether or not the items decompose. How will you see the items? You may need to research composting in books, magazines, or on the Internet.

4. Prepare a data table in your Science Journal to record your observations.

5. **Identify** all constants, variables, and controls of the experiment.

Do

1. Make sure your teacher approves of your plan and your data table before you start.

2. Set up your experiment and collect data as planned.

3. While doing the experiment, record your observations and complete your data tables in your Science Journal.

Analyze Your Data

1. **Describe** your results. Did all of the items decompose? If not, which did and which did not?

2. Were your predictions correct? Explain.

3. Was there a difference in how fast items decomposed? If so, which items decomposed fastest and which took longer?

Draw Conclusions

1. What general statement(s) can you make about what types of items can be composted and which cannot? What about the speed of decomposition?

2. Do your results support your hypothesis?

3. What might happen to your compost pile if antibiotics were added to it? Explain.

4. **Describe** what you think happens in a landfill to items similar to those that you tested.

*C*ommunicating
Your Data

Write a letter to the editor of the local newspaper describing what you have learned about composting and encouraging your neighbors to do more composting.

ACTIVITY   B ◆ 23

✓*Assessment*

Performance With permission, have students plan and construct a school compost pile in a corner of the school property. Use **Performance Assessment in the Science Classroom,** p. 105.

*C*ommunicating
Your Data

Encourage students to access the Glencoe Science Web site to gather information on local landfills, compost sites, and recycling centers.

Expected Outcome

Student results should show various degrees of decay for the food items, natural fiber clothing, and paper. Nonbiodegradable items will not show significant signs of decay.

Analyze Your Data

1. Food items, paper, and clothing made of natural fibers will show various signs of decay, but nondegradable items will not.

2. Answers will vary with results.

3. The food items will decay most rapidly, followed by clothing made of natural fibers. Moist items will decay more rapidly than drier items.

Error Analysis

To avoid confusion when examining the composted items, students should use initially new items and make a record of the appearance of each item before it is composted.

Draw Conclusions

1. Materials made of natural ingredients can be composted, but artificial items will not compost. Aerating the soil and keeping the compost moist increases decay.

2. Answers will vary.

3. Bacteria are the primary decomposing agents in compost piles. Killing bacteria would slow or stop the decay process.

4. Landfill items are frequently buried more deeply, are exposed to less moisture, and receive little or no aeration. Thus items would decay more slowly in a landfill.

Content Background

There are many bacteria species that thrive in extreme environmental conditions. Thermophiles are bacteria that thrive at temperatures between 50°C to 60°C. Some can even live in hot springs and ocean hydrothermal vents, where temperatures can reach 110°C. Other bacteria, called psychrophiles, are most comfortable at temperatures of 15°C to 20°C. Psychrophiles that live in the soil and water of Arctic regions can survive temperatures as low as 0°C. Bacteria that live under extreme pressure are called barophiles. Barophiles that live on the ocean floor at a depth of 7 km cannot survive at atmospheric pressure. Some species of bacteria, called acidophiles, can survive in highly acidic environments. These bacteria can survive in a pH as low as 1 and are found in water that drains from coal mines, which contains high amounts of sulfuric acid and in hydrothermal vents.

Discussion

What advantages do unusual bacteria have over other types of bacteria? Possible answer: These bacteria can survive in extreme environmental conditions.

Activity

Have students research different methods of food preservation, such as refrigeration, pasteurization, sterilization, pH alteration, radiation, and chemical preservatives, and discuss how the form of preservation relates to the basic survival or environmental requirements of many bacteria.

Science Stats

Unusual Bacteria

Did you know...

...The hardiest bacteria, *Deinococcus radiodurans* (DE no KO kus·RA de oh DOOR anz), has a nasty odor, which has been described as similar to rotten cabbage. It might have an odor, but it can survive 3,000 times more radiation than humans because it quickly repairs damage to its DNA molecule. These bacteria were discovered in canned meat when they survived sterilization by radiation.

...The smallest bacteria, nanobes (NAN obes), are Earth's smallest living things. These miniature creatures live far below the ocean floor and are 20 to 150 nanometers long. That means, depending on their size, it would take about 6,500,000 to 50,000,000 nanobes lined up to equal 1 m!

...Nanobes were discovered in ancient stone about 5 km beneath the ocean floor in petroleum exploration wells near Australia. To understand just how deep this is, first picture the bottom of the ocean. Then imagine a hole in the bottom of the ocean that's deep enough to bury about 13 Empire State Buildings stacked on top of each other.

SCIENCE
Online
Internet Addresses

_____
_____
_____

Explore the Glencoe Science Web site at **science.glencoe.com** to find out more about topics in this feature.

...The largest bacterium on Earth,

Thiomargarita namibiensis (THE oh ma ga RE ta·nah ME be yen sis), is about the same size as the period at the end of this sentence. Its name means, "Sulfur Pearl of Namibia," and describes its appearance. The sulfur inside its cells reflects white light. The cells form strands that look like strings of pearls.

T. namibiensis

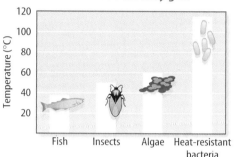

How hot can they get?

Temperature (°C) / Organisms: Fish, Insects, Algae, Heat-resistant bacteria

...Earth's oldest living bacteria

are thought to be 250 million years old. These ancient bacteria were revived from a crystal of rock salt buried 579 m below the desert floor in New Mexico.

Do the Math

1. The smallest and the oldest bacteria were found beneath Earth's surface. Which was deeper? How many meters deeper was it found?
2. What is the difference in size between the smallest nanobe and the largest nanobe?
3. A rad is a unit for measuring radiation. *Deinococcus radiodurans* can withstand a maximum of 1.5 million rads of radiation. How many rads would be deadly to humans?

Go Further

Do library research about halophiles, the bacteria that can live in salty environments. What is the maximum salt concentration in which they can survive? How does this compare to the maximum salt concentration bacteria that are not halophiles can survive?

Do the Math

Teaching Strategies

- Have students recall how to convert km to m by multiplying km by 1000.
- Have students recall how to set up an equation to solve for an unknown variable.

Answers

1. smallest, 4421 m
2. 130 nanometers
3. 500 rads

Go Further

Have students list locations where halophiles can be found. ocean, Great Salt Lake, Dead Sea, salt licks, brine vats, salt flats Have students make a chart of the different types of halophiles, the salt concentration in which they can survive, and the number of times higher that is than the concentration in which nonhalophiles.
IS Logical-Mathematical

Visual Learning

How hot can they get? How much higher temperatures can heat-resistant bacteria withstand than insects? about 60°C What is the minimum temperature needed to sterilize foods such as canned goods against heat-resistant bacteria? 120°C

Reviewing Main Ideas

Preview

Students can answer the questions in their Science Journals. Discuss the answers as you go through the chapter. [S] **Linguistic**

Review

Students can write their answers, then compare them with those of other students. [S] **Interpersonal**

Reteach

Students can look at the illustrations and describe details that support the main ideas of the chapter. [S] **Visual-Spatial**

Answers to Chapter Review

SECTION 1

1. cocci
5. When cyanobacteria die, aerobic bacteria decompose them and use up all available oxygen in the water. Fish and other organisms die.

SECTION 2

1. Certain bacteria are able to use oil as an energy source. These bacteria could be sprayed on the spill in order to digest it.
3. Vaccinations protect you from the effects of pathogens.

Reviewing Main Ideas

Section 1 What are bacteria?

1. Bacteria can be found almost everywhere. They have three basic shapes—cocci, bacilli, and spirilli. *What shape of bacteria is shown here?*

2. Bacteria are prokaryotic cells that usually reproduce by fission. All bacteria contain DNA, ribosomes, and cytoplasm but lack a membrane-bound nucleus.

3. Most bacteria are consumers, but some can make their own food. Anaerobes are bacteria that are able to live without oxygen, but aerobes need oxygen to survive.

4. Cell shape and structure, how they get food, if they use oxygen, and their waste products can be used to classify eubacteria.

5. Cyanobacteria are producer eubacteria. They are an important source of food and oxygen for some aquatic organisms. *How does a bloom of cyanobacteria affect other aquatic organisms?*

6. Archaebacteria are bacteria that often exist in extreme conditions, such as near ocean vents and in hot springs.

Section 2 Bacteria in Your Life

1. Most bacteria are helpful. They aid in recycling nutrients, fixing nitrogen, or helping in food production. They even can be used to break down harmful pollutants. *How could bacteria be used to clean up this oil spill?*

2. Some bacteria that live in your body help you stay healthy and survive.

3. Other bacteria are harmful because they can cause disease in the organisms they infect. *Why are vaccinations important to your health?*

4. Pasteurization is one process that can prevent the growth of harmful bacteria in food.

FOLDABLES Reading & Study Skills

After You Read

Using the information on your Foldable, write about the characteristics these two kingdoms of bacteria have in common under the *Both* tab.

FOLDABLES Reading & Study Skills

After You Read

After students have read the chapter and completed the Foldable described in Before You Read, have them do the activity on the student page.

Dinah Zike

Chapter ① Study Guide

Visualizing Main Ideas

Complete the following concept map on how bacteria affect the environment.

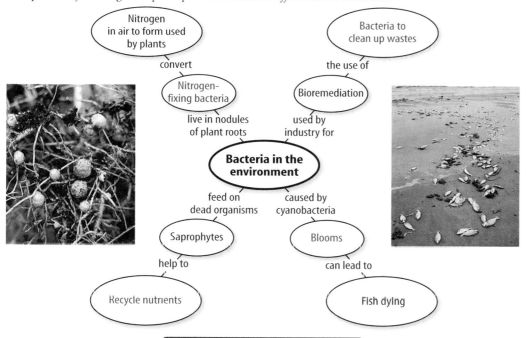

Nitrogen in air to form used by plants
↓ convert
Nitrogen-fixing bacteria
↓ live in nodules of plant roots

Bacteria to clean up wastes
↓ the use of
Bioremediation
↓ used by industry for

Bacteria in the environment

feed on dead organisms → Saprophytes → help to → Recycle nutrients

caused by cyanobacteria → Blooms → can lead to → Fish dying

Visualizing Main Ideas

See student page.

Vocabulary Review

Using Vocabulary

1. saprophyte
2. vaccine
3. pathogen
4. aerobe
5. fission
6. Nitrogen-fixing bacteria
7. anaerobe

Vocabulary Review

Vocabulary Words

a. aerobe
b. anaerobe
c. antibiotic
d. endospore
e. fission
f. flagella
g. nitrogen-fixing bacteria
h. pathogen
i. saprophyte
j. toxin
k. vaccine

THE PRINCETON REVIEW **Study Tip**

Make flash cards for new vocabulary words. Put the word on one side and the definition on the other. Then use them to quiz yourself.

Using Vocabulary

Replace the underlined words with the correct vocabulary word(s).

1. An <u>aerobe</u> uses dead organisms as a food source.

2. A <u>toxin</u> can prevent some bacterial diseases.

3. A <u>saprophyte</u> causes disease.

4. A bacterium that needs oxygen to carry out respiration is a(n) <u>pathogen</u>.

5. Bacteria reproduce using <u>flagella</u>.

6. <u>Anaerobes</u> are bacteria that convert nitrogen in the air to a form used by plants.

7. A(n) <u>flagella</u> can live without oxygen.

Chapter 1 Assessment

Checking Concepts

1. D
2. B
3. A
4. D
5. A
6. A
7. B
8. C
9. D
10. A

Thinking Critically

11. Nitrogen would no longer be available in a form that plants could use; therefore, the plants would die unless fertilizer was added.
12. Bacteria can reproduce quickly, have means of moving, and can form endospores to survive extreme conditions. They can also exchange DNA, providing the population with variations that may be helpful.
13. Crops like beans, peas, and peanuts have nitrogen-fixing bacteria. These crops help to increase soil fertility.
14. spheres
15. Using fresh foods and keeping them refrigerated, washing hands and all surfaces and utensils, and properly cooking foods are ways to prevent food poisoning.

Checking Concepts

Choose the word or phrase that best answers the question.

1. What is a way of cleaning up an ecosystem using bacteria to break down harmful compounds?
   A) landfill   C) toxic waste dumps
   B) waste storage D) bioremediation

2. What do bacterial cells contain?
   A) nucleus   C) mitochondria
   B) DNA   D) four chromosomes

3. What pigment do cyanobacteria need to make food?
   A) chlorophyll   C) plasmids
   B) chromosomes   D) ribosomes

4. Which of the following terms describes most bacteria?
   A) anaerobic   C) many-celled
   B) pathogens   D) beneficial

5. What is the name for rod-shaped bacteria?
   A) bacilli   C) spirilla
   B) cocci   D) colonies

6. What structure allows bacteria to stick to surfaces?
   A) capsule   C) chromosome
   B) flagella   D) cell wall

7. What organisms can grow as blooms in ponds?
   A) archaebacteria C) cocci
   B) cyanobacteria   D) viruses

8. Which of these organisms are recyclers in the environment?
   A) producers   C) saprophytes
   B) flagella   D) pathogens

9. Which of the following is caused by a pathogenic bacterium?
   A) an antibiotic C) nitrogen fixation
   B) cheese   D) strep throat

10. Which organisms do not need oxygen to survive?
    A) anaerobes   C) humans
    B) aerobes   D) fish

Thinking Critically

11. What would happen if nitrogen-fixing bacteria could no longer live on the roots of some plants?

12. Why are bacteria capable of surviving in almost all environments of the world?

13. Farmers often rotate crops such as beans, peas, and peanuts with other crops such as corn, wheat, and cotton. Why might they make such changes?

14. One organism that causes bacterial pneumonia is called pneumococcus. What is its shape?

15. What precautions can be taken to prevent food poisoning?

Developing Skills

16. **Making and Using Graphs** Graph the data from the table below. Using the graph, determine where the doubling rate would be at 20°C.

Bacterial Reproduction Rates	
Temperature (°C)	Doubling Rate Per Hour
20.5	2.0
30.5	3.0
36.0	2.5
39.2	1.2

17. **Interpreting Data** What is the effect of temperature in question 16?

Chapter ✓Assessment Planner

Portfolio Encourage students to place in their portfolios one or two items of what they consider to be their best work. Examples include:
- Science Journal, p. 11
- Cultural Diversity, p. 16
- Science Journal, p. 20

Performance Additional performance assessments, Performance Task Assessment Lists, and rubrics for evaluating these activities can be found in Glencoe's **Performance Assessment in the Science Classroom.**

18. Concept Mapping Complete the following events-chain concept map about the events surrounding a cyanobacteria bloom.

Nutrients, such as farm runoff or fertilizer, are added to pond.

Cyanobacteria increase in number to form a bloom.

Available resources including oxygen are used up.

The pond's organisms die.

19. Identifying and Manipulating Variables and Controls How would you decide if a kind of bacteria could grow anaerobically?

20. Communicating Describe the nitrogen-fixing process in your own words, using numbered steps. You will probably have more than four steps.

Performance Assessment

21. Poster Create a poster that illustrates the effects of bacteria. Use photos from magazines and your own drawings.

22. Poem Write a poem that demonstrates your knowledge of the importance of bacteria to human health.

TECHNOLOGY

Go to the Glencoe Science Web site at **science.glencoe.com** or use the **Glencoe Science CD-ROM** for additional chapter assessment.

THE PRINCETON REVIEW **Test Practice**

In science class, Melissa's homework assignment was to look up five diseases that are caused by bacteria. She was to find the name of the bacterium that causes the disease and how it is transmitted to humans. The results of her research are listed in the chart below.

Infectious Diseases		
Disease	**Source**	**Bacterium**
Cholera	Contaminated water	*Vibrio cholerae*
Botulism	Improperly canned foods	*Clostridium botulinum*
Legionnaires' disease	Air vents	*Legionella pneumophila*
Lyme disease	Tick bites	*Borrelia burgdorferi*
Tuberculosis	Airborne from humans	*Mycobacterium tuberculosis*

Study the chart and answer the following questions.

1. According to the chart, which disease-causing bacterium can be transmitted to humans by a bite from another animal?
   A) *Vibrio cholerae*
   B) *Clostridium botulinum*
   C) *Borrelia burgdorferi*
   D) *Legionella pneumophila*

2. Based on the information in the chart, which disease can be prevented by purifying water that is used for drinking, cooking, or washing fruits and vegetables?
   F) cholera   **H)** Legionnaires'
   G) botulism   **J)** tuberculosis

THE PRINCETON REVIEW **Test Practice**

The Test-Taking Tip was written by The Princeton Review, the nation's leader in test preparation.
1. C
2. F

Developing Skills

16. Graph should increase until a peak is reached, then decrease. Doubling rate will be almost 2.0 at 20°C.

17. Doubling rate increases until an optimal temperature of approximately 30.5 °C is reached. After this temperature, the doubling rate decreases as the temperature increases.

18. See student page.

19. Place the organism in an environment without oxygen and measure its growth rate.

20. (1) Root hairs curl before infection by nitrogen-fixing bacteria. (2) Bacteria enter roots through an infection thread. (3) Pocketlike spaces within the root form and the cells begin to grow and divide. (4) Root nodules containing nitrogen-fixing bacteria form on the roots of legumes. (5) Atmospheric nitrogen is fixed and becomes available for other living things.

Performance Assessment

21. Posters should show beneficial and harmful effects of bacteria. Use **PASC**, p. 145.

22. Poems should demonstrate knowledge of the importance of bacteria to human health. Use **PASC**, p. 157.

✓*Assessment* Resources

Section/Objectives	Standards		Activities/Features
	National	**State/Local**	
Chapter Opener	See p. 5T for a Key to Standards.		**Explore Activity:** Dissect a mushroom, p. 31 **Before You Read,** p. 31
Section 1 Protists 🕐 3 sessions 📦 1.5 blocks 1. **Describe** the characteristics shared by all protist. 2. **Compare and contrast** the three groups of protists. 3. **List** examples of each of the three protist groups. 4. **Explain** why protists are so difficult to classify.	National Content Standards: UCP1, UCP5, A1, C1, C5		**Science Online,** p. 36 **Health Integration,** p. 39 **MiniLAB:** Observing Slime Molds, p. 40 **Problem-Solving Activity:** Is it a fungus or a protist?, p. 41 **Activity:** Comparing Algae and Protozoans, p. 43
Section 2 Fungi 🕐 4 sessions 📦 2 blocks 1. **Identify** the characteristics shared by all fungi. 2. **Classify** fungi into groups based on their methods of reproduction. 3. **Differentiate** between the imperfect fungi and all other fungi.	National Content Standards: UCP1, UCP5, A1, C1, C2, C5, F5, G1		**Science Online,** p. 45 **MiniLAB:** Interpreting Spore Prints, p. 47 **Visualizing Lichens as Air Quality Indicators,** p. 49 **Environmental Science Integration,** p. 50 **Activity:** Creating a Fungus Field Guide, p. 52–53 **Science and Society:** Chocolate SOS, p. 54–55

NATIONAL GEOGRAPHIC

Teacher's Corner

PRODUCTS AVAILABLE FROM GLENCOE
To order call 1-800-334-7344:
CD-ROM
NGS PictureShow: The Cell
Transparency Set
NGS PicturePack: The Cell

PRODUCTS AVAILABLE FROM NATIONAL GEOGRAPHIC SOCIETY
To order call 1-800-368-2728:
Videos
Protists: Threshold of Life
INDEX TO NATIONAL GEOGRAPHIC SOCIETY
The following articles may be used
for research relating to this chapter:
"Leafcutters: Gardeners of the Ant World," by Mark W. Moffet, July 1995.
"Slime Mold: The Fungus That Walks," by Douglas B. Lee, July 1981.
"The Wild World of Compost," by Cecil E. Johnson, August 1980.

Activity Materials	Reproducible Resources	Section Assessment	Technology
Explore Activity: mushroom, hand lens	**Chapter Resources Booklet** Foldables Worksheet, p. 15 Directed Reading Overview, p. 17 Note-taking Worksheets, pp. 29–30	GLENCOE'S **ASSESSMENT** ADVANTAGE	
MiniLAB: live specimen of *Physarum polycephaalum*, hand lens **Activity:** cultures of *Paramecium, Amoeba, Euglena,* and *Spirogyra*; prepared slide of slime mold, 4 microscope slides, 4 coverslips, microscope, dropper	**Chapter Resources Booklet** Transparency Activity, p. 40 MiniLAB, p. 3 Enrichment, p. 27 Reinforcement, p. 25 Directed Reading, p. 18 Transparency Activity, pp. 43–44 Activity Worksheet, pp. 5–6 **Cultural Diversity,** p. 3 **Science Inquiry Labs,** p. 3	Portfolio Science Journal, p. 34 Health Integration, p. 39 Performance MiniLAB, p. 40 Problem-Solving Activity, p. 41 Skill Builder Activities, p. 42 Content Section Assessment, p. 42	Section Focus Transparency Teaching Transparency Interactive CD-ROM Guided Reading Audio Program
MiniLAB: several grocery-store mushrooms, unlined white paper **Activity:** Collection jars, hand lens, microscope, microscope slides and coverslips, field guide to fungi or club fungi, art supplies *Need materials?* Contact Science Kit at 1-800-828-7777 or www.sciencekit.com on the Internet.	**Chapter Resources Booklet** Transparency Activity, p. 41 MiniLAB, p. 4 Enrichment, p. 28 Reinforcement, p. 26 Directed Reading, pp. 19, 20 Lab Activities, pp. 9–10, 11–13 Activity Worksheet, pp. 7–8 **Mathematics Skill Activities,** p. 5 **Reading and Writing Skill Activities,** p. 37 **Lab Management and Safety,** p. 58	Portfolio MiniLAB, p. 47 Performance MiniLAB, p. 47 Skill Builder Activities, p. 51 Content Section Assessment, p. 51	Section Focus Transparency Interactive CD-ROM Guided Reading Audio Program

End of Chapter Assessment

Blackline Masters	Technology	Professional Series
Chapter Resources Booklet Chapter Review, pp. 33–34 Chapter Tests, pp. 35–38 **Standardized Test Practice by The Princeton Review,** pp. 39–42	MindJogger Videoquiz Interactive CD-ROM Vocabulary PuzzleMakers ExamView Pro Test Bank Interactive Lesson Planner Interactive Teacher Edition	Performance Assessment in the Science Classroom (PASC)

Transparencies

Section Focus

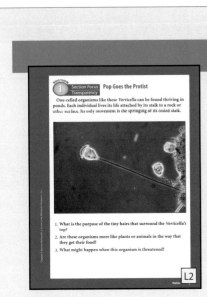

Section Focus Transparency 1 — Pop Goes the Protist

One-celled organisms like these *Vorticella* can be found thriving in ponds. Each individual lives its life attached by its stalk to a rock or other surface. Its only movement is the springing of its coiled stalk.

1. What is the purpose of the tiny hairs that surround the *Vorticella's* top?
2. Are these organisms more like plants or animals in the way that they get their food?
3. What might happen when this organism is threatened?

L2

Section Focus Transparency 2 — Dig It

Care for a truffle! Highly prized in Europe as a delicacy, truffles are a rare, fragrant, and flavorful variety of fungi. Because they can grow as much as 30 centimeters underground, people have trained pigs and dogs to hunt them by scent. The rarest truffles can be worth $3,000 per kilogram!

1. Do you think that truffles are classified as plants? Explain.
2. What other organisms resemble truffles?

L2

This is a representation of key blackline masters available in the Teacher Classroom Resources. See Resource Manager boxes within the chapter for additional information.

Key to Teaching Strategies

The following designations will help you decide which activities are appropriate for your students.

L1 — Level 1 activities should be appropriate for students with learning difficulties.

L2 — Level 2 activities should be within the ability range of all students.

L3 — Level 3 activities are designed for above-average students.

ELL — ELL activities should be within the ability range of English Language Learners.

COOP LEARN — Cooperative Learning activities are designed for small group work.

LS — Multiple Learning Styles logos are used throughout to indicate strategies that address different learning styles.

P — These strategies represent student products that can be placed into a best-work portfolio.

Assessment

Assessment Transparency — Protists and Fungi

Directions: Carefully review the table and answer the following questions.

Types of Fungi		
Type	**Features**	**Examples**
Club fungi	Produce spores inside club-shaped basidium structure	Mushrooms, toadstools
Sac fungi	Produce spores inside tiny sacs	Mildew, yeast, Dutch elm disease
Zygote fungi	Produce spores in cases at top of thin stalks	Black mold
Imperfect fungi	Reproduce asexually	Athlete's foot fungus, ringworm

1. According to the table, which kind of fungus is a mushroom?
   A club fungus C zygote fungus
   B sac fungus   D imperfect fungus
2. According to the table, the fungus responsible for making bread rise is a ___.
   F club fungus H zygote fungus
   G sac fungus   J imperfect fungus
3. According to the table, a black fungus growing on old celery is most likely a ___.
   A club fungus C zygote fungus
   B sac fungus   D imperfect fungus

L2

Teaching

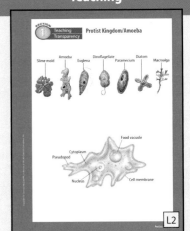

Teaching Transparency — Protist Kingdom/Amoeba

Slime mold Amoeba Euglena Dinoflagellate Paramecium Diatom Macroalga

Food vacuole
Cytoplasm
Pseudopod
Nucleus
Cell membrane

L2

Hands-on Activities

Activity Worksheets

Activity — Comparing Algae and Protozoans

Lab Preview
Directions: Answer these questions before you begin the Activity.

1. What must you do after handling algae and protozoans?

2. How will you observe the wet mounts?

Algae and protozoan cells have characteristics that are similar enough to place them in the same group—the protists. However, the variety of protists forms is great. In this activity, you can observe many of the differences among protists.

What You'll Investigate
What are the differences between algae and protozoans?

Materials
cultures of *Paramecium, Amoeba, Euglena,* and *Spirogyra*
prepared slides of the organisms listed above
prepared slide of slime mold
microscope slides (4)
coverslips (4)
microscope
stereomicroscope
dropper
Alternate materials

Goals
• Draw and label the organisms you examine.
• Observe the differences between algae and protozoans.

Safety Precautions
Make sure to wash your hands after handling algae and protozoans.

Procedure
1. Record your drawings and observations in the table in the Data and Observations section.
2. Make a wet mount of the *Paramecium* culture. If you need help, refer to Student Resources at the back of the book.
3. **Observe** the wet mount first under low and then under high power. Record your observations in the data table on the next page. Draw and label the organism that you observed.
4. Repeat steps 2 and 3 with the other cultures. Return all preparations to your teacher and wash your hands.
5. Observe the slide of slime mold under low and high power. Record your observations.

L2

Laboratory Activities

Laboratory Activity 1 — Molds

Molds are fungi that need food for energy. They contain no chlorophyll, so they cannot make their own food. Molds grow on almost any surface that provides them with food. Will they grow only on surfaces that provide certain conditions?

Strategy
You will build an apparatus to test for mold growth.
You will test the conditions in which mold will grow by using different foods.
You will test light conditions, and different amounts of moisture.
You will observe and record the conditions in which molds grew.

Materials
spoon
potato flakes (dried)
8 baby food jars (with lids)
paper towels
mold source

Procedure
1. Your teacher will assign a group with which you will work. Your group will prepare eight jars for testing mold growth.
2. Your teacher will supply you with mold. Observe and record in the Data and Observations section the appearance of the mold.
3. Rub a cotton swab over the surface of the mold and then rub it over the surface of four paper towels. Rub the swab over the surface of the mold again. Then rub it over the surface of four spoonfuls of potato flakes. CAUTION: Give all swabs to your teacher for proper disposal. Always wash your hands after handling microbes.
4. Put a spoonful of dry potatoes in four baby food jars. Crumple the paper towels and place one in each of the other four jars. Wash your hands.
5. Put 5 mL of water into two of the potato jars and into two of the paper towel jars.
6. Seal all the jars with lids. Label the jars with your name and the date, and the growth conditions for the jar on each label: dry-dark, dry-light, wet-dark, wet-light.
7. Place one dry potato jar in the light and the other dry potato jar in the dark. Place one wet potato jar in the light and the other in the dark. Do the same for the wet and dry paper towel jars.
8. Observe the jars every day for one week. Record your daily observations in the table in the Data and Observations section. CAUTION: Give all jars to your teacher for proper disposal.

L2

RESOURCE MANAGER

Meeting Different Ability Levels

Content Outline

L2

Reinforcement

L2

Directed Reading

L1

Assessment

Chapter Tests

L2

Enrichment

L3

Spanish Directed Reading

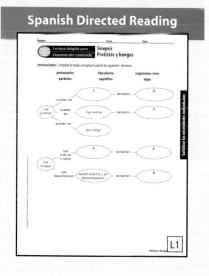

L1

Test Practice Workbook

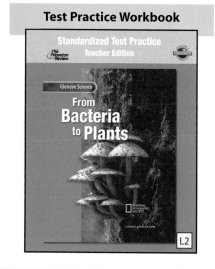

Standardized Test Practice
Teacher Edition

Glencoe Science

From
Bacteria
to Plants

NATIONAL GEOGRAPHIC

science.glencoe.com

L2

Chapter Review

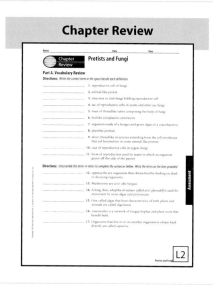

L2

Science Content Background

SECTION 1

Protists

Evolution of Protists

Convenience is the primary reason for grouping all eukaryotes that are not animals, plants, or fungi into a single kingdom. Because the phyla of Kingdom Protista appear to have evolved independently from one another, protists pose several problems for taxonomists. One of the major theories of evolution explains how eukaryotic cells evolved. According to this theory, chloroplasts evolved from a cyanobacterium taken up by an ancestor. Mitochondria and other organelles are thought to have evolved from aerobic heterotrophic prokaryotes. In these cases, the prokaryotes evolved into the organelles through symbiotic relationships in which the smaller prokaryotes lived inside larger prokaryotes. These symbiotic relationships are somewhat similar to the symbiotic relationships that exist between humans and the anaerobic protists living in the human digestive tract.

Plantlike Protists

The chloroplasts of diatoms in the phylum Bacillariophyta most resemble those of the brown algae and dinoflagellates. Diatoms store their food reserves as a type of oil. This oil provides buoyancy to the diatoms, keeping them near the surface of the water, and thus near sunlight. Dinoflagellates are characterized by unique chromosomes and by an unusual form of mitosis that takes place within a nucleus whose nuclear membrane does not degenerate. Dinoflagellates are widespread as symbionts of corals. In this relationship, the dinoflagellates are responsible for much of the productivity of coral reefs.

The extreme diversity of the green algae in the phylum Chlorophyta is reflected by their abundance in marine, freshwater, and damp terrestrial environments, such as on tree trunks and in soil. Red algae lack centrioles and flagellated cells. For this reason, most taxonomists hypothesize that these organisms descended from the most ancient eukaryotes. Red algae have complex life cycles that involve alternation of generations. Brown algae also have alternating generations, with small gametophytes and large sporophytes.

Animal-like Protists

Most flagellates are nonparasitic. But some of the parasitic flagellates can be quite harmful to humans. These harmful parasites include *Trypanosoma*, which live in the bloodstreams of many vertebrates. These protozoans cause diseases such as sleeping sickness. They protect themselves from attack by the host's immune system by changing the molecular structure of their coats frequently.

Funguslike Protists

Phylum Myxomycota contains plasmodial slime molds. These slime molds form round spore-containing capsules under unfavorable environmental conditions such as starvation. These capsules then release spores that may undergo meiosis.

Fun Fact

A plasmodial slime mold can reach several centimeters in length and contain many nuclei, although it is one cell. A slime mold often has a web-like appearance, which allows it to increase its surface area (increasing its contact with food, water, and oxygen) and helps distribute nutrients and oxygen to different parts of the slime mold.

Fun Fact

Phylum Oomycota, the oomycetes, occur in water or as plant parasites. A member of this phylum caused the Irish potato famine of the mid-nineteenth century. Oomycotes have a filamentous structure similar to that of fungi, and they exhibit alternation of generations.

SCIENCE *Online*

For additional content background on this topic, go to the Glencoe Science Web site at science.glencoe.com.

SECTION 2

Fungi

Club Fungi

Basidiomycota includes about 25,000 species of mushrooms, puffballs, shelf fungi, and rusts. Some species of this phylum form mycorrhizae. Others are plant parasites that cause considerable damage each year. Basidiomycotes are named for club-shaped structures that form the sexual spores.

Sac Fungi

Ascomycota is the largest group of fungi accounting for 75 percent of all described fungi. These fungi are named for the sac in which their sexual spores are produced. Yeast are sac fungi that are important in baking and brewing.

Zygote Fungi

Phylum Zygomycota is made up of about 600 species of fungi, including mycorrhizae, an important group that forms mutually beneficial relationships with the roots of most species of plants. Sexual reproduction in this group occurs when appropriate mating strains grow together and produce resistant spores called zoosporangia.

Imperfect Fungi

Fungal species with no known method of sexual reproduction are classified in the phylum Deuteromycota. Some members of this phylum are responsible for producing the colors and flavors of several types of cheese.

Fun Fact

Truffles grow underground and are associated with tree roots. They are one of the most prized of edible fungi. Truffle hunters have traditionally used pigs to hunt truffles because the pigs can smell them. In more recent times, the hunters have begun to train dogs to hunt truffles because, unlike pigs, dog don't try to eat the truffles.

Antman/The Image Works

Protists and Fungi

Chapter Vocabulary

protist, p. 32
algae, p. 33
flagellum, p. 34
protozoan, p. 37
cilia, p. 37
pseudopod, p. 38
hyphae, p. 44
saprophyte, p. 44
spore, p. 45
basidium, p. 46
ascus, p. 46
budding, p. 46
sporangium, p. 47
lichen, p. 48
mycorrhizae, p. 48

What do you think?

Science Journal The picture shows the surface of a diatom, a kind of photosynthetic protist called an alga. Diatoms have intricately etched walls made of silica.

Protists and Fungi

How many protists helped form this limestone cliff, and how did they do it? Did you know that fungi help to make hot dog buns? Some fungi can be seen only through a microscope but others are more than 100 m long. In this chapter, you will learn what characteristics separate protists and fungi from bacteria, plants, and animals. You also will learn why protists and fungi are important to you and the environment.

What do you think?

Science Journal Look at the picture below with a classmate. Discuss what you think this might be. Here's a hint: *This organism is visible only under a microscope.* Write your answer or best guess in your Science Journal.

30 ◆ B

Theme Connection

Systems and Interactions Changes over time and ecological relationships of protists and fungi are discussed.

EXPLORE ACTIVITY

It is hard to tell by a mushroom's appearance whether it is safe to eat or is poisonous. Some edible mushrooms are so highly prized that people keep their location a secret for fear that others will find their treasure. Do the activity below to learn about the parts of mushrooms.

Dissect a mushroom

WARNING: *Wash your hands after handling mushrooms. Do not eat any lab materials.*

1. Obtain a mushroom from your teacher.
2. Using a magnifying glass, observe the underside of the mushroom cap where the stalk is connected to it. Then carefully pull off the cap and observe the gills, which are the thin, tissuelike structures. Hundreds of thousands of tiny reproductive structures called spores will form on these gills.
3. Use your fingers to pull the stalk apart lengthwise. Continue this process until the pieces are as small as you can get them.

Poisonous or edible?

Observe

In your Science Journal, write a description of the parts of the mushroom, and make a labeled drawing of the mushroom and its parts.

Before You Read

Making a Compare and Contrast Study Fold Make the following Foldable to help you see how protists and fungi are similar and different.

1. Place a sheet of paper in front of you so the short side is at the top. Fold the top of the paper down and the bottom up.
2. Open the paper and label the three rows *Protists, Protists and Fungi,* and *Fungi.*
3. As you read the chapter, write information about each type of organism in the appropriate row and information that they share in the middle row.

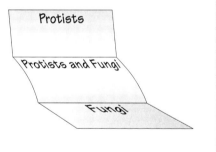

B ◆ 31

Before You Read

FOLDABLES Reading & Study Skills

Dinah Zike Study Fold

Purpose Students will make a Foldable for listing characteristics of protists and fungi during reading. They will use data collected to compare and contrast these forms of life after reading.

For additional help, see Foldables Worksheet, p. 15 in **Chapter Resources Booklet,** or go to the Glencoe Science Web site at **science.glencoe.com.** See After You Read in the Study Guide at the end of this chapter.

EXPLORE ACTIVITY

Purpose Use the Explore Activity to introduce students to fungi. They will learn more about fungi in this chapter. [L1]

ELL COOP LEARN

IS Visual-Spatial

Preparation Buy enough mushrooms for each student to have one.

Materials mushroom, hand lens

Teaching Strategies

• The best mushrooms to use will be those that have the membrane of the cap just separated from the stalk as opposed to those that are still tightly closed.
• Encourage students to examine the mushroom gills thoroughly with the hand lens.
• Tell students not to eat anything used in the lab.

Observe

Parts identified are cap, gills, spores, and stalk. Drawings will vary, but should include all parts.

✓ Assessment

Oral Have students hypothesize how fungi became so widespread in the environment. Their spores are light, numerous, and easily carried by air currents. Use **Performance Assessment in the Science Classroom,** p. 93.

SECTION

Protists

1 Motivate

Bellringer Transparency

Display the Section Focus Transparency for Section 1. Use the accompanying Transparency Activity Master. L2 ELL

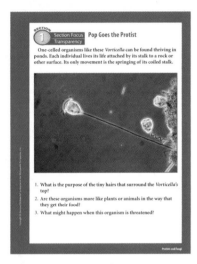

Section Focus Transparency Pop Goes the Protist

One-celled organisms like these *Vorticella* can be found thriving in ponds. Each individual lives its life attached by its stalk to a rock or other surface. Its only movement is the springing of its coiled stalk.

1. What is the purpose of the tiny hairs that surround the *Vorticella's* top?
2. Are these organisms more like plants or animals in the way that they get their food?
3. What might happen when this organism is threatened?

Protists and Fungi

Tie to Prior Knowledge

Review classification with students. Explain that protists have some characteristics of animals, plants, and fungi.

SECTION

1 Protists

As You Read

What You'll Learn

- **Describe** the characteristics shared by all protists.
- **Compare and contrast** the three groups of protists.
- **List** examples of each of the three protist groups.
- **Explain** why protists are so difficult to classify.

Vocabulary

protist   protozoan
algae   cilia
flagellum   pseudopod

Why It's Important

Many protists are important food sources for other organisms.

What is a protist?

Look at the organisms in **Figure 1**. Do you see any similarities among them? As different as they appear, all of these organisms belong to one kingdom—the protist kingdom. A **protist** is a one- or many-celled organism that lives in moist or wet surroundings. All protists are made up of eukaryotic cells—cells that have a nucleus and other internal, membrane-bound structures. Some protists are plantlike. They contain chlorophyll and make their own food. Other protists are animal-like. They do not have chlorophyll and can move. Some protists have a solid or a shell-like structure on the outside of their bodies.

Protist Reproduction One-celled protists usually reproduce asexually. In protists, asexual reproduction requires only one parent organism and occurs by the process of cell division. During cell division, the hereditary material in the nucleus is duplicated before the nucleus divides. After the nucleus divides, the cytoplasm divides. The result is two new cells that are genetically identical. In asexual reproduction of many-celled protists, parts of the large organism can break off and grow into entire new organisms by the process of cell division.

Most protists also can reproduce sexually. During sexual reproduction, the process of meiosis produces sex cells. Two sex cells join to form a new organism that is genetically different from the two organisms that were the sources of the sex cells. How and when sexual reproduction occurs depends on the specific type of protist.

Figure 1
The protist kingdom is made up of a variety of organisms. Many are difficult to classify. *What characteristics do the organisms shown here have in common?*

Slime mold	Amoeba	Euglena	Dinoflagellate	Paramecium	Diatom	Macroalga

---

Section ✔*Assessment* Planner

PORTFOLIO	**CONTENT ASSESSMENT**
Science Journal, p. 34	Section, p. 42
Health Integration, p. 39	Challenge, p. 42
PERFORMANCE ASSESSMENT	Chapter, pp. 58–59
MiniLAB, p. 40	
Skill Builder Activities, p. 42	
See page 58 for more options.	

Classification of Protists

Not all scientists agree about how to classify the organisms in this group. Protists usually are divided into three groups—plantlike, animal-like, and funguslike—based on whether they share certain characteristics with plants, animals, or fungi. **Table 1** shows some of these characteristics. As you read this section, you will understand some of the problems of grouping protists in this way.

Evolution of Protists

Although protists that produce a hard outer covering have left many fossils, other protists lack hard parts so few fossils of these organisms have been found. But, by studying the genetic material and structure of modern protists, scientists are beginning to understand how they are related to each other and to other organisms. Scientists hypothesize that the common ancestor of most protists was a one-celled organism with a nucleus and other cellular structures. However, evidence suggests that protists with the ability to make their own food could have had a different ancestor than protists that cannot make their own food.

Plantlike Protists

Protists in this group are called plantlike because, like plants, they contain the pigment chlorophyll in chloroplasts and can make their own food. Many of them have cell walls like plants, and some have structures that hold them in place just as the roots of a plant do, but these protists do not have roots.

Plantlike protists are known as **algae** (AL jee) (singular, *alga*). As shown in **Figure 2,** some are one cell and others have many cells. Even though all algae have chlorophyll, not all of them look green. Many have other pigments that cover up their chlorophyll.

Table 1 Characteristics of Protist Groups

Plantlike	Animal-Like	Funguslike
Contain chlorophyll and make their own food using photosynthesis	Cannot make their own food; capture other organisms for food	Cannot make their own food; absorb food from their surroundings
Have cell walls	Do not have cell walls	Some organisms have cell walls; others do not
No specialized ways to move from place to place	Have specialized ways to move from place to place	Have specialized ways to move from place to place

Magnification: 3,100×

Figure 2
Algae exist in many shapes and sizes. **A** Microscopic algae are found in freshwater and salt water. **B** You can see some types of green algae growing on rocks, washed up on the beach, or floating in the water.

② Teach

What is a protist?

Caption Answer
Figure 1 All are eukaryotic and live in a moist or wet environment.

Visual Learning

Table 1 Use information presented here to lead a discussion of the characteristics of the groups of protists. Allow students to compare and contrast the groups using these characteristics.

Plantlike Protists

Activity

Have students bring in pond water. Allow students to observe wet mount slides of the water. They should observe a variety of algae. Use a dichotomous key to identify the algae. L2 ELL
IS Visual-Spatial

Make a Model

After students have looked at various algae under the microscope, have them make models to show what they look like. Materials for models might include clay, polystyrene, or plaster of paris. L2 ELL
IS Kinesthetic

Figure 3
The cell walls of diatoms contain silica, the main element in glass. The body of a diatom is like a small box with a lid. The pattern of dots, pits, and lines on the wall's surface is different for each species of diatom.

Magnification: 3,000×

Magnification: 2,866×

Diatoms Extremely large populations of diatoms exist. Diatoms, shown in **Figure 3,** are found in freshwater and salt water. They have a golden-brown pigment that covers up the green chlorophyll. Diatoms secrete glasslike boxes around themselves. When the organisms die, these boxes sink. Over thousands of years, they can collect and form deep layers.

Dinoflagellates Another group of algae is called the dinoflagellates, which means "spinning flagellates." Dinoflagellates, as shown in **Figure 4A,** have two flagella. A **flagellum** (plural, *flagella*) is a long, thin, whiplike structure used for movement. One flagellum circles the cell like a belt, and another is attached to one end like a tail. As the two flagella move, they cause the cell to spin. Because many of the species in this group produce a chemical that causes them to glow at night, they are known as fire algae. Almost all dinoflagellates live in salt water. While most contain chlorophyll, some do not and must feed on other organisms.

Figure 4
A Dinoflagellates usually live in the sea. Some are free living and others live in the tissues of animals like coral and giant clams.
B How are euglenoids similar to plants and animals?

Euglenoids Protists that have characteristics of both plants and animals are known as the euglenoids (yew GLEE noydz). Many of these one-celled algae have chloroplasts, but some do not. Those with chloroplasts, like *Euglena* shown in **Figure 4B,** can produce their own food. However, when light is not present, *Euglena* can feed on bacteria and other protists. Although *Euglena* has no cell wall, it does have a strong, flexible layer inside the cell membrane that helps it move and change shape. Many euglenoids move by whipping their flagella. An eyespot, an adaptation that is sensitive to light, helps photosynthetic euglenoids move toward light.

Magnification: 180×   Magnification: 50×

Red Algae Most red algae are many-celled and, along with the many-celled brown and green algae, sometimes are called seaweeds. Red algae contain chlorophyll, but they also produce large amounts of a red pigment. Some species of red algae can live up to 200 m deep in the ocean. They can absorb the limited amount of light at those depths to carry out the process of photosynthesis. **Figure 5** shows the depths at which different types of algae can live.

Green Algae Due to the diversity of their traits, about 7,000 species of green algae have been classified. These algae, shown in **Figure 6A,** contain large amounts of chlorophyll. Green algae can be one-celled or many-celled. They are the most plantlike of all the algae. Because plants and green algae are similar in their structure, chlorophyll, and how they undergo photosynthesis, some scientists hypothesize that plants evolved from ancient, many-celled green algae. Although most green algae live in water, you can observe types that live in other moist environments, including on damp tree trunks and wet sidewalks.

Brown Algae As you might expect from their name, brown algae contain a brown pigment in addition to chlorophyll. They usually are found growing in cool, saltwater environments. Brown algae are many-celled and vary greatly in size. An important food source for many fish and invertebrates is a brown alga called kelp, as shown in **Figure 6B.** Kelp forms a dense mat of stalks and leaflike blades where small fish and other animals live. Giant kelp is the largest organism in the protist kingdom and can grow to be 100 m in length.

✔ **Reading Check**   *What is kelp?*

Figure 5
Green algae are found closer to the surface. Brown algae can grow from a depth of about 35 m. Red algae are found in the deepest water at 175 m to 200 m.

Figure 6
🅐 Green algae often can be seen on the surface of ponds in the summer. 🅑 Giant kelp, a brown alga, can form forests like this one located off the coast of California. Extracts from kelp add to the smoothness and spreadability of products such as cheese spreads and mayonnaise.

SECTION 1 Protists **B** ◆ **35**

Importance of Algae

Activity

Have students research how satellites are used to capture images of red tides. L3

SCIENCE Online
Internet Addresses

_____

_____

_____

_____

Explore the Glencoe Science Web site at science.glencoe.com to find out more about topics in this section.

Extension

Each year, more than 200,000 metric tons of diatomaceous earth is mined in a quarry in California. Ask students what this means in terms of the number of diatoms it took to accumulate such a deposit and where the ocean was located at one time. This indicates that, at one time, this area may have been under water.

✔ Reading Check

Answer Possible answer: algae is used in food and cosmetics.

SCIENCE Online

Research Visit the Glencoe Science Web site at **science.glencoe.com** for more information about red tides. Determine whether there is an area or time of year in which red tides occur more frequently. Communicate to your class what you learned.

Figure 7
Carrageenan, a substance extracted from the red alga Irish moss, is used for thickening dairy products such as chocolate milk.

36 ◆ B

Importance of Algae

Have you thought about how important grasses are as a food source for animals that live on land? Cattle, deer, zebras, and many other animals depend on grasses as their main source of food. Algae sometimes are called the grasses of the oceans. Most animals that live in the oceans eat either algae for food or other animals that eat algae. You might think many-celled, large algae like kelp are the most important food source, but the one-celled diatoms and dinoflagellates claim that title. Algae, such as *Euglena*, also are an important source of food for organisms that live in freshwater.

Algae and the Environment Algae are important in the environment because they produce oxygen as a result of photosynthesis. The oxygen produced by green algae is important for most organisms on Earth, including you.

Under certain conditions, algae can reproduce rapidly and develop into what is known as a bloom. Because of the large number of organisms in a bloom, the color of the water appears to change. Red tides that appear along the east and Gulf coasts of the United States are the result of dinoflagellate blooms. Toxins produced by the dinoflagellates can cause other organisms to die and can cause health problems in humans.

Algae and You People in many parts of the world eat some species of red and brown algae. You probably have eaten foods or used products made with algae. Carrageenan (kar uh JEE nuhn), a substance found in the cell walls of red algae, has gelatinlike properties that make it useful to the cosmetic and food industries. It is usually processed from the red alga Irish moss, shown in **Figure 7.** Carrageenan gives toothpastes, puddings, and salad dressings their smooth, creamy textures. Another substance, algin (AL juhn), found in the cell walls of brown algae, also has gelatinlike properties. It is used to thicken foods such as ice cream and marshmallows. Algin also is used in making rubber tires and hand lotion.

Ancient deposits of diatoms are mined and used in insulation, filters, and road paint. The cell walls of diatoms produce the sparkle that makes some road lines visible at night and the crunch you feel in toothpaste.

✔ Reading Check *What are some uses by humans of algae?*

Curriculum Connection

Geography Have students plot on a United States map the major areas where diatomite, or diatomaceous earth, is mined. Leading producers in the United States are California, Nevada, Arizona, Washington, and Florida. L2 ELL

Science Journal

News Item Have students write in their Science Journals an item that might appear on a news program to warn people about red tides. The item should contain information about the organisms that are causing the problem and health precautions to prevent poisoning. L2
N Linguistic

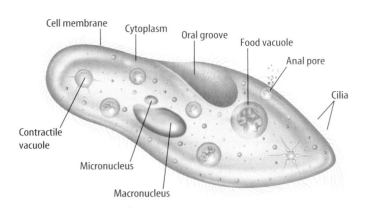

Cell membrane   Cytoplasm   Oral groove   Food vacuole

Anal pore

Cilia

Contractile vacuole

Micronucleus

Macronucleus

Magnification: 107×

Figure 8
Paramecium is a typical ciliate found in many freshwater environments. These rapidly swimming protists consume bacteria. *Locate the contractile vacuoles in the photo. What is their function?*

Animal-Like Protists

One-celled, animal-like protists are known as **protozoans.** Usually protozoans are classified by how they move. These complex organisms live in or on other living or dead organisms that are found in water or soil. Many protozoans have specialized vacuoles for digesting food and getting rid of excess water.

Ciliates As their name suggests, these protists have **cilia** (SIHL ee uh)—short, threadlike structures that extend from the cell membrane. Ciliates can be covered with cilia or have cilia grouped in specific areas on the surface of the cell. The cilia beat in a coordinated way. As a result, the organism moves swiftly in any direction. Organisms in this group include some of the most complex, one-celled protists and some of the largest, one-celled protists.

A typical ciliate is *Paramecium,* shown in **Figure 8.** *Paramecium* has two nuclei—a macronucleus and a micronucleus—another characteristic of the ciliates. The micronucleus is involved in reproduction. The macronucleus controls feeding, the exchange of oxygen and carbon dioxide, the amount of water and salts entering and leaving *Paramecium,* and other functions of *Paramecium.*

Ciliates usually feed on bacteria that are swept into the oral groove by the cilia. Once the food is inside the cell, a vacuole forms around it and the food is digested. Wastes are removed through the anal pore. Freshwater ciliates, like *Paramecium,* also have a structure called the contractile vacuole that helps get rid of excess water. When the contractile vacuole contracts, excess water is ejected from the cell.

SECTION 1 Protists   **B** ◆ **37**

Quick Demo

Use model plant and animal cells to illustrate the organelles in common between algae and plants and between protozoans and animals. **IS** **Visual-Spatial**

Teacher FYI

Recent research suggests that some termite species can digest wood without their flagellated mutualists. However, wood digestion is more efficient with the mutualists than without them.

Discussion

Have groups of students research a particular parasitic protozoan such as *Plasmodium*, *Trypanosoma*, *Giardia*, or *Trichomona*. During class have them share their findings about location of outbreaks, numbers of cases, and disease symptoms. **L2**
COOP LEARN **IS** **Interpersonal**

Quick Demo

Squash a termite's abdomen in a saline solution that is isotonic for insects, making a wet mount. Allow students to observe the flagellates in the termite's gut.

Caption Answer

Figure 10 It is a one-celled consumer, has no cell wall, and moves by using pseudopods.

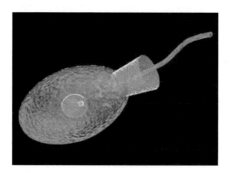

Figure 9
Proterospongia is a rare, freshwater protist. Some scientists hypothesize that it might share an ancestor with ancient animals.

Figure 10
In many areas of the world, a disease-causing species of amoeba lives in the water. If it enters a human body, it can cause dysentery—a condition that can lead to a severe form of diarrhea. *Why is an amoeba classified as a protozoan?*

Magnification: 2,866×

Flagellates Protozoans called flagellates move through their watery environment by whipping their long flagella. Many species of flagellates live in freshwater, though some are parasites that harm their hosts.

Proterospongia, shown in **Figure 9,** is a member of one group of flagellates that might share an ancestor with ancient animals. These flagellates often grow in colonies of many cells that are similar in structure to cells found in animals called sponges. Like sponge cells, when *Proterospongia* cells are in colonies, they perform different functions. Moving the colony through the water and dividing which increases the colony's size, are two examples of jobs that the cells of *Proterospongia* carry out.

Movement with Pseudopods Some protozoans move through their environments and feed using temporary extensions of their cytoplasm called **pseudopods** (SEWD uh pahdz). The word *pseudopod* means "false foot." These organisms seem to flow along as they extend their pseudopods. They are found in freshwater and saltwater environments, and certain types are parasites in animals.

The amoeba shown in **Figure 10** is a typical member of this group. To obtain food, an amoeba extends the cytoplasm of a pseudopod on either side of a food particle such as a bacterium. Then the two parts of the pseudopod flow together and the particle is trapped. A vacuole forms around the trapped food. Digestion takes place inside the vacuole.

Although some protozoans of this group, like the amoeba, have no outer covering, others secrete hard shells around themselves. The white cliffs of Dover, England are composed mostly of the remains of some of these shelled protozoans. Some shelled organisms have holes in their shells through which the pseudopods extend.

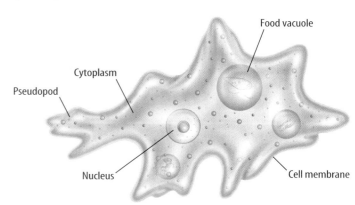

Food vacuole

Cytoplasm

Pseudopod

Nucleus

Cell membrane

LAB DEMONSTRATION

✔️*Assessment*

Purpose to observe how amoebas capture prey
Materials amoeba culture, small ciliates, projecting microscope, slide and coverslip, dropper
Preparation Have all necessary equipment set up before class starts. Pre-dyed amoebas and ciliates may be helpful to obtain.

Procedure A drop of amoeba and a drop of prey per slide are sufficient. Observe under low power, then high power with the projecting microscope.

Expected Outcome Students should observe amoebas extending pseudopodia and capturing prey in food vacuoles.

When is the organism captured? when the pseudopod completely envelopes it **Is the prey still alive after capture?** The prey lives for some time before digestive fluids kill it.

Figure 11
Asexual reproduction takes place inside a human host. Sexual reproduction takes place in the intestine of a mosquito.

Magnification: 11×

Uninfected female mosquitoes can become infected if they bite someone who has malaria.

Liver

Plasmodium lives in the salivary glands of certain female mosquitoes. The parasite can be transferred to a human's blood if an infected mosquito bites them.

After it is in the body, the parasite travels to the liver and then to the red blood cells where it reproduces and releases more parasites into the blood.

Other Protozoans One group of protozoans has no way of moving on their own. All of the organisms in this group are parasites of humans and other animals. These protozoans have complex life cycles that involve sexual and asexual reproduction. They often live part of their lives in one animal and part in another. The parasite that causes malaria is an example of a protozoan in this group. **Figure 11** shows the life cycle of the malaria parasite.

Importance of Protozoans

Like the algae, some protozoans are an important source of food for larger organisms. When some of the shelled protozoans die, they sink to the bottom of bodies of water and become part of the sediment. Sediment is a buildup of plant and animal remains and rock and mineral particles. The presence of these protists in sediments is used sometimes by field geologists as an indicator species. This tells them where petroleum reserves might be found beneath the surface of Earth.

✔ **Reading Check** *Why are shelled protozoans important?*

One type of flagellated protozoan lives with bacteria in the digestive tract of termites. Termites feed mainly on wood. These protozoans and bacteria produce wood-digesting enzymes that help break down the wood. Without these organisms, the termites would be unable to use the chemical energy stored in wood.

Health
INTEGRATION

The flagellate *Trypanosoma* is carried by the tsetse fly in Africa and causes African sleeping sickness in humans and other animals. It is transmitted to other organisms during bites from the fly. The disease affects the central nervous system. Research this disease and create a poster showing your results.

Importance of Protozoans

Health
INTEGRATION

African sleeping sickness is prevalent in sub-Saharan Africa. Some regions are uninhabitable because of the risk of becoming infected. There are several varieties, caused by different species of protozoa, which differ slightly in their symptoms and severity. Early symptoms usually include fever and inflammation of the lymph nodes. More advanced symptoms may include a sensation of pain, severe headaches, mental dullness and apathy, tremors, paralysis, chorea, and profound sleepiness. These symptoms are often followed by coma and death, though in some cases the individual develops a tolerance and lives for many years as a carrier. Posters may relate the numbers of cases each year, the number of deaths, the vector, and locations of infestations. Some students may research possible cures. P

✔ **Reading Check**

Answer The presence of these organisms in sediment can indicate where petroleum may be found.

Curriculum Connection

Math Have students analyze the following story by making a graph. A person who contracted malaria had the following body temperatures (°C) at the given times. Day 1: 1:00 P.M., 39.4° (chills); 6:00 P.M., 38.3° (sweating); Day 2: 1:00 A.M., 36.1°; 6:00 A.M., 36.7°; 1:00 P.M., 36.1°; 6:00 P.M., 37.2°; Day 3: 1:00 A.M., 38.3° (chills); 6:00 A.M., 39.4°; 1:00 P.M., 39.4°; 6:00 P.M., 38.3° (sweating). **When will the person have chills next?** The person will have the chills next at 1:00 P.M. on Day 5. L2 IS **Logical-Mathematical**

Resource Manager

Chapter Resources Booklet
Enrichment, p. 27
Transparency Activity, pp. 43–44

Funguslike Protists

Mini LAB

Purpose to observe the growth of slime molds and predict the best conditions for their growth L2 IS **Visual-Spatial**

Materials slime mold specimens, magnifying glass, pencil, paper

Teaching Strategy Obtain live specimens of slime mold from a biological supply company. *Physarum polycephalum* produces good results.

Analysis

Lower temperatures and reduced humidity or the presence of food will result in the growth of the spore-producing form.

✓Assessment

Performance To assess students' understanding of slime molds, have them try to grow slime mold cultures on different surfaces with different nutrients. Use **Performance Assessment in the Science Classroom**, p. 97.

Caption Answer

Figure 12 Slime molds move and behave like animal-like protists during part of their life cycle, but, like fungi, they are decomposers that reproduce with spores.

Mini LAB

Observing Slime Molds

Procedure

1. Obtain live specimens of the slime mold *Physarum polycephaalum* from your teacher. Wash your hands.
2. Observe the mold once each day for four days.
3. Using a **magnifying glass,** make daily drawings and observations of the mold as it grows.

Analysis

Predict the growing conditions under which the slime mold will change from the amoeboid form to the spore-producing form.

Figure 12
Slime molds come in many different forms and colors ranging from brilliant yellow or orange to rich blue, violet, pink, and jet black. *How are slime molds similar to protists and fungi?*

Disease in Humans The protozoans that are most important to you are the ones that cause diseases in humans. In tropical areas, flies or other biting insects transmit many of the parasitic flagellates to humans. A flagellated parasite called *Giardia* can be found in water that is contaminated with wastes from humans or wild or domesticated animals. If you drink water directly from a stream, you could get this diarrhea-causing parasite.

Some amoebas also are parasites that cause disease. One parasitic amoeba, found in ponds and streams, can lead to a brain infection and death.

Funguslike Protists

Funguslike protists include several small groups of organisms such as slime molds, water molds, and downy mildews. Although all funguslike protists produce spores like fungi, most of them can move from place to place using pseudopods like the amoeba. All of them must take in food from an outside source.

Slime Molds As shown in **Figure 12,** slime molds are more attractive than their name suggests. Slime molds form delicate, weblike structures on the surface of their food supply. Often these structures are brightly colored. Slime molds have some protozoan characteristics. During part of their life cycle, slime molds move by means of pseudopods and behave like amoebas.

Most slime molds are found on decaying logs or dead leaves in moist, cool, shady environments. One common slime mold sometimes creeps across lawns and mulch as it feeds on bacteria and decayed plants and animals. When conditions become less favorable, reproductive structures form on stalks and spores are produced.

Magnification: 3×

Magnification: 5.25×

Inclusion Strategies

Learning Disabled After having students observe the movement of a slime mold under the microscope, have them perform these same movements as a group. The cytoplasm streams in one direction and then slows to a stop. Then the cytoplasm flows in the opposite direction, but not as far, before stopping. In this way, the slime mold creeps across a surface. L1 IS **Kinesthetic**

Water Molds and Downy Mildews

Most members of this large, diverse group of funguslike protists live in water or moist places. Like fungi, they grow as a mass of threads over a plant or animal. Digestion takes place outside of these protists, then they absorb the organism's nutrients. Unlike fungi, the spores these protists produce have flagella. Their cell walls more closely resemble those of plants than those of fungi.

Some water molds are parasites of plants, and others feed on dead organisms. Most water molds appear as fuzzy, white growths on decaying matter. **Figure 13** shows a parasitic water mold that grows on aquatic organisms. If you have an aquarium, you might see water molds attack a fish and cause its death. Another important type of protist is a group of plant parasites called downy mildew. Warm days and cool, moist nights are ideal growing conditions for them. They can live on aboveground parts of many plants. Downy mildews weaken plants and even can kill them.

Figure 13
Water mold, the threadlike material seen in the photo, grows on a dead salamander. In this case, the water mold is acting as a decomposer. This important process will return nutrients to the water.

 Reading Check *How do water molds affect organisms?*

Problem-Solving Activity

Is it a fungus or a protist?

Slime molds, such as the pipe cleaner slime shown in the photograph to the right, can be found covering moist wood. They can be white or bright red, yellow, or purple. If you look at a piece of slime mold on a microscope slide, you will see that the cell nuclei move back and forth as the cytoplasm streams along. This streaming of the cytoplasm is how a slime mold creeps over the wood.

Identifying the Problem

Should slime molds be classified as protists or as fungi?

Solving the Problem

1. What characteristics do slime molds share with protists? How are slime molds similar to protozoans and algae?

2. What characteristics do slime molds share with fungi? What characteristics do slime molds have that are different from fungi?

3. What characteristics did you compare to decide what group slime molds should be classified in? What other characteristics could scientists examine to help classify slime molds?

SECTION 1 Protists   **B** ◆ 41

Importance of the Funguslike Protists

Activity

Have students make a chart listing the positive and negative effects of funguslike protists.

Reteach

Have students examine photographs or illustrations of various protists and identify the life cycle phase of each. [L2]

[IS] **Visual-Spatial**

Challenge

What are the causes and effects of a red tide? A red tide is caused by a population explosion of dinoflagellates. Millions of these organisms cause the water to look red. Some species release a nerve toxin that can kill fish and humans.

✔ ***Assessment***

Performance Have students write a statement in their Science Journals comparing the environments of slime molds and water molds. Use **Performance Assessment in the Science Classroom,** p. 175.

Figure 14
Downy mildews can have a great impact on agriculture and economies when they infect potatoes, sugar beets, grapes, and melons like those above.

Importance of the Funguslike Protists

Some of the organisms in this group are important because they help break down dead organisms. However, most funguslike protists are important because of the diseases they cause in plants and animals. One species of water mold that causes lesions in fish can be a problem when the number of organisms in a given area is high. Fish farms and salmon spawning in streams can be greatly affected by a water mold spreading throughout the population. Water molds cause disease in other aquatic organisms including worms and even diatoms.

Economic Effects Downy mildews can have a huge effect on economies as well as social history. A downy mildew infection of grapes in France during the 1870s nearly wiped out the entire French wine industry. One of the most well-known members of this group is a downy mildew, which caused the Irish potato famine during the 1840s. Potatoes were Ireland's main crop and the primary food source for its people. When the potato crop became infected with downy mildew, potatoes rotted in the fields, leaving many people with no food. Downy mildews, as shown in **Figure 14,** continue to infect crops such as lettuce, corn, and cabbage, as well as tropical avocados and pineapples.

Section ① Assessment

1. What are the characteristics common to all protists?
2. Compare and contrast the different characteristics of animal-like, plantlike, and funguslike protists.
3. How are plantlike protists classified into different groups?
4. How are protozoans classified into different groups?
5. **Think Critically** Why are there few fossils of certain groups of protists?

Skill Builder Activities

6. **Making and Using Tables** Make a table of the positive and negative effects that protists have on your life and health. **For more help, refer to the** Science Skill Handbook.
7. **Using an Electronic Spreadsheet** Use a spreadsheet to make a table that compares the characteristics of the three groups of protozoans. Include *example organisms, method of transportation,* and *other characteristics.* **For more help, refer to the** Technology Skill Handbook.

Answers to Section Assessment

1. single-celled or many-celled organisms that live in moist or wet surroundings; possess membrane-bound nuclei; protists may be plantlike, animal-like, or funguslike
2. Algae are plantlike protists with chloroplasts and cell walls. Protozoans are single-celled animal-like protists that lack cell walls and cannot produce their own food. Funguslike protists are all consumers that produce spores.
3. by their structure and the pigments they contain
4. by their method of movement
5. Protists are small and do not have hard parts that are fossilized easily. The protists decay rapidly, leaving no trace of their existence.
6. Check student tables for accuracy.
7. Tables should accurately display information from this section.

Activity

Comparing Algae and Protozoans

Algae and protozoans have characteristics that are similar enough to place them in the same group—the protists. However, the variety of protist forms is great. In this activity, you can observe many of the differences among protists.

What You'll Investigate
What are the differences between algae and protozoans?

Materials
cultures of *Paramecium, Amoeba, Euglena,* and *Spirogyra*
*prepared slides of the organisms listed above
prepared slide of slime mold
microscope slides (4)
coverslips (4)
microscope
*stereomicroscope
dropper
*Alternate materials

Goals
■ **Draw and label** the organisms you examine.
■ **Observe** the differences between algae and protozoans.

Safety Precautions

Make sure to wash your hands after handling algae and protozoans.

Procedure
1. Copy the data table in your Science Journal.
2. Make a wet mount of the *Paramecium* culture. If you need help, refer to Student Resources at the back of the book.

Magnification: 50×

Protist Observations		
Protist	Drawing	Observations
Paramecium		
Amoeba	Student drawings	
Euglena	should resemble group features	
Spirogyra	described in this section.	
Slime mold		

3. **Observe** the wet mount first under low and then under high power. Record your observations in the data table. Draw and label the organism that you observed.
4. **Repeat** steps 2 and 3 with the other cultures. Return all preparations to your teacher and wash your hands.
5. **Observe** the slide of slime mold under low and high power. Record your observations.

Conclude and Apply
1. Which structure was used for movement by each organism that could move?
2. Which protists make their own food? Explain how you know that they can make their own food.
3. Identify the protists you observed with animal-like characteristics.

Communicating Your Data
Share the results of this activity with your classmates. **For more help, refer to the Science Skill Handbook.**

ACTIVITY **B ◆ 43**

Resource Manager

Chapter Resources Booklet
Activity Worksheet, pp. 5–6

Communicating Your Data
Students should have similar results. They may communicate by using drawings or written descriptions of their observations.

Activity

BENCH TESTED

Purpose to observe the differences between algae and protozoans L2 **IS Visual-Spatial**

Process Skills observing and inferring, classifying, making and using tables, comparing and contrasting

Time Required 50 minutes

Materials Prepared slides of protozoans and algae may be used. All live specimens should be obtained from a reputable supply house. No parasitic forms should be used.

Safety Precautions Remind students to be careful when plugging and unplugging the microscope. Water should be kept away from the outlet.

Teaching Strategies
• Use a videotape of the organisms to prepare students for what they will see.
• Remind students that algae and protozoans are protists.

Troubleshooting Maintain separate cultures for each organism. Prevent students from using the same dropper for more than one culture.

Answers to Questions
1. Paramecia use cilia; amoebas use pseudopods; euglenas use flagella.
2. *Spirogyra* and *Euglena* make their own food; they contain chloroplasts for photosynthesis.
3. *Paramecium, Euglena, Amoeba,* slime mold

Assessment

Performance To further assess students' abilities to classify algae and protozoans, have them make and view wet mounts of scrapings from fish tanks. Use **PASC,** p. 121.

SECTION

2 Fungi

1 Motivate

Bellringer Transparency

Display the Section Focus Transparency for Section 2. Use the accompanying Transparency Activity Master. L2

ELL

Tie to Prior Knowledge

Have students relate examples of fungi they know about. Students will likely know about toadstools and fungi used in food. Explain that fungi are in a kingdom separate from other organisms.

SECTION

2 Fungi

As You Read

What You'll Learn

- **Identify** the characteristics shared by all fungi.
- **Classify** fungi into groups based on their methods of reproduction.
- **Differentiate** between the imperfect fungi and all other fungi.

Vocabulary

hyphae
saprophyte
spore
basidium
ascus

budding
sporangium
lichen
mycorrhizae

Why It's Important

Fungi are important sources of food and medicines, and they help recycle Earth's wastes.

What are fungi?

Do you think you can find any fungi in your house or apartment? You have fungi in your home if you have mushroom soup or fresh mushrooms. What about that package of yeast in the cupboard? Yeasts are a type of fungus used to make some breads and cheeses. You also might find fungus growing on a loaf of bread or mildew fungus growing on your shower curtain.

Origin of Fungi Although fossils of fungi exist, most are not useful in determining how fungi are related to other organisms. Some scientists hypothesize that fungi share an ancestor with ancient, flagellated protists and slime molds. Other scientists hypothesize that their ancestor was a green or red alga.

Structure of Fungi Most species of fungi are many-celled. The body of a fungus is usually a mass of many-celled, thread-like tubes called **hyphae** (HI fee), as shown in **Figure 15.** The hyphae produce enzymes that help break down food outside of the fungus. Then, the fungal cells absorb the digested food. Because of this, most fungi are known as saprophytes. **Saprophytes** are organisms that obtain food by feeding on dead or decaying tissues of other organisms. Other fungi are parasites. They obtain their food directly from living things.

Figure 15
The hyphae of fungi are involved in the digestion of food, as well as reproduction.

A The body of a fungus is visible to the unaided eye.

B Threadlike, microscopic hyphae make up the body of a fungus.

C The internal structure of hyphae.

Section ✓Assessment Planner

PORTFOLIO
Try at Home MiniLAB, p. 47
PERFORMANCE ASSESSMENT
Try at Home MiniLAB, p. 47
Skill Builder Activities, p. 51
See page 58 for more options.

CONTENT ASSESSMENT
Section, p. 51
Challenge, p. 51
Chapter, pp. 58–59

Other Characteristics of Fungi What other characteristics do all fungi share? Because fungi grow anchored in soil and have a cell wall around each cell, fungi once were classified as plants. But fungi don't have the specialized tissues and organs of plants, such as leaves and roots. Unlike plants, fungi cannot make their own food because they don't contain chlorophyll.

Fungi grow best in warm, humid areas, such as tropical forests or between toes. You need a microscope to see some fungi, but in Michigan one fungus was found growing underground over an area of about 15 hectares. In the state of Washington, another type of fungus found in 1992 was growing throughout nearly 600 hectares of soil.

Reproduction Asexual and sexual reproduction in fungi usually involves the production of spores. A **spore** is a waterproof reproductive cell that can grow into a new organism. In asexual reproduction, cell division produces spores. These spores will grow into new fungi that are genetically identical to the fungus from which the spores came.

Fungi are not identified as either male or female. Sexual reproduction can occur when the hyphae of two genetically different fungi of the same species grow close together. If the hyphae join, a reproductive structure will grow, as shown in **Figure 16.** Following meiosis in these structures, spores are produced that will grow into fungi. These fungi are genetically different from either of the two fungi whose hyphae joined during sexual reproduction. Fungi are classified into three main groups based on the type of structure formed by the joining of hyphae.

✔ **Reading Check** *How are fungi classified?*

SCIENCE Online

Research Visit the Glencoe Science Web site at **science.glencoe.com** for more information about the gigantic fungus *Armillaria ostoyae* and other unusual fungi. Communicate to your class what you learned.

A Two hyphae fuse.

− +

B Reproductive structure forms.

Figure 16
A When two genetically different fungi of the same species meet, B a reproductive structure, in this case a zygospore, will be formed. The new fungi will be genetically different from either of the two original fungi.

Club Fungi

Sac Fungi

Figure 17
A Club fungi, like this mushroom, form a reproductive structure called a basidium. Each basidium produces four balloonlike structures called basidiospores. **B** Spores will be released from these as the final step in sexual reproduction.

Spores

Club Fungi

The mushrooms shown in **Figure 17** are probably the type of fungus that you are most familiar with. The mushroom is only the reproductive structure of the fungus. Most of the fungus grows as hyphae in the soil or on the surface of its food source. These fungi commonly are known as club fungi. Their spores are produced in a club-shaped structure called a **basidium** (buh SIHD ee uhm) (plural, *basidia*).

Sac Fungi

Yeasts, molds, morels, and truffles are all examples of sac fungi—a diverse group containing more than 30,000 different species. The spores of these fungi are produced in a little, saclike structure called an **ascus** (AS kus), as shown in **Figure 18A**.

Although most fungi are many-celled, yeasts are one-celled organisms. Yeasts reproduce by forming spores and reproduce asexually by budding, as illustrated in **Figure 18B**. **Budding** is a form of asexual reproduction in which a new organism forms on the side of an organism. The two organisms are genetically identical.

Figure 18
A The spores of a sac fungus are released when the tip of an ascus breaks open.
B Yeasts can reproduce by forming buds off their sides. A bud pinches off and forms an identical cell.

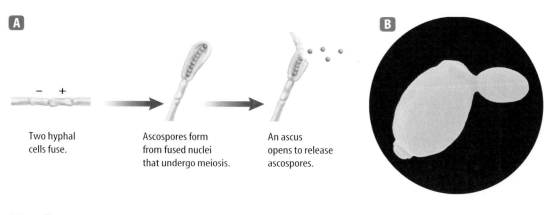

A

− +

Two hyphal cells fuse.

Ascospores form from fused nuclei that undergo meiosis.

An ascus opens to release ascospores.

B

Fun Fact

One of the largest organisms in the world is a fungus growing under acres of forest floor in Michigan. It is estimated to weigh at least 100 tons.

Curriculum Connection

Math The fairy ring toadstool (a type of mushroom) advances outward from the center at a rate of about 30 cm per year. One ring is estimated to be 150 years old. **How many meters in diameter is this fairy ring?** 150 years × 30 cm/year × 2 radii/diameter = 9,000 cm = 90 meters
L2 IS **Logical-Mathematical**

Figure 19
The black mold found growing on bread or fruit is a type of zygospore fungus.

Magnification: 100×

 B The zygospores shown here produce sporangia that hold the individual spores.

 A This black mold produces zygospores during sexual reproduction.

Zygote Fungi and Other Fungi

The fuzzy black mold that you sometimes find growing on a piece of fruit or an old loaf of bread as shown in **Figure 19,** is a type of zygospore fungus. Fungi that belong to this group produce spores in a round spore case called a **sporangium** (spuh RAN jee uhm) (plural, *sporangia*) on the tips of upright hyphae. When each sporangium splits open, hundreds of spores are released into the air. Each spore will grow and reproduce if it lands in a warm, moist area that has a food supply.

✔ **Reading Check** *What is a sporangium?*

Some fungi either never reproduce sexually or never have been observed reproducing sexually. Because of this, these fungi are difficult to classify. They usually are called imperfect fungi because there is no evidence that their life cycle has a sexual stage. Imperfect fungi reproduce asexually by producing spores. When the sexual stage of one of these fungi is observed, the species is classified immediately in one of the other three groups.

Penicillium is a fungus that is difficult to classify. Some scientists classify *Penicillium* as an imperfect fungi. Others believe it should be classified as a sac fungus based on the type of spores it forms during asexual reproduction. Another fungus, which causes pneumonia, has been classified recently as an imperfect fungus. Like *Penicillium*, scientists do not agree about which group to place it in.

TRY AT HOME
Mini LAB

Interpreting Spore Prints

Procedure

1. Obtain several **mushrooms from the grocery store** and let them age until the undersides look brown.
2. Remove the stems. Place the mushroom caps with the gills down on a piece of **unlined white paper.** Wash your hands.
3. Let the mushroom caps sit undisturbed overnight and remove them from the paper the next day. Wash your hands.

Analysis

1. Draw and label the results in your **Science Journal.** Describe the marks on the page and what made them.
2. How could you estimate the number of new mushrooms that could be produced from one mushroom cap?

Zygote Fungi and Other Fungi

Make a Model

After students have observed bread mold with a dissecting microscope or hand lens, have them construct a model of the structures they observe. Students should show spores, hyphae, and so on. L2 **IS Kinesthetic**

✔ **Reading Check**

Answer a round spore case

TRY AT HOME
Mini LAB

Purpose to observe spore prints L1 **ELL IS Visual-Spatial** P

Materials mushrooms, unlined white paper

Teaching Strategy Caution students not to disturb the mushrooms while spore prints are being made.

Safety Precautions Remind students not to eat anything used in the lab.

Analysis

1. Sketches will vary. Brown lines will be parallel or concentric rings made by falling spores.
2. Count a few spores in one area and multiply by the total area of spore production.

✔ Assessment

Performance To further assess understanding of mushrooms, have students carefully tease apart a bit of gill from under the cap and make a wet mount of an extremely small piece. Students should draw and describe what they see in their Science Journals. Use **PASC,** p. 127.

Resource Manager

Chapter Resources Booklet
   MiniLAB, p. 4
Home and Community Involvement, p. 43

Inclusion Strategies

Learning Disabled Have students make flash cards with the name of a group of fungi and a picture on one side and the characteristics and an example on the other. Allow students to practice learning the fungi by using their flash cards. L1 **IS Linguistic**

Figure 20
Lichens can look like a crust on bare rock, appear leafy, or grow upright. All three forms can grow near each other. *What is one way lichens might be classified?*

Figure 22
Many plants, such as these orchids, could not survive without mycorrhizae to help absorb water and important minerals from soil.

Lichens

The colorful organisms in **Figure 20** are lichens. A **lichen** (LI kun) is an organism that is made of a fungus and either a green alga or a cyanobacterium. These two organisms have a relationship in which they both benefit. The alga or cyanobacterium lives among the threadlike strands of the fungus. The fungus gets food made by the green alga or cyanobacterium. The green alga or cyanobacterium gets a moist, protected place to live.

Importance of Lichens For many animals, including caribou and musk oxen, lichens are an important food source.

Lichens also are important in the weathering process of rocks. They grow on bare rock and release acids as part of their metabolism. The acids help break down the rock. As bits of rock accumulate and lichens die and decay, soil is formed. This soil supports the growth of other species.

Scientists also use lichens as indicator organisms to monitor pollution levels, as shown in **Figure 21.** Many species of lichens are sensitive to pollution. When these organisms show a decline in their health or die quickly, it alerts scientists to possible problems for larger organisms.

Fungi and Plants

Some fungi interact with plant roots. They form a network of hyphae and roots known as **mycorrhizae** (mi kuh RI zee). About 80 percent of plants develop mycorrhizae. The fungus helps the plant absorb more of certain nutrients from the soil better than the roots can on their own, while the plant supplies food and other nutrients to the fungi. Some plants, like the lady's slipper orchids shown in **Figure 22,** cannot grow without the development of mycorrhizae.

✔ Reading Check   *Why are mycorrhizae so important to plants?*

Science Journal

Erosion Have students research the importance of fungi in erosion and write a paragraph about it in their Science Journals. Wind, water, temperature changes, and living things such as fungi are the main forces of erosion. Explain that all landforms—mountains, rivers, valleys, and plains—show visible results of erosional forces. L2 IS **Linguistic**

Figure 21

Widespread, slow-growing, and long-lived, lichens come in many varieties. Lichens absorb water and nutrients mainly from the air rather than the soil. Because certain types are extremely sensitive to toxic environments, lichens make natural, inexpensive air-pollution detectors.

A lichen consists of a fungus and an alga or cyanobacterium living together in a partnership that benefits both organisms. In this cross section of a lichen (50x), reddish-stained bits of fungal tissue surround blue-stained algal cells.

Can you see a difference between these two red alder tree trunks? White lichens cover one trunk but not the other. Red alders are usually covered with lichens such as those seen in the photo on the left. Lichens could not survive on the tree on the right because of air pollution.

Evernia lichens, left, sicken and die when exposed to sulfur dioxide, a common pollutant emitted by coal-burning industrial plants such as the one above.

Visualizing Lichens as Air Quality Indicators

Have students examine the pictures and read the captions. Then ask the following questions.

If a tree has no lichens on its trunk, what does that indicate about the air quality in that area? Possible answer: The tree is in an area that has a source of air pollution.

Where do lichens get most of their nutrients? Lichens absorb water and nutrients from the air.

Activity

Have students make a map of the area surrounding the school. The area should encompass about 5 square km. Then have them indicate on the map which areas would most likely contain lichens. If there are no lichens in the area, have students discuss why that may be.

IS Naturalist

Extension

Many current studies are trying to determine the effect that air pollution has on lichens. Have students research several different species of lichens and determine whether the lichens are sensitive to certain types of air pollution.

Resource Manager

Chapter Resources Booklet
  Enrichment, p. 28

Fungi and Plants,
continued

Earth Science
INTEGRATION

The fossilized fungus was mycorrhizae. In addition to providing evidence of how plants could have made the transition to land, the fossil also provided evidence of fungi that are scarce in the fossil record.

Importance of Fungi

Activity

Allow students to work in groups to develop and carry out interviews with local physicians concerning the role of fungi in the health field. Students will learn that fungi can cause infection in humans, but that some fungi are also used in the production of medicines. L2
COOP LEARN **Interpersonal**

Environmental Science
INTEGRATION

Some fungi form sticky nets that can be used to trap microscopic nematodes—roundworms that can be detrimental to plants.

Environmental Science
INTEGRATION

Although fungi can have negative effects on agriculture, they can be used to help farmers. Some farmers are using fungi as natural pesticides. Fungi can control a variety of pests including termites, rice weevils, tent caterpillars, aphids, and citrus mites.

Figure 23
A Rusts can infect the grains used to make many cereals including wheat, barley, rye, and oats. **B** Not all fungi are bad for agriculture. Some are natural pesticides. This grasshopper is infected with a fungal parasite.

Earth Science
INTEGRATION

Fossilized Fungus In 1999, scientists discovered a fossilized fungus in a 460 million-year-old rock. The fossil was a type of fungus that forms associations with plant roots. Scientists have known for many years that the first plants could not have survived moving from water to land alone. Early plants did not have specialized roots to absorb nutrients. Also, tubelike cells used for transporting water and nutrients to leaves were too simple.

Scientists have hypothesized that early fungi attached themselves to the roots of early plants, passing along nutrients taken from the soil. Scientists suggest that it was this relationship that allowed plants to move successfully from water onto land about 500 million years ago. Until the discovery of this fossil, no evidence had been found that this type of fungus existed at that time.

Importance of Fungi

As mentioned in the beginning of this chapter, some fungi are eaten for food. Cultivated mushrooms are an important food crop. However, wild mushrooms never should be eaten because many are poisonous. Some cheeses are produced using fungi. Yeasts are used in the baking industry. Yeasts use sugar for energy and produce alcohol and carbon dioxide as waste products. The carbon dioxide causes doughs to rise.

Agriculture Many fungi are important because they cause diseases in plants and animals. Many sac fungi are well known by farmers because they damage or destroy plant crops. Diseases caused by sac fungi are Dutch elm disease, apple scab, and ergot disease of rye. Smuts and the rust, shown in **Figure 23A,** are club fungi. They cause billions of dollars worth of damage to food crops each year.

✔ Active Reading

Quickwrites This strategy, sometimes called freewrites, lets students use spontaneous writing to discover what they already know. Have students write a list of ideas about a topic, then share these ideas with the class. Next, have students write their ideas freely in a paragraph without worrying about punctuation, spelling, and grammar. Have students use a Quickwrite to discover what they know about the importance of fungi.

Resource Manager

Chapter Resources Booklet
Reinforcement, p. 26
Lab Activities, pp. 9–10, 11–13

Health and Medicine Fungi are responsible for causing diseases in humans and animals. Ringworm and athlete's foot are two infections of the skin caused by species of imperfect fungi. Other fungi can cause respiratory infections. The effects of fungi on health and medicine are not all negative. Some species of fungi naturally produce antibiotics that keep bacteria from growing on or near them.

The antibiotic penicillin is produced by the imperfect fungi *Penicillium*. This fungus is grown commercially, and the antibiotic is collected to use in fighting bacterial infections. Cyclosporin, an important drug used to help fight the body's rejection of transplanted organs, also is derived from a fungus. There are many more examples of breakthroughs in medicine as a result of studying and discovering new uses of fungi. In fact, there is a worldwide effort among scientists who study fungi to investigate soil samples to find more useful drugs.

Decomposers As important as fungi are in the production of different foods and medicines, they are most important as decomposers that break down organic materials. Food scraps, clothing, and dead plants and animals are made of organic material. Often found on rotting logs, as shown in **Figure 24,** fungi break down these materials. The chemicals in these materials are returned to the soil where plants can reuse them. Fungi, along with bacteria, are nature's recyclers. They keep Earth from becoming buried under mountains of organic waste materials.

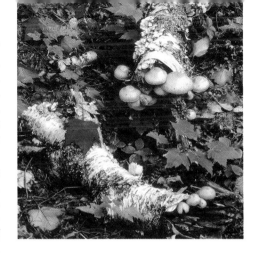

Figure 24
Fungi have an important role as decomposers in nature.

③ Assess

Reteach

Show students various illustrations of fungi. Ask them to identify the parts of each fungus. L2 **IS Visual-Spatial**

Challenge

Why is it beneficial for fungi to reproduce both sexually and asexually? Asexual reproduction allows fungi to take full and rapid advantage of a food source. Sexual reproduction provides genetic variation for surviving in different environments.

✔Assessment

Oral What has never been observed in any of the imperfect fungi? a sexual stage **How do the imperfect fungi reproduce if they don't have a sexual stage?** asexual spores Use **Performance Assessment in the Science Classroom,** p. 143.

Section ② Assessment

1. List characteristics common to all fungi.
2. How are fungi classified into different groups?
3. Differentiate between the imperfect fungi and all other fungi.
4. Why are lichens important to the environment?
5. **Think Critically** If an imperfect fungus were found to produce basidia under certain environmental conditions, how would the fungus be reclassified?

Skill Builder Activities

6. **Comparing and Contrasting** What are the similarities and differences among the characteristics of the four groups of fungi and lichens? **For more help, refer to the** Science Skill Handbook.
7. **Using Proportions** Of the 100,000 fungus species, approximately 30,000 are sac fungi. What percentage of fungus species are sac fungi? **For more help, refer to the** Math Skill Handbook.

Answers to Section Assessment

1. Fungi cannot make their own food. Most fungi are many-celled saprophytes with a body made of hyphae. They grow anchored in soil and have cell walls.
2. by the structure formed by the joining of hyphae
3. Imperfect fungi have no known sexual stage in their life cycle; all other fungi do.
4. Lichens are an important food source for many animals, they help break down rocks into soil, and they are used to monitor pollution levels.
5. It would be reclassified as a club fungus belonging to division Basidiomycota.
6. Zygote fungi: round spore cases on upright stalks; sac fungi: spores grow in a protective sac; club fungi: spores grow in a club-shaped structure; imperfect fungi: no sexual stage has been observed; lichens: crusty, leafy or upright; closely associated with algae or cyanobacteria. See information in section 2 under: What are fungi?; Club fungi; Sac Fungi; Zygote Fungi and other Fungi; Lichens
7. 30,000/100,000 × 100% = 30%

Activity

Recognize the Problem

Purpose

Students identify fungi and design a field guide for fungi in their area. **[IS] Kinesthetic and Visual-Spatial**

Process Skills

identifying, classifying, analyzing, and designing

Time Required

three class periods

Thinking Critically

Discussion

Tell students to think about methods for observing fungi. Have them consider features in their field guides that they would want to use to make identifying fungi easier. How will they group the organisms in the book? What type of diagrams or photographs will they include? How can they waterproof the pages of the field guide? What size should the field guide be?

Possible Materials

Provide a wide selection of containers and other collection equipment. Provide students with detailed guidebooks to help them identify their discoveries. Encourage students to use a wide variety of art mediums including color pencils, markers, pastels, charcoal, paints, and photography.

Safety Precautions

Caution students never to eat any fungi they collect and to thoroughly wash their hands after handling fungi.

Activity — Model and Invent

Creating a Fungus Field Guide

Magnification: 18×

Cross section of club fungus

Whether they are hiking deep into a rain forest in search of rare tropical birds, diving to coral reefs to study marine worms, or peering into microscopes to identify strains of bacteria, scientists all over the world depend on reliable field guides. Field guides are books that identify and describe certain types of organisms or the organisms living in a specific environment. Scientists find field guides for a specific area especially helpful. In this activity, you will create your own field guide for the club fungi found in your area.

Recognize the Problem

How could you create a field guide for the club fungi living in your area?

Thinking Critically

What information would you include in a field guide of club fungi?

Possible Materials

collection jars
magnifying glass
microscopes
microscope slides and coverslips
field guide to fungi or club fungi
art supplies

Goals

- ■ **Identify** the common club fungi found in the woods or grassy areas near your home or school.
- ■ **Create** a field guide to help future science students identify these fungi.

Data Source

SCIENCE*Online* Go to the Glencoe Science Web site at **science.glencoe.com** for more information about club fungi.

Safety Precautions

Be certain not to eat any of the fungi you collect. Wash your hands after handling any fungus collected. Do not touch your face during the activity.

52 ◆ B CHAPTER 2 Protists and Fungi

SCIENCE *Online*
Internet Addresses

_____
_____
_____

Explore the Glencoe Science Web site at **science.glencoe.com** to find out more about topics in this activity.

Resource Manager

Chapter Resources Booklet
  Activity Worksheet, pp. 7–8
Lab Management and Safety, p. 58

Planning the Model

1. Decide on the locations where you will conduct your search.

2. Select the materials you will need to collect and survey club fungi.

3. Design a data table in your Science Journal to record the fungi you find.

4. Decide on the layout of your field guide. What information about the fungi you will include? What drawings you will use? How will you group the fungi?

Check Model Plans

1. **Describe** your plan to your teacher and ask your teacher how it could be improved.

2. **Present** your ideas for collecting and surveying fungi, and your layout ideas for your field guide to the class. Ask your classmates to suggest improvements in your plan.

Making the Model

1. Search for samples of club fungi. **Record** the organisms you find in your data table. Use a fungus field guide to identify the fungi you discover. Do not pick or touch any fungi that you find unless you have permission.

2. Using your list of organisms, complete your field guide of club fungi as planned.

3. When finished, give your field guide to a classmate to identify a club fungus.

Analyzing and Applying Results

1. **Compare** the number of fungi you found to the total number of organisms listed in the field guide you used to identify the organisms.

2. **Infer** why your field guide would be more helpful to future science students in your school than the fungus field guide you used to identify organisms.

3. **Analyze** the problems you had while collecting and identifying your fungi. Suggest steps you could take to improve your collection and identification methods.

4. **Analyze** the problems you had while creating your field guide. Suggest ways your field guide could be improved.

Communicating Your Data

Compare your field guide with the field guides assembled by your classmates. Combine all the information on local club fungi compiled by your class to create a classroom field guide to club fungi.

ACTIVITY   B ◆ 53

Planning the Model

Teaching Strategies

• Assign each student a "buddy." Students should be responsible for staying with their buddies at all times.

• Review any poisonous fungi found in your area. Emphasize that students should not touch these organisms.

Making the Model

Expected Outcome Students will design and create a field guide that illustrates and identifies the types of fungi found in local woods and grassy areas.

Analyzing and Applying Results

Student answers will vary depending upon individual research. Accept all reasonable answers.

Assessment

Portfolio Ask students to draw a large colored picture of one of their fungi. Use **PASC**, p. 127.

Communicating Your Data

Offer students who are interested the opportunity to purchase color photocopies of the classroom field guide.

Content Background

The cacao tree is a perennial that yields several harvests annually. It was introduced to Europe in the sixteenth century after being cultivated in South America. On average the cacao stands 20 feet tall with 12-inch long shiny leaves. The cacao tree's pods contain beans with a high level of fat and are pulverized into a residue we commonly refer to as cocoa. Other uses for the cocoa bean include medication, cosmetics, and soap.

Of the three fungi mentioned, witches' broom is the most destructive. This fungus infects the pods, making them unusable. Brazil was once the top producer of cacao beans but because of this blight has fallen into eighth place in the last five years. Hard hit by this agricultural problem are the 5 to 6 million small farmers who depend heavily on production of the cacao tree for their financial survival. The Agricultural Research Service has developed new ways of combating the effects of fungi, including spraying with copper-based fungicides, breeding trees for resistance, pruning diseased trees, and cleaning up infected pods and branches.

TIME SCIENCE AND Society

SCIENCE ISSUES THAT AFFECT YOU!

Chocolate SOS

Can a fungus protect cacao trees under attack?

Chocolate is made from seeds (cocoa beans) that grow in the pods of the tropical cacao tree. To grow large crops more efficiently, farmers plant only a couple of the many varieties of cacao. They also use pesticides to protect the trees from destructive insect pests. These modern farming methods have produced huge crops of cocoa beans. But they also have helped destructive fungi sweep through cacao fields. There are fewer healthy cacao trees today than there were several years ago. And unless something stops the fungi that are destroying the trees, there could be a lot less chocolate in the future.

Pods contain dozens of beans.

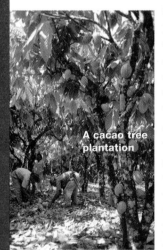

A cacao tree plantation

Losing Beans

Three types of fungi (witches' broom, blackpod rot, and frosty pod rot) are now killing cacao trees. The monoculture (growing one type of crop) of modern fields helps fungi spread quickly. A disease that attacks one plant of a species in a monoculture will rapidly spread to all plants in the monoculture. If a variety of plant species is present, the disease won't spread as quickly or as far.

54 ◆ B

Resources for Teachers and Students

"Fighting a Fungal Siege on Cacao Farms." November 1999. *Agricultural Research*.

"No Fun Fungi." May 26, 2000. *St. Louis Post-Dispatch*.

A diseased pod from a cacao tree

Since the blight began in the late 1980s and early 1990s, the world has lost 3 million tons of cocoa beans. Brazil was the top cocoa bean exporter in South America. In 1985, the United States alone bought 430,000 tons of cocoa beans from Brazil. In 1999, the whole Brazilian harvest contained just 130,000 tons, mostly because of the witches' broom fungus. The 2000 harvest was only 80,000 tons—the smallest in 30 years.

A Natural Cure

Farmers were using traditional chemical sprays to fight the fungus, but they were ineffective because in tropical regions, the sprays were washed away by rain. Now agriculture experts are working on a "natural" solution to the problem. They are using several types of "good" fungi to fight the "bad" fungi attacking the trees. When sprayed on infected trees, the good fungi (strains of *Trichoderma*) attack and stop the spread of the bad fungi. Scientists are already testing the fungal spray on trees in Brazil and Peru. The treatments have reduced the destruction of the trees by between 30 percent and 50 percent.

Don't expect your favorite chocolate bars to disappear from stores anytime soon. Right now, world cocoa bean supplies still exceed demand. But if the spread of the epidemic can't be stopped, those chocolate bars could become slightly more expensive and a little harder to find.

A fungus-infested cacao tree

CONNECTIONS Concept Map What are the steps in making chocolate—from harvesting cacao beans to packing chocolate products for sale? Use library and other sources to find out. Then draw a concept map that shows the steps. Compare your concept map with those of your classmates.

Online

For more information, visit science.glencoe.com

Discussion

What are farmers currently doing to fight the fungal attacks on the cacaos? Possible answer: Using "good" fungi called *Trichoderma* to stop the spread of the "bad" fungi that is destroying the cacao trees.

Activity

Use the Irish potato famine to illustrate how crop shortages can have devastating effects on a population. Use a team activity model. Have one group research the timetable for the famine. When did it start? Another group should focus on what caused the potatoes to become diseased and ultimately disappear as a resource. Another group should focus on the statistics of the famine. Who was affected? How many people died as a result? Another group should be responsible for an illustration representing the time period. Finally, after each group has presented, lead a discussion on how the two crop shortages are similar and how they differ.

Investigate the Issue

Lead a short discussion of the importance of each step that goes into cacao processing. To spur discussion, ask: **Would we still have easy access to chocolate bars if one group or part of the process was eliminated?**

CONNECTIONS Continue a dialogue asserting the necessity of each person in the process of making and distributing this product. Emphasize the role of the small farmers in the process. Try to convey their potential for loss if the amount of cacao that is diseased is great.

Online

Internet Addresses

_____

_____

_____

Explore the Glencoe Science Web site at **science.glencoe.com** to find out more about topics in this feature.

Chapter ② Study Guide

Reviewing Main Ideas

Preview

Students can answer the questions in their Science Journals. Discuss the answers as you go through the chapter. **Linguistic**

Review

Students can write their answers, then compare them with those of other students. **Interpersonal**

Reteach

Students can look at the illustrations and describe details that support the main ideas of the chapter. **Visual-Spatial**

Answers to Chapter Review

SECTION 1

2. Algae obtain energy through photosynthesis.

6. Downy mildews can kill plants, sometimes having a great economic impact.

SECTION 2

4. *Pencillium* does not appear to have a sexual stage, the primary characteristic used to classify fungi.

Reviewing Main Ideas

Section 1 Protists

1. Protists are one-celled or many-celled eukaryotic organisms. They can reproduce asexually, resulting in two new cells that are genetically identical. Protists also can reproduce sexually and produce genetically different organisms.

2. The protist kingdom has members that are plantlike, animal-like, and funguslike. *How do plantlike protists like the one shown below obtain food?*

3. Protists are thought to have evolved from a one-celled organism with a nucleus and other cellular structures.

4. Plantlike protists have cell walls and contain chlorophyll.

5. Animal-like protists can be separated into groups by how they move.

6. Funguslike protists have characteristics of protists and fungi. *What is the importance of funguslike protists such as the downy mildew shown below?*

Section 2 Fungi

1. Most species of fungi are many-celled. The body of a fungus consists of a mass of threadlike tubes.

2. Fungi are saprophytes or parasites—they feed off other things because they cannot make their own food.

3. Fungi reproduce using spores.

4. The three main groups of fungi are club fungi, sac fungi, and zygote fungi. Fungi that cannot be placed in a specific group are called imperfect fungi. Fungi are placed into one of these groups according to the structures in which they produce spores. *Why are fungi such as the* Penicillium *shown below so hard to classify?*

5. A lichen is an organism that consists of a fungus and a green alga or cyanobacterium.

FOLDABLES Reading & Study Skills

After You Read

Using what you have learned, write about similarities and differences of protists and fungi on the back of your Compare and Contrast Study Fold.

FOLDABLES Reading & Study Skills

After You Read

After students have read the chapter and completed the Foldable described in Before You Read, have them do the activity on the student page.

Dinah Zike

Visualizing Main Ideas

Complete the following concept map on a separate sheet of paper.

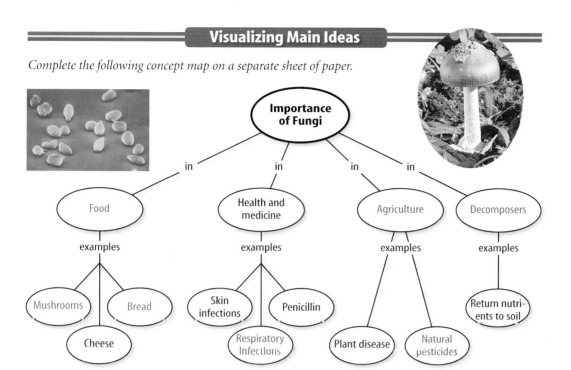

```
                    Importance
                    of Fungi
        in        in          in         in
    Food    Health and    Agriculture    Decomposers
            medicine
  examples   examples      examples       examples

Mushrooms    Bread    Skin        Penicillin              Return nutri-
                      infections                          ents to soil
      Cheese         Respiratory        Plant disease    Natural
                     infections                          pesticides
```

Visualizing Main Ideas

See student page.

Vocabulary Review

Using Vocabulary

1. spore
2. protist
3. cilia
4. algae
5. lichen
6. ascus
7. hyphae
8. pseudopod

Vocabulary Review

Vocabulary Words

a. algae
b. ascus
c. basidium
d. budding
e. cilia
f. flagellum
g. hyphae
h. lichen
i. mycorrhizae
j. protist
k. protozoan
l. pseudopod
m. saprophyte
n. sporangium
o. spore

THE PRINCETON REVIEW **Study Tip**

Make sure to read over your class notes after each lesson. Reading them will help you better understand what you've learned, as well as prepare you for the next day's lesson.

Using Vocabulary

Write the vocabulary word that matches each of these descriptions.

1. reproductive cell of a fungus

2. organisms that are animal-like, plantlike, or funguslike

3. threadlike structures used for movement

4. plantlike protists

5. organism made up of a fungus and an alga or a cyanobacterium

6. reproductive structure made by sac fungi

7. threadlike tubes that make up the body of a fungus

8. structure used for movement formed by oozing cytoplasm

Checking Concepts

1. D
2. B
3. D
4. D
5. B
6. A
7. D
8. B
9. B
10. C

Thinking Critically

11. no warmth, low humidity, low moisture
12. Accessory pigments help chlorophyll to be more efficient during photosynthesis.
13. Funguslike protists produce spores and take in food from an outside source like fungi. Unlike fungi, the funguslike protists usually move by using pseudopods.
14. When in association with certain mutualistic fungi, some plants are able to take in materials from their environment.
15. Fungi can digest food outside the organism. This mold secrets the enzymes, which help digest the fruit. Then the cells absorb the nutrients.

Checking Concepts

Choose the word or phrase that best answers the question.

1. Which of the following is an alga?
   A) *Paramecium*   C) *Amoeba*
   B) lichen   D) diatom

2. Which type of protist captures food, does not have cell walls, and can move from place to place?
   A) algae   C) fungi
   B) protozoans   D) lichens

3. Which of the following organisms cause red tides when found in large numbers?
   A) *Euglena*   C) *Ulva*
   B) diatoms   D) dinoflagellates

4. Algae are important for which of the following reasons?
   A) They are a food source for many aquatic organisms.
   B) Parts of algae are used in foods that humans eat.
   C) Algae produce oxygen as a result of the process of photosynthesis.
   D) all of the above

5. Which of the following moves using cilia?
   A) *Amoeba*   C) *Giardia*
   B) *Paramecium*   D) *Euglena*

6. Where would you most likely find funguslike protists?
   A) on decaying logs C) on dry surfaces
   B) in bright light   D) on metal surfaces

7. Decomposition is an important role of which organisms?
   A) protozoans   C) plants
   B) algae   D) fungi

8. Where are spores produced in mushrooms?
   A) sporangia   C) ascus
   B) basidia   D) hyphae

9. Which of the following is used as an indicator organism?
   A) club fungus   C) slime mold
   B) lichen   D) imperfect fungus

10. Which of the following is sometimes classified as an imperfect fungus?
    A) mushroom   C) *Penicillium*
    B) yeast   D) lichen

Thinking Critically

11. What kind of environment is needed to prevent fungal growth?

12. Why do algae contain pigments other than just chlorophyll?

13. Compare and contrast the features of fungi and funguslike protists.

14. What advantages do some plants have when they form associations with fungi?

15. Explain the adaptations of fungi that enable them to get food. *How does this mold obtain food?*

Developing Skills

16. **Recognizing Cause and Effect** A leaf sitting on the floor of the rain forest will decompose in just six weeks. A leaf on the floor of a temperate forest, located in areas that have four seasons, will take up to a year to decompose. Explain how this is possible.

17. **Classifying** Classify these organisms based on their method of movement: *Euglena*, water molds, *Amoeba*, dinoflagellates, *Paramecium*, slime molds, and *Giardia*.

Chapter ✓*Assessment* Planner

Portfolio Encourage students to place in their portfolios one or two items of what they consider to be their best work. Examples include:
- Science Journal, p. 34
- Health Integration, p. 39
- Try at Home MiniLAB, p. 47

Performance Additional performance assessments, Performance Task Assessment Lists, and rubrics for evaluating these activities can be found in Glencoe's **Performance Assessment in the Science Classroom.**

18. Comparing and Contrasting Make a chart comparing and contrasting the different ways protists and fungi can obtain food.

19. Making and Using Tables Complete the following table that compares the different groups of fungi.

Fungi Comparisons		
Fungi Group	**Structure Where Sexual Spores Are Produced**	**Examples**
Club fungi	Basidium	Mushroom
Sac fungi	Ascus	Truffles
Zygospore fungi	Sporangium	Bread mold
Imperfect fungi	No sexual spores produced	*Penicillium*

20. Identifying and Manipulating Variables and Controls You find a new and unusual fungus growing in your refrigerator. Design an experiment to determine what fungus group it belongs to.

Performance Assessment

21. Poster Research the different types of fungi found in the area where you live. Determine to which group each fungus belongs. Create a poster to display your results and share them with your class.

22. Poem Write a poem about protists or fungi. Include facts about characteristics, types of movement, and ways of feeding.

TECHNOLOGY

Go to the Glencoe Science Web site at **science.glencoe.com** or use the **Glencoe Science CD-ROM** for additional chapter assessment.

 Test Practice

Kingdom Protista includes a wide variety of organisms. Some can make their own food and others might get food from their environment. Two groups of protists are shown in the boxes below.

Group A   **Group B**

Study the pictures in the two boxes above and answer the following questions.

1. The protists in Group B are different from the protists in Group A because only the protists in Group B _____ .
A) have chlorophyll
B) are many-celled
C) can move
D) have a nucleus

2. Which of the following organisms would belong in Group A above?
F) bacteria   H) grass
G) kelp   J) fish

3. Which of the following is NOT characteristic of Group A?
A) cell membrane
B) contain chlorophyll
C) live in a watery environment
D) one-celled

 Test Practice

The Test-Taking Tip was written by The Princeton Review, the nation's leader in test preparation.
1. C
2. G
3. D

Developing Skills

16. Warm, moist environments such as those found in the rain forest are ideal for the growth of fungi. Therefore, fungi decompose dead organic materials more rapidly in rain forests than in cooler, drier temperate forests.
17. flagella—*Euglena*, water molds, dinoflagellates, *Giardia*; pseudopods—*Amoeba*, slime molds; cilia—*Paramecium*.
18. Check charts for accuracy.
19. See student page.
20. Design will vary. Designs should include comparing the fungus with characteristics of different fungi and observing its sexual reproduction.

Performance Assessment

21. Posters will vary. Most will have photos or drawings of various mushrooms or slime molds. Posters should contain information about the groups of fungi. Use **PASC**, p. 145.
22. Poems will vary but should indicate characteristics and types of organisms studied in this chapter. Use **PASC**, p. 157.

✔*Assessment* Resources

 Reproducible Masters

Chapter Resources Booklet
Chapter Review, pp. 33–34
Chapter Tests, pp. 35–38
Assessment Transparency Activity, p. 45

Glencoe Science Web site
Interactive Tutor
Chapter Quizzes

Glencoe Technology
Assessment Transparency
Interactive CD-ROM Chapter Quizzes
ExamView Pro Test Bank
Vocabulary PuzzleMaker Software
MindJogger Videoquiz

Section/Objectives	Standards		Activities/Features
Chapter Opener	**National**	**State/Local**	**Explore Activity:** Determine how you use plants, p. 61 **Before You Read,** p. 61
	See p. 5T for a Key to Standards.		
Section 1 An Overview of Plants 🕐 2 sessions 📦 1 block 1. **Identify** characteristics common to all plants. 2. **Explain** which plant adaptations make it possible for plants to survive on land. 3. **Compare and contrast** vascular and nonvascular plants.	National Content Standards: UCP1, C1, C5		**Chemistry Integration,** p. 64 **Visualizing Plant Classification,** p. 66
Section 2 Seedless Plants 🕐 2 sessions 📦 1 block 1. **Distinguish** between characteristics of seedless nonvascular plants and seedless vascular plants. 2. **Identify** the importance of some nonvascular and vascular plants.	National Content Standards: UCP5, A1, C1, C5, F4		**MiniLAB:** Measuring Water Absorption by a Moss, p. 69 **Science Online,** p. 70 **Problem-Solving Activity:** What is the value of rain forests?, p. 70
Section 3 Seed Plants 🕐 3 sessions 📦 1.5 blocks 1. **Identify** the characteristics of seed plants. 2. **Explain** the structures and functions of roots, stems, and leaves. 3. **Describe** the main characteristics and importance of gymnosperms and angiosperms. 4. **Compare** similarities and differences between monocots and dicots.	National Content Standards: UCP5, A1, C1, C5, E2, F5, G2		**MiniLAB:** Observing Water Moving in a Plant, p. 75 **Health Integration,** p. 77 **Science Online,** p. 81 **Activity:** Identifying Conifers, p. 83 **Activity:** Plants as Medicine, pp. 84–85 **Oops! Accidents in Science:** A Loopy Idea Inspires "Fasten-ating" Invention, pp. 86–87

■ NATIONAL GEOGRAPHIC   Teacher's Corner

PRODUCTS AVAILABLE FROM GLENCOE
To order call 1-800-334-7344:
CD-ROMs
NGS PictureShow: Plants: What It Means to Be Green
Curriculum Kit
GeoKit: Plants

Transparency Sets
NGS PicturePack: Plants: What It Means to Be Green
VideoDisc
STV: Plants

PRODUCTS AVAILABLE FROM NATIONAL GEOGRAPHIC SOCIETY
To order call 1-800-368-2728:
Videos
Plant Classification

Activity Materials	Reproducible Resources	Section Assessment	Technology
Explore Activity: old magazines, scissors	**Chapter Resources Booklet** Foldables Worksheet, p. 13 Directed Reading Overview, p. 15 Note-taking Worksheets, pp. 29–31	*GLENCOE'S ASSESSMENT ADVANTAGE*	
Need materials? Contact Science Kit at 1-800-828-7777 or www.sciencekit.com on the Internet.	**Chapter Resources Booklet** Transparency Activity, p. 40 Enrichment, p. 26 Reinforcement, p. 23 Directed Reading, p. 16 **Cultural Diversity,** p. 19 **Life Science Critical Thinking/ Problem Solving,** p. 9 **Earth Science Critical Thinking/ Problem Solving,** p. 17 **Performance Assessment in the Science Classroom,** p. 55	Portfolio Activity, p. 65 Performance Skill Builder Activities, p. 67 Content Section Assessment, p. 67	Section Focus Transparency Interactive CD-ROM Guided Reading Audio Program
MiniLAB: *sphagnum* moss, cheesecloth, spring scales, graduated cylinder, water, container for water	**Chapter Resources Booklet** Transparency Activity, p. 41 MiniLAB, p. 3 Enrichment, p. 27 Reinforcement, p. 24 Directed Reading, p. 17 **Home and Community Involvement,** p. 42 **Math Skill Activities,** p. 5	Portfolio Make a Model, p. 71 Performance MiniLAB, p. 69 Skill Builder Activities, p. 73 Content Section Assessment, p. 73	Section Focus Transparency Interactive CD-ROM Guided Reading Audio Program
MiniLAB: clear container, water, metric ruler, red food coloring, green onion, hand lens **Activity:** short branches of pine, cedar, spruce, Douglas fir, hemlock, fir, redwood, arborvitae, juniper **Activity:** no materials needed	**Chapter Resources Booklet** Transparency Activity, p. 42 MiniLAB, p. 4 Enrichment, p. 28 Reinforcement, p. 25 Directed Reading, pp. 17, 18 Activity Worksheets, pp. 5–6, 7–8 Transparency Activity, pp. 43–44 Lab Activities, pp. 9–10, 11–12 **Performance Assessment in the Science Classroom,** p. 61 **Lab Management and Safety in the Science Classroom,** p. 61	Portfolio Curriculum Connection, p. 77 Performance MiniLAB, p. 75 Skill Builder Activities, p. 82 Content Section Assessment, p. 82	Section Focus Transparency Teaching Transparency Interactive CD-ROM Guided Reading Audio Program

End of Chapter Assessment

GLENCOE'S ASSESSMENT ADVANTAGE

Blackline Masters	Technology	Professional Series
Chapter Resources Booklet Chapter Review, pp. 33–34 Chapter Tests, pp. 35–38 **Standardized Test Practice by The Princeton Review,** pp. 43–46	MindJogger Videoquiz Interactive CD-ROM Vocabulary PuzzleMakers ExamView Pro Test Bank Interactive Lesson Planner Interactive Teacher Edition	Performance Assessment in the Science Classroom (PASC)

Transparencies

Section Focus

A Lot Can Happen in 4,000 Years

Bristlecone pines live a very long time. The oldest one is thought to be over 4,600 years old. From the time the pyramids at Giza were built through this very moment, it has lived in a quiet spot in eastern California. Bristlecones are usually found at high altitudes where it is very dry.

1. Looking at the picture, describe the bristlecone pine's environment.
2. What might some advantages be to the bristlecone's habitat? What might be disadvantages?

L2

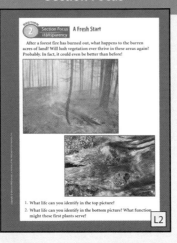

A Fresh Start

After a forest fire has burned out, what happens to the barren acres of land? Will lush vegetation ever thrive in these areas again? Probably. In fact, it could even be better than before!

1. What life can you identify in the top picture?
2. What life can you identify in the bottom picture? What function might these first plants serve?

L2

Rooted in Nature

Bonsai is an ancient method of growing trees or shrubs in small containers. The plants are kept small by pruning the branches and roots. Because some types of plants used for bonsai can live for more than 100 years, they are passed from generation to generation.

1. What are some advantages to having bonsai plants? What might some disadvantages be?
2. What qualities do you think would be important in practicing bonsai?

L2

This is a representation of key blackline masters available in the Teacher Classroom Resources. See Resource Manager boxes within the chapter for additional information.

Assessment

Plants

Directions: *Carefully review the table and answer the following questions.*

Day	Plant A with no water	Plant B watered monthly	Plant C watered weekly	Plant D watered daily
1	10 cm	11 cm	12 cm	8 cm
5	10 cm	12 cm	13 cm	12 cm
10	10 cm	12 cm	15 cm	18 cm
15	10 cm	13 cm	17 cm	19 cm
20	10 cm	13 cm	20 cm	23 cm
25	10 cm	?	22 cm	27 cm

Watering and Plant Growth

1. According to the table, which plant was the tallest on Day 5?
   A Plant A
   B Plant B
   C Plant C
   D Plant D
2. According to the table, which plant grew the most between Day 1 and Day 20?
   F Plant A   H Plant C
   G Plant B   J Plant D
3. If everything remains the same, what is a reasonable prediction for the height of Plant B on Day 25?
   A 10 cm   C 18 cm
   B 14 cm   D 24 cm

L2

Teaching

Monocots and Dicots

Monocot   Dicot

Vascular bundles   Vascular bundle

Cotyledon   Cotyledon

L2

Key to Teaching Strategies

The following designations will help you decide which activities are appropriate for your students.

L1 Level 1 activities should be appropriate for students with learning difficulties.

L2 Level 2 activities should be within the ability range of all students.

L3 Level 3 activities are designed for above-average students.

ELL ELL activities should be within the ability range of English Language Learners.

COOP LEARN Cooperative Learning activities are designed for small group work.

LS Multiple Learning Styles logos are used throughout to indicate strategies that address different learning styles.

P These strategies represent student products that can be placed into a best-work portfolio.

Hands-on Activities

Activity Worksheets

Identifying Conifers

Lab Preview
Directions: Answer these questions before you begin the Activity.
1. Identify the two types of conifer leaves.

2. Why will you need a separate sheet of paper for this activity?

How can you tell a pine from a spruce or a cedar from a juniper? One way is to observe their leaves. The leaves of most conifers are either needlelike—shaped like needles—or scalelike—like the scales on a fish or snake. Examine some conifer branches and identify them using the key to classify leaves.

What You'll Investigate
How can leaves be used to classify conifers?

Materials
short branches of the following conifers:
pine
cedar
spruce
Douglas fir
hemlock
fir
redwood
arborvitae
juniper
*Illustrations of the conifers above
*Alternate materials

Goals
• Identify the difference between needlelike and scalelike leaves.
• Classify conifers according to their leaves.

Safety Precautions
Wash your hands after handling leaves.

Procedure
1. Observe the leaves or illustrations of each conifer, then use the key at the right to identify it.
2. Write the number and name of each conifer you identify in the table in the Data and Observations section.

Key to Classifying Leaves
1. All leaves are needlelike
   a. no, go to 2
   b. no, go to 8
2. Needles are in clusters.
   a. yes, go to 3
   b. no, go to 4
3. Clusters contain 2, 3, or 5 needles.
   a. yes, pine
   b. no, cedar
4. Needles grow on all sides of the stem.
   a. yes, go to 5
   b. no, go to 7
5. Needles grow from a woody peg.
   a. yes, spruce
   b. no, go to 6
6. Needles appear to grow from the branch.
   a. yes, Douglas fir
   b. no, hemlock
7. Most of the needles grow upward.
   a. yes, fir
   b. no, redwood
8. All the leaves are scalelike but not prickly.
   a. yes, arborvitae
   b. no, juniper

L2

Laboratory Activities

Root Structure and Functions

Roots hold a plant in the ground. They also absorb, store, and transport water and minerals. They have small threadlike side roots with root hairs that absorb water and minerals from the soil. Taproots, such as carrots, have a primary root that grows straight down into the soil. Taproots look very different from fibrous roots, such as grasses, which have many small roots branching out in different directions.

Strategy
You will examine a dissected carrot root.
You will label a diagram of a root and list the function of each part.

Materials
carrot sliced crosswise
carrot sliced lengthwise
hand lens

Procedure
1. Your teacher will prepare a crosswise slice of a carrot for you.
2. Hold the slice up to the light. Compare what you see with Figure 1 under Data and Observations.
3. Examine the lengthwise slice of the carrot. Use the hand lens. Look at both the inner and outer parts.
4. The outside layer of the root is the epidermis. Lateral roots grow from the epidermal cells and root hairs grow from them. Label the epidermis, lateral roots, and root hairs if all of these structures are present.
5. Inside the epidermis, you will find several layers of large, loosely packed cells that store food. This is the cortex. Food stored in the cortex can be used by other cells of the plant. Label the cortex.
6. Inside the cortex are tubelike cells from xylem vessels that carry water and minerals in the plant. Label the xylem cells.
7. Other tubelike cells inside the cortex carry food to the plant. These cells are called phloem cells. Label the phloem cells.

Data and Observations

Figure 1

L2

Meeting Different Ability Levels

Content Outline

Reinforcement

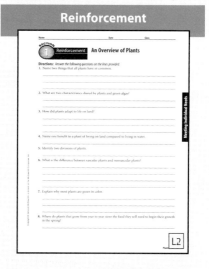

Directed Reading

(L1)

Assessment

Chapter Tests

Enrichment

Spanish Directed Reading

Test Practice Workbook

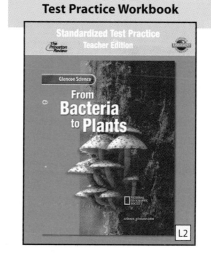

Standardized Test Practice
Teacher Edition

Glencoe Science

From Bacteria to Plants

NATIONAL GEOGRAPHIC SOCIETY

science.glencoe.com

Chapter Review

Part A. Vocabulary Review

Science Content Background

SECTION 1 An Overview of Plants
Origin and Evolution of Plants

Plants probably share an ancestor with multicellular Chlorophyta, the green algae. Common characteristics of plants and green algae include pigments such as chlorophyll a and b and carotenoids, cell walls that consist primarily of cellulose, starch as the primary food-storage product, and similar cell division. Some plants, including mosses, liverworts, and ferns, have free-swimming sperm and require water for fertilization—another feature they have in common with green algae.

Fun Fact

Luminous mosses glow with a greenish light. These mosses are found in caves and have cells shaped like tiny lenses that focus small amounts of light on the chloroplast.

Adaptations to Land

Fibers are long, slender cells that are found in the vascular tissue of some plants. They usually contain an organic substance called lignin that makes the walls tough and hard. Fibers add extra support to many terrestrial plants. People weave the fibers of some plants to make products such as rope and cloth.

Classification of Plants

Classification of plants traditionally has been based on morphological characteristics such as the number and arrangement of leaves and the structure of flowers and fruit. Recently, genetic studies have been used to make minor changes in the classification of some plants. However, derived characteristics such as vascular tissue and seed formation and similar, easily observable characteristics are reliable features for classification.

For many years plants have been separated into divisions, but in 1993 the International Botanical Congress made the term *phylum* an acceptable alternative. You may wish to introduce the alternate term to your students.

SECTION 2 Seedless Plants
Less Familiar Plants

Liverworts and hornworts are leafy with creeping gametophyte forms. Mosses have distinct leaflike and stemlike structures, but because they do not contain vascular tissue, they are not homologous to the leaves and stems of vascular plants. Some liverworts produce structures called gemma cups on their surfaces. Groups of cells in these structures are washed out of the cup when it rains. These cells can grow into new liverwort plants.

Seedless vascular plants include whisk ferns (Psilophyta), club mosses (Lycopoda), horsetails (Sphenophyta), and ferns (Pterophyta). In each of these divisions, motile sperm require water to swim to the egg.

Pat Watson/The Image Works

Seed Plants

Origins

Seed plants appeared suddenly about 65 million years ago at the beginning of the Cretaceous Period. These plants dominated the land. They developed sperm-containing pollen grains that could be transported from plant to plant without water. The development of an embryo inside a protective seed coat allowed seeds to survive harsh conditions for long periods. About 200,000 of the more than 260,000 species of plants in existence today are seed plants.

Vascular Tissue

The first vascular plants appeared no later than the early Silurian Period, some 430 million years ago. Early vascular plants had stems formed as a result of primary growth—growth from plant tips. Stems had vascular cylinders with conducting functions, as they do in modern vascular plants. Secondary growth, found in conifers and some dicots, is an important early development. It arises by mitotic divisions of cambium tissues and increases the plant's girth.

Xylem tissue is made of tracheids and vessel elements that carry water and dissolved minerals. Tracheids are found in all plants with vascular tissue, but vessel elements are limited almost exclusively to angiosperms. Both are long, tubelike cells that have thick cell walls. Small openings called pits allow water to seep through the cell walls from tracheid to tracheid. Vessels lack transverse end walls and are continuous pipelines through which water can flow.

John Gerlach/Tom Stack & Associates

Fun Fact

An aphid drinks sap from plants by piercing the plant's phloem with its hollow mouthpart.

Unlike xylem tissue, phloem tissue is living. It is composed mostly of sieve-tube elements and companion cells. Sieve-tube elements are cells that carry the products of photosynthesis throughout the plant. Their cell walls are thinner than those of cells found in xylem. Cytoplasm extends from one sieve-tube element to the next through structures called sieve plates. Since mature sieve-tube cells have no nuclei, companion cells help with their metabolism.

SCIENCE *Online*

For additional content background on this topic, go to the Glencoe Science Web site at science.glencoe.com.

Plants

Chapter Vocabulary

cuticle, p. 64
cellulose, p. 64
vascular plant, p. 67
nonvascular plant, p. 67
rhizoid, p. 68
pioneer species, p. 69
stomata, p. 75
guard cell, p. 75
xylem, p. 77
phloem, p. 77
cambium, p. 77
gymnosperm, p. 78
angiosperm, p. 79
monocot, p. 80
dicot, p. 80

What do you think?

Science Journal Indian pipe is the common name of the plant in this picture. Unlike most plants, Indian pipe plants are not green.

Plants

Go outside and look around. Where do you see plants? Plants cover almost every available surface in a tropical rain forest but only some areas of a desert. Plants are found nearly everywhere on Earth.

Take a close look at a plant. When you look at an animal, you expect to see eyes, a mouth, and maybe even legs. What do you expect to see when you look at a plant? Do all plants have leaves, roots, and flowers?

In this chapter, you'll learn what characteristics plants have and how they are classified. You'll also learn why plants are important.

What do you think?

Science Journal Look at the picture below with a classmate. Discuss what you think this might be or what is happening. Here's a hint: *Most of its relatives are green.* Write your answer or your best guess in your Science Journal.

Theme Connection

Stability and Change This chapter emphasizes plant adaptations that allow these organisms to adapt, survive, and reproduce in various environments.

EXPLORE ACTIVITY

Plants are just about everywhere—in parks and gardens, by streams, on rocks, in houses, and even on dinner plates. Do you use plants for things other than food? In the following activity, find out how plants are used. Then, in the pages that follow, learn about plant life.

Determine how you use plants

1. Brainstorm with two other classmates and make a list of everything that you use in a day that comes from plants.

2. Compare your list with those of other groups in your class.

3. Search through old magazines for images of the items on your list.

4. As a class, build a bulletin board of the magazine images.

Observe

In your Science Journal, list things that were made from plants 100 years or more ago but today are made from plastics, steel, or some other material.

Before You Read

FOLDABLES
Reading & Study Skills

Making a Know-Want-Learn Study Fold It would be helpful to identify what you already know and what you want to know. Make the following Foldable to help you focus on reading about plants.

1. Place a sheet of paper in front of you so the long side is at the top. Fold the paper in half from top to bottom.

2. Fold both sides in to divide the paper into thirds. Unfold the paper so three columns show.

3. Through the top thickness of paper, cut along each of the fold lines to the top fold, forming three tabs.

4. Draw and label *Know, Want,* and *Learned* across the front of the paper as shown.

5. Before you read the chapter, write what you know under the left tab. Under the middle tab, write what you want to know.

6. As you read the chapter, write what you learn under the right tab.

 EXPLORE ACTIVITY

Purpose Use the Explore Activity to introduce students to the many uses of plants. L2
COOP LEARN **IS** **Interpersonal**

Preparation Provide books, magazines, and other resources from which students can get ideas.

Teaching Strategy Offer suggestions of additional items from plants to students who need help.

Observe

Examples include building materials, clothing fibers, dyes, paper, resins, paints, and inks.

✔ *Assessment*

Process Show students a picture of a desert succulent with plump water-filled leaves. Have them infer how desert animals might use this plant. The plant could provide water to animals in a dry environment. Use **Performance Assessment in the Science Classroom,** p. 89.

FOLDABLES
Reading & Study Skills

Before You Read

Dinah Zike Study Fold

Purpose This Foldable will provide students an opportunity to review what they know about plants and make them question what they would like to know. The Foldable can be used as an assessment tool at the end of the chapter to determine what students have learned.

📁 For additional help, see Foldables Worksheet, p. 13 in **Chapter Resources Booklet,** or go to the Glencoe Science Web site at **science.glencoe.com.** See After You Read in the Study Guide at the end of this chapter.

SECTION

An Overview of Plants

1 Motivate

Bellringer Transparency

Display the Section Focus Transparency for Section 1. Use the accompanying Transparency Activity Master. L2 ELL

Tie to Prior Knowledge

Ask students to visualize a common plant and list its major parts. Students should know that most plants have the following parts in common: roots, stems, leaves, and often flowers and fruits. Display a common flowering plant, such as a geranium, and have students point out the parts they know.

An Overview of Plants

As You Read

What You'll Learn
- **Identify** characteristics common to all plants.
- **Explain** which plant adaptations make it possible for plants to survive on land.
- **Compare and contrast** vascular and nonvascular plants.

Vocabulary
cuticle
cellulose
vascular plant
nonvascular plant

Why It's Important
Plants produce food and oxygen used by most organisms on Earth.

What is a plant?

What is the most common sight you see when you walk along nature trails in parks like the one shown in **Figure 1?** Maybe you've taken off your shoes and walked barefoot on soft, cool grass. Perhaps you've climbed a tree to see what things look like from high in its branches. In each instance, plants surrounded you.

If you named all the plants that you know, you probably would include trees, flowers, vegetables, fruits, and field crops like wheat, rice, or corn. Between 260,000 and 300,000 plant species have been discovered and identified. Scientists think more are still to be found, mainly in tropical rain forests. Some of these plants are important food sources to humans and other consumers. Without plants, most life on Earth as we know it would not be possible.

Plant Characteristics Plants range in size from microscopic water ferns to giant sequoia trees that are sometimes more than 100 m in height. Most have roots or rootlike structures that hold them in the ground or onto some other object like a rock or another plant. Plants are adapted to nearly every environment on Earth. Some grow in frigid, ice-bound polar regions and others grow in hot, dry deserts. All plants need water, but some plants cannot live unless they are submerged in either freshwater or salt water.

Figure 1
All plants are many-celled and nearly all contain chlorophyll. Grasses, trees, shrubs, mosses, and ferns are all plants.

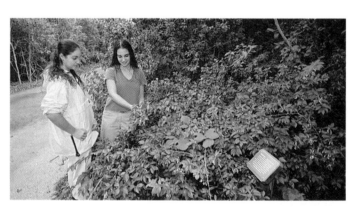

Section ✓*Assessment* Planner

PORTFOLIO	**CONTENT ASSESSMENT**
Activity, p. 65	Section, p. 67
PERFORMANCE ASSESSMENT	Challenge, p. 67
Skill Builder Activities, p. 67	Chapter, pp. 90–91
See page 90 for more options.	

Plant Cells Like other living things, plants are made of cells. A plant cell has a cell membrane, a nucleus, and other cellular structures. In addition, plant cells have cell walls that make them different from animal cells. Cell walls provide structure and protection for plant cells.

Many plant cells contain the green pigment chlorophyll (KLOR uh fihl) so most plants are green. Plants need chlorophyll to make food using a process called photosynthesis. Chlorophyll is found in a cell structure called a chloroplast. Plant cells from green parts of the plant usually contain many chloroplasts.

Most plant cells have a large, membrane-bound structure called the central vacuole that takes up most of the space inside of the cell. This structure plays an important role in regulating the water content of the cell. Many substances are stored in the vacuole such as the pigments that make some flowers red, blue, or purple.

Origin and Evolution of Plants

Have plants always existed on land? The first plants that lived on land probably could survive only in damp areas. Their ancestors were probably ancient green algae that lived in the sea. Green algae are one-celled or many-celled organisms that use photosynthesis to make food. Today, plants and green algae have the same types of chlorophyll and carotenoids (kuh RAH tun oydz) in their cells. Carotenoids are red, yellow, or orange pigments that also are used for photosynthesis. This has led scientists to think that plants and green algae have a common ancestor.

 Reading Check *How are plants and green algae alike?*

Fossil Record The fossil record for plants is not like that for animals. Most animals have bones or other hard parts that can fossilize. Plants usually decay before they become fossilized. But, the oldest fossil plants are about 420 million years old. **Figure 2** shows *Cooksonia,* a fossil of one of these plants. Other fossils of early plants are similar to the ancient green algae. Scientists hypothesize that some of these kinds of plants evolved into the plants that exist today.

Cone-bearing plants, such as pines, probably evolved from a group of plants that grew about 350 million years ago. Fossils of these plants have been dated to about 300 million years ago. It is estimated that flowering plants did not exist until about 120 million years ago. However, the exact origin of flowering plants is not known.

Figure 2
This is a fossil of a plant named *Cooksonia.* These plants grew about 420 million years ago and were about 2.5 cm tall.

 SECTION 1 An Overview of Plants **B ◆ 63**

2 Teach

What is a plant?

Visual Learning
Figure 1 Which features of the organisms in the photo suggest they are plants? They are green, grow from soil, and have leaves and stems.

IDENTIFYING
Misconceptions

Students may think that all plants produce seeds in flowers. Explain that some plants are seedless and do not make seeds, others produce seeds in cones.

Origin and Evolution of Plants

✔ **Reading Check**

Answer Both have similar chlorophyll and carotenoids.

Inclusion Strategies

Learning Disabled and Visually Impaired If possible, provide petrified wood or fossil casts of plants. Ask students what clues they have that these fossils were once living plants. The fossils may be shaped like plant stems or leaves. **LS Kinesthetic**

Resource Manager

Chapter Resources Booklet
Note-taking Worksheets, pp. 29–31
Transparency Activity, p. 40
Cultural Diversity, p. 19

Life on Land

Adaptations to Land

Reading Check

Answer to slow the loss of water

Quick Demo

Use a spray mister to mist water onto a plant leaf that has a thick cuticle. Allow students to observe how the water beads up and runs off.

Activity

Set up stations around the class that contain different plant parts. Have students write the name of each plant part and important information about each as they move from one station to another. [L1]

Visual-Spatial

Chemistry
INTEGRATION

Plant cell walls are made mostly of cellulose, which is made of long chains of glucose molecules $(C_6H_{12}O_6)$. More than half of the carbon in plants is found in cellulose. Raw cotton is more than 90 percent cellulose. What physical property of cellulose makes it ideal for helping plants survive on land?

Figure 3
The alga *Spirogyra*, like all algae, must have water to survive. If the pool where it lives dries up, it will die.

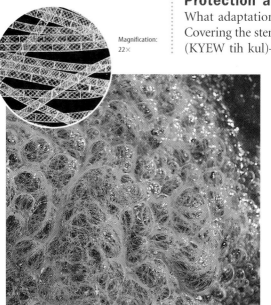

Magnification: 22×

Life on Land

Life on land has some advantages for plants. More sunlight and carbon dioxide—needed for photosynthesis—are available on land than in water. During photosynthesis, plants give off oxygen. Long ago, as more and more plants adapted to life on land, the amount of oxygen in Earth's atmosphere increased. This paved the way for organisms that depend on oxygen.

Adaptations to Land

What is life like for green algae, shown in **Figure 3,** as they float in a shallow pool? The water in the pool surrounds and supports them as the algae make their own food through the process of photosynthesis. Because materials can enter and leave through their cell membranes and cell walls, the algae cells have everything they need to survive as long as they have water.

Now, imagine a summer drought. The pool begins to dry up. Soon, the algae are on damp mud and are no longer supported by water. As long as the soil stays damp, materials can move in and out through the algae's cell membranes and cell walls. As the soil becomes drier and drier, the algae will lose water too because water moves through their cell membranes and cell walls from where there is more water to where there is less water. Without enough water in their environment, the algae will die.

Protection and Support Water is important for plants. What adaptations would help a plant conserve water on land? Covering the stems, leaves, and flowers of many plants is a **cuticle** (KYEW tih kul)—a waxy, protective layer secreted by cells onto the surface of the plant. The cuticle slows the loss of water. The cuticle and other adaptations shown in **Figure 4** enable plants to survive on land.

Reading Check *What is the function of a plant's cuticle?*

Supporting itself is another problem for a plant on land. Like all cells, plant cells have cell membranes, but they also have rigid cell walls outside the membrane. Cell walls contain **cellulose** (SEL yuh lohs), which is a chemical compound that plants can make out of sugar. Long chains of cellulose molecules form tangled fibers in plant cell walls. These fibers provide structure and support.

Teacher FYI

Almost all of the oxygen in our atmosphere has been produced by the release of oxygen during photosynthesis. Plants also absorb carbon dioxide from the atmosphere during photosynthesis. Thus, the destruction of vast areas of tropical forest may negatively impact the balance of these gases in the atmosphere.

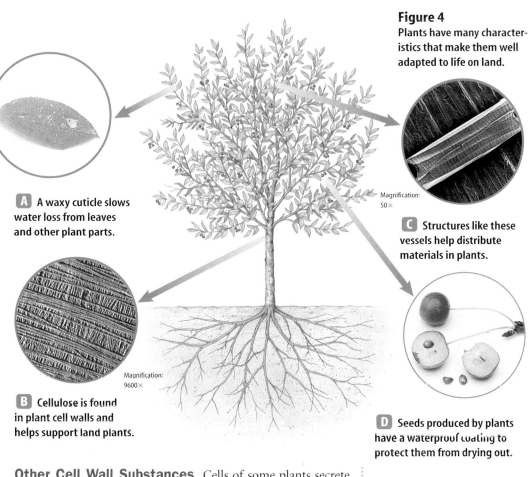

Figure 4
Plants have many characteristics that make them well adapted to life on land.

A A waxy cuticle slows water loss from leaves and other plant parts.

Magnification: 50×

C Structures like these vessels help distribute materials in plants.

Magnification: 9600×

B Cellulose is found in plant cell walls and helps support land plants.

D Seeds produced by plants have a waterproof coating to protect them from drying out.

Other Cell Wall Substances Cells of some plants secrete other substances into the cellulose that make the cell wall even stronger. Trees, such as oaks and pines, could not grow without these strong cell walls. Wood can be used for construction mostly because of strong cell walls.

Life on land means that each plant cell is not surrounded by water. The plant cannot depend on water to move substances from one cell to the next. Through adaptations, structures developed in many plants that distribute water, nutrients, and food throughout the plant. These structures also help provide support for the plant.

Reproduction Changes in reproduction were necessary if plants were to survive on land. The presence of water-resistant spores helped some plants reproduce successfully. Other plants adapted by producing water-resistant seeds in cones or in flowers that developed into fruits.

SECTION 1 An Overview of Plants   **B ◆ 65**

Use Science Words

Word Meaning Have students compare the meaning of the word cuticle in relation to plants (protective layer on plant surface) and in relation to the human body (hardened skin at the base of nails). Both are derived from the Latin *cutis* meaning "skin." L2
IS Linguistic

Activity

Have students prepare posters that show examples of plant adaptations to life on land. L2
IS Visual-Spatial P

Use an Analogy

Explain that vascular tissue in plants is somewhat like the plumbing in a building. Some pipes, analogous to xylem, bring water up into the building. Other pipes, analogous to phloem, transport materials away. Reinforce that phloem does NOT carry water—it carries nutrients.

LAB DEMONSTRATION

Purpose to model the function of plant cuticles

Materials water, paper towels, wax paper, paper clips, string

Preparation Tie the string so it forms a line on which the towels can hang. Cut the towels and wax paper into 10-cm squares. Obtain a bowl of water for wetting the towels

Procedure Wet three towel squares. Leave one uncovered. Cover one side of another with wax paper. Sandwich a third between two sheets of wax paper. Hang all three with clips. Have students observe how long it takes each towel to dry.

Expected Outcome Uncovered towels dry more quickly than covered towels.

How are towels covered with wax paper like plant leaves with cuticles?
Wax paper prevents the towel from drying, as the cuticle prevents water loss from plants.

Visualizing Plant Classification

Have students examine the pictures and read the captions. Then ask the following question.

How might an injury to the stem of a vascular plant affect the rest of the plant? Possible answer: Since the stem transports water and nutrients absorbed by the roots to the rest of the plant, an injury could result in the plant becoming dry or some leaves dying from lack of nutrients.

Activity

Provide students with hand lenses and the seeds of a variety of plants, such as sunflower, coconut, peanut, apple, orange, peach and common garden plants. Have students examine the samples to identify similarities and differences. If fern spores are available, have students compare and contrast these structures with seeds. L2
LS Visual-Spatial

Extension

Have students investigate how nonvascular plants transport food and water to cells. Nonvascular plants have rhizoids, root-like structures, that collect water and nutrients from soil. The plants transport the materials throughout the rest of the body in one of two ways. Water and nutrients spread by diffusion or are carried by simple conducting tissues. Because both of these methods are very slow, plant size is limited. Usually nonvascular plants are no more than 2 cm in height.

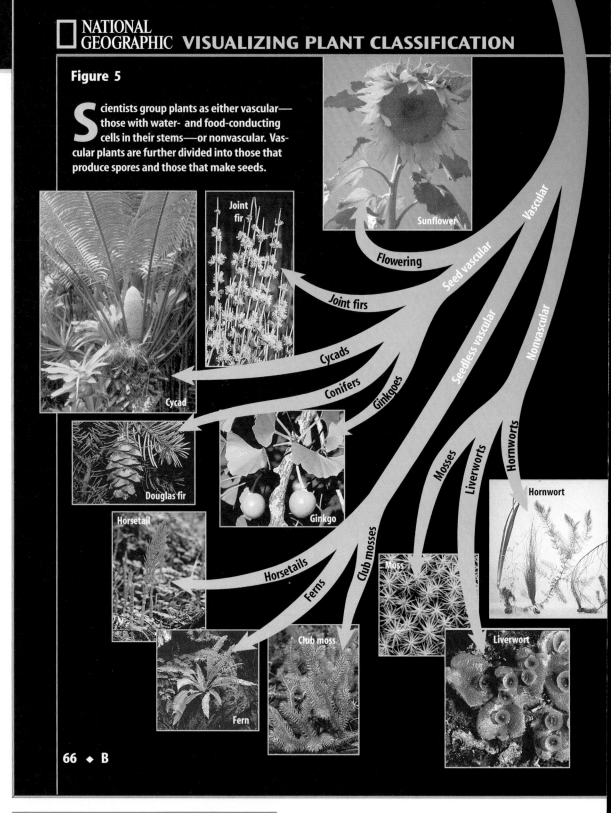

◻ NATIONAL GEOGRAPHIC VISUALIZING PLANT CLASSIFICATION

Figure 5

Scientists group plants as either vascular—those with water- and food-conducting cells in their stems—or nonvascular. Vascular plants are further divided into those that produce spores and those that make seeds.

Sunflower · Vascular · Flowering · Seed vascular · Joint fir · Joint firs · Cycads · Nonvascular · Seedless vascular · Cycad · Conifers · Ginkgoes · Hornworts · Mosses · Liverworts · Douglas fir · Ginkgo · Hornwort · Horsetail · Club mosses · Horsetails · Moss · Ferns · Club moss · Liverwort · Fern

66 ◆ B

Resource Manager

Chapter Resources Booklet
  Reinforcement, p. 23
  Directed Reading for Content Mastery,
    pp. 15, 16
**Performance Assessment in the Science
  Classroom,** p. 55

Classification of Plants

The plant kingdom is classified into major groups called divisions. A division is the same as a phylum in other kingdoms. Another way to group plants is as vascular (VAS kyuh lur) or nonvascular plants, as illustrated in **Figure 5**. **Vascular plants** have tubelike structures that carry water, nutrients, and other substances throughout the plant. **Nonvascular plants** do not have these tubelike structures and use other ways to move water and substances.

Naming Plants Are biologists trying to show off when they call a pecan tree *Carya illinoiensis* or a white oak *Quercus alba*? Although it might seem so, they are just using words that accurately name the plant. In the third century B.C., most plants were grouped as trees, shrubs, or herbs and placed into smaller groups by leaf characteristics. This simple system survived until late in the eighteenth century when a Swedish botanist, Carolus Linnaeus, developed a new system. His new system used many characteristics to classify a plant. He also developed a way to name plants called binomial nomenclature (bi NOH mee ul • NOH mun klay chur). Under this system, every plant species is given a unique two-word name like the names above for the pecan tree and white oak and for the two daisies in **Figure 6**.

Shasta daisy, *Chrysanthemum maximum*

African daisy, *Dimorphotheca aurantiaca*

Figure 6
Although these two plants are called daisies, they are not the same species of plant. Using their binomial names helps eliminate the confusion that might come from using their common names.

Assess

Reteach
Obtain a sunflower with stem and leaves, or a large color photograph of one. Direct students to pick out the characteristics that would help this plant survive on land. thin cuticle that protects leaves and stem from drying out, tall stem supported by cellulose, vascular structures to distribute materials throughout the plant, seeds protected by hard covering L2

Challenge
How might animals have been affected if plants had not adapted to live on land? Life would probably not have been possible for animals on land, because plants are the foundation of all land food chains and they produce much of the atmospheric oxygen that land animals need to live.

Assessment

Oral Have students write additional questions not included in the Section Assessment and quiz each other. Use **Performance Assessment in the Science Classroom,** p. 91.

Section 1 Assessment

1. List the characteristics of plants.
2. Compare and contrast vascular and nonvascular plants.
3. Name three adaptations that allow plants to survive on land.
4. Why is binomial nomenclature used to name plants?
5. **Think Critically** If you left a board lying on the grass for a few days, what would happen to the grass underneath the board? Why?

Skill Builder Activities

6. **Forming Hypotheses** Make a hypothesis about what adaptations land plants might undergo if they lived submerged in water instead of on land. **For more help, refer to the Science Skill Handbook.**
7. **Communicating** One of the oldest surviving plant species is *Ginkgo biloba*. Research the history of this species, then write about it in your Science Journal. **For more help, refer to the Science Skill Handbook.**

Answers to Section Assessment

1. eukaryotic cells with cell walls; pigments for photosynthesis; most have roots, stems, and leaves
2. Both have eukaryotic cells with cell walls and carry out photosynthesis. Vascular plants have tubelike structures to carry materials; nonvascular plants do not.
3. Adaptations listed may include the cuticle, vascular tissue, and seeds.
4. It gives every species of plant a unique two-word name.
5. The grass might die. Light is needed for photosynthesis.
6. Possible answers: A thicker cuticle or a system for pumping water from

cells could be needed; some might have a long stem to raise leaves above the water.
7. Students' reports could include: The tree (also called the maidenhair tree) is the only surviving member of a group of plants that flourished millions of years ago. It is native to China.

1 Motivate

Bellringer Transparency

Display the Section Focus Transparency for Section 2. Use the accompanying Transparency Activity Master. L2

ELL

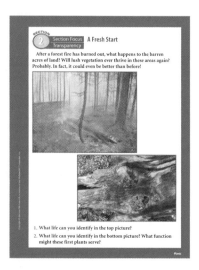

Tie to Prior Knowledge

Students may already be familiar with some seedless plants. Point out that wreaths often contain club mosses, gardeners use peat moss to keep young plants from drying out, and ferns are common as house plants.

SECTION

2 Seedless Plants

As You Read

What You'll Learn

- **Distinguish** between characteristics of seedless nonvascular plants and seedless vascular plants.
- **Identify** the importance of some nonvascular and vascular plants.

Vocabulary
rhizoid
pioneer species

Why It's Important
Seedless plants are often the first to grow in damaged or disturbed environments.

Figure 7
The seedless nonvascular plants include mosses, liverworts, and hornworts.

Seedless Nonvascular Plants

If you were asked to name the parts of a plant, you probably would list roots, stems, leaves, and flowers. You also might know that many plants grow from seeds. However, some plants, called nonvascular plants, don't grow from seeds and they do not have all of these parts. **Figure 7** shows some common types of nonvascular plants.

Nonvascular plants are usually just a few cells thick and only 2 cm to 5 cm in height. Most have stalks that look like stems and green, leaflike growths. Instead of roots, threadlike structures called **rhizoids** (RI zoydz) anchor them where they grow. Most nonvascular plants grow in places that are damp. Therefore, water is absorbed and distributed directly through their cell membranes and cell walls. Nonvascular plants also do not have flowers or cones that produce seeds. They reproduce by spores. Mosses, liverworts, and hornworts are examples of nonvascular plants.

Mosses Most nonvascular plants are classified as mosses, like the ones in **Figure 7A.** They have green, leaflike growths arranged around a central stalk. Their rhizoids are made of many cells. Sometimes stalks with caps grow from moss plants. Reproductive cells called spores are produced in the caps of these stalks. Mosses often grow on tree trunks and rocks or the ground. Although they commonly are found in damp areas, some are adapted to living in deserts.

A Close-up of moss plants   **B** Close-up of a liverwort   **C** Close-up of a hornwort

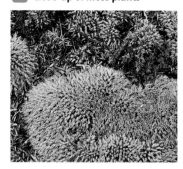

Section ✓Assessment Planner

PORTFOLIO
Make a Model, p. 71
PERFORMANCE ASSESSMENT
MiniLab, p. 69
Skill Builder Activities, p. 73
See page 90 for more options.

CONTENT ASSESSMENT
Section, p. 73
Challenge, p. 73
Chapter, pp. 90–91

Liverworts In the ninth century, liverworts were thought to be useful in treating diseases of the liver. The suffix -*wort* means "herb," so the word *liverwort* means "herb for the liver." Liverworts are rootless plants with flattened, leaflike bodies, as shown in **Figure 7B.** They usually have one-celled rhizoids.

Hornworts Most hornworts are less than 2.5 cm in diameter and have a flattened body like liverworts, as shown in **Figure 7C.** Unlike other nonvascular plants, almost all hornworts have only one chloroplast in each of their cells. Hornworts get their name from their spore-producing structures, which look like tiny horns of cattle.

Nonvascular Plants and the Environment Mosses and liverworts are important in the ecology of many areas. Although they require moist conditions to grow and reproduce, many of them can withstand long, dry periods. They can grow in thin soil and in soils where other plants could not grow, as shown in **Figure 8.**

Spores of mosses and liverworts are carried by the wind. They will grow into plants if enough water is available and other growing conditions are right. Often, they are among the first plants to grow in new or disturbed environments, such as lava fields or after a forest fire. Organisms that are the first to grow in new or disturbed areas are called **pioneer species.** As pioneer plant species grow and die, decaying material builds up. This, along with the slow breakdown of rocks, builds soil. As a result, other organisms can move into the area.

✔ **Reading Check** *Why are pioneer plant species important in disturbed environments?*

Mini LAB

Measuring Water Absorption by a Moss

Procedure 🖾 🦺 ⬚

1. Place a few teaspoons of *Sphagnum* moss on a piece of **cheesecloth.** Gather the corners of the cloth and twist, then tie them securely to form a ball.
2. Weigh the ball.
3. Put 200 mL of **water** in a **container** and add the ball.
4. After 15 min, remove the ball and drain the excess water into the container.
5. Weigh the ball and measure the amount of water left in the container.
6. Wash your hands after handling the moss.

Analysis
In your **Science Journal,** calculate how much water was absorbed by the *Sphagnum* moss.

② Teach

Seedless Nonvascular Plants

Mini LAB

Purpose Students measure absorption capacity of *Sphagnum* moss. L2

IS **Logical-Mathematical**

Materials *Sphagnum* moss, cheesecloth, scale, graduated cylinder, beaker, water

Teaching Strategies
• Remind students that 1 mL of water has a mass of 1 g.
• Have students predict how much water the moss will hold and then check their predictions at the end.

Analysis
1. *Sphagnum* moss will soak up about 100 g (100 mL) of water.

✔ Assessment

Performance Growers often root plants in a mix of equal parts clean sand to *Sphagnum* moss. Have students design an experiment to test this rooting method. Use **PASC,** p. 95.

✔ Reading Check

Answer They help form soil and create conditions that allow other plants to grow.

Curriculum Connection

History Because peat mosses contain chemicals that kill germs, they were used during World War I as dressings for wounds. Have students research mosses to find out some of their other uses in the past. Possible answer: Some Native Americans used peat mosses for diapers because of their absorbency. It has also been used for lamp wicks, bedding, and stable litter. L2

Resource Manager

Chapter Resources Booklet
  Transparency Activity, p. 41
  MiniLAB, p. 3
Home and Community Involvement, p. 42

Seedless Vascular Plants

Quick Demo

Show a variety of fern fronds. If possible, include some with sori. Have students note differences in color, size, and location among sori.

Extension

Have motivated students read natural history books to find out why ferns have such common names as Boston fern, maidenhair fern, staghorn fern, cinnamon fern, hay-scented fern, and bracken fern. These names have to do with the shapes or scents of their leaves. L3

Problem-Solving Activity

National Math Standards

Correlation to Mathematics Objectives
5–10

Answers

1. Brazil
2. Answers should include some of the countries shaded on the map.
3. Some plants may become extinct before they can be studied.

Teacher FYI

The active ingredient in aspirin, the acetylsalicylic acid also found in willow bark, interferes with the body's production of prostaglandins. These hormonelike substances aid transmission of pain signals to the brain and help raise body temperature to fight infection. That is why taking aspirin helps dull pain and fight fever.

SCIENCE Online

Research Visit the Glencoe Science Web site at **science.glencoe.com** for more information about medicinal plants. In your Science Journal, list four medicinal plants and their uses.

Seedless Vascular Plants

The fern in **Figure 9** is growing next to some moss plants. Ferns and mosses are alike in one way. Both reproduce by spores instead of seeds. However, ferns are different from mosses because they have vascular tissue. The vascular tissue in the seedless vascular plants, like ferns, is made up of long, tubelike cells. These cells carry water, minerals, and food to cells throughout the plant. Why is having cells like these an advantage to a plant? Remember that nonvascular plants like the moss are usually only a few cells thick. Each cell absorbs water directly from its environment. As a result, these plants cannot grow large. Vascular plants, on the other hand, can grow bigger and thicker because the vascular tissue distributes water and nutrients.

Problem-Solving Activity

What is the value of rain forests?

Throughout history, cultures have used plants for medicines. Some cultures used willow bark to cure headaches. Willow bark contains salicylates (suh LIH suh layts), the main ingredient in aspirin. Heart problems were treated with foxglove, which is the main source of digitalis (dih juh TAH lus), a drug prescribed for heart problems. Have all medicinal plants been identified?

Identifying the Problem

Tropical rain forests have the largest variety of organisms on Earth. Many plant species are unknown. These forests are being destroyed rapidly. The map below shows the rate of destruction of the rain forests.

Some scientists estimate that most tropical rain forests will be destroyed in 30 years.

Solving the Problem

1. What country has the most rain forest destroyed each year?
2. Where can scientists go to study rain forest plants before the plants are destroyed?
3. Predict how the destruction of rain forests might affect research on new drugs from plants.

Deforested annually (km²)
- more than 15,000
- 2,000 to 14,800
- 100 to 1,900

SCIENCE Online

Internet Addresses

_____

_____

_____

Explore the Glencoe Science Web site at **science.glencoe.com** to find out more about topics in this section.

Inclusion Strategies

Visually Impaired Prepare samples of mosses, liverworts, and ferns for the class labeled with large print. Provide large magnifying glasses for closer observation of the plants.

Types of Seedless Vascular Plants

Besides ferns, seedless vascular plants include ground pines, spike mosses, and horsetails. About 1,000 species of ground pines, spike mosses, and horsetails are known to exist. Ferns are more abundant, with at least 12,000 known species. Many species of seedless vascular plants are known only from fossils. They flourished during the warm, moist period 360 million to 286 million years ago. Fossil records show that some horsetails grew 15 m tall, unlike modern species, which grow only 1 m to 2 m tall.

Ferns The largest group of seedless vascular plants is the ferns. They include many different varieties, as shown in **Figure 10.** They have stems, leaves, and roots. Fern leaves are called fronds. Ferns produce spores in structures that usually are found on the underside of their fronds. Thousands of species of ferns now grow on Earth, but many more existed long ago. From clues left in rock layers, scientists know that about 360 million years ago much of Earth was tropical. Steamy swamps covered large areas. The tallest plants were species of ferns. The ancient ferns grew as tall as 25 m—as tall as the tallest fern species alive today. The tallest modern tree ferns are about 3 m to 5 m in height, as shown in **Figure 10C,** and grow in tropical areas.

Figure 9
The mosses and ferns in this picture are seedless plants. *Why can the fern grow taller than the moss?*

Figure 10
Ferns come in many different shapes and sizes.

A The sword fern has a typical fern shape. Spores are produced in structures on the back of the frond.

B This fern grows on other plants, not in the soil. *Why do you think it's called the staghorn fern?*

C Tree ferns, like this one in Hawaii, grow in tropical areas.

Fun Fact

The stems of tree ferns are harvested and sold as plant supports. The dry, fibrous parts of some ferns have been used as mattress stuffing.

Make a Model

Have students construct a shoe box model of what they think a tropical forest dominated by ferns may have looked like millions of years ago. L2
ELL **Kinesthetic** P

Caption Answers

- **Figure 9** Ferns have vascular tissues that transport materials and provide support; mosses do not.
- **Figure 10B** because of the shape of its leaves

Teacher FYI

Ferns are found mostly in damp shady areas in most parts of the world. In the United States, ferns are found mostly in the Southeast and the Pacific Northwest along streams in forests. In the tropics, ferns grow on tree trunks and branches. There are about 12,000 species of ferns on Earth today.

Resource Manager

Chapter Resources Booklet
Enrichment, p. 27
Mathematics Skill Activities, p. 5

Discussion

How can you tell the difference between true mosses and club mosses? True mosses produce spores in capsules on stalks. Club mosses produce spores at the end of stems in structures that look like tiny pine cones.

✔ Reading Check

Answer at the ends of stems in structures that look like pine cones

Quick Demo

Obtain horsetail plants. Demonstrate (and allow students to feel) how the grittiness of the silica in the plant's cell walls could be useful for scouring. L2 IS Kinesthetic

Caption Answer

Figure 12 in a conelike structure at the tips of some stems

Importance of Seedless Plants

Use Science Words

Word Usage Provide each student with a list of terms that can be used to describe nonvascular and seedless vascular plants. Have students write paragraphs that compare and contrast these plants using the terms given. Terms might include *nonvascular, vascular, moss, rhizoid, moist, liverwort, ferns, leaves, roots,* and *horsetails.* L2 IS Linguistic

Figure 11
Photographers once used the dry, flammable spores of club mosses as flash powder. It burned rapidly and produced the light that was needed to take photographs.

Figure 12
Most horsetails grow in damp areas and are less than 1 m tall. *Where would spores be produced on this plant?*

Club Mosses Ground pines and spike mosses are groups of plants that often are called club mosses. They are related more closely to ferns than to mosses. These seedless vascular plants have needle-like leaves. Spores are produced at the end of the stems in structures that look like tiny pine cones. Ground pines, shown in **Figure 11,** are found from arctic regions to the tropics, but never in large numbers. In some areas, they are endangered because they have been over collected to make wreaths and other decorations.

✔ Reading Check *Where are spores in club mosses produced?*

Spike mosses resemble ground pines. One species of spike moss, the resurrection plant, is adapted to desert conditions. When water is scarce, the plant curls up and seems dead. When water becomes available, the resurrection plant unfurls its green leaves and begins making food again. The plant can repeat this process whenever necessary.

Horsetails The stem structure of horsetails is unique among the vascular plants. The stem is jointed and has a hollow center surrounded by a ring of vascular tissue. At each joint, leaves grow out from around the stem. In **Figure 12,** you can see these joints. If you pull on a horsetail stem, it will pop apart in sections. Like the club mosses, spores from horsetails are produced in a conelike structure at the tips of some stems. The stems of the horsetails contain silica, a gritty substance found in sand. For centuries, horsetails have been used for polishing objects, sharpening tools, and scouring cooking utensils. Another common name for horsetails is scouring rush.

Importance of Seedless Plants

When many ancient seedless plants died, they became submerged in water and mud before they decomposed. As this plant material built up, it became compacted and compressed and eventually turned into coal—a process that took millions of years.

Today, a similar process is taking place in bogs, which are poorly drained areas of land that contain decaying plants. The plants in bogs are mostly seedless plants like mosses and ferns.

Resource Manager

Chapter Resources Booklet
  Reinforcement, p. 24
  Directed Reading for Content Mastery, p. 17

Visual Learning

Figure 13 If possible, have students examine samples of peat and coal. Remind them that peat is the first stage of coal formation. **How does the appearance of peat differ from that of coal?** Peat is lighter in color and isn't as rocklike as coal.

Peat When plants die, the decay process is slow because waterlogged soil does not contain oxygen. Over time, these decaying plants are compressed into a substance called peat. Peat, which forms from the remains of sphagnum moss, is mined from bogs to use as a low-cost fuel in places such as Ireland and Russia, as shown in **Figure 13.** Peat supplies about one third of Ireland's energy requirements. Scientists hypothesize that over time, if additional layers of soil bury, compact, and compress the peat, it will become coal.

Uses of Seedless Vascular Plants Many people keep ferns as houseplants. Ferns also are sold widely as landscape plants for shady areas. Peat and sphagnum mosses also are used for gardening. Peat is an excellent soil conditioner, and sphagnum moss often is used to line hanging baskets. Ferns also are used for weaving material and basketry.

Although most mosses are not used for food, parts of many other seedless vascular plants can be eaten. The rhizomes and young fronds of some ferns are edible. The dried stems of one type of horsetail can be ground into flour. Seedless plants have been used as folk medicines for hundreds of years. For example, ferns have been used to treat bee stings, burns, fevers, and even dandruff.

Figure 13
Peat is cut from bogs and used for a fuel in some parts of Europe.

Section Assessment

1. What are the similarities and differences between mosses and ferns?
2. What do fossil records show us about some seedless plants?
3. Under what growing conditions would you expect to find pioneer plants such as mosses and liverworts?
4. What do vascular tissues provide for plants that have them?
5. **Think Critically** The electricity that you use every day might be produced by burning coal. What is the connection between electricity production and seedless nonvascular and seedless vascular plants?

Skill Builder Activities

6. **Concept Mapping** Make a concept map showing how seedless nonvascular and seedless vascular plants are related. Include these terms in the concept map: *plant kingdom, seedless nonvascular plants, seedless vascular plants, ferns, ground pines, horsetails, liverworts, hornworts, mosses,* and *spike mosses.* **For more help, refer to the** Science Skill Handbook.
7. **Using Fractions** Approximately 8,000 species of liverworts and 9,000 species of mosses exist today. Estimate what fraction of these seedless nonvascular plants are mosses. **For more help, refer to the** Math Skill Handbook.

Answers to Section Assessment

1. alike: reproduce by spores; different: unlike mosses, ferns have vascular tissue
2. Seedless plants dominated Earth long ago and grew much larger than they grow today.
3. in disturbed or new environments
4. The vascular system carries water, minerals, and food to plant cells.

This allows the plant to grow bigger and thicker. The cells of vascular tissue provide support, also.
5. Seedless plants (both vascular and nonvascular) formed ancient forests that decayed and became the coal we burn today as fuel.
6. Students should begin the concept map with *plant kingdom*. Branching

from that should be *seedless nonvascular plants* and *vascular plants. Mosses, hornworts,* and *liverworts* branch from *seedless nonvascular plants. Spike mosses, ground pines, horsetails,* and *ferns* branch from *seedless vascular plants.*
7. 9/17

1 Motivate

Bellringer Transparency

Display the Section Focus Transparency for Section 3. Use the accompanying Transparency Activity Master. L2

ELL

Tie to Prior Knowledge

Invite students to brainstorm a list of plant seeds that they eat or see regularly. Possible answers: any type of edible nut, sunflower seeds, sesame or poppy seeds, coconuts, seeds inside fruits

---

As You Read

What You'll Learn

- **Identify** the characteristics of seed plants.
- **Explain** the structures and functions of roots, stems, and leaves.
- **Describe** the main characteristics and importance of gymnosperms and angiosperms.
- **Compare** similarities and differences between monocots and dicots.

Vocabulary

stomata
guard cell
xylem
phloem
cambium

gymnosperm
angiosperm
monocot
dicot

Why It's Important

We depend on seed plants for food, clothing, and shelter.

Characteristics of Seed Plants

What foods from plants have you eaten today? Apples? Potatoes? Carrots? Peanut butter and jelly sandwiches? All of these foods and more come from seed plants.

Most of the plants you are familiar with are seed plants. Most seed plants have leaves, stems, roots, and vascular tissue. They produce seeds, which usually contain an embryo and stored food. The stored food is the source of energy for the embryo's early growth as it develops into a plant. Most of the plant species that have been identified in the world today are seed plants. Seed plants generally are classified into two major groups—gymnosperms (JIHM nuh spurmz) and angiosperms (AN jee uh spurmz).

Leaves Most seed plants have leaves—the organs of the plant where the food-making process—photosynthesis—usually occurs. Leaves come in many shapes, sizes, and colors. Examine the structure of a typical leaf, shown in **Figure 14.**

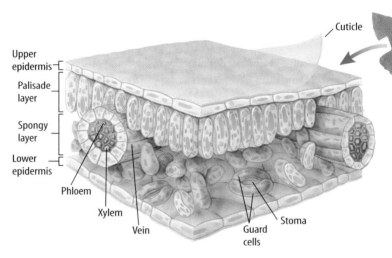

Upper epidermis
Palisade layer
Spongy layer
Lower epidermis
Phloem
Xylem
Vein
Guard cells
Stoma
Cuticle

Figure 14
The structure of a typical leaf is adapted for photosynthesis. *Why do cells in the palisade layer have more chloroplasts than cells in the spongy layer?*

Section ✔ Assessment Planner

PORTFOLIO
Curriculum Connection, p. 77
PERFORMANCE ASSESSMENT
Try at Home MiniLAB, p. 75
Skill Builder Activities, p. 82
See page 90 for more options.

CONTENT ASSESSMENT
Section, p. 82
Challenge, p. 82
Chapter, pp. 90–91

Leaf Cell Layers A typical leaf is made of different layers of cells. On the upper and lower surfaces of a leaf is a thin layer of cells called the epidermis, which covers and protects the leaf. A waxy cuticle coats the epidermis of some leaves. Most leaves have small openings in the epidermis called **stomata** (STOH muh tuh) (singular, *stoma*). Stomata allow carbon dioxide, water, and oxygen to enter into and exit from a leaf. Each stoma is surrounded by two **guard cells** that open and close it.

Just below the upper epidermis is the palisade layer. It consists of closely packed, long, narrow cells that usually contain many chloroplasts. Most of the food produced by plants is made in the palisade cells. Between the palisade layer and the lower epidermis is the spongy layer. It is a layer of loosely arranged cells separated by air spaces. In a leaf, veins containing vascular tissue are found in the spongy layer.

Stems The trunk of a tree is really the stem of the tree. Stems usually are located above ground and support the branches, leaves, and flowers. Materials move between leaves and roots through the vascular tissue in the stem. Stems also can have other specialized functions, as shown in **Figure 15.**

Plant stems are either herbaceous (hur BAY shus) or woody. Herbaceous stems usually are soft and green, like the stems of a tulip, while trees and shrubs have hard, rigid, woody stems. Lumber comes from woody stems.

Figure 15
Some plants have stems with special functions.

A These potatoes are stems that grow underground and store food for the plant.

B The stems of this cactus store water and can carry on photosynthesis.

C Some stems of this grape plant help it climb on other plants.

SECTION 3 Seed Plants **B ◆ 75**

Teacher FYI

Sweet potatoes are fleshy roots; white potatoes are fleshy underground stems (tubers). Both are structures that store food.

Quick Demo

Germinate some bean or corn seeds to demonstrate that the mass of the roots becomes larger than the rest of the plant very quickly.

Activity

Have students make posters that illustrate the different functions of roots and stems. For example, the roots of some orchids and the stems of cacti can photosynthesize. L2

IS Visual-Spatial

Caption Answer

Figure 16 to anchor the tree and to take in enough water and nutrients to support the above ground parts of the plant

✔ Reading Check

Answer Roots take in water and nutrients from soil, anchor the plant, and store food and water. Some plants have roots that take in oxygen from the air.

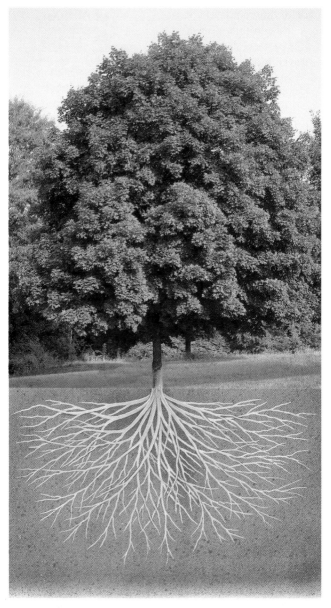

Figure 16
The root system of a tree is as long as the tree can be tall. *Why would the root system of a tree need to be so large?*

Roots Imagine a lone tree growing on top of a hill. What is the largest part of this plant? Maybe you guessed the trunk or the branches. Did you consider the roots? The root systems of most plants are as large or larger than the aboveground stems and leaves, as shown in **Figure 16.**

Roots are important to plants. Water and other substances enter a plant through its roots. Roots have vascular tissue in which water and dissolved substances move from the soil through the stems to the leaves. Roots also act as anchors, preventing plants from being blown away by wind or washed away by moving water. Each root system must support the other plant parts that are aboveground—the stem, branches, and leaves of a tree. Sometimes, part of or all of the roots are aboveground, too.

Roots can store food. When you eat carrots or beets, you eat roots that contain stored food. Plants that grow from year to year use this stored food to begin their growth in the spring. Plants that grow in dry areas often have roots that store water.

Root tissues also can perform functions such as absorbing oxygen that is used in the process of respiration. Because water does not contain as much oxygen as air does, plants that grow with their roots in water might not be able to absorb enough oxygen. Some swamp plants have roots that grow partially out of the water and take in oxygen from the air. In order to perform all these functions, the root systems of plants must be large.

✔ Reading Check *What are several functions of roots in plants?*

Resource Manager

Chapter Resources Booklet
Enrichment, p. 28
Transparency Activity, pp. 43–44

Visual Learning

Figure 16 How could planting a large tree such as this close to a building cause a problem? Students should infer that its extensive root system could interfere with the building's foundation or pipes leading into the building.

Vascular Tissue Three tissues usually make up the vascular system in a seed plant. **Xylem** (ZI lum) tissue is made up of hollow, tubular cells that are stacked one on top of the other to form a structure called a vessel. These vessels transport water and dissolved substances from the roots throughout the plant. The thick cell walls of xylem are also important because they help support the plant.

Phloem (FLOH em) is a plant tissue also made up of tubular cells that are stacked to form structures called tubes. Tubes are different from vessels. Phloem tubes move food from where it is made to other parts of the plant where it is used or stored.

In some plants, a cambium is between xylem and phloem. **Cambium** (KAM bee um) is a tissue that produces most of the new xylem and phloem cells. The growth of this new xylem and phloem increases the thickness of stems and roots. All three tissues are illustrated in **Figure 17.**

Health INTEGRATION

Plants have vascular tissue, and you have a vascular system. Your vascular system transports oxygen, food, and wastes through blood vessels. Instead of xylem and phloem, your blood vessels include veins and arteries. In your Science Journal write a paragraph describing the difference between veins and arteries.

Figure 17
The vascular tissue of some seed plants includes xylem, phloem, and cambium.
Which of these tissues transports food throughout the plant?

Phloem   Xylem

Xylem transports water and dissolved substances other than sugar throughout the plant.

Cambium

Cambium produces xylem and phloem as the plant grows.

Phloem transports dissolved sugar throughout the plant.

Health INTEGRATION

Arteries carry blood away from the heart; veins carry blood toward the heart. Except for those vessels going to and from the lungs, arteries carry oxygen-rich blood, and veins carry oxygen-poor blood.

Quick Demo

Demonstrate the appearance of vascular tissue in woody plants by showing students a photo of a tree trunk cross-section, or by bringing a cut woody stem to class.

Extension

Foresters measure quantities of timber in board feet. Have students research the size of this unit. A board foot is a volume measure of lumber. A board measuring 12″ × 12″ × 1″ is one board foot. Challenge students to find out how many board feet of lumber are consumed by a common activity, such as building a house or producing pulp for a certain amount of newsprint. [L3]

Caption Answer
Figure 17 phloem

Curriculum Connection

History Theophrastus (ca. 372–ca. 287 B.C.) is known as the father of botany. His botanical works were so complete that nearly 1,800 years passed before any new discoveries were made. Have students research the name and contributions of other botanists and compile their findings into one time line. Bauhin, Linnaeus, Bailey, Gesner, Hales, Nageli, and Ray are botanists students may name. **P**

Teacher FYI

The pattern of rings in tree trunks provides information about a tree's life. Good growth years produce wide rings. Slower growth, due to less favorable conditions, forms a narrower ring. If there is an extended dry period between two wet periods, two rings will be produced. Rings are wider on the sunny side of a tree.

Gymnosperms

Discussion

Is an apple tree a gymnosperm? Explain. No, it has seeds encased in fruits. Is a maple tree whose leaves turn golden and red in fall a gymnosperm? Explain. No, its seeds are enclosed in a dry, winged fruit.

Activity

If possible, ask each student to find and bring to class a cone from a conifer in the area. Cones may be found in yards, in parks, and along routes to and from school. Have them compare and contrast the cones in class and make sketches and written descriptions of each type of cone. Discuss how the cones are alike and different. Although they have the same basic structure, they differ in size, color, and shape. L1
IS Visual-Spatial

Caption Answer

Figure 18D Most gymnosperms do not lose all of their leaves in the fall.

✔ **Reading Check**

Answer Cones are the reproductive structures of the plants; seeds develop on female cones.

Figure 18
The gymnosperms include four divisions of plants.

A Conifers are the largest, most diverse division. Most conifers are evergreen plants, such as this ponderosa pine.

C About 100 species of cycads exist today. Only one genus is native to the United States.

B More than half of the 70 species of gnetophytes, such as this joint fir, are in one genus.

D The ginkgoes are represented by one living species. Ginkgoes lose their leaves in the fall. *How is this different from most gymnosperms?*

Field **GUIDE**

Can you identify conifers by looking at their cones? To find out more about cones, see the **Cones Field Guide** at the back of the book.

Gymnosperms

The oldest trees alive are gymnosperms. A bristlecone pine tree in the White Mountains of eastern California is estimated to be 4,900 years old. **Gymnosperms** are vascular plants that produce seeds that are not protected by fruit. The word *gymnosperm* comes from the Greek language and means "naked seed." Another characteristic of gymnosperms is that they do not have flowers. Leaves of most gymnosperms are needlelike or scalelike. Many gymnosperms are called evergreens because some green leaves always remain on their branches.

Four divisions of plants—conifers, cycads, ginkgoes, and gnetophytes (NE tuh fites)—are classified as gymnosperms. **Figure 18** shows examples of the four divisions. You are probably most familiar with the division Coniferophyta (kuh NIH fur uh fi tuh), the conifers. Pines, firs, spruces, redwoods, and junipers belong to this division. It contains the greatest number of gymnosperm species. All conifers produce two types of cones—male and female. Both types usually are found on the same plant. Cones are the reproductive structures of conifers. Seeds develop on the female cone but not on the male cone.

✔ **Reading Check** *What is the importance of cones to gymnosperms?*

Inclusion Strategies

Learning Disabled Bring branches from different conifers to class. Identify the branches and then have students feel the differences in texture and shape of the leaves. Encourage students to compare and contrast the smells and textures associated with each. L1 IS **Kinesthetic**

✔ Active Reading

Think-Pair-Share This strategy encourages students to think first before discussing their ideas or thoughts about a topic. Ask students to respond to a question. After recording ideas, have partners share responses to the question. Finally, ask students to share responses with the class. Have students become involved in a Think-Pair-Share about seed plants.

Angiosperms

When people are asked to name a plant, most name an angiosperm. An **angiosperm** is a vascular plant that flowers and has a fruit that contains one or more seeds, such as the peach in **Figure 19A.** The fruit develops from a part or parts of one or more flowers. Angiosperms are familiar plants no matter where you live. They grow in parks, fields, forests, jungles, deserts, freshwater, salt water, and cracks of sidewalks. You might see them dangling from wires or other plants, and one species of orchid even grows underground. Angiosperms make up the plant division Anthophyta (AN thoh fi tuh). More than half of the known plant species belong to this division.

Flowers The flowers of angiosperms vary in size, shape, and color. Duckweed, an aquatic plant, has a flower that is only 0.1 mm long. A plant in Indonesia has a flower that is nearly 1 m in diameter and can weigh 9 kg. Nearly every color can be found in some flower, although some people would not include black. Multicolored flowers are common. Some plants have flowers that are not recognized easily as flowers, such as those shown in **Figure 19B.**

Some flower parts develop into fruit. Most fruits contain seeds, like an apple, or have seeds on their surface, like a strawberry. If you think all fruits are juicy and sweet, there are some that are not. The fruit of the vanilla orchid, as shown in **Figure 19C,** contains seeds and is dry.

Angiosperms are divided into two groups—the monocots and the dicots—shortened forms of the words *monocotyledon* (mah nuh kah tul EE dun) and *dicotyledon* (di kah tul EE dun).

Figure 19
Angiosperms have a wide variety of flowers and fruits.

 The fruit of the vanilla orchid is the source of vanilla flavoring.

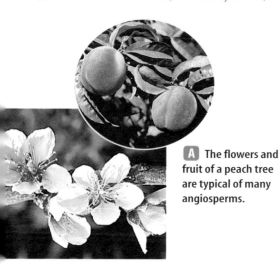

A The flowers and fruit of a peach tree are typical of many angiosperms.

B Ash flowers are not large and colorful. Their fruits are small and dry.

Angiosperms

Teacher FYI

Botanically, a fruit is any plant organ that grows from female flower parts. Therefore, tomatoes, green beans, squash, cucumbers, and peppers are fruit—although they're not necessarily sweet.

Science Journal

Nutritious Grains Have students research one of the major grains eaten in the United States and write a short report that includes what the plant looks like, what parts of it we eat, and where it is grown. Some students might also visit a supermarket to report on the number and kinds of foods containing the grain. Encourage students to include photos and diagrams in their reports, and to share their findings in class. Students could research corn, wheat, oats, or rice. [L2]
IS Linguistic

Cultural Diversity

Food for Thought People from different cultures rely on plants native to their part of the world for food. Have each student choose a country and prepare a poster that shows the main plants that are part of the diet there. After presenting each poster, encourage students to compare and contrast these foods with those that are commonly eaten in the United States.

Resource Manager

Chapter Resources Booklet
Directed Reading for Content Mastery, pp. 17, 18

Angiosperms, continued

Activity

Prepare several lab stations to demonstrate different monocot or dicot characteristics. Have students rotate through the stations, making notes and sketches of each characteristic. When everyone has completed the activity, have students discuss how monocots and dicots are similar and different. L2
IS Interpersonal

Extension

Have students survey the plants they find at a home and garden store, a grocery store, or a florist shop. Tell them to sketch the leaves and flowers of one monocot and one dicot and bring the sketches to class. Remind them to write down the names of the plants on the back of each sketch and whether the plant is a monocot or dicot. Have each student present his or her two sketches in class. Quiz class members on whether the plants are monocots or dicots, and have students give reasons for their choices. L1
IS Visual-Spatial

Monocots and Dicots A cotyledon is part of a seed often used for food storage. The prefix *mono* means "one," and *di* means "two." Therefore, **monocots** have one cotyledon inside their seeds and **dicots** have two. The flowers, leaves, and stems of monocots and dicots are shown in **Figure 20.**

Many important foods come from monocots, including corn, rice, wheat, and barley. If you eat bananas, pineapple, or dates, you are eating fruit from monocots. Lilies and orchids also are monocots.

Dicots also produce familiar foods such as peanuts, green beans, peas, apples, and oranges. You might have rested in the shade of a dicot tree. Most shade trees, such as maple, oak, and elm, are dicots.

Figure 20
By observing a monocot and a dicot, you can determine their plant characteristics.

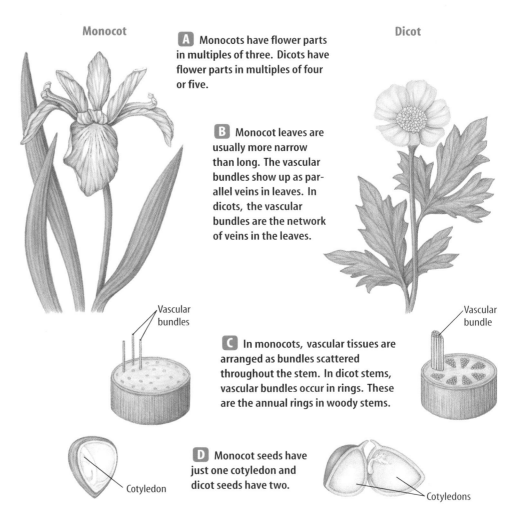

Monocot

A Monocots have flower parts in multiples of three. Dicots have flower parts in multiples of four or five.

Dicot

B Monocot leaves are usually more narrow than long. The vascular bundles show up as parallel veins in leaves. In dicots, the vascular bundles are the network of veins in the leaves.

Vascular bundles

C In monocots, vascular tissues are arranged as bundles scattered throughout the stem. In dicot stems, vascular bundles occur in rings. These are the annual rings in woody stems.

Vascular bundle

D Monocot seeds have just one cotyledon and dicot seeds have two.

Cotyledon

Cotyledons

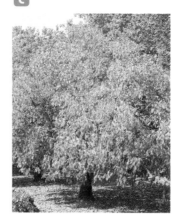

Life Cycles of Angiosperms Flowering plants vary greatly in appearance. Their life cycles are as varied as the kinds of plants, as shown in **Figure 21.** Some angiosperms grow from seeds to mature plants with their own seeds in less than a month. The life cycles of other plants can take as long as a century. If a plant's life cycle is completed within one year, it is called an annual. These plants must be grown from seeds each year.

Plants called biennials (bi EH nee ulz) complete their life cycles within two years. Biennials such as parsley store a large amount of food in an underground root or stem for growth in the second year. Biennials produce flowers and seeds only during the second year of growth. Angiosperms that take more than two years to grow to maturity are called perennials. Herbaceous perennials such as peonies appear to die each winter but grow and produce flowers each spring. Woody perennials such as fruit trees produce flowers and fruits on stems that survive for many years.

Importance of Seed Plants

What would a day at school be like without seed plants? One of the first things you'd notice is the lack of paper and books. Paper is made from pulp that comes from trees, which are seed plants. Are the desks and chairs at your school made of wood? They'll need to be made of something else if no seed plants exist. Clothing that is made from cotton would not exist because cotton comes from seed plants. When it's time for lunch, you'll have trouble finding something to eat. Bread, fruits, and potato chips all come from plants. Milk, hamburgers, and hot dogs all come from animals that eat seed plants. Unless you like to eat plants such as mosses and ferns, you'll go hungry. Without seed plants, your day at school would be different.

Figure 21
Life cycles of angiosperms include annuals, biennials, and perennials. **A** These petunias, which are annuals, complete their life cycle in one year.
B Parsley plants, which are biennials, do not produce flowers and seeds the first year.
C Perennials, such as this pecan tree, flower and produce fruits year after year.

Research Visit the Glencoe Science Web site at **science.glencoe.com** for recent news or magazine articles about the timber industry's efforts to replant conifer trees. In your Science Journal, list the types of trees that are replanted.

Discussion

Why might it be a good idea to plant a flower garden with a mix of annuals and perennials? Students should infer that, aside from the desirability of variety in types of flowers, a garden of all annuals would be a lot of work because it would have to be replanted each year. A mix would include annuals that must be replanted and perennials that will bloom year after year.

Activity

Have the class observe the life cycle of an angiosperm by planting seeds of an annual that will germinate, grow, and bloom within a few weeks. Check with a florist or someone at a home and garden store in your area for suggestions on plants to use. L1

Discussion

Lead a discussion with students about why plants are important. You might ask each student to identify an important aspect of plants in general or the importance of a particular plant. L2

Internet Addresses
_____
_____
_____
Explore the Glencoe Science Web site at **science.glencoe.com** to find out more about topics in this section.

Resource Manager

Chapter Resources Booklet
Reinforcement, p. 25

Performance Assessment in the Science Classroom, p. 61

Emphasize the important characteristics that distinguish gymnosperms from angiosperms, or monocots from dicots. Prepare flash cards with a written or visual characteristic of one of the groups on each one. Quiz students by having them quickly respond as you hold up each card. L2

Challenge

If you only know that a plant contains 12 petals, why can't you say for sure whether it is a monocot or dicot? Monocots have petals in multiples of three; dicots have petals in multiples of four or five. Since 12 is divisible by three and four, this characteristic alone won't provide the answer.

✓ *Assessment*

Performance Assess students' abilities to classify food plants by plant part. Give them several common fruits and vegetables and have students classify them as roots, stems, leaves, fruits, or flowers. roots: yams, beets, carrots; stems: asparagus, white potatoes, ginger; leaves: spinach, lettuce; fruits: tomatoes, cherries; flowers: broccoli, cauliflower Use **Performance Assessment in the Science Classroom,** p. 121. ELL

Table 1 Some Products of Seed Plants

From Gymnosperms	From Angiosperms	
lumber, paper, soap, varnish, paints, waxes, perfumes, edible pine nuts, medicines		foods, sugar, chocolate, cotton cloth, linen, rubber, vegetable oils, perfumes, medicines, cinnamon, flavorings (toothpaste, chewing gum, candy, etc.), dyes, lumber	

Products of Seed Plants Conifers are the most economically important gymnosperms. Most of the wood used for construction and for paper production comes from conifers such as pines and spruces. Resin, a waxy substance secreted by conifers, is used to make chemicals found in soap, paint, varnish, and some medicines.

The most economically important plants on Earth are the angiosperms. They form the basis of diets for most animals. Angiosperms were the first plants that humans grew. They included grains, such as barley and wheat, and legumes, such as peas and lentils. Angiosperms are also the source of many of the fibers used in clothing. Besides cotton, linen fabrics come from plant fibers. **Table 1** shows just a few of the products of angiosperms and gymnosperms.

Section ③ Assessment

1. What are the characteristics of a seed plant?
2. Compare and contrast the characteristics of gymnosperms and angiosperms.
3. If you are looking at a flower with five petals, is it from a monocot or dicot?
4. Explain why the root system might be the largest part of a plant.
5. **Think Critically** The cuticle and epidermis of leaves are transparent. If they weren't, what might be the result?

Skill Builder Activities

6. **Forming Hypotheses** Examine the leaf diagram in **Figure 14** in this section. What cell structure is found in the guard cells but not in the other epidermal cells? Hypothesize about what guard cells might produce. **For more help, refer to the** Science Skill Handbook.
7. **Using a Word Processor** Use a word-processing program to outline the structures and functions that are associated with roots, stems, and leaves. **For more help, refer to the** Technology Skill Handbook.

Answers to Section Assessment

1. Seed plants have roots, stems, leaves, vascular tissue, and produce seeds.
2. Gymnosperms produce seeds not protected by fruit; most have needle-like, evergreen leaves. Angiosperms produce flowers that become fruits that enclose seeds.
3. It is from a dicot.
4. Roots must absorb large amounts of water and nutrients and anchor plants.
5. Less light would reach the chloroplasts, which would reduce the rate of photosynthesis.
6. Chloroplasts; guard cells produce food (sugar).
7. Answers will vary. Partial sample outline:
   I. Roots
     A. Vascular Tissue
       1. Moves water.
       2. Moves minerals.

Identifying Conifers

How can you tell a pine from a spruce or a cedar from a juniper? One way is to observe their leaves. The leaves of most conifers are either needlelike—shaped like needles—or scale-like—like the scales on a fish or snake. Examine some conifer branches and identify them using the key to classifying leaves.

What You'll Investigate
How can leaves be used to classify conifers?

Materials
short branches of the following conifers:

pine	fir
cedar	redwood
spruce	arborvitae
Douglas fir	juniper
hemlock	

*illustrations of the conifers above
*Alternate materials

Goals
- **Identify** the difference between needlelike and scalelike leaves.
- **Classify** conifers according to their leaves.

Safety Precautions

Wash your hands after handling leaves.

Communicating Your Data
Use the information from the key to identify any conifers that grow on your school grounds. Draw a map that locates and identifies these conifers. Post the map for other students in your school to see. **For more help, refer to the** Science Skill Handbook.

Procedure
1. **Observe** the leaves or illustrations of each conifer, then use the key below to identify it.
2. **Write** the number and name of each conifer you identify in your Science Journal.

Conclude and Apply
1. What are two traits of hemlock leaves?
2. How are pine and cedar leaves alike?

Key to Classifying Conifer Leaves

1. All leaves are needlelike.
  a. yes, go to 2
  b. no, go to 8

2. Needles are in clusters.
  a. yes, go to 3
  b. no, go to 4

3. Clusters contain two, three, or five needles.
  a. yes, pine
  b. no, cedar

4. Needles grow on all sides of the stem.
  a. yes, go to 5
  b. no, go to 7

5. Needles grow from a woody peg.
  a. yes, spruce
  b. no, go to 6

6. Needles appear to grow from the branch.
  a. yes, Douglas fir
  b. no, hemlock

7. Most of the needles grow upward.
  a. yes, fir
  b. no, redwood

8. All the leaves are scalelike but not prickly.
  a. yes, arborvitae
  b. no, juniper

ACTIVITY   B ◆ 83

Resource Manager
Chapter Resources Booklet
Lab Activities, pp. 9–10, 11–12
Activity Worksheet, pp. 5–6

Communicating Your Data
If possible, have students use a software program to draw their maps. Students can also use a word processing program to make a table that lists the types of conifers and their locations in and around the school grounds.

BENCH TESTED

Purpose Students observe and classify conifer leaves. L2 ELL

Logical-Mathematical

Process Skills observing, classifying, comparing and contrasting

Time Required 50 minutes

Safety Precautions Remind students not to eat any plant parts, and to wash their hands thoroughly after handling the leaves.

Teaching Strategy Provide hand lenses for students who want to have a closer look at the structures of the leaves.

Answers to Questions
1. Leaves are needlelike; needles grow on all sides of the stem.
2. Both have needlelike leaves with needles in clusters.

Assessment

Process Direct students to come up with a classification chart similar to the one on this page to classify several broad leaves with very different characteristics. Have students test each other's classification systems. Use **Performance Assessment in the Science Classroom,** p. 121.

Activity

Recognize the Problem

Internet Students will use Internet sites that can be accessed through the Glencoe Science Web site at **science. glencoe.com.** They will investigate plants that are used as medicine.

Non-Internet Sources Collect materials describing alternative medicines from nutritionists.

Time Required

three to six days

Preparation

Internet Access the Glencoe Science Web site at **science. glencoe.com** to run through the steps that the students will follow.

Non-Internet Collect books and brochures about plants used as medicine.

Form a Hypothesis

Possible Hypotheses

Students will identify plants that are used as medicine, then hypothesize about their effectiveness. For example, *Echinacea* eases common cold symptoms and peppermint helps an upset stomach.

Activity *Use the Internet*

Plants as Medicine

You may have read about using peppermint to relieve an upset stomach, or taking *Echinacea* to boost your immune system and fight off illness. But did you know that pioneers brewed a cough medicine from lemon mint? In this activity, you will explore plants and their historical use in treating illness, and the benefits and risks associated with using plants as medicine.

Echinacea

Recognize the Problem

How are plants used in maintaining good health?

Form a Hypothesis

How do you know that a particular plant helps you stay healthy? If there is conflicting data, how would you evaluate the use of that plant? Form a hypothesis about how to evaluate a plant's use as a medicine.

Goals

■ **Identify** two plants that can be used as a treatment for illness or as a supplement to support good health.

■ **Research** the cultural and historical use of each of the two selected plants as medical treatments.

■ **Review** multiple sources to understand the effectiveness of each of the two selected plants as a medical treatment.

■ **Compare and contrast** the research and form a hypothesis about the medicinal effectiveness of each of the two plants.

Data Source

SCIENCE*Online* Go to the Glencoe Science Web site at **science.glencoe.com** to get more information about plants that can be used for maintaining good health and for data collected by other students.

Monarda

Resource Manager

Chapter Resources Booklet
   Activity Worksheet, pp. 7–8
Lab Management and Safety, p. 61

Test Your Hypothesis

Plan

1. Search for information about plants that are used as medicine and identify two plants to investigate.

2. **Research** how these plants are currently recommended for use as medicine or to promote good health. Find out how each has been used historically.

3. **Explore** how other cultures used these plants as a medicine.

Do

1. Make sure your teacher approves your plan before you start.

2. **Record** data you collect about each plant in your Science Journal.

Mentha

Analyze Your Data

1. **Write** a description of how different cultures have used each plant as medicine.

2. How have the plants you investigated been used as medicine historically?

3. **Record** all the uses suggested by different sources for each plant.

4. **Record** the side effects of using each plant as a treatment.

Draw Conclusions

1. After conducting your research, what do you think are the benefits and drawbacks of using these plants as alternative medicines?

2. **Describe** any conflicting information about using each of these plants as medicine.

3. Based on your analysis, would you recommend the use of each of these two plants to treat illness or promote good health? Why or why not?

4. What would you say to someone who was thinking about using any plant-based, over-the-counter, herbal supplement?

*C*ommunicating Your Data

SCIENCE Online Find this *Use the Internet* activity on the Glencoe Science Web site at **science. glencoe.com** Post your data for the two plants you investigated in the tables provided. **Compare** your data to those of other students. Review data that other students have entered about other plants that can be used as medicine.

Test Your Hypothesis

Teaching Strategies

Students should identify plants by common names and scientific names.

Troubleshooting Remind students that they may find conflicting information among their references.

Analyze Your Data

Answers will be subjective and based on students' individual research.

Draw Conclusions

Answers will be individualized and often based on students' opinions of their research. Look for depth and quality of research performed.

✔*Assessment*

Portfolio Have students create a guide describing each of the plants they investigated. The guide should include a picture of the plant, how they promote good health, and a summary of the plant's effectiveness. Use **PASC**, p. 129.

SCIENCE Online

Internet Addresses

_____

_____

_____

Explore the Glencoe Science Web site at **science.glencoe.com** to find out more about topics in this activity.

*C*ommunicating Your Data

Suggest that students use a combination of their data and that obtained from others to draw their conclusions.

Oops! Accidents in SCIENCE

SOMETIMES GREAT DISCOVERIES HAPPEN BY ACCIDENT!

Content Background

Hook-and-loop tape was not quickly or easily accepted as a useful invention. George deMestral faced tremendous financial difficulty and great frustration while trying to promote hook-and-loop tape to clothing manufacturers, who saw the fastener as ugly. Astronauts were some of the first to use hook-and-loop tape. It was used to attach food pouches to the walls of spacecraft and astronaut's boots to the floor of the spacecraft. Hook-and-loop tape was slowly accepted as a useful addition to sportswear and equipment. Children's clothing manufacturers then began to view hook-and-loop tape as a useful and attractive material to use.

Discussion

After deMestral had his idea for a new fastener based on the properties of cockleburs, he experimented for years to design hook-and-loop tape. Have students hypothesize why it took years for the idea to become reality. Possible answers: Scientists and inventors must find a material to build their invention with, they might have another job that keeps them from devoting long hours to their project, and many details must be worked out of any design before it takes shape as a product.

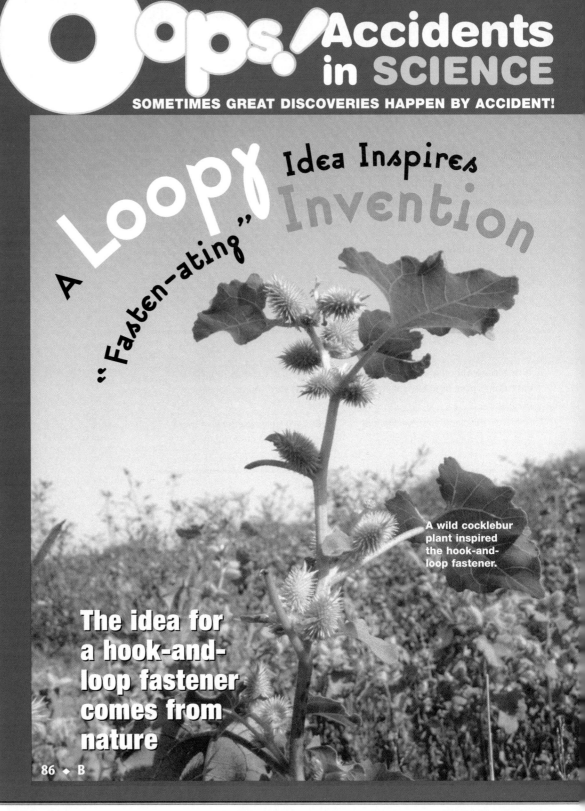

A "Fasten-ating" Idea Inspires A Loopy Invention

A wild cocklebur plant inspired the hook-and-loop fastener.

The idea for a hook-and-loop fastener comes from nature

86 ◆ B

Resources for Teachers and Students

Why Didn't I think of That?, by Allyn Freeman and Bob Golden, John Wiley & Sons, Inc., 1997.

Mistakes that Worked, by Charlotte Foltz Jones, Doubleday, 1991.

Inventing, Inventions and Inventors: A Teaching Resource Book, by Jerry D. Flack, Teacher Ideas Press, 1989.

Scientists often spend countless hours in the laboratory dreaming up useful inventions. Sometimes, however, the best ideas hit them in unexpected places at unexpected times. That's why scientists are constantly on the lookout for things that spark their curiosity.

One day in 1948, a Swiss inventor named George deMestral strolled through a field with his dog. When they returned home, deMestral discovered that the dog's fur was covered with cockleburs, parts of a prickly plant. These burs were also stuck to deMestral's jacket and pants. Curious about what made the burs so sticky, the inventor examined one under a microscope.

DeMestral noticed that the cocklebur was covered with lots of tiny hooks. By clinging to animal fur and fabric, this plant is carried to other places. While studying these burs, he got the idea to invent a new kind of fastener that could do the work of buttons, snaps, zippers, and laces—but better!

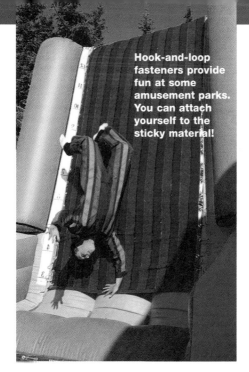

Hook-and-loop fasteners provide fun at some amusement parks. You can attach yourself to the sticky material!

After years of experimentation, deMestral came up with a strong, durable hook-and-loop fastener made of two strips of nylon fabric. One strip has thousands of small, stiff hooks; the other strip is covered with soft, tiny loops. Today, this hook-and-loop fastening tape is used on shoes and sneakers, watchbands, hospital equipment, space suits, clothing, book bags, and more. You may have one of those hook-and-loop fasteners somewhere on you right now. They're the ones that go ripppppppp when you open them.

So, if you ever get a fresh idea that clings to your mind like a hook to a loop, stick with it and experiment! Who knows? It may lead to a fabulous invention that changes the world!

This photo provides a close-up view of a hook-and-loop fastener.

Activity
Students should work in groups to examine a small sample of hook-and-loop tape with a hand lens. If possible, provide a cocklebur for the students to examine as well. Student groups should make a visual that describes the fastener with words or diagrams.

Analyze the Event
Ask students what characteristics allowed George deMestral to develop his hook-and-loop fastener. Possible answers: He was observant, he persevered through years of developing the invention, he was determined to have his invention accepted by clothing manufacturers. Stress that deMestral faced great personal difficulty while developing his product. It was financially very difficult, and many of his friends told him to give up his idea. Point out that the road from invention to finished product is not simple or easy.

CONNECTIONS | **List** Make a list of at least ten ways that hook-and-loop tape is used today. Think of three new uses for it. Since you can buy strips of hook-and-loop fastening tape in most hardware and fabric stores, you could even try out some of your favorite ideas.

SCIENCE *Online*
For more information, visit science.glencoe.com

CONNECTIONS Encourage students to think creatively when making their lists of uses and potential uses for hook-and-loop tape. Possible answers for today's uses of hook-and-loop tape include clothing, shoes, backpacks, toys and watches. What potential uses can students think of that don't involve clothing? How about ideas that involve automotive design, the arts, musical composition, or engineering?

SCIENCE *Online*

Internet Addresses
_____
_____
_____

Explore the Glencoe Science Web site at **science.glencoe.com** to find out more about topics in this feature.

Chapter ③ Study Guide

Chapter ③ Study Guide

Reviewing Main Ideas

Preview

Students can answer the questions in their Science Journals. Discuss the answers as you go through the chapter. **Linguistic**

Review

Students can write their answers, then compare them with those of other students. **Interpersonal**

Reteach

Students can look at the illustrations and describe details that support the main ideas of the chapter. **Visual-Spatial**

Answers to Chapter Review

SECTION 1

3. Possible answers: cuticle, vascular tissue, seeds, ability to store water, spines

SECTION 2

3. spores

SECTION 3

3. Needlelike leaves reduce water loss; seeds are produced in cones.

Reviewing Main Ideas

Section 1 An Overview of Plants

1. Plants are made up of eukaryotic cells and vary greatly in size and shape.

2. Plants usually have some form of leaves, stems, and roots.

3. As plants evolved from aquatic to land environments, changes in structure and function occurred. Changes included how they reproduced, supported themselves, and moved substances from one part of the plant to another. *What adaptations does the plant shown above need to survive?*

4. The plant kingdom is classified into groups called divisions.

Section 2 Seedless Plants

1. Seedless plants include nonvascular and vascular types.

2. Seedless nonvascular plants have no true leaves, stems, or roots. Reproduction usually is by spores.

3. Club mosses, horsetails, and ferns are seedless vascular plants. They have vascular tissues that move substances throughout the plant. These plants may reproduce by spores. *What is produced in these fern structures?*

4. Many ancient forms of these plants underwent a process that resulted in the formation of coal.

Section 3 Seed Plants

1. Seed plants are adapted to survive in nearly every environment on Earth.

2. Seed plants produce seeds and have vascular tissue, stems, roots, and leaves. Vascular tissues transport food, water, and dissolved substances in the roots, stems, and leaves.

3. The two major groups of seed plants are gymnosperms and angiosperms. Gymnosperms generally have needlelike leaves and some type of cone. Angiosperms are plants that flower and are classified as monocots or dicots. *What is the importance of these structures to gymnosperms?*

4. Seed plants provide food, shelter, clothing, and many other products. They are the most economically important plants on Earth.

FOLDABLES
Reading & Study Skills

After You Read

Use the information that you recorded in your Know-Want-Learned Study Fold to explain the characteristics of plants you see every day.

FOLDABLES
Reading & Study Skills

After You Read

After students have read the chapter and completed the Foldable described in Before You Read, have them do the activity on the student page.

Dinah Zike

Visualizing Main Ideas

Complete the following concept map about the seed plants.

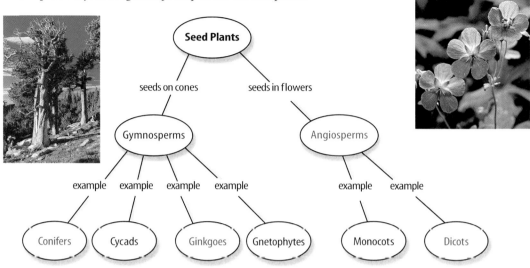

Vocabulary Review

Vocabulary Words

a. angiosperm
b. cambium
c. cellulose
d. cuticle
e. dicot
f. guard cell
g. gymnosperm
h. monocot
i. nonvascular plant
j. phloem
k. pioneer species
l. rhizoid
m. stomata
n. vascular plant
o. xylem

THE PRINCETON REVIEW **Study Tip**

Don't just memorize definitions. Write complete sentences using new vocabulary words to be certain you understand what they mean.

Using Vocabulary

Complete each analogy by providing the missing vocabulary word.

1. Angiosperm is to flower as _____ is to cone.
2. Dicot is to two seed leaves as _____ is to one seed leaf.
3. Root is to fern as _____ is to moss.
4. Phloem is to food transport as _____ is to water transport.
5. Vascular plant is to horsetail as _____ is to liverwort.
6. Cellulose is to support as _____ is to protect.
7. Fuel is to ferns as _____ is to bryophytes.
8. Cuticle is to wax as _____ is to fibers.

Chapter **3** Study Guide

Visualizing Main Ideas

See student page.

Vocabulary Review

Using Vocabulary

1. gymnosperm
2. monocot
3. rhizoid
4. xylem
5. nonvascular plant
6. cuticle
7. pioneer species
8. cellulose

Chapter ③ Assessment

Checking Concepts

1. C
2. A
3. C
4. B
5. D
6. C
7. A
8. D
9. C
10. A

Thinking Critically

11. The plant might lose so much water that it would wilt or die.
12. Flowering plants all have vascular tissue.
13. Succulents grow naturally in dry environments.
14. They must grow in moist environments because they don't have vascular tissue for water or nutrient transport. All of their cells must absorb water from the environment.
15. Pioneer species help to break down rocks and make small pockets of soil needed by other, larger plants.

Checking Concepts

Choose the word or phrase that best answers the question.

1. Which of the following is a seedless vascular plant?
   A) moss
   B) liverwort
   C) horsetail
   D) pine

2. What are the small openings in the surface of a leaf surrounded by guard cells called?
   A) stomata
   B) cuticles
   C) rhizoids
   D) angiosperms

3. What are the plant structures that anchor the plant called?
   A) stems
   B) leaves
   C) roots
   D) guard cells

4. Where is most of a plant's new xylem and phloem produced?
   A) guard cell
   B) cambium
   C) stomata
   D) cuticle

5. What group has plants that are only a few cells thick?
   A) gymnosperms
   B) cycads
   C) ferns
   D) mosses

6. Which of the following plant parts is found only on gymnosperms?
   A) flowers
   B) seeds
   C) cones
   D) fruit

7. What kinds of plants have structures that move water and other substances?
   A) vascular
   B) protist
   C) nonvascular
   D) bacterial

8. In what part of a leaf does most photosynthesis occur?
   A) epidermis
   B) cuticle
   C) stomata
   D) palisade layer

9. Which one of the following do ferns have?
   A) cones
   B) rhizoids
   C) spores
   D) seeds

10. Which of these is an advantage to life on land for plants?
    A) more direct sunlight
    B) less carbon dioxide
    C) greater space to grow
    D) less competition for food

Thinking Critically

11. What might happen if a land plant's waxy cuticle were destroyed?

12. On a walk through the woods with a friend, you find a plant neither of you has seen before. The plant is herbaceous and has yellow flowers. Your friend says it is a vascular plant. How does your friend know this?

13. Plants called succulents store large amounts of water in their leaves, stems, and roots. In what environments would you expect to find succulents growing naturally?

14. Explain why mosses are usually found in moist areas.

15. How do pioneer species change environments so that other plants can grow there?

Developing Skills

16. **Interpreting Data** What do the data in this table tell you about where gas exchange occurs in each plant leaf?

Stomata (per mm²)		
Plant	Upper Surface	Lower Surface
Pine	50	71
Bean	40	281
Fir	0	228
Tomato	12	13

17. **Making and Using Graphs** Make two circle graphs using the table in question 16.

Chapter ✔Assessment Planner

Portfolio Encourage students to place in their portfolios one or two items of what they consider to be their best work. Examples include:
- Activity, p. 65
- Make a Model, p. 71
- Curriculum Connection, p. 77

Performance Additional performance assessments, Performance Task Assessment Lists, and rubrics for evaluating these activities can be found in Glencoe's **Performance Assessment in the Science Classroom.**

18. Concept Mapping Complete this map for the seedless plants of the plant kingdom.

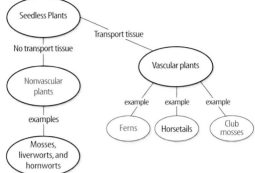

19. Interpreting Scientific Illustrations Using **Figure 20** in this chapter, compare and contrast the number of cotyledons, bundle arrangement in the stem, veins in leaves, and number of flower parts for monocots and dicots.

20. Concept Mapping Put the following events in order to show how coal is formed from plants: *living seedless plants, coal is formed, dead seedless plants decay,* and *peat is formed.*

Performance Assessment

21. Poem Choose a topic in this chapter that interests you. Look it up in a reference book, in an encyclopedia, or on a CD-ROM. Write a poem to share what you learn.

TECHNOLOGY

Go to the Glencoe Science Web site at **science.glencoe.com** or use the **Glencoe Science CD-ROM** for additional chapter assessment.

THE PRINCETON REVIEW — Test Practice

Maria and Josh are studying how different environmental factors affect the growth of plants. They set up four pots. Each pot contains a different plant growing in a standard potting soil. They record their data in the following table.

Plant Growth Data			
Type of Plant	Hours of Light	Amount of Water (mL)	Percent Growth
Moss	0	100	2%
Lettuce	4	100	15%
Tree Seedling	8	100	40%
Grape Vine	12	100	65%

Study the table and answer the following questions.

1. According to this information, which is the most likely cause of the differences in plant growth?
   A) light
   B) water
   C) plant type
   D) soil

2. How could this experiment be improved?
   F) Vary the amount of water each plant receives.
   G) Record plant growth in cm.
   H) Use only one kind of plant.
   J) Expose each plant to the same number of hours of light.

THE PRINCETON REVIEW — Test Practice

The Test-Taking Tip was written by The Princeton Review, the nation's leader in test preparation.
1. A
2. H

Developing Skills

16. Gas exchange for pine and tomato leaves is nearly the same on both the upper and lower surfaces because the number of stomata on each are about equal. Most of the gas exchange for bean leaves occurs on the lower surface. All gas exchange for fir needles happens on the lower surface.
17. The upper-surface graph should show 177° for pine, 141° for bean, and 42° for tomato. The lower-surface graph should show 43° for pine, 171° for bean, 138° for fir, and 8° for tomato.
18. See student page.
19. Monocots have one seed leaf, scattered vascular bundles, parallel veins in leaves, and flower parts in multiples of three. Dicots have two seed leaves, vascular bundles in rings, a network of veins in leaves, and flower parts in multiples of four or five.
20. Living seedless plants, dead seedless plants decay, peat is formed, coal is formed.

Performance Assessment

21. Have students share their poems with the class. Use **PASC**, p. 157.

✔ Assessment Resources

 Reproducible Masters

Chapter Resources Booklet
Chapter Review, pp. 33–34
Chapter Tests, pp. 35–38
Assessment Transparency Activity, p. 45

Glencoe Science Web site
Interactive Tutor
Chapter Quizzes

Glencoe Technology
- Assessment Transparency
- Interactive CD-ROM Chapter Quizzes
- ExamView Pro Test Bank
- Vocabulary PuzzleMaker Software
- MindJogger Videoquiz

Section/Objectives	Standards		Activities/Features
Chapter Opener	**National**	**State/Local**	**Explore Activity:** Predict where seeds are found, p. 93 **Before You Read,** p. 93
	See p. 5T for a Key to Standards.		
Section 1 Introduction to Plant Reproduction 🕐 2 sessions 📦 1 block 1. **Distinguish** between the two types of plant reproduction. 2. **Describe** the two stages in a plant's life cycle.	National Content Standards: UCP3, A1, C1, C2		**MiniLAB:** Observing Asexual Reproduction, p. 95 **Science Online,** p. 96
Section 2 Seedless Reproduction 🕐 2 sessions 📦 1 block 1. **Examine** the life cycles of a moss and a fern. 2. **Explain** why spores are important to seedless plants. 3. **Identify** some special structures used by ferns for reproduction.	National Content Standards: UCP5, A1, C1, C2, C5		**Physics Integration,** p. 100 **Activity:** Comparing Seedless Plants, p. 102
Section 3 Seed Reproduction 🕐 3 sessions 📦 1.5 blocks 1. **Examine** the life cycles of typical gymnosperms and angiosperms. 2. **Describe** the structure and function of the flower. 3. **Discuss** methods of seed dispersal in seed plants.	National Content Standards: UCP5, A1, C1, C2, C5, E2, F5		**Science Online,** p. 104 **Environmental Science Integration,** p. 106 **MiniLAB:** Modeling Seed Dispersal, p. 110 **Visualizing Seed Dispersal,** p. 111 **Math Skills Activity:** Calculating the Number of Seeds That Will Germinate, p. 112 **Activity:** Germination Rate of Seeds, pp. 114–115 **Science and Society:** Genetic Engineering, pp. 116–117

NATIONAL GEOGRAPHIC

Teacher's Corner

PRODUCTS AVAILABLE FROM GLENCOE
To order call 1-800-334-7344:
CD-ROM: NGS PictureShow: *Plants: What It Means to Be Green*
Transparency Set
NGS PicturePack: *Plants: What It Means to Be Green*

PRODUCTS AVAILABLE FROM NATIONAL GEOGRAPHIC SOCIETY
To order call 1-800-368-2728:
Video: *Pollination*

INDEX TO NATIONAL GEOGRAPHIC SOCIETY
The following articles may be used for research relating to this chapter:

"Bats—The Cactus Connection," by Merlin D. Tuttle, June 1991; "Hummingbirds: The Nectar Connection," by Paul W. Ewald, Feb. 1982; "The Exquisite Orchids," by Luis Marden, April 1971; "The Wasp That Plays Cupid to a Fig," by Robert F. Sisson, Nov. 1970; "Crossroads of the Insect World," by J.W. MacSwain, Dec. 1966.

Activity Materials	Reproducible Resources	Section Assessment	Technology
Explore Activity: 2 different types of grapes, plastic knife, paper towels	**Chapter Resources Booklet** Foldables Worksheet, p. 15 Directed Reading Overview, p. 17 Note-taking Worksheets, pp. 31–33	GLENCOE'S **ASSESSMENT** ADVANTAGE	
MiniLAB: scissors, coleus or other houseplant, cup, water, small container of soil	**Chapter Resources Booklet** Transparency Activity, p. 42 MiniLAB, p. 3 Enrichment, p. 28 Reinforcement, p. 25 Directed Reading, p. 18 **Cultural Diversity,** p. 19	Portfolio Assessment, p. 97 Performance MiniLAB, p. 95 Skill Builder Activities, p. 97 Content Section Assessment, p. 97	Section Focus Transparency Interactive CD-ROM Guided Reading Audio Program
Activity: live mosses, liverworts, and ferns with gametophytes and sporophytes; hand lens; forceps; dropper; microscope slide and coverslip (2); microscope; dissecting needle; pencil with eraser	**Chapter Resources Booklet** Transparency Activity, p. 43 Enrichment, p. 29 Reinforcement, p. 26 Directed Reading, p. 18 Transparency Activity, pp. 45–46 Activity Worksheet, pp. 5–6	Portfolio Make a Model, p. 100 Performance Skill Builder Activities, p. 101 Content Section Assessment, p. 101	Section Focus Transparency Teaching Transparency Interactive CD-ROM Guided Reading Audio Program
MiniLAB: buttons, glue, paper, string, other common materials **Activity:** seeds, water, salt, potting soil, plant trays or plastic cups, thermometer, graduated cylinder, beakers	**Chapter Resources Booklet** Transparency Activity, p. 44 MiniLAB, p. 4 Enrichment, p. 30 Reinforcement, p. 27 Directed Reading, pp. 19, 20 Lab Activity, pp. 9–12, 13–14 Activity Worksheet, pp. 7–8 **Lab Management and Safety,** p. 38	Portfolio Activity, p. 105 Performance MiniLAB, p. 110 Math Skills Activity, p. 112 Skill Builder Activities, p. 113 Content Section Assessment, p. 113	Section Focus Transparency Interactive CD-ROM Guided Reading Audio Program

Need materials? Contact Science Kit at 1-800-828-7777 or www.sciencekit.com on the Internet.

End of Chapter Assessment

GLENCOE'S **ASSESSMENT** ADVANTAGE

Blackline Masters	Technology	Professional Series
Chapter Resources Booklet Chapter Review, pp. 35–36 Chapter Tests, pp. 37–40 **Standardized Test Practice by The Princeton Review,** pp. 47–50	MindJogger Videoquiz Interactive CD-ROM Vocabulary PuzzleMakers ExamView Pro Test Bank Interactive Lesson Planner Interactive Teacher Edition	Performance Assessment in the Science Classroom (PASC)

Transparencies

Section Focus

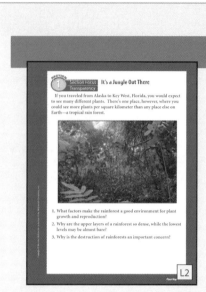

1 Section Focus Transparency — **It's a Jungle Out There**

If you traveled from Alaska to Key West, Florida, you would expect to see many different plants. There's one place, however, where you could see more plants per square kilometer than any other place on Earth—a tropical rain forest.

1. What factors make the rainforest a good environment for plant growth and reproduction?
2. Why are the upper layers of a rainforest so dense, while the lowest levels may be almost bare?
3. Why is the destruction of rainforests an important concern?

L2

2 Section Focus Transparency — **It's Raining, It's Sporing**

While flowering plants use seeds to reproduce, mosses use a different strategy. As seen below, one part of moss reproduction involves releasing spores into the environment. Each spore is capable of growing into a new plant.

1. Judging from the picture, how are moss spores dispersed?
2. Why does the moss produce so many spores?

L2

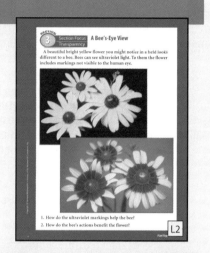

3 Section Focus Transparency — **A Bee's-Eye View**

A beautiful bright yellow flower you might notice in a field looks different to a bee. Bees can see ultraviolet light. To them the flower includes markings not visible to the human eye.

1. How do the ultraviolet markings help the bee?
2. How do the bee's actions benefit the flower?

L2

This is a representation of key blackline masters available in the Teacher Classroom Resources. See Resource Manager boxes within the chapter for additional information.

Key to Teaching Strategies

The following designations will help you decide which activities are appropriate for your students.

L1 Level 1 activities should be appropriate for students with learning difficulties.

L2 Level 2 activities should be within the ability range of all students.

L3 Level 3 activities are designed for above-average students.

ELL ELL activities should be within the ability range of English Language Learners.

COOP LEARN Cooperative Learning activities are designed for small group work.

LS Multiple Learning Styles logos are used throughout to indicate strategies that address different learning styles.

P These strategies represent student products that can be placed into a best-work portfolio.

Assessment

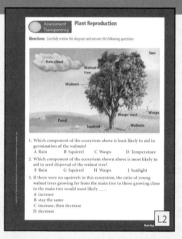

Assessment Transparency — **Plant Reproduction**

Directions: Carefully review the diagram and answer the following questions.

1. Which component of the ecosystem above is least likely to aid in germination of the walnuts?
   A Rain   B Squirrel   C Wasps   D Temperature
2. Which component of the ecosystem shown above is most likely to aid in seed dispersal of the walnut tree?
   F Rain   G Squirrel   H Wasps   J Sunlight
3. If there were no squirrels in this ecosystem, the ratio of young walnut trees growing far from the main tree to those growing close to the main tree would most likely ____.
   A increase
   B stay the same
   C increase, then decrease
   D decrease

L2

Teaching

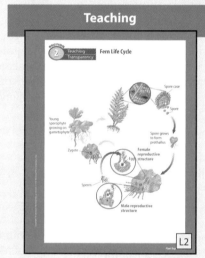

2 Teaching Transparency — **Fern Life Cycle**

L2

Hands-on Activities

Activity Worksheets

Activity — Comparing Seedless Plants

L2

Laboratory Activities

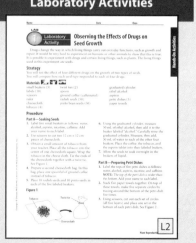

1 Laboratory Activity — **Observing the Effects of Drugs on Seed Growth**

L2

RESOURCE MANAGER

Meeting Different Ability Levels

Content Outline

L2

Reinforcement

L2

Directed Reading

L1

Assessment

Chapter Tests

L2

Enrichment

L3

Spanish Directed Reading

L1

Test Practice Workbook

Standardized Test Practice
Teacher Edition

Glencoe Science

From Bacteria to Plants

NATIONAL GEOGRAPHIC SOCIETY

science.glencoe.com

L2

Chapter Review

L2

Science Content Background

SECTION

Introduction to Plant Reproduction

Types of Reproduction

Asexual reproduction is a common method of reproduction in plants. Asexual reproduction works best in appropriate environments that change little over long periods of time. The advantage of asexual reproduction is the ability to produce large numbers of offspring that have the same genetic makeup as the parent plant. Such asexual reproduction is cloning. Many commercially grown plants, such as orchids and African violets, are routinely cloned.

> ### Fun Fact
> Of the approximate 230,000 known species of flowering plants, the *Wolffia augusta* is one of the tiniest. One will easily fit through the eye of an ordinary sewing needle. Five thousand will easily fit in a sewing thimble.

The genetic diversity of plants is increased through sexual reproduction. Sexual reproduction allows plants to evolve and invade new habitats or adapt when the environment changes.

Haploid and Diploid Stages

In all plant life cycles, there are haploid and diploid stages. In some plants, the stages are separate and unique and referred to as an alternation of generations. Alternation of generations evolved with the ancestors of the plant kingdom, the ancient Chlorophyta, or green algae. A diploid sporophyte ($2n$) generation alternates with a haploid gametophyte generation (n). *Sporophyte* means "spore-producing" and *gametophyte* means "gamete-producing." These terms indicate the reproductive function of the plant. In some plants these are distinct organisms, but in others they are part of the larger organism.

Meiosis occurs in specialized cells of the sporophyte, the spore mother cells, and results in the production of spores. Spores produce the gametophyte by mitosis. In time, gametophytes produce haploid gametes. A male and a female gamete unite to form a diploid zygote, the first cell in the multicellular sporophyte.

SECTION

Seedless Reproduction

Seedless Plants

In mosses, liverworts, and hornworts, the gametophyte is the familiar plant that makes its own food by photosynthesis. The sporophyte generation in mosses is found at the tip of the gametophyte and consists of a stalk with a capsule in which spores are produced by meiosis.

Fern spores germinate into a filamentous

D. Cavagnaro/DRK Photo

plant that eventually grows into an inconspicuous heart-shaped gametophyte called a prothallus. The gametophyte is independent and carries on photosynthesis. Fern sporophytes have leaves called fronds. Fronds produce spores in specialized packets called sori (singular, *sorus*) that are often misidentified as a plant disease.

D. Cavagnaro/DRK Photo

SECTION 3
Seed Reproduction
Gymnosperm Reproduction

Gymnosperms are unique among seed plants because the ovules of their seeds are not completely enclosed by tissue produced by the sporophyte.

The sporophytes, or $2n$ generations of gymnosperms, are familiar trees and shrubs like pines, junipers, and spruces. Ovulate cones and pollen-bearing cones are produced on separate stems. The female cones of gymnosperms vary from the familiar woody cones to fleshy, berry-like cones. Berrylike cones are often colorful, such as the red ones on yews and the bluish ones on junipers. Many gymnosperm cones complete their life cycle in one year, but some take two or three years for maturation.

All but about 35,000 of the 235,000 species of plants today are characterized by their production of seeds.

Germination

Seeds are efficient units of dispersal for plants, and many have elaborate adaptations for moving away from the parent plant. Germination, the growth of a plant from a seed, is affected by many factors, such as temperature, amount of light, presence of moisture and presence of oxygen. Some seeds lay dormant, waiting for the appropriate set of conditions for germination.

Fun Fact

The number of seeds per fruit ranges from one—in fruits such as peaches and plums—to several hundred in pumpkins and other squashes. It has been reported that a tropical plant, *Rafflesia keithii*, produced a fruit with 273,000 seeds.

SCIENCE Online

For additional content background on this topic, go to the Glencoe Science Web site at science.glencoe.com.

Chapter Vocabulary

gametophyte stage, p. 97
spore, p. 97
sporophyte stage, p. 97
frond, p. 100
rhizome, p. 100
sori, p. 100
prothallus, p. 100
pollen grain, p. 103
pollination, p. 103
ovule, p. 105
stamen, p. 107
pistil, p. 107
ovary, p. 107
germination, p. 112

What do you think?

Science Journal The photo shows a flower of grass. This is not the typical showy flower most students are familiar with, but many plants have flowers of this type.

CHAPTER
4

Plant Reproduction

Saplings and other plants grow among the remains of trees that were destroyed by fire. Where did these new plants come from? Did they grow from seeds that survived the fire? Perhaps they grew from plant roots and stems that survived underground. In either case, these plants are the result of plant reproduction. In this chapter, you will learn how different groups of plants reproduce and how plants can be dispersed from place to place.

What do you think?

Science Journal Look at the picture below with a classmate. Discuss what this might be. Here's a hint: *In many plants these are colorful and have pleasant aromas.* Write your answer or best guess in your Science Journal.

Theme Connection

Systems and Interactions This chapter emphasizes the mechanisms and systems of reproduction in plants.

You might know that most plants grow from seeds. Seeds are usually found in the fruits of plants. When you eat watermelon, it can contain many small seeds. Do all fruits contain seeds? Do this activity to find out.

Predict where seeds are found

1. Obtain two grapes from your teacher. Each grape should be from a different plant.
2. Split each grape in half and examine the insides of each grape. **WARNING:** *Do not eat the grapes.*

Observe

Were seeds found in both grapes? Hypothesize how new grape plants could be grown if no seeds are produced. In your Science Journal list three other fruits you know of that do not contain seeds.

Before You Read

Making a Venn Diagram Study Fold **Make the following Foldable to compare and contrast sexual and asexual characteristics of a plant.**

1. Place a sheet of paper in the front of you so the long side is at the top. Fold the paper in half from top to bottom.
2. Fold both sides in. Unfold the paper so three sections show.
3. Through the top thickness of the paper, cut along each of the fold lines to the top fold, forming three tabs. Label each tab *Sexual, Both,* and *Asexual* as shown.
4. Before you read the chapter, draw circles across the front of the page, as shown.
5. As you read the chapter write information about sexual and asexual reproduction under the left and right tabs.

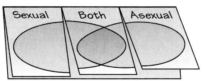

B ◆ 93

Purpose Use the Explore Activity to introduce students to the ideas of sexual and asexual reproduction. Inform students that they will learn more about plant reproduction in this chapter. L1 ELL **Visual-Spatial**

Preparation Purchase both seedless and seeded grapes.

Materials grapes, plastic knife, paper towels

Teaching Strategies
- Be sure each student has both a seedless and a seeded grape.
- Have students cover their work surfaces with a paper towel.
- Be sure students wash their hands after handling the grapes.

Observe

A seed was found in only one of the grapes. Hypotheses should indicate that some method other than seeds is responsible for producing seedless grape plants. Seedless fruits include bananas, some watermelons, and some oranges.

Process Show students several fruits—some with seeds and some without. Have them classify the plants from which the fruits came as able to reproduce sexually or only asexually. Use **Performance Assessment in the Science Classroom,** p. 121.

Before You Read

Dinah Zike Study Fold

Purpose Students make and use a Foldable to collect information on sexual and asexual reproduction in plants. They then use what they have learned to compare and contrast the two.

📁 For additional help, see Foldables Worksheet, p. 15 in **Chapter Resources Booklet,** or go to the Glencoe Science Web site at **science.glencoe.com.** See After You Read in the Study Guide at the end of this chapter.

1 Motivate

Bellringer Transparency

Display the Section Focus Transparency for Section 1. Use the accompanying Transparency Activity Master. L2 ELL

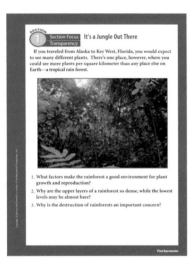

SECTION
1 Section Focus Transparency It's a Jungle Out There

If you traveled from Alaska to Key West, Florida, you would expect to see many different plants. There's one place, however, where you could see more plants per square kilometer than any place else on Earth—a tropical rain forest.

1. What factors make the rainforest a good environment for plant growth and reproduction?
2. Why are the upper layers of a rainforest so dense, while the lowest levels may be almost bare?
3. Why is the destruction of rainforests an important concern?

Plant Reproduction

Tie to Prior Knowledge

Ask students if they have ever seen a plant being rooted from a leaf cutting. Students may have seen an African violet or similar plant being propagated in this way. Explain that what they have observed is a form of asexual reproduction and that this is one way some plants reproduce.

1 Introduction to Plant Reproduction

As You Read

What You'll Learn
- **Distinguish** between the two types of plant reproduction.
- **Describe** the two stages in a plant's life cycle.

Vocabulary
spore
gametophyte stage
sporophyte stage

Why It's Important
You can grow new plants without using seeds.

Types of Reproduction

Do people and plants have anything in common? You don't have leaves or roots, and a plant doesn't have a heart or a brain. Despite these differences, you are alike in many ways—you need water, oxygen, energy, and food to grow. Like humans, plants also can reproduce and make similar copies of themselves. Although humans have only one type of reproduction, most plants can reproduce in two different ways, as shown in **Figure 1.**

Sexual reproduction in plants and animals requires the production of sex cells—usually called sperm and eggs—in reproductive organs. The offspring produced by sexual reproduction are genetically different from either parent organism.

A second type of reproduction is called asexual reproduction. This type of reproduction does not require the production of sex cells. During asexual reproduction, one organism produces offspring that are genetically identical to it. Most plants have this type of reproduction, but humans and most other animals don't.

Figure 1
Many plants reproduce sexually with flowers that contain male and female parts.

A In crocus flowers, bees and other insects help get the sperm to the egg.

B Other plants can reproduce asexually. A cutting from this impatiens plant can be placed in water and will grow new roots. This new plant can then be planted in soil.

94 ◆ B   CHAPTER 4 Plant Reproduction

Section ✓Assessment Planner

PORTFOLIO
Assessment, p. 97

PERFORMANCE ASSESSMENT
Try at Home MiniLAB, p. 95
Skill Builder Activities, p. 97
See page 120 for more options.

CONTENT ASSESSMENT
Section, p. 97
Challenge, p. 97
Chapter, pp. 120–121

Figure 2
Asexual reproduction in plants takes many forms.

A The eyes on these potatoes have begun to sprout. If a potato is cut into pieces, each piece that contains an eye can be planted and will grow into a new potato plant.

B The grass plants spread by reproducing asexually.

Asexual Plant Reproduction Do you like to eat oranges and grapes that have seeds, or do you like seedless fruit? If these plants do not produce seeds, how do growers get new plants? Growers can produce new plants by asexual reproduction because many plant cells have the ability to grow into a variety of cell types. New plants can be grown from just a few cells in the laboratory. Under the right conditions, an entire plant can grow from one leaf or just a portion of the stem or root. When growers use these methods to start new plants, they must make sure that the leaf, stem, or root cuttings have plenty of water and anything else that they need to survive.

Asexual reproduction has been used to produce plants for centuries. The white potatoes shown in **Figure 2A** were probably produced asexually. Many plants, such as lawn grasses shown in **Figure 2B,** can spread and cover wide areas because their stems grow underground and produce new grass plants asexually along the length of the stem.

Sexual Plant Reproduction Although plants and animals have sexual reproduction, there are differences in the way that it occurs. An important event in sexual reproduction is fertilization. Fertilization occurs when a sperm and egg combine to produce the first cell of the new organism, the zygote. How do the sperm and egg get together in plants? In some plants, water or wind help bring the sperm to the egg. For other plants, animals such as insects help bring the egg and sperm together.

 Reading Check *How does fertilization occur in plants?*

Mini LAB

Observing Asexual Reproduction

Procedure

1. Using a pair of **scissors**, cut a stem with at least two pairs of leaves from a **coleus or another houseplant.**
2. Carefully remove the bottom pair of leaves.
3. Place the cut end of the stem into a **cup that is half-filled with water** for two weeks. Wash your hands.
4. Remove the new plant from the water and plant it in a small **container** of **soil.**

Analysis

1. Draw and label your results in your **Science Journal.**
2. Predict how the new plant and the plant from which it was taken are genetically related.

Teacher FYI

Tissue culture allows many plants to be grown quickly from one plant with a desirable trait. This method also produces disease-free plants. Plants routinely cloned using tissue culture include orchids, tobacco, chrysanthemums, potatoes, strawberries, asparagus, and gladioli.

---

2 Teach

Types of Reproduction

Mini LAB

Purpose Students will observe the asexual reproduction of a houseplant. L2 ELL

IS Kinesthetic

Materials coleus plant, glass of water, scissors, container of soil

Teaching Strategy Tell students to choose a young stem rather than a tougher, older one.

Analysis

1. Drawings should show the growth of a new plant in the soil. Plants should have roots, stems, and leaves.
2. The plants are genetically identical.

✔ Assessment

Performance Have students repeat the activity with a different plant that can be propagated from a leaf or a root. Use **PASC,** p. 97.

Quick Demo

Show students a strawberry plant with runners. Explain that runners are one means of reproducing asexually.

Extension

If there is a university nearby, arrange a field trip to see a tissue culture laboratory, or have individual students arrange such a visit and report their observations to the class.

 Reading Check

Answer Wind, water, or animals may carry the sperm to the egg in plants.

Types of Reproduction, continued

Extension

Have students research cloning as it relates to asexual reproduction of plants and write about how cloning is an important activity in tree farming.

SCIENCE *Online*
Internet Addresses

_____

_____

_____

Explore the Glencoe Science Web site at science.glencoe.com to find out more about topics in this section.

Plant Life Cycles

Use Science Words

Word Meaning Have students research the meanings of the prefixes and suffixes that make up the words *sporophyte* and *gametophyte*. *Spor-* is derived from a Greek word meaning "seed;" *-phyte* from a Greek word meaning "plant;" *gamet-* from a Greek word meaning "to marry." Thus the gametophytes produce sex cells that will "marry" to form the sporophyte, or seed-producing stage in a plant's life cycle. L2 **LS Linguistic**

A Flowers of pea plants contain male and female structures, and each flower can fertilize itself.

B These holly flowers contain only male reproductive structures, so they can't fertilize themselves.

C Compare the flowers of this female holly plant to those of the male plant.

SCIENCE *Online*

Research Visit the Glencoe Science Web site at **science.glencoe.com** to find out more about male and female plants. In your Science Journal, list four plants that have male and female reproductive structures on separate plants.

Reproductive Organs A plant's female reproductive organs produce eggs and male reproductive organs produce sperm. Depending on the species, these reproductive organs can be on the same plant or on separate plants, as shown in **Figure 3.** If a plant has both organs, it usually can reproduce by itself. However, some plants that have both sex organs still must exchange sex cells with other plants of the same type to reproduce.

In some plant species, the male and female reproductive organs are on separate plants. For example, holly plants are either female or male. For fertilization to occur, holly plants with flowers that have different sex organs must be near each other. In that case, after the eggs in female holly flowers are fertilized, berries can form.

Another difference between you and a plant is how and when plants produce sperm and eggs. You will begin to understand this difference as you examine the life cycle of a plant.

Plant Life Cycles

All organisms have life cycles. Your life cycle started when a sperm and an egg came together to produce the zygote that would grow and develop into the person you are today. A plant also has a life cycle. It can start when an egg and a sperm come together, eventually producing a mature plant.

Resource Manager

Chapter Resources Booklet
Note-taking Worksheets, pp. 31–33
Enrichment, p. 28
Reinforcement, p. 25
Cultural Diversity, p. 19

Visual Learning

Figure 4 Plant life cycles can be very confusing. Help students break down the words *haploid* and *diploid* and relate them to the numbers of chromosomes contained in the cells of each plant stage. haploid—half the number of chromosomes; diploid—full number of chromosomes

Two Stages During your life cycle, all structures in your body are formed by cell division and made up of diploid cells—cells with a full set of chromosomes. However, sex cells form by meiosis and are haploid—they have half a set of chromosomes.

Plants have a two-stage life cycle, as shown in **Figure 4.** The two stages are the gametophyte (guh MEE tuh fite) stage and the sporophyte (SPOHR uh fite) stage.

Gametophyte Stage When cells in reproductive organs undergo meiosis and produce haploid cells called **spores,** the **gametophyte stage** begins. Some plants release spores into their surroundings. Spores divide by cell division to form plant structures or an entire new plant. The cells in these structures or plants are haploid. Some of these cells undergo cell division and form sex cells.

Sporophyte Stage Fertilization—the joining of haploid sex cells—begins the **sporophyte stage.** Cells formed in this stage have the diploid number of chromosomes. Meiosis occurs in some of these plant structures to form spores, and the cycle begins again.

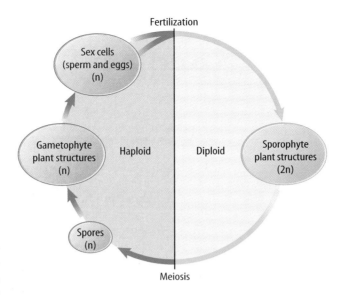

Figure 4
Plants produce diploid and haploid plant structures.

Section ① **Assessment**

1. Name two types of plant reproduction.
2. Compare and contrast the gametophyte stage and the sporophyte stage.
3. Describe how plants can be grown using asexual reproduction.
4. Explain how sexual reproduction is different in plants and animals.
5. **Think Critically** You see a plant that you like and want to grow an identical one. What type of plant reproduction would you use? Why?

Skill Builder Activities

6. **Drawing Conclusions** You use a microscope to observe the nuclei of several cells from a plant. Each one has only half the number of chromosomes you would expect. What do you conclude about this stage of its life cycle? **For more help, refer to the** Science Skill Handbook.
7. **Communicating** In your Science Journal write your own analogy about the diploid and haploid stages of a plant life cycle. **For more help,** refer to the Science Skill Handbook.

Reteach

Have students work in small groups to prepare three multiple-choice questions about the general types of plant reproduction. Have groups take turns asking and answering each other's questions. COOP LEARN

Challenge

Work with students to make a list of the advantages and disadvantages of asexual reproduction. When the list has been compiled, have students debate this statement: Asexual reproduction has no advantages over sexual reproduction. Advantages—asexual reproduction is usually faster than sexual reproduction; it takes only one plant, so there is no need to find a "mate"; and in a stable environment, lack of genetic variation may be advantageous. Disadvantages—asexual reproduction does not provide genetic diversity because there is no genetic recombination.

✔Assessment

Portfolio Have students write a poem that includes information about sexual and asexual reproduction. Use **Performance Assessment in the Science Classroom,** p. 151. P

Answers to Section Assessment

1. asexual and sexual
2. The gametophyte stage is haploid. The sporophyte stage is diploid.
3. Some plants grow asexually from leaves, stems, roots, runners, or other plant parts.
4. In animals, only sex cells are haploid. In plants, all the cells in the gametophyte stage of the life cycle are haploid.

5. A type of asexual reproduction (stem, leaf, or tip cutting); plants produced through these methods are identical to the parent plant.
6. Based on the number of chromosomes, students should conclude that it is in the haploid stage.

7. Answers will vary. Analogies should have alternating parts such as up and down, or in and out, for example.

1 Motivate

Bellringer Transparency

Display the Section Focus
Transparency for Section 2.
Use the accompanying Trans-
parency Activity Master. L2
ELL

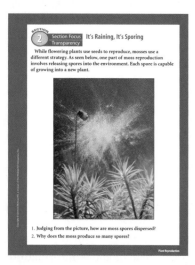

Tie to Prior Knowledge

Ask students to tell where
they have seen mosses growing
in nature. Most will indicate
that they have seen these plants
growing in damp places in
wooded areas. Tell students that
in this section, they will learn
why these plants need to be in
damp areas.

Seedless Reproduction

As You Read

What You'll Learn
- **Examine** the life cycles of a moss and a fern.
- **Explain** why spores are important to seedless plants.
- **Identify** some special structures used by ferns for reproduction.

Vocabulary
frond   sori
rhizome   prothallus

Why It's Important
Seedless plants have adaptations for reproduction on land.

Figure 5
Spores come in a variety of shapes. All spores are small and have a waterproof coating. Some, like the horsetail spores, have winglike structures that uncoil and allow them to be blown easily by the wind.

The Importance of Spores

If you want to grow plants like ferns and moss plants, you can't go to a garden store and buy a package of seeds—they don't produce seeds. You could, however, grow them from spores. These plants produce haploid spores at the end of their sporophyte stage in structures called spore cases. When the spore case breaks open, the spores are released and spread by wind or water. The spores, shown in **Figure 5,** can grow into plants that will produce sex cells.

Seedless plants include all nonvascular plants and some vascular plants. Nonvascular plants do not have structures that transport water and substances throughout the plant. Instead, water and substances simply move from cell to cell. Vascular plants have tubelike cells that transport water and substances throughout the plant.

Nonvascular Seedless Plants

If you walked in a damp, shaded forest, you probably would see mosses covering the ground or growing on a log. Mosses, liverworts, and hornworts are all nonvascular plants.

The sporophyte stage of most nonvascular plants is so small that it can be easily overlooked. Moss plants have a life cycle that is typical of how sexual reproduction occurs in this plant group.

Magnification: 200×

Moss spores   Magnification: 64×

Horsetail spores   Fern spores   Magnification: 150×

98 ◆ B CHAPTER 4 Plant Reproduction

Section ✓*Assessment* Planner

PORTFOLIO	**CONTENT ASSESSMENT**
Make a Model, p. 100	Section, p. 101
PERFORMANCE ASSESSMENT	Challenge, p. 101
Skill Builder Activities, p. 101	Chapter, pp. 120–121
See page 120 for more options.	

The Moss Life Cycle You recognize mosses as green, low-growing masses of plants. This is the gametophyte stage, which produces the sex cells. But the next time you see some moss growing, get down and look at it closely. If you see any brownish stalks growing up from the tip of the gametophyte plants, you are looking at the sporophyte stage. The sporophyte stage does not carry on photosynthesis. It depends on the gametophyte for nutrients and water. On the tip of the stalk is a tiny capsule. Inside the capsule millions of spores have been produced. When environmental conditions are just right, the capsule opens and the spores either fall to the ground or are blown away by the wind. New moss gametophytes can grow from each spore and the cycle begins again, as shown in **Figure 6.**

Figure 6
The life cycle of a moss alternates between gametophyte and sporophyte stages. *What is produced by the gametophyte stage?*

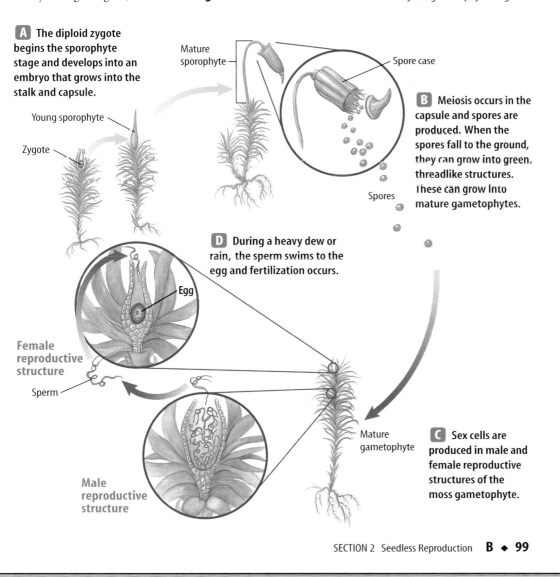

A The diploid zygote begins the sporophyte stage and develops into an embryo that grows into the stalk and capsule.

Mature sporophyte

Spore case

Young sporophyte

Zygote

B Meiosis occurs in the capsule and spores are produced. When the spores fall to the ground, they can grow into green, threadlike structures. These can grow into mature gametophytes.

Spores

D During a heavy dew or rain, the sperm swims to the egg and fertilization occurs.

Egg

Female reproductive structure

Sperm

Mature gametophyte

C Sex cells are produced in male and female reproductive structures of the moss gametophyte.

Male reproductive structure

2 Teach

Nonvascular Seedless Plants

Discussion

Explain that a single moss capsule may release 50 million spores. Ask students what advantages the production of so many spores provides to moss plants. It increases the likelihood that some spores will find a suitable environment and develop into new moss plants, thus aiding in the survival of the species.

Caption Answer

Figure 6 sex cells (eggs and sperm)

Activity

Have the class make a terrarium that includes mosses. Have students observe these plants as they grow, mature, and produce spores from their capsules.

Visual Learning

Figure 6 Have students trace the different stages in the diagram, following the arrows. Again emphasize that the gametophyte produces sex cells (egg and sperm) that unite to form the sporophyte, which produces spores. Review with students the number of chromosomes contained by cells at each stage. Then give student pairs drawings of the stages of moss life cycle on 3 × 5 cards. Have students sequence and label the drawings.

Teacher FYI

Some mosses possess strands of vascular tissue. This tissue is not arranged or differentiated to the extent found in other vascular plants.

Curriculum Connection

History Have students find out how humans have used moss gametophytes historically. Have students make posters to present their findings. Mosses were once used as bandages during wars because of their absorbency and antiseptic properties.

Resource Manager

Chapter Resources Booklet
Transparency Activity, p. 43
Directed Reading for Content Mastery, p. 18
Enrichment, p. 29

Nonvascular Seedless Plants, continued

Visual Learning

Figure 7 Ask students to explain why the balls of cells that grow in the cups shown in the picture are a form of asexual reproduction. These balls of cells do not need to be fertilized in order to grow into a new plant. Thus, they are a form of asexual reproduction.

Make a Model

Have students make drawings, flowcharts, or other models to show the stages of a moss's or fern's life cycle. Their models should include both gametophyte and sporophyte generations.

Vascular Seedless Plants

Discussion

Ask students to hypothesize how much time a plant spends in each phase of its life cycle. Allow them to explain their answers. Nonvascular plants spend most of their life cycle in the gametophyte phase. Most vascular plants spend most of their life cycle in the sporophyte stage.

Physics INTEGRATION

Possible answers: machines that toss tennis balls and skeet throwers

✔ Reading Check

Answer prothallus

Figure 7
Small balls of cells grow in cuplike structures on the surface of the liverwort.

Physics INTEGRATION

Catapults have been used by humans for thousands of years to launch objects. The spore cases of ferns act like tiny catapults as they eject their spores. In your Science Journal list tools, toys, and other objects that use catapult technology to work.

Nonvascular Plants and Asexual Reproduction Nonvascular plants also can reproduce asexually. For example, if a piece of a moss gametophyte plant breaks off, it can grow into a new plant. Liverworts can form small balls of cells on the surface of the gametophyte plant, as shown in **Figure 7.** These are carried away by water and grow into new gametophyte plants if they settle in a damp environment.

Vascular Seedless Plants

Millions of years ago most plants on Earth were vascular seedless plants. Today they are not as widespread.

Most vascular seedless plants are ferns. Other plants in this group include horsetails and club mosses. All of these plants have vascular tissue to transport water from their roots to the rest of the plant. Unlike the nonvascular plants, the gametophyte of vascular seedless plants is the part that is small and often overlooked.

The Fern Life Cycle The fern plants that you see in nature or as houseplants are fern sporophyte plants. Fern leaves are called **fronds.** They grow from an underground stem called a **rhizome.** Roots that anchor the plant and absorb water and nutrients also grow from the rhizome. Fern sporophytes make their own food by photosynthesis. Fern spores are produced in structures called **sori** (singular, *sorus*), usually located on the underside of the fronds. Sori can look like crusty rust-, brown-, or dark-colored bumps. Sometimes they are mistaken for a disease or for something growing on the fronds.

If a fern spore lands on damp soil or rocks, it can grow into a small, green, heart-shaped gametophyte plant called a **prothallus** (proh THA lus). A prothallus is hard to see because most of them are only about 5 mm to 6 mm in diameter. The prothallus contains chlorophyll and can make its own food. It absorbs water and nutrients from the soil. The life cycle of a fern is shown in **Figure 8.**

✔ Reading Check   *What is the gametophyte plant of a fern called?*

Ferns may reproduce asexually, also. Fern rhizomes grow and form branches. New fronds and roots develop from each branch. The new rhizome branch can be separated from the main plant. It can grow on its own and form more fern plants.

Resource Manager

Chapter Resources Booklet
Reinforcement, p. 26
Transparency Activity, pp. 45–46
Activity Worksheet, pp. 5–6

Science Journal

Using Definitions *Frond* is the name given to leaves of ferns and palms. Have students look in a dictionary to find the derivation and meaning of the word *frond* and then write a paragraph in their journals to suggest why the word is used for these leaves. *Frond comes from the Latin word for leaf.*

Figure 8

A fern's life cycle and a moss's are similar. However, the fern sporophyte and gametophyte are photosynthetic and can grow on their own.

A Meiosis takes place inside each spore case to produce thousands of spores.

Spore case

Spore

B Spores are ejected and fall to the ground. Each can grow into a prothallus, which is the gametophyte plant.

Young sporophyte growing on gametophyte

Spore grows to form prothallus

Zygote

Female reproductive structure

Egg

E The zygote is the beginning of the sporophyte stage and grows into the familiar fern plant.

Sperm

D Water is needed for the sperm to swim to the egg. Fertilization occurs and a zygote is produced.

Male reproductive structure

C The prothallus contains the male and female reproductive structures where sex cells form.

Section 2 Assessment

1. Describe the life cycle of mosses.
2. Explain the stages in the life cycle of a fern.
3. Compare and contrast the gametophyte plant of the moss with the gametophyte plant of the fern.
4. List several ways that seedless plants reproduce asexually.
5. **Think Critically** Why might some seedless plants reproduce only asexually during dry times of the year?

Skill Builder Activities

6. **Concept Mapping** Use an events-chain concept map to show the events in the life cycle of either a moss or fern. **For more help, refer to the** Science Skill Handbook.
7. **Solving One-Step Equations** Moss spores are usually no more than 0.1 mm in diameter. About how many spores would it take to equal the diameter of a penny? **For more help, refer to the** Math Skill Handbook.

Visual Learning

Figure 8 Again, have students trace with their fingers the sequence of events in a fern's life cycle. This time, have students explain the difference between the sporophyte and the gametophyte generations.

3 Assess

Reteach

Provide students with a list of the terms used in this section. Have students identify each term as being part of the moss life cycle, fern life cycle, or both. L2 ELL COOP LEARN **IS** **Interpersonal**

Challenge

Have students write essays that describe, compare, and contrast the life cycles of mosses and ferns. **IS** **Linguistic**

✓ Assessment

Performance Give each student a 3 × 5 card on which is written a description of a fern or moss structure. Have each student identify his or her structure. Then divide the class into groups (two for each plant)—one for students whose structure is part of the sporophyte stage, and one for students whose structure is part of the gametophyte stage of their plant's life cycle. Have students work together to arrange themselves into a physical model of their plant's life cycle. Use **PASC**, p. 123.

Answers to Section Assessment

1. Spores land on the ground and grow into upright leafy gametophytes, which produce sex cells. Sperm swim in water to reach the egg, forming a zygote. The zygote grows and develops into a spore-producing sporophyte.
2. A spore grows into a heart-shaped gametophyte. The gametophyte produces sex cells that unite to form a zygote. The zygote grows into a spore-producing sporophyte.
3. A moss gametophyte is larger than the sporophyte and photosynthetic; ferns produce small, photosynthetic gametophytes.
4. Seedless plants reproduce asexually from plant parts, small balls of cells that form on the gametophyte, or from rhizomes.
5. Sexual reproduction in these plants requires water.
6. The chain should summarize **Figure 6** or **Figure 8**.
7. A penny is approximately 20 mm in diameter, so about 200 spores would be needed.

Activity
BENCH TESTED

Purpose Students will observe the stages in the life cycles of liverworts, mosses, and ferns. L2

ELL   COOP LEARN   IS **Visual-Spatial**

Process Skills observing, classifying, comparing and contrasting

Time Required 50 minutes

Safety Precautions Remind students not to eat any plant parts and to be careful when using microscopes.

Teaching Strategy Be sure students have properly focused their microscopes.

Troubleshooting If moss spores are not liberated using water, add an equal amount of glycerin to the water. This mixture allows the spores to come out of the capsule more easily.

Answers to Questions

1. Moss gametophyte: green, low-growing structure with leaves in a whorl around a stalk; liverwort gametophyte: green, flat, leaflike form. Sporophytes of mosses are a non-green stalk with a spore-containing capsule at the top. Liverwort sporophytes form on the gametophytes as green umbrella-like structures with spores in cases underneath. Fern gametophytes: green, heart-shaped structures; their sporophytes are familiar green plants.
2. gametophyte, sporophyte, rhizoid, spores, leaflike structures
3. Many spores do not land where conditions are right for growth. The greater the number of spores produced, the greater the chances that some will grow.

Activity

Comparing Seedless Plants

All seedless plants have specialized structures that produce spores. Although these sporophyte structures have a similar function, they look different. The gametophyte plants also are different from each other. Do this activity and observe the similarities and differences among three groups of seedless plants.

What You'll Investigate
How are the gametophyte stages and the sporophyte stages of liverworts, mosses, and ferns similar and different?

Materials
live mosses, liverworts, and ferns
    with gametophytes and sporophytes
hand lens
forceps
dropper
microscope slides and coverslips (2)
microscope
dissecting needle
pencil with eraser

Goals
■ **Describe** the sporophyte and gametophyte forms of liverworts, mosses, and ferns.
■ **Identify** the spore-producing structures of liverworts, mosses, and ferns.

Safety Precautions

Procedure
1. Obtain a gametophyte of each plant. With a hand lens, observe the rhizoids, leafy parts, and stemlike parts, if any are present.
2. Obtain a sporophyte of each plant and use a hand lens to observe it.

102 ◆ B   CHAPTER 4 Plant Reproduction

3. Locate the spore structure on the moss plant. Remove it and place it in a drop of water on the slide. Place a coverslip over it. Use the eraser of a pencil to gently push on the coverslip to release the spores. **WARNING:** *Do not break the coverslip.* Observe the spores under low and high power.
4. Make labeled drawings of all observations in your Science Journal.
5. Repeat steps 3 and 4 using a fern.

Conclude and Apply
1. For each plant, compare the gametophyte's appearance to the sporophyte's appearance.
2. **List** structure(s) common to all three plants.
3. **Hypothesize** about why each plant produces a large number of spores.

*C*ommunicating
Your Data

Prepare a bulletin board that shows differences between the sporophyte and gametophyte stages of liverworts, mosses, and ferns. **For more help,** refer to the Science Skill Handbook.

*C*ommunicating
Your Data

The bulletin board should illustrate differences between the life cycle stages of the plants examined. Encourage students to use Internet sources to research photographs and information for the bulletin board.

✔*A*ssessment

Performance Assess students' understanding of the parts of mosses, liverworts, and ferns by having them identify parts of living specimens and by describing the functions of each. Use **Performance Assessment in the Science Classroom**, p. 89.

SECTION 3

Seed Reproduction

The Importance of Pollen and Seeds

All the plants described so far have been seedless plants. However, the fruits and vegetables that you eat come from seed plants. Oak, maple, and other shade trees are also seed plants. All flowers are produced by seed plants. In fact, most of the plants on Earth are seed plants. How do you think they became such a successful group? Reproduction that involves pollen and seeds is part of the answer.

Pollen In seed plants, some spores develop into small structures called pollen grains. A **pollen grain,** as shown in **Figure 9,** has a water-resistant covering and contains gametophyte parts that can produce the sperm. The sperm of seed plants do not need to swim to the female part of the plant. Instead, they are carried as part of the pollen grain by gravity, wind, water currents, or animals. The transfer of pollen grains to the female part of the plant is called **pollination.**

After the pollen grain reaches the female part of a plant, sperm and a pollen tube are produced. The sperm moves through the pollen tube, then fertilization can occur.

As You Read

What You'll Learn
- **Examine** the life cycles of typical gymnosperms and angiosperms.
- **Describe** the structure and function of the flower.
- **Discuss** methods of seed dispersal in seed plants.

Vocabulary

pollen grain	pistil
pollination	ovary
ovule	germination
stamen	

Why It's Important
Seeds from cones and flowers produce most plants on Earth.

Figure 9
The waterproof covering of a pollen grain is unique and can be used to identify the plant that it came from. This pollen from a ragweed plant is a common cause of hay fever.

Magnification: 3,000×

SECTION 3   Seed Reproduction   **B** ◆ **103**

SECTION 3

Seed Reproduction

1 Motivate

Bellringer Transparency

Display the Section Focus Transparency for Section 3. Use the accompanying Transparency Activity Master. L2
ELL

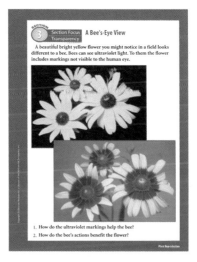

Tie to Prior Knowledge

Ask students to recall a time when they dispersed seeds. One answer may be when they were eating fruit such as watermelon. Others may have actually planted seeds in a garden. Still others may have walked through a field and found seeds stuck to their clothing.

Section ✔Assessment Planner

PORTFOLIO
Activity, p. 105
PERFORMANCE ASSESSMENT
Try at Home MiniLAB, p. 110
Skill Builder Activities, p. 113
See page 120 for more options.

CONTENT ASSESSMENT
Section, p. 113
Challenge, p. 113
Chapter, pp. 120–121

Resource Manager

Chapter Resources Booklet
Transparency Activity p. 44
Directed Reading for
Content Mastery, pp. 19, 20

The Importance of Pollen and Seeds

IDENTIFYING
Misconceptions

Many students assume that plants fertilize themselves. Point out that many plants must be cross-pollinated in order to reproduce.

Caption Answer

Figure 10 Wings allow seeds to catch the wind and be dispersed farther from the parent plant.

✔ Reading Check

Answer seed coat, stored food, embryo

Internet Addresses

Explore the Glencoe Science Web site at **science.glencoe.com** to find out more about topics in this section.

Figure 10
Seeds have three main parts—a seed coat, stored food, and an embryo. This pine seed also has a wing.
What is the function of the wing?

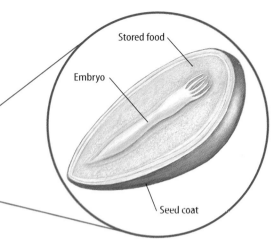
Stored food
Embryo
Seed coat

SCIENCE *Online*

Research Seed banks conserve seeds of many useful and endangered plants. Visit the Glencoe Science Web site at **science.glencoe.com** to find out more about seed banks. In your Science Journal list three organizations that manage seed banks.

Field GUIDE

Do all gymnosperm plants produce the same type of cones? To find out more about cones, see the **Cones Field Guide** at the back of this book.

Seeds Following fertilization, the female part can develop into a seed. A seed consists of an embryo, stored food, and a protective seed coat, as shown in **Figure 10.** The embryo has structures that eventually will produce the plant's stem, leaves, and roots. In the seed, the embryo grows to a certain stage and then stops until the seed is planted. The stored food provides energy that is needed when the plant embryo begins to grow into a plant. Because the seed contains an embryo and stored food, a new plant can develop more rapidly from a seed than from a spore.

✔ Reading Check *What are the three parts of a seed?*

Gymnosperms (JIHM nuh spurmz) and angiosperms are seed plants. One difference between the two groups is the way seeds develop. In gymnosperms, seeds usually develop in cones—in angiosperms, seeds develop in flowers.

Gymnosperm Reproduction

If you have collected pine cones or used them in a craft project, you probably noticed that many shapes and sizes of cones exist. You probably also noticed that some cones contain seeds. Cones are the reproductive structures of gymnosperms. Each gymnosperm species has a different cone.

Gymnosperm plants include pines, firs, cedars, cycads, and ginkgoes. The pine is a familiar gymnosperm. Production of seeds in pines is typical of most gymnosperms.

Cones A pine tree or shrub is a sporophyte plant that produces male cones and female cones as shown in **Figure 11.** Male and female gametophyte structures are produced in the cones but you'd need a magnifying glass to see these structures clearly.

104 ◆ **B** CHAPTER 4 Plant Reproduction

Curriculum Connection

Geography Gymnosperms are the dominant plant of the taiga biome. In North America, most of this area is located between 45° and 60° north latitude. Have students locate on a world map countries where taiga is the primary biome. Then have students list the climactic conditions of these areas. Canada, Norway, Sweden, and Russia are examples. These countries experience harsh winters and short summers. L2

Resource Manager

Reading and Writing Skill Activities, p. 1

Life Science Critical Thinking/Problem Solving, p. 8

A mature female cone consists of a spiral of woody scales on a short stem. At the base of each scale are two ovules. The egg is produced in the **ovule.** Pollen grains are produced in the smaller male cones. In the spring, clouds of pollen are released from the male cones. Anything near pine trees might be covered with the yellow, dustlike pollen.

Figure 11
Seed formation in pines, as in most gymnosperms, involves male and female cones.

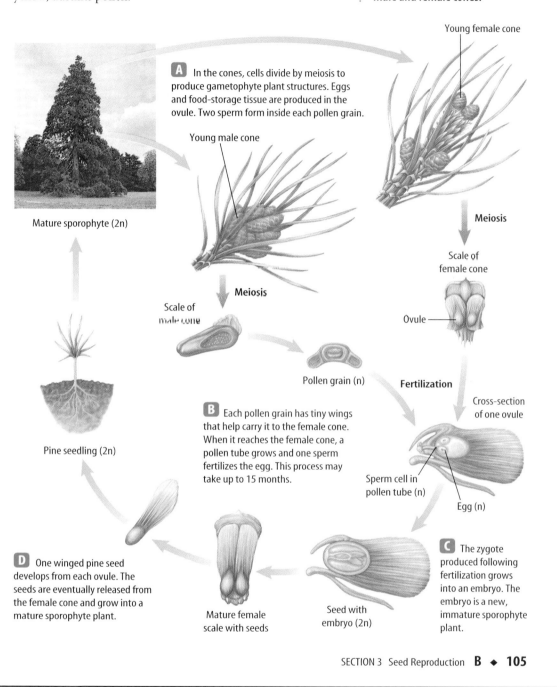

Mature sporophyte (2n)

A In the cones, cells divide by meiosis to produce gametophyte plant structures. Eggs and food-storage tissue are produced in the ovule. Two sperm form inside each pollen grain.

Young male cone

Young female cone

Meiosis

Scale of female cone

Meiosis

Scale of male cone

Ovule

Pollen grain (n)

Fertilization

Cross-section of one ovule

B Each pollen grain has tiny wings that help carry it to the female cone. When it reaches the female cone, a pollen tube grows and one sperm fertilizes the egg. This process may take up to 15 months.

Pine seedling (2n)

Sperm cell in pollen tube (n)

Egg (n)

D One winged pine seed develops from each ovule. The seeds are eventually released from the female cone and grow into a mature sporophyte plant.

Mature female scale with seeds

Seed with embryo (2n)

C The zygote produced following fertilization grows into an embryo. The embryo is a new, immature sporophyte plant.

SECTION 3 Seed Reproduction **B** ◆ **105**

Gymnosperm Reproduction

Visual Learning

Figure 11 Have students discuss the primary differences in the life cycles of nonseed plants and gymnosperms. In gymnosperms and other seed plants, the gametophyte stage is usually microscopic. In nonseed plants, this stage can be larger than the sporophyte.

Activity

Have students write a description of a cone for someone who is visually impaired. After reviewing all the descriptions, share the best two or three with the class. **LS** **Linguistic** P

Extension

Have students visit a botanical garden to identify plants from your area and around the world. Ask students to make drawings of the plants they observe and to note any unique features of the plants. Students can present their drawings and a summary of their observations in an oral presentation.

✔ Active Reading

Double-Bubble Map This strategy utilizes two bubble maps to compare concepts. Each cluster has ideas that are unique to that idea. In the middle are connecting ideas shared by both clusters. Have students design a Double-Bubble Map summarizing gymnosperm and angiosperm reproduction. A sample is shown.

**Environmental
Science**

INTEGRATION

Without forest fires, cones would not open and new plants would not grow.

Angiosperm Reproduction

Teacher FYI

Self-pollinating plants usually produce flowers that are either not attractive to insects or have structures that hinder the movement of pollen from one plant to another. Genetic recombination in self pollinating plants generally is not as extensive as in cross pollinating plants.

Figure 12
Seed development can take more than one year in pines. The female cone looks different at various stages of the seed-production process.

Cone at pollination | Cone at the end of the first year | Mature, second-year cone

**Environmental
Science**

INTEGRATION

Some gymnosperm seeds will not germinate until the heat of a fire causes the cones to open and release the seeds. Without fires, these plants cannot reproduce. In your Science Journal, explain why some forest fires could be good for the environment.

Gymnosperm Seeds Wind usually carries the pollen from male cones to female cones. However, most of the pollen falls on other plants, the ground, and bodies of water. To be useful, the pollen has to be blown between the scales of a female cone. There it can be trapped in the sticky fluid secreted by the ovule. If the pollen grain and the female cone are the same species, fertilization and the formation of a seed can take place.

If you are near a pine tree when the female cones release their seeds, you might hear a crackling noise as the cones' scales open. It can take a long time for seeds to be released from a female pine cone. From the moment a pollen grain falls on the female cone until the seeds are released, can take two or three years, as shown in **Figure 12.** In the right environment, each seed can grow into a new pine sporophyte.

Angiosperm Reproduction

You might not know it, but you are already familiar with angiosperms. If you had cereal for breakfast or bread in a sandwich for lunch, you ate parts of angiosperms. Flowers that you send or receive for special occasions are from angiosperms. Most of the seed plants on Earth today are angiosperms.

All angiosperms have flowers. The sporophyte plant produces the flowers. Flowers are important because they contain the reproductive organs that contain gametophyte structures that produce sperm or eggs for sexual reproduction.

106 ◆ B CHAPTER 4 Plant Reproduction

LAB DEMONSTRATION

Purpose to identify the parts of a flower
Materials a variety of monocot and dicot flowers, plastic knives, tape, paper
Preparation Collect or purchase enough flowers so that each student can have one flower.
Safety Caution students to be careful with the knives.

Procedure Give each student a flower to dissect. As they work, have students tape each different type of flower part in a line on the paper. Have students compare and contrast their dissections.
Expected Outcome Students should identify flower parts and note differences among flowers.

✓Assessment

Have students describe any differences they have observed. The numbers of flower parts vary from plant to plant. Dicot flower parts occur in fours and fives; monocot flower parts occur in threes.

The Flower When you think of a flower, you probably imagine something with a pleasant aroma and colorful petals. Although many such flowers do exist, some flowers are drab and have no aroma, like the flowers of the maple tree shown in **Figure 13.** Why do you think such variety among flowers exists?

Most flowers have four main parts—petals, sepals, stamen, and pistil—as shown in **Figure 14.** Generally, the colorful parts of a flower are the petals. Outside the petals are usually leaflike parts called sepals. Sepals form the outside of the flower bud. Sometimes petals and sepals are the same color.

Inside the flower are the reproductive organs of the plant. The **stamen** is the male reproductive organ. Pollen is produced in the stamen. The **pistil** is the female reproductive organ. The **ovary** is the swollen base of the pistil where ovules are found. Not all flowers have every one of the four parts. Remember the holly plants you learned about at the beginning of the chapter? What flower part would be missing on a flower from a male holly plant?

✔ Reading Check *Where are ovules found in the flower?*

Figure 13
Maple trees produce clusters of flowers early in the spring. *How are these flowers different from those of the crocus seen earlier?*

Figure 14
The color of a flower's petals can attract insect pollinators. *What are the male and female parts of this flower?*

A pistil consists of a sticky stigma where pollen grains land, a long stalklike style, and an ovary. Ovules are the part of the ovary where meiosis occurs to produce gametophyte structures. Eggs are produced in the ovules.

A stamen consists of an anther and a thin stalk called the filament. Pollen grains form inside the anther by meiosis. Sperm develop in each pollen grain.

Petals are usually the most colorful part of the flower.

stigma
anther
stamen
filament
pistil
style
ovary
ovule
sepal

Sepals are often small, green, leaflike parts. In some flowers, the sepals are as colorful and as large as the petals.

Scarlet pimpernel

SECTION 3 Seed Reproduction **B ◆ 107**

Section 3 Seed Reproduction **B ◆ 107**

Text Question Answers

- Possible response: Having great variety helps flowers attract different types of insects or other animals that may aid in pollination or dispersal of seeds.
- pistil (stigma, style, and ovary)

Caption Answers

- **Figure 13** The flowers produced by the maple tree are very different from crocus flowers in appearance. The maple flower is not brightly colored.
- **Figure 14** Male parts are stamens (pollen, anthers, and filaments). Female parts are pistils (stigma, style, ovary, and ovule). Petals and sepals are neither male nor female.

✔ Reading Check

Answer in the ovary, which is at the base of the pistil

Teacher FYI

Flowers may be perfect or imperfect. Perfect flowers possess both stamens and pistils. Imperfect flowers may be either male (if they have only stamens) or female (if they have only pistils).

Activity

Have students use **Figure 14** as a guide to make models of the structures of a flower. Allow students to select the materials from which they will make their models.

Inclusion Strategies

Visually Impaired Provide visually impaired students with large plastic models of flowers so that they can tactilely identify the flower's structures. Allow these students to smell the scents of a variety of flowers to enrich their experience.
⬛ Kinesthetic

Resource Manager

Science Inquiry Labs, pp. 7, 13

Earth Science Critical Thinking/Problem Solving, p. 7

Visual Learning

Figure 15 After students have studied the pollination mechanisms shown, have them work in teams to write a short story about a particular kind of flower and its pollination mechanism. The story should include a day in the life of a flower. L2

COOP LEARN ⓚ **Linguistic**

Fun Fact

It would take more than ten million orchid seeds to equal the mass of a single coconut.

✔ Reading Check

Answer An animal may pick up pollen as it eats the flower, its nectar, or its pollen. The pollen is then spread to other flowers that the animal visits.

Figure 15
Looking at flowers will give you a clue about how each one is pollinated.

A Honeybees are important pollinators. They are attracted to brightly colored flowers, especially blue and yellow flowers.

B Flowers that are pollinated at night, like this cactus flower being pollinated by a bat, are usually white.

C Flowers that are pollinated by hummingbirds usually are brightly colored, especially bright red and yellow.

D Flowers that are pollinated by flies usually are dull red or brown. They often have a strong odor like rotten meat.

E The flower of this wheat plant does not have a strong odor and is not brightly colored. Wind, not an animal, is the pollinator of wheat and most other grasses.

Importance of Flowers The appearance of a plant's flowers can tell you something about the life of the plant. Large flowers with brightly colored petals often attract insects and other animals, as shown in **Figure 15.** These animals might eat the flower, its nectar, or pollen. As they move about the flower, the animals get pollen on their wings, legs, or other body parts. Later, these animals spread the flower's pollen to other plants that they visit. Other flowers depend on wind, rain, or gravity to spread their pollen. Their petals can be small or absent. Flowers that open only at night, such as the cactus flower in **Figure 15B,** usually are white or yellow and have strong scents to attract animal pollinators. Following pollination and fertilization, the ovules of flowers can develop into seeds.

✔ **Reading Check** *How do animals spread pollen?*

Resource Manager

Chapter Resources Booklet
   Enrichment, p. 30
Home and Community Involvement, p. 41

Inclusion Strategies

Learning Disabled Play "plant bingo." Have students make a game board by writing all the bold-faced terms from this section in squares on a sheet of paper. Then read a definition of a plant term. Students who can correctly identify the term can cover that term on their board. The first student to have all terms covered wins.

Angiosperm Seeds The development of angiosperm seeds is shown in **Figure 16.** Pollen grains reach the stigma in a variety of ways. Pollen is carried by wind, rain, or animals such as insects, birds, and mammals. A flower is pollinated when pollen grains land on the sticky stigma. A pollen tube grows from the pollen grain down through the style. The pollen tube enters the ovary and reaches an ovule. The sperm then travels down the pollen tube and fertilizes the egg in the ovule. A zygote forms and grows into the plant embryo.

Visual Learning

Figure 16 After students have read and discussed the information, have them make an events chain concept map to summarize seed formation in angiosperms.
L2 ℕ **Visual-Spatial**

Teacher FYI

Bees and flowers have a symbiotic, or mutually beneficial, relationship. More flowers are pollinated by bees than any other kind of insect. Many flowers also have a highly complicated structure that discourages self-pollination and encourages cross-pollination of plants with single flowers. This means that while a bee is getting nectar from the flower, it is able to touch the pistil, but not the stamen. As the bee is leaving, however, it is able to touch the stamen, but not the pistil. This way, the bee leaves pollen from another flower rather than the pollen from the flower from which the bee is taking nectar.

Figure 16
In angiosperms, seed formation begins with the formation of sperm and eggs in the male and female flower parts.

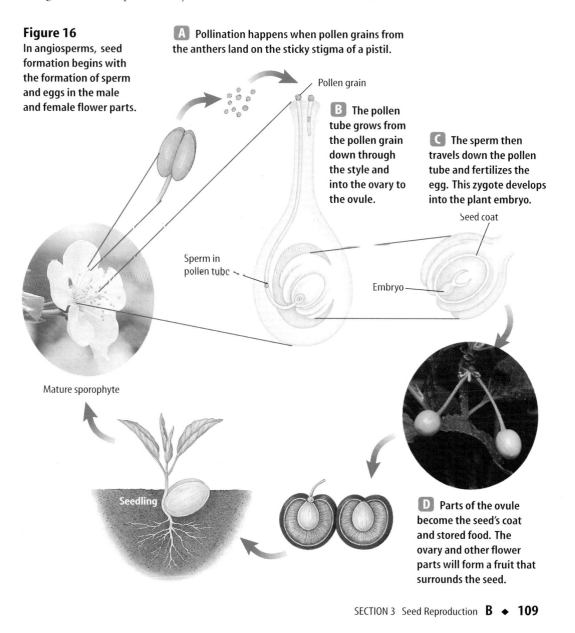

A Pollination happens when pollen grains from the anthers land on the sticky stigma of a pistil.

B The pollen tube grows from the pollen grain down through the style and into the ovary to the ovule.

C The sperm then travels down the pollen tube and fertilizes the egg. This zygote develops into the plant embryo.

Pollen grain

Seed coat

Sperm in pollen tube

Embryo

Mature sporophyte

Seedling

D Parts of the ovule become the seed's coat and stored food. The ovary and other flower parts will form a fruit that surrounds the seed.

SECTION 3 Seed Reproduction **B** ◆ **109**

Cultural Diversity

Drip Irrigation Crop production on a Navajo reservation in Arizona was once limited because of the scarcity of water. In 1984, David Mazigh, manager of an experimental farm in Israel, was invited to visit the reservation. Mazigh shared his knowledge of drip irrigation with the Navajos. Some Israeli farmers use drip irrigation to get water to plants in their desert lands. Water is pumped from a well and mixed with fertilizer. The fertilizer solution travels in thick pipes to thin drip lines that lie beside rows of planted seeds in the fields. Small nozzles allow the solution to drip out, providing plants with a slow and constant supply of water and fertilizer. Encourage students to visit a garden store and examine the drip irrigation systems available for home use.

Seed Dispersal

Use an Analogy

The way many seeds attach themselves to passing animals is like the way that two pieces of hook and loop tape stick together. In fact, hook and loop tape was inspired by the mechanism cockleburs use to stick to fur and clothing.

✔ **Reading Check**

Answer Small seeds may become airborne when the plant releases them. Some seeds have structures that allow them to move with air currents.

Figure 17
Seeds of land plants are capable of surviving unfavorable environmental conditions.
1. Immature plant
2. Cotyledon(s)
3. Seed coat
4. Endosperm

Seed Development Parts of the ovule develop into the stored food and the seed coat that surround the embryo, and a seed is formed, as shown in **Figure 17.** In the seeds of some plants, like beans and peanuts, the food is stored in structures called cotyledons. The seeds of other plants, like corn and wheat, have food stored in a tissue called endosperm.

Seed Dispersal

Earth Science INTEGRATION

Sometimes, plants just seem to appear. They probably grew from a seed, but where did the seed come from? Plants have many ways of dispersing their seeds, as shown in **Figure 18.** Most seeds grow only when they are placed on or in soil. Do you know how seeds naturally get to the soil? For many seeds, gravity is the answer. They fall onto the soil from the parent plant on which they grew. However, in nature some seeds can be spread great distances from the parent plant.

Wind dispersal usually occurs because a seed has an attached structure that moves it with air currents. Sometimes, small seeds become airborne when released by the plant.

✔ **Reading Check** *How can wind be used to disperse seeds?*

Animals can disperse many seeds. Some seeds are eaten with fruits, pass through an animal's digestive system, and are dispersed as the animal moves from place to place. Seeds can be carried great distances and stored or buried by animals. Hitch-hiking on fur, feathers, and clothing is another way that animals disperse seeds.

Water also disperses seeds. Raindrops can knock seeds out of a dry fruit. Some fruits and seeds float on flowing water or ocean currents. When you touch the seedpod of an impatiens flower, it explodes. The tiny seeds are ejected and spread some distance from the plant.

Teacher FYI

Seeds of maples, milkweed, elms, pines, cottonwoods, and other plants are dispersed by the wind.

Figure 18

Plants have many adaptations for dispersing seeds, often enlisting the aid of wind, water, or animals.

▲ **Equipped with tiny hooks, burrs cling tightly to fur and feathers.**

▼ **Dandelion seeds are easily dislodged and sail away on a puff of wind.**

▲ **Pressure builds within the seedpods of this jewelweed plant until the pod bursts, flinging seeds far and wide.**

▼ **Some seeds buried by animals, such as this squirrel, go uneaten and sprout the next spring.**

▲ **Encased in a thick, buoyant husk, a coconut may be carried hundreds of kilometers by ocean currents.**

▶ **Blackberry seeds eaten by this white-footed mouse will pass through its digestive tract and be deposited in a new location.**

SECTION 3 Seed Reproduction **B ◆ 111**

NATIONAL GEOGRAPHIC

Visualizing Seed Dispersal

Have students examine the pictures and read the captions. Then ask the following question.

What advantage does wide dispersal of seeds give a plant species? Possible answers: less competition for resources between parent plant and offspring, better chance of finding a suitable environment for growth

Activity

Have students complete a chart of the different methods of seed dispersal illustrated and give more examples for each method. Sample chart:

Dispersal Method	Examples
In Fur of Animals	burdock, burr clover, foxtails, sticktights
Buried by Animals	oak
Excreted by Animals	raspberries, strawberries, tomatoes
Floating	red mangroves, sedge
Shotgun Dispersal	mistletoe, "touch-me-not" (impatiens), "squirting cucumbers" (ecballium), sandbox tree
Wind Dispersal	maple, orchids, milkweed, tumbleweeds

Extension

Have students research the importance of bats and their role in pollination and seed dispersal in rain forests around the world. Have them make posters showing their results. Possible research findings: Bats are important in seed dispersal as they excrete seeds from the fruits they consume. Bats also are important in pollination of plants in tropical areas. Plants that rely on bats for pollination only bloom at night, when bats are active.

Resource Manager

Chapter Resources Booklet
MiniLAB, p. 4
Lab Activity, pp. 9–12, 13–14
Mathematics Skill Activities, p. 5

Teacher FYI

Force may be defined as a push or a pull. Some dry fruits open with such great force when ripe, that their seeds are dispersed some distance from the plants. Witch hazel seeds may be propelled more than 12 m by the force of its splitting ripe fruit.

Seed Dispersal,
continued

Discussion

Why might some gardeners soak their bean seeds before planting? Soaking softens the seed coat and speeds germination.

Activity

Have students collect as many different kinds of seeds as possible. Once collected, students can germinate the seeds and draw pictures of differences they note among the germinating seeds. They also can record and graph the various rates of germination. [L2] [ELL] [LS] **Kinesthetic and Visual-Spatial**

Germination A series of events that results in the growth of a plant from a seed is called **germination.** When dispersed from the plant, some seeds germinate in just a few days and other seeds take weeks or months to grow. Some seeds can stay in a resting stage for hundreds of years. In 1982, seeds of the East Indian lotus sprouted after 466 years.

Seeds will not germinate until environmental conditions are right. Temperature, the presence or absence of light, availability of water, and amount of oxygen present can affect germination. Sometimes the seed must pass through an animal's digestive system before it will germinate. Germination begins when seed tissues absorb water. This causes the seed to swell and the seed coat to break open.

Math Skills Activity

Calculating the Number of Seeds That Will Germinate

Example Problem

The label on a packet of carrot seeds says that it contains about 200 seeds. It also claims that 95 percent of the seeds will germinate. How many seeds should germinate if the packet is correct?

1 *This is what you know:*
quantity = 200
percentage = 95

2 *This is what you need to find:*
95 percent of 200

3 *This is the equation you need to use:*
$$\frac{95}{100} = \frac{x}{200}$$

4 *Solve the equation for* x:
$$x = \frac{95 \times 200}{100}$$

Check your answer by dividing by 200 then multiplying by 100. Do you get the original percentage of 95?

Practice Problem

The label on a packet of 50 corn kernels claims that 98 percent will germinate. How many kernels will germinate if the packet is correct?

For more help, refer to the Math Skill Handbook.

Inclusion Strategies

Learning Disabled To reinforce the conditions needed for germination, have students carry out this activity. Place a sponge in a shallow dish with enough water to soak the sponge. Be sure the sponge rises above the water level. Sprinkle a small amount of birdseed on the sponge. Pat the seeds into the sponge. Place the sponge in a bright but not sunny location. Add water to keep the sponge moist. Have students use hand lenses to examine the sponge each day. Have them record their observations as drawings with explanatory labels. Be sure they note when they see cracking in the seeds and the sprouting of the embryo. In five to seven days, the seedlings can be scraped off the sponge and into a container of potting soil. Continue to have students monitor growth of the young plants. [L1] [ELL] [LS] **Kinesthetic**

Figure 19
Although germination in all seeds is similar, some differences exist.

Cotyledon

Seed coat

Cotyledons

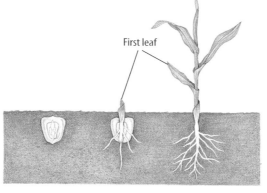

First leaf

A In bean seeds, the cotyledons can be raised above the soil. As the stored food is used up, the cotyledons shrivel and fall off.

B In corn, the stored food in the endosperm remains in the soil and is gradually used up as the young plant grows.

Next, a series of chemical reactions occurs that releases energy from the stored food in the cotyledons or endosperm for growth. Eventually, a root grows from the seed, followed by a stem and leaves as shown in **Figure 19.** After the plant emerges from the soil, photosynthesis can begin. Photosynthesis provides food as the plant continues to grow.

Section 3 Assessment

1. Compare and contrast life cycles of angiosperms and gymnosperms.
2. Diagram a flower that has all four parts and label them.
3. List three methods of seed dispersal in plants.
4. Describe the three parts of a seed and give the function of each.
5. **Think Critically** Some conifers have female cones on the top half of the tree and male cones on the bottom half. Why would this arrangement of cones on a tree be important?

Skill Builder Activities

6. **Researching Information** Find out what conditions are needed for seed germination of three different garden plants, such as corn, peas, and beans. How long does each type of seed take to germinate? **For more help, refer to the** Science Skill Handbook.

7. **Communicating** Observe live specimens of several different types of flowers. In your Science Journal, describe their structures. Include numbers of petals, sepals, stamens, and pistil. **For more help, refer to the** Science Skill Handbook.

BENCH TESTED

Recognize the Problem

Purpose

Students design and carry out an experiment to explore how germination rate varies with an environmental factor. L2 COOP LEARN

N Logical-Mathematical

Process Skills

designing an experiment; collecting, interpreting and analyzing data; drawing conclusions; communicating; making and using tables and graphs; comparing and contrasting; recognizing cause and effect; forming a hypothesis; separating and controlling variables; measuring in SI

Time Required

one class period, plus 10 minutes per day for two weeks

Alternate Materials

Use any fast-germinating seeds. Epsom salts may be substituted for table salt. Seedling warming cables provide another variable to test.

Safety Precautions

Have students review safety symbols and precautions on the student page.

Form a Hypothesis

Possible Hypotheses

Students may predict that seeds will germinate at a higher rate with water than with salt solutions. They may predict that warmer soil will increase the rate of germination. The presence and absence of light and planting depth are other variables that may be tested.

Germination Rate of Seeds

Many environmental factors affect the germination rate of seeds. Among these are soil temperature, air temperature, moisture content of soil, and salt content of soil. What happens to the germination rate when one of these variables is changed? Can you determine a way to predict the best conditions for seed germination?

Recognize the Problem

How do environmental factors affect seed germination?

Form a Hypothesis

Based on your knowledge of seed germination, state a hypothesis about how environmental factors affect germination rates.

Possible Materials

seeds
water
salt
potting soil
plant trays or plastic cups
seedling warming cables
thermometer
graduated cylinder
beakers
Alternate materials

Goals

- **Design** an experiment to test the effect of an environmental factor on seed germination rate.
- **Compare** germination rates under different conditions.

Safety Precautions

Some kinds of seeds are poisonous. Do not place any seeds in your mouth. Be careful when using any electrical equipment to avoid shock hazards.

Test Your Hypothesis

Possible Procedures

Students will plant seeds in shallow trays or plastic cups. They may test one variable in their procedure. Students using salt solutions should be encouraged to use at least two solution strengths with distilled water as the control. If students use the warming cables as a variable, then seeds without added heat will be the control. If planting depth is the variable, the control is the recommended depth.

Test Your Hypothesis

Plan

1. As a group, agree upon and write your hypothesis and decide how you will test it. Identify which results will confirm the hypothesis.

2. **List** the steps you need to take to test your hypothesis. Be specific, and describe exactly what you will do at each step. List your materials.

3. **Prepare** a data table in your Science Journal to record your observations.

4. Reread your entire experiment to make sure that all of the steps are in a logical order.

5. **Identify** all constants, variables, and controls of the experiment.

Do

1. Make sure your teacher approves your plan and your data table before you proceed.

2. Use the same type and amount of soil in each tray.

3. While the experiment is going on, record your observations accurately and complete the data table in your Science Journal.

Analyze Your Data

1. **Compare** the germination rate in the two groups of seeds.

2. **Compare** your results with those of other groups.

3. Did changing the variable affect germination rates? Explain.

4. Make a bar graph of your experimental results.

Draw Conclusions

1. **Interpret** your graph to estimate the conditions that give the best germination rate.

2. What things affect the germination rate?

 Communicating
Your Data

Write a short article for a local newspaper telling about this experiment. Give some ideas about when and how to plant seeds in the garden and the conditions needed for germination.

SECTION 3   Seed Reproduction   **B** ◆ **115**

Teaching Strategy

Have students examine seed packets to gain additional information about normal germination rates.

Troubleshooting Students may confuse rate of germination (how quickly seeds germinate) with germination rate (the percent of seeds that actually germinate).

Expected Outcome

Some environmental conditions enhance seed germination; others do not.

Analyze Your Data

1. One group should have had a higher germination rate than the other.
2. Groups testing the same variable should have similar results.
3. Rates of germination and germination rates vary with environmental conditions for each variable, depending on species of plant tested.
4. Graphs should accurately reflect experimental data.

Error Analysis

Have students try to explain differences in their results from others who tested the same variable.

Draw Conclusions

1. Graphs will vary, but each should indicate a range for best germination of the variable tested.
2. Answers may include water quality, amount of water, planting depth, and other similar variables.

 Assessment

Performance Have students test other temperatures, chemicals, or light conditions and compare their results to those obtained in this activity. Use **Performance Assessment in the Science Classroom,** p. 97.

Communicating
Your Data

Have students include graphs in their articles.

TIME
SCIENCE AND Society

TIME SCIENCE AND Society

Content Background

Genetic engineering is possible because all living organisms, from viruses and single-celled bacteria to humans, use the same genetic code. This allows the possibility of combining DNA from various organisms. The resulting product is called *recombinant DNA*. Organisms that contain DNA from different species are called *transgenic*.

Bacteria contain circular chromosomes called *plasmids*. Favorable genes can be spliced into these plasmids and replicated in great numbers as the bacteria undergo cell division. When the plasmids are introduced to other species, the new gene is transferred to the recipient's DNA, making it possible for the organism to produce a new protein with a certain desired effect. This technique is often used in transferring genes to plant species.

Viruses are little more than molecules of DNA surrounded by a protein coat. Many viruses are specialized and target specific tissues in plants and animals. Viruses work by injecting their DNA into a cell. The viral DNA then is spliced into the recipient's DNA and can be replicated in the host's body. The part of the viral DNA that causes disease can be disabled, making it non-infectious. Favorable genes are spliced into this DNA and then injected into a host. The virus will then target a specific cell type and deliver its modified DNA, allowing the cell to produce an otherwise missing protein. This technique is being developed as a potential means for curing a number of genetic disorders. Favorable results have been seen in this kind of treatment of muscular dystrophy, diabetes, and cystic fibrosis.

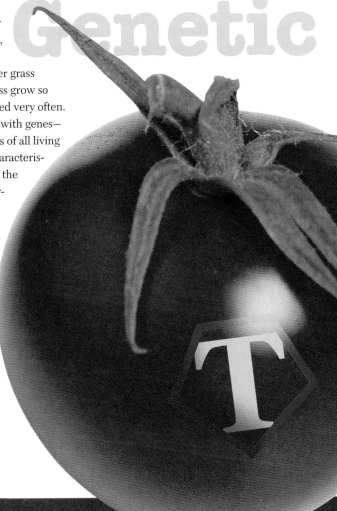

What would happen if you crossed a cactus with a rose? Well, you'd either get an extra spiky flower, or a bush that didn't need to be watered very often. Until recently, this sort of mix was the stuff science fiction was made of. But now, with the help of genetic engineering, it may be possible.

Genetic engineering is a way of taking genes from one species and giving them to another. One purpose of genetic engineering is to transfer an organism's traits. For example, scientists have changed grass by adding to it the gene from another grass species. This gene makes the grass grow so slowly, it doesn't have to be mowed very often.

How is this done? It all starts with genes—sections of DNA found in the cells of all living things. Genes produce certain characteristics, or traits, in an organism, like the color of a flower or whether a person has blond hair or black hair. Scientists have found a way to exchange genes and their traits among bacteria, viruses, plants, animals, and even humans. In 1983, the first plant was genetically modified, or changed. Since then, many crops in the U.S. have been modified in this way, including soybeans, potatoes, and tomatoes.

One common genetically engineered crop is corn. To modify it, scientists took a gene from a particular bacterium.

The gene "instructed" the bacterium to produce a natural toxin that killed certain insects. This gene was placed into another bacterium, which was placed into a corn plant. This bacterial "taxi" carried the gene into the plant's DNA, giving it the new trait. The seeds from the genetically modified corn produced crops that resisted harmful insects.

Genetic

Resources for Teachers and Students

The Food Safety Educator, Available from: USDA/FSIS/Food Safety Education, Room 2944-South Building, 1400 Independence Ave., SW, Washington, DC 20250-3700

Genetic Engineering: Fast Forwarding to Future Foods, by John Henkel, April 1995, *FDA Consumer Magazine.*

"Are Bioengineered Foods Safe?," by Larry Thompson, January-February 2000, *FDA Consumer Magazine.*

"Methods For Genetically Engineering a Plant," January-February 2000, *FDA Consumer Magazine.*

Clifton Poodry: Biologist

Clifton Poodry was born in Buffalo, New York, on the Tonawanda Seneca Indian reservation. On the reservation, Native Americans took a great deal of pride in free thinking. "This way of thinking helps if you want to do scientific research," said Poodry. "As a scientist, one thing you get to do is pursue a question that is of interest to you, even if it is not of interest to someone else."

In graduate school, Poodry studied how cells were organized and how they develop structures in the human body.

He was especially interested in learning how an organism develops from one cell to an organism with many different cells. He based his work on the fruit fly.

But equally exciting to Poodry was the fact that in college he shared the labs with men and women from many different ethnic backgrounds—all of whom were interested in research and science. That excitement, and the idea of many people coming together to share knowledge, led him to become a university professor. Today, he works to increase the number of minority students who go into scientific research. He heads the Division of Minority Opportunities in Research, a part of the National Institutes of Health.

Engineering

In addition to making plants resist insects, genetic engineering can make plants grow bigger and faster. Genetic engineering also has produced herbicide-resistant plants. This allows farmers to produce more crops with less chemicals. Scientists predict that genetic engineering will soon produce crops that are more nutritious and that can resist cold, heat, or even drought. This will help farmers increase their harvests and make more food available.

However, not everyone thinks genetic engineering is so great. Since it is a relatively new process, some people are worried about the long-term risks. One concern is that people might be allergic to modified foods and not realize it until it's too late. Other people say that genetic engineering is unnatural. Also, farmers must purchase the patented genetically modified seeds each growing season from the companies that make them, rather than saving and replanting the seeds from their current crops.

Genetically modified "super" tomatoes and "super" corn can resist heat, cold, drought, and insects.

People in favor of genetic engineering reply that there are always risks with new technology, but proper precautions are being taken. Each new plant is tested and then approved by U.S. governmental agencies. And they say that most "natural" crops aren't really natural. They are really hybrid plants bred by agriculturists, and they couldn't survive on their own.

As genetic engineering continues, so does the debate.

CONNECTIONS Debate Research the pros and cons of genetic engineering on the Glencoe Science Web site and in your school's media center. Decide whether you are for or against genetic engineering. Debate your conclusions with your classmates.

SCIENCE
Online
For more information, visit science.glencoe.com

SCIENCE
Online

Internet Addresses

_____

_____

_____

Explore the Glencoe Science Web site at **science.glencoe.com** to find out more about topics in this feature.

Discussion

What other methods could be used to transfer genes from one species to another without using viruses? Possible answer: A so-called gene gun can be used to "shoot" microscopic metallic pellets coated with plasmids into a cell.

What are some of the fears associated with the technology of genetic engineering? Possible answers: Bacteria and viruses that have been disabled may regain their ability to cause disease after they are injected; some viruses that are used cause very serious diseases prior to being disabled for such a use.

Extension

Have students research which human conditions may be beneficially treated with gene therapy. Suggest students make a collage of pictures and descriptions of these disorders that demonstrates the potential benefits of genetic medicine in the future.
IS Visual-Spatial

Investigate the Issue

Many of the fears regarding genetic engineering involve the use of this technology in altering many food items. Have students research and identify the foods that have already been subjected to this engineering. **What are the goals of this work?** Many possible answers: tomatoes with longer shelf life; corn and wheat with resistance to insects, etc. Some fears are that modified foods will produce new allergies, cause diseases, result in crop pests that are resistant to insecticides.

Reviewing Main Ideas

Preview

Students can answer the questions in their Science Journals. Discuss the answers as you go through the chapter. **LS Linguistic**

Review

Students can write their answers, then compare them with those of other students. **LS Interpersonal**

Reteach

Students can look at the illustrations and describe details that support the main ideas of the chapter. **LS Visual-Spatial**

Answers to Chapter Review

SECTION 1

2. They are identical.

SECTION 2

3. The production of many spores increases the chances that some will encounter an environment suitable for germination and growth.

SECTION 3

3. Orchid flowers are usually pollinated by insects.

Reviewing Main Ideas

Section 1 Introduction to Plant Reproduction

1. Plants reproduce sexually and asexually. Sexual reproduction involves the formation of sex cells and fertilization.

2. Asexual reproduction does not involve sex cells and produces plants genetically identical to the parent plant. *How do fern plants produced from the same rhizome compare genetically?*

3. Plant life cycles include a gametophyte and a sporophyte stage. The gametophyte stage begins with meiosis. The sporophyte stage begins when the egg is fertilized by a sperm.

4. In some plant life cycles, the sporophyte and gametophyte stages are separate and not dependent on each other. In other plant life cycles, they are part of the same organism.

Section 2 Seedless Reproduction

1. For liverworts and mosses, the gametophyte stage is the familiar plant form. The sporophyte stage produces spores.

2. In ferns, the sporophyte stage, not the gametophyte stage, is the familiar plant form.

3. Seedless plants, like mosses and ferns, use sexual reproduction to produce spores. *Why do seedless plants such as these produce so many small spores?*

Section 3 Seed Reproduction

1. In seed plants the male reproductive organs produce pollen grains that eventually contain sperm. Eggs are produced in the ovules of the female reproductive organs.

2. The male and female reproductive organs of gymnosperms are called cones. Wind usually moves pollen from the male cone to the female cone for pollination.

3. The reproductive organs of angiosperms are in a flower. The male reproductive organ is the stamen, and the female reproductive organ is the pistil. Gravity, wind, rain, and animals can pollinate a flower. *How would these flowers become pollinated?*

4. Seeds of gymnosperms and angiosperms are dispersed in many ways. Wind, water, and animals spread seeds. Some plants can eject their seeds.

5. Germination is a series of events that results in the growth of a plant from a seed.

FOLDABLES Reading & Study Skills

After You Read

On the front of your Venn Diagram Study Fold where the circles overlap, write common characteristics of sexual and asexual reproduction.

FOLDABLES Reading & Study Skills

After You Read

After students have read the chapter and completed the Foldable described in Before You Read, have them do the activity on the student page.

Dinah Zike

Visualizing Main Ideas

Complete the following table that compares reproduction in different plant groups.

Plant Reproduction

Plant Group	Seeds?	Pollen?	Cones?	Flowers?
Mosses	No	No	No	No
Ferns	No	No	No	No
Gymnosperms	Yes	Yes	Yes	No
Angiosperms	Yes	Yes	No	Yes

Vocabulary Review

Vocabulary Words

a. frond
b. gametophyte stage
c. germination
d. ovary
e. ovule
f. pistil
g. pollen grain
h. pollination
i. prothallus
j. rhizome
k. sori
l. spore
m. sporophyte stage
n. stamen

THE PRINCETON REVIEW

Study Tip

Read the chapter before you go over it in class. Being familiar with the material before your teacher explains it gives you better understanding and an opportunity to ask questions.

Using Vocabulary

Replace the underlined word or phrase with the correct vocabulary word(s).

1. A <u>sori</u> is the leaf of a fern.

2. In seed plants, the <u>anther</u> contains the egg.

3. The plant structures in the <u>sporophyte stage</u> are made up of haploid cells.

4. The green, leafy moss plant is part of the <u>prothallus</u> in the moss life cycle.

5. Two parts of a sporophyte fern are <u>stamen</u> and <u>pistil</u>.

6. The female reproductive organ of the flower is the <u>rhizome</u>.

7. The <u>ovule</u> is the swollen base of the pistil.

CHAPTER STUDY GUIDE B ◆ 119

Visualizing Main Ideas

See student page.

Vocabulary Review

Using Vocabulary

1. frond
2. ovule
3. gametophyte stage
4. gametophyte stage
5. frond; rhizome; sori (any two)
6. pistil
7. ovary

Chapter 4 Assessment

Checking Concepts

1. A
2. A
3. A
4. A
5. A
6. C
7. C
8. D
9. D
10. D

Thinking Critically

11. Large numbers of pollen grains increase the chances that any one pollen grain will be blown to a female cone and fertilize an ovule.
12. No; the embryo is the young plant; without it, no plant can grow.
13. Nonvascular plants and ferns require water to transport the sperm to egg cells.
14. The sporophyte is not photosynthetic, so it depends on the photosynthetic gametophyte for nutrition.
15. Brightly colored structures, scents, and flower form help to ensure pollination by specialized pollinators.

Checking Concepts

Choose the word or phrase that best answers the question.

1. How are colorful flowers usually pollinated?
   A) insects
   B) wind
   C) clothing
   D) gravity

2. What type of reproduction produces plants that are genetically identical?
   A) asexual
   B) sexual
   C) spore
   D) flower

3. Which of the following terms describes the cells in the gametophyte stage?
   A) haploid
   B) prokaryote
   C) diploid
   D) missing a nucleus

4. What structures do ferns form when they reproduce sexually?
   A) spores
   B) anthers
   C) seeds
   D) flowers

5. What contains food for the plant embryo?
   A) endosperm
   B) pollen grain
   C) stigma
   D) root

6. What disperses most dandelion seeds?
   A) rain
   B) animals
   C) wind
   D) insects

7. What is the series of events that results in a plant growing from a seed?
   A) pollination
   B) prothallus
   C) germination
   D) fertilization

8. In plants, meiosis is used to produce what before fertilization?
   A) prothallus
   B) seeds
   C) flowers
   D) spores

9. Ovules and pollen grains take part in what process?
   A) germination
   B) asexual reproduction
   C) seed dispersal
   D) sexual reproduction

10. What part of the flower receives the pollen grain from the anther?
    A) sepal
    B) petal
    C) stamen
    D) stigma

Thinking Critically

11. Explain why male cones produce so many pollen grains.

12. Could a seed without an embryo germinate? Explain your answer.

13. Discuss the importance of water in the sexual reproduction of nonvascular plants and ferns.

14. In mosses, why is the sporophyte stage dependent on the gametophyte stage?

15. What features of flowers ensure pollination?

Developing Skills

16. **Making and Using Graphs** Make a bar graph for the following data table about onion seeds. Put days on the horizontal axis and temperature on the vertical axis.

Onion Seed Data						
Temperature (°C)	10	15	20	25	30	35
Days to Germinate	13	7	5	4	4	13

17. **Comparing and Contrasting** Describe the differences and similarities between the fern sporophyte and gametophyte stages.

Chapter ✓Assessment Planner

Portfolio Encourage students to place in their portfolios one or two items of what they consider to be their best work. Examples include:
• Assessment, p. 97
• Make a Model, p. 100
• Activity, p. 105

Performance Additional performance assessments, Performance Task Assessment Lists, and rubrics for evaluating these activities can be found in Glencoe's **Performance Assessment in the Science Classroom.**

18. **Predicting** Observe pictures of flowers or actual flowers and predict how they are pollinated. Explain your prediction.

19. **Interpreting Scientific Illustrations** Using **Figure 16**, sequence these events.
    pollen is trapped on the stigma
    pollen tube reaches the ovule
    fertilization
    pollen released from the anther
    pollen tube forms through the style
    a seed forms

20. **Concept Mapping** Complete this concept map of a typical plant life cycle.

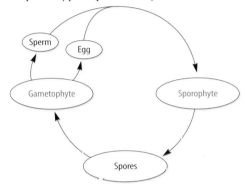

Performance Assessment

21. **Seed Mosaic** Collect several different types of seeds and use them to make a mosaic picture of a flower.

22. **Newspaper Story** Write a newspaper story to tell people about the importance of gravity, water, wind, insects, and other animals in plant life cycles.

TECHNOLOGY

Go to the Glencoe Science Web site at **science.glencoe.com** or use the **Glencoe Science CD-ROM** for additional chapter assessment.

Test Practice

Four groups containing 15 plants each were set up to determine how many flowers were pollinated in a 24-h period. Each plant had five flowers. A botanist recorded the data in the following table.

Plant Group (15 plants per group)	Number of Bees	Number of Birds	Number of Flowers Pollinated after 24 hrs.
1	5	1	16
2	10	1	35
3	15	1	49
4	20	1	73

Study the table and answer the following questions.

1. Which hypothesis probably is being tested in this experiment?
   A) A greater number of bees increases the rate of pollination.
   B) Birds increase the chance of pollination.
   C) A combination of birds and bees gives the best chance of successful pollination.
   D) Increasing the number of plants in a group results in increased pollination.

2. The pollination that is taking place in this experiment is part of which process?
   F) asexual reproduction
   G) sexual reproduction
   H) seed dispersal
   J) germination

Test Practice

The Test-Taking Tip was written by The Princeton Review, the nation's leader in test preparation.
1. A
2. G

Developing Skills

16. Onion Seed Germination

17. Haploid gametophyte stage—small and inconspicuous; diploid sporophyte stage—large and conspicuous; both stages are independent and photosynthetic.
18. Answers will vary depending on flowers observed.
19. 1—pollen is released from the anther; 2—pollen is trapped on the stigma; 3—pollen tube forms through style; 4—pollen tube reaches the ovule; 5—fertilization; 6—a seed forms
20. See student page.

Performance Assessment

21. Seed mosaics will vary depending on seed selection and flower chosen. Look for all parts of a flower in the mosaics. Use **PASC**, p. 135.
22. Stories should include information about plant life cycles and the importance of mechanisms of pollination. Use **PASC**, p. 141.

✓Assessment Resources

📁 **Reproducible Masters**

Chapter Resources Booklet
Chapter Review, pp. 35–36
Chapter Tests, pp. 37–40
Assessment Transparency Activity, p. 47

Glencoe Science Web site
Interactive Tutor
Chapter Quizzes

Glencoe Technology
Assessment Transparency
Interactive CD-ROM Chapter Quizzes
ExamView Pro Test Bank
Vocabulary PuzzleMaker Software
MindJogger Videoquiz

Section/Objectives	Standards		Activities/Features
Chapter Opener	**National**	**State/Local**	**Explore Activity:** Infer how plants lose water, p. 123 **Before You Read,** p. 123
	See p. 5T for a Key to Standards.		
Section 1 Photosynthesis and Respiration ⏱ 2 sessions 📦 1 block 1. **Explain** how plants take in and give off gases. 2. **Compare and contrast** relationships between photosynthesis and respiration. 3. **Discuss** why photosynthesis and respiration are important.	National Content Standards: UCP1, A1, C1, C3		**Health Integration,** p. 125 **MiniLAB:** Inferring What Plants Need to Produce Chlorophyll, p. 126 **Science Online,** p. 128 **Activity:** Stomata in Leaves, p. 132
Section 2 Plant Responses ⏱ 3 sessions 📦 1.5 blocks 1. **Identify** the relationship between a stimulus and a tropism in plants. 2. **Compare and contrast** long-day and short-day plants. 3. **Explain** how plant hormones and responses are related.	National Content Standards: UCP1, A1, C1, C3, G1		**Physics Integration,** p. 134 **Math Skills Activity:** Calculating Averages, p. 135 **MiniLAB:** Observing Ripening, p. 136 **Visualizing Plant Hormones,** p. 137 **Science Online,** p. 138 **Activity:** Tropism in Plants, pp. 140–141 **Science and Language Arts:** Sunkissed: An Indian Legend, pp. 142–143

NATIONAL GEOGRAPHIC

Teacher's Corner

PRODUCTS AVAILABLE FROM GLENCOE
To order call 1-800-334-7344:
CD-ROM
NGS PictureShow: Plants: What It Means to Be Green
Curriculum Kit
GeoKits: Plants

Transparency Set
NGS PicturePack: Plants: What It Means to Be Green
Videodisc
STV: Plants

PRODUCTS AVAILABLE FROM NATIONAL GEOGRAPHIC SOCIETY
To order call 1-800-368-2728:
Video
Photosynthesis: Life Energy

Activity Materials	Reproducible Resources	Section Assessment	Technology
Explore Activity: self-sealing plastic bag, aluminum foil, small potted plant	**Chapter Resources Booklet** Foldable Worksheet, p. 15 Directed Reading Overview, p. 17 Note-taking Worksheets, pp. 29–31	*GLENCOE'S* **ASSESSMENT** *ADVANTAGE*	
MiniLAB: black construction paper, plant with leaves, scissors, tape **Activity:** lettuce in dish of water, coverslip, microscope, microscope slide, salt solution, forceps *Need materials?* Contact Science Kit at 1-800-828-7777 or www.sciencekit.com on the Internet.	**Chapter Resources Booklet** Transparency Activity, p. 40 MiniLAB, p. 3 Enrichment, p. 27 Reinforcement, p. 25 Directed Reading, p. 18 Activity Worksheet, pp. 5–6 Transparency Activity, pp. 43–44 Lab Activity, pp. 9–10 **Science Inquiry Labs,** p. 35 **Life Science Critical Thinking/ Problem Solving,** p. 8	Portfolio Science Journal, p. 127 Performance MiniLAB, p. 127 Skill Builder Activities, p. 131 Content Section Assessment, p. 131	Section Focus Transparency Interactive CD-ROM Teaching Transparency Guided Reading Audio Program
MiniLAB: 2 green bananas, paper bag **Activity:** paper towel, 30 × 30-cm sheet of aluminum foil, water, mustard seeds, marking pen, 1-L clear glass or plastic jar	**Chapter Resources Booklet** Transparency Activity, p. 41 MiniLAB, p. 4 Enrichment, p. 28 Reinforcement, p. 26 Directed Reading, pp. 19, 20 Activity Worksheet, pp. 7–8 Lab Activity, pp. 11–14 **Home and Community Involvement,** p. 45 **Lab Management and Safety,** p. 58	Portfolio Curriculum Connection, p. 138 Reteach, p. 139 Performance MiniLAB, p. 136 Skill Builder Activities, p. 139 Content Section Assessment, p. 139	Section Focus Transparency Interactive CD-ROM Guided Reading Audio Program

End of Chapter Assessment

GLENCOE'S **ASSESSMENT** *ADVANTAGE*

Blackline Masters	Technology	Professional Series
Chapter Resources Booklet Chapter Review, pp. 33–34 Chapter Tests, pp. 35–38 **Standardized Test Practice by The Princeton Review,** pp. 51–54	MindJogger Videoquiz Interactive CD-ROM Vocabulary PuzzleMakers ExamView Pro Test Bank Interactive Lesson Planner Interactive Teacher Edition	Performance Assessment in the Science Classroom (PASC)

Transparencies

Section Focus

Assessment

Teaching

This is a representation of key blackline masters available in the Teacher Classroom Resources. See Resource Manager boxes within the chapter for additional information.

Key to Teaching Strategies

The following designations will help you decide which activities are appropriate for your students.

L1 Level 1 activities should be appropriate for students with learning difficulties.

L2 Level 2 activities should be within the ability range of all students.

L3 Level 3 activities are designed for above-average students.

ELL ELL activities should be within the ability range of English Language Learners.

COOP LEARN Cooperative Learning activities are designed for small group work.

LS Multiple Learning Styles logos are used throughout to indicate strategies that address different learning styles.

P These strategies represent student products that can be placed into a best-work portfolio.

Hands-on Activities

Activity Worksheets

Laboratory Activities

RESOURCE MANAGER

Meeting Different Ability Levels

Content Outline

Reinforcement

Directed Reading

Assessment

Chapter Tests

Enrichment

Spanish Directed Reading

Test Practice Workbook

Chapter Review

Science Content Background

SECTION 1

Photosynthesis and Respiration
The Food-Making Process

During the light-dependent cycle, a chemical reaction occurs between light and chlorophyll. Electrons from this reaction combine with hydrogen ions from water and stored chemical energy called NADPH + H^+. The NADPH is the source of energy for the light-independent cycle. During this cycle, most plants utilize the NADPH energy to synthesize carbohydrates, including glucose, from carbon dioxide.

Respiration, the mechanism by which energy is released from stored fuel, is always preceded by glycolysis. Glycolysis, which occurs in cell cytoplasm, breaks down one glucose molecule into two molecules of pyruvic acid, producing only a small amount of energy. If oxygen is not required or is unavailable during respiration, the process continues as anaerobic reactions, sometimes producing lactic acid. If alcohol is produced, the process is called fermentation. These two inefficient processes extract only a small amount of energy from the pyruvic acid. Aerobic respiration uses oxygen and releases all the energy in the chemical bonds of pyruvic acid. The end products of this process are carbon dioxide, water, and energy.

Jean Paul/FPG International

Student Misconception

Plants do not take in oxygen or give off carbon dioxide.

Refer to the facing page for teaching strategies to address this misconception. Refer to pages 127–129 for content related to this topic.

SECTION 2

Plant Responses
Types of Responses

Plant responses to external stimuli, called tropisms, are slow, permanent, directed growth movements. Plant responses to internal stimuli are faster and reversible.

Plant Hormones

Plant hormones, chemicals produced in specific plant cells, are transported to other sites in the plant, where they cause physiological changes. The hormone auxin causes cell walls to become more elastic and to stretch during active cell growth, controls suppression of lateral bud growth, and prevents leaf abscission, or leaf drop. Ethylene regulates ripening of fruits. Abscisic acid, produced mainly in leaves and fruits, causes buds to become dormant. Gibberellins and cytokinins affect plant growth.

SCIENCE *Online*

For additional content background on this topic, go to the Glencoe Science Web site at science.glencoe.com.

IDENTIFYING Misconceptions

Students may think that . . .

- **Plants do not take in oxygen or give off carbon dioxide.**

- **Photosynthesis is a plant's way of breathing.**

Textbooks and science activity books frequently include diagrams showing a cycle in which plants produce oxygen and take in carbon dioxide and animals take in oxygen while giving off carbon dioxide. From diagrams like these, students draw the conclusion that plants exist to give off oxygen for the benefit of animals. They also equate photosynthesis with breathing because it involves taking in one gas and giving off another. Students who do know that plants can give off carbon dioxide often believe it only occurs in the dark, when the plant cannot get sunlight.

Activity
Write the words *oxygen, carbon dioxide, plant, animal, glucose, light,* and *water* on the board. Ask students to copy the words and then construct concept maps showing how all these terms interrelate. Students will most likely make diagrams showing oxygen moving from plant to animal and carbon dioxide moving from animal to plant. They may not know where to place glucose and water.

Demonstrations
After students have learned that glucose is a product of photosynthesis, ask them why they think plants make glucose. A possible answer may be "Plants make glucose for animals to eat." The following demonstrations will help students understand that plants make glucose for their own use.

- Show students a soaked bean seed. Open the seed and apply iodine as a test for starch. After several minutes the starchy endosperm of the seed should turn blue-black. Use a diagram or snap-lock beads to help explain that starch molecules are chains of glucose molecules. Explain that the bean plant stored starch in the bean seed. Ask students what advantage this might have for the plant. Some students may think that the starch is food for animals, while others may understand that it is food for the embryonic plant.

- Place viable bean seeds in a flask until it is one-third full. Add enough water to completely cover the seeds. Insert a stopper with a glass tube. Attach one end of a length of rubber tubing to the glass tube. Insert the other end into a small flask of limewater. Let the apparatus sit in a warm, well-lighted place. As the seeds absorb water and begin germination, they will metabolize the stored starch in their endosperm and will give off carbon dioxide. Carbon dioxide bubbling slowly through the limewater will cause the liquid to turn cloudy.

After completing the chapter, see *Identifying Misconceptions* in the Study Guide.

CHAPTER 5

Plant Processes

Chapter Vocabulary

What do you think?

Science Journal The picture shows *Elodea* leaves giving off oxygen bubbles. Oxygen is a by-product of the process of photosynthesis, which requires light.

CHAPTER 5
Plant Processes

From crabgrass to giant sequoias, many plants start as small seeds. Some trees may grow to be more than 20 m tall. One tree can be cut up to produce many pieces of lumber. Where does all that wood come from? You may have seen a plant on a windowsill with all its leaves growing toward the window. Why do they grow that way? In this chapter, find the answers to these questions. In addition, learn how plants are essential to the survival of all animals on Earth—including you!

What do you think?

Science Journal Look at the picture below with a classmate. Discuss what you think this might be or what is happening. Here's a hint: *This would never happen without light.* Write your answer or best guess in your Science Journal.

Theme Connection

Systems and Interactions The systems and structures involved in the processes of photosynthesis and respiration work together. Through interactions, these processes, along with the stimuli-response mechanisms discussed in the second part of the chapter, allow a plant to maintain homeostasis.

Plants are similar to other living things because they are made of cells, reproduce, make and use substances, and need water. If you forgot to water a houseplant, what do you think would happen? From your own experiences, you probably know that the houseplant would wilt. Do the following activity to discover one way plants lose water.

Infer how plants lose water

1. Obtain a self-sealing plastic bag, some aluminum foil, and a small potted plant from your teacher.

2. Using the foil, carefully cover the soil around the plant in the pot. Place the potted plant in the plastic bag.

3. Seal the bag and place it in a sunny window. Wash your hands.

4. Look at the plant at the same time every day for a few days.

Observe

In your Science Journal, describe what happens in the bag. If enough water is lost by a plant and not replaced, predict what will happen to the plant.

Before You Read

FOLDABLES
Reading & Study
Skills

Making a Compare and Contrast Study Fold As you study plant processes, use the following Foldable to help you compare and contrast plant respiration and animal respiration.

1. Place a sheet of paper in front of you so the long side is at the top. Fold the paper in half from top to bottom.

2. Write *Respiration* across the front, as shown.

3. Unfold the paper. Draw a picture of an animal on the top half and a plant on the bottom half. Leave room to write below the drawings.

4. Before you read the chapter write what you know about animal respiration and plant respiration on the appropriate flaps.

5. As you read the chapter, add to or change your information.

Respiration

Purpose Use the Explore Activity to introduce students to plant processes. Inform students that they will be learning more about plant processes as they read the chapter. ELL **IS Kinesthetic**

Preparation The seedlings should be large enough to transpire an observable amount of water.

Materials large self-sealing plastic bags, seedling plants in pots, aluminum foil

Teaching Strategies

- Have students record their hypotheses about what will happen after the plants are sealed in the plastic bags.

- Discuss why the soil is covered with foil. *to reduce evaporation from the soil*

Observe

Students should explain that most of the water that gathers in the bag came from the plant. The plant will wilt or even die if it loses too much water.

✔*Assessment*

Process Have students diagram the pathway of water through a plant, drawing on prior knowledge to label their diagrams with terms such as *roots*, *stems*, *vascular tissue*, and *xylem*. Use **Performance Assessment in the Science Classroom**, p. 127.

Before You Read

FOLDABLES
Reading & Study
Skills

Dinah Zike Study Fold

Purpose Students make and use a Foldable to collect information on plant respiration. Students use this information to compare and contrast plant and animal respiration. How are they the same? How do they differ?

📁 For additional help, see Foldables Worksheet, p. 15 in **Chapter Resources Booklet,** or go to the Glencoe Science Web site at **science.glencoe.com.** See After You Read in the Study Guide at the end of this chapter.

SECTION

Photosynthesis and Respiration

SECTION

Photosynthesis and Respiration

As You Read

What You'll Learn

- **Explain** how plants take in and give off gases.
- **Compare and contrast** relationships between photosynthesis and respiration.
- **Discuss** why photosynthesis and respiration are important.

Vocabulary

stomata   photosynthesis
chlorophyll   respiration

Why It's Important

Understanding photosynthesis and respiration in plants will help you understand how life is maintained on Earth.

Figure 1
Plants take in raw materials through their roots and leaves and get rid of wastes through their leaves.

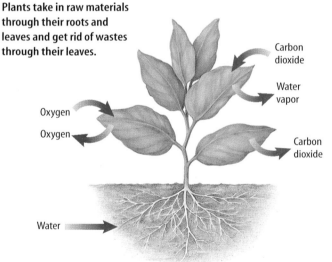

Carbon dioxide

Water vapor

Oxygen

Oxygen

Carbon dioxide

Water

Taking in Raw Materials

Sitting in the cool shade under a tree, you finish eating your lunch. The food you eat is one of the raw materials that you need to grow. Oxygen is another. It enters your lungs and eventually reaches every cell in your body. Your cells use oxygen to help release the energy from the food that you eat. The process that uses oxygen to release the energy from food produces carbon dioxide and water as wastes. These wastes move in your blood to your lungs where they are removed as gases when you exhale. You look up at the tree and wonder, "Does a tree need to eat? Does it use oxygen? How does a tree get rid of wastes?"

Movement of Materials in Plants No one packs a sack lunch for the tree. Trees and other plants don't take in foods the way you do. Plants make their own foods using the raw materials water, carbon dioxide, and inorganic chemicals in the soil. Just like you, plants also produce waste products.

Most of the water used by plants is taken in through roots, as shown in **Figure 1.** Water moves into root cells and then up through the plant to where it is used. When you pull up a plant, some of its roots are damaged. If you replant it, the plant will need extra water until new roots grow to replace those that were damaged.

Leaves, instead of lungs, are where most gas exchange occurs in plants. Most of the water taken in through the roots exits through the leaves of a plant. Carbon dioxide, oxygen, and water vapor exit and enter the plant through the leaf. The leaf's structure helps explain how it functions in gas exchange.

Section ✓ Assessment Planner

PORTFOLIO
Science Journal, p. 127
PERFORMANCE ASSESSMENT
MiniLAB, p. 127
Skill Builder Activities, p. 131
See page 146 for more options.

CONTENT ASSESSMENT
Section, p. 131
Challenge, p. 131
Chapter, pp. 146–147

Figure 2
A leaf's structure determines its function. Food is made in the inner layers. Most stomata are found on the lower epidermis.

Upper epidermis
Cuticle
Palisade layer
Spongy layer
Lower epidermis
Guard cells

A Closed stomata

B Open stomata

Leaf Structure and Function A leaf is made up of many different layers, as shown in **Figure 2.** The outer cell layer of the leaf is the epidermis. A waxy cuticle that helps keep the leaf from drying out covers the epidermis. Because the epidermis is nearly transparent, sunlight—which is used to make food—reaches the cells inside the leaf. If you examine the epidermis under a microscope, you will see that it contains many small openings. These openings, called **stomata** (stoh MAH tuh) (singular, *stoma*), act as doorways for raw materials such as carbon dioxide, water vapor, and waste gases to enter and exit the leaf. Stomata also are found on the stems of many plants. More than 90 percent of the water plants take in through their roots is lost through the stomata. In one day, a growing tomato plant can lose up to 1 L of water.

Two cells called guard cells surround each stoma and control its size. As water moves into the guard cells, they swell and bend apart, opening a stoma. When guard cells lose water, they deflate, closing the stoma. **Figures 2A** and **2B** show closed and open stomata.

Stomata usually are open during the day when most plants need to take in raw materials to make food. They usually are closed at night when food making slows down. Stomata also close when a plant is losing too much water. This adaptation conserves water, because less water vapor escapes from the leaf.

Inside the leaf are two layers of cells, the spongy layer and the palisade layer. Carbon dioxide and water vapor, which are needed in the food-making process, fill the spaces of the spongy layer. Most of the food is made in the palisade layer.

Health
INTEGRATION

Vitamins are substances needed for good health. You get most of the vitamins you need from the plants you eat. Research to learn about four vitamins and the plant foods you would need to eat to get them. Display your results on a poster.

②Teach

Taking in Raw Materials

Quick Demo
Demonstrate how guard cells change shape. Show students an uninflated oblong balloon along whose length you have placed a strip of cellophane tape. Blow up the balloon, and again show it to the class. Explain that when the balloon is inflated, its shape changes just like a guard cell's shape changes when it swells with water. The guard cell takes this shape because it has a thickened cell wall on the side next to the stoma.

Make a Model
Have students use two balloons like the one in the demo above to model how two guard cells bracket a stoma. Point out the tape, which represents the thickened cell wall that adjoins the stoma.

Health
INTEGRATION

Answer Answers will vary, but should include four vitamins, their sources, and their functions.

Visual Learning

Figure 2 Make sure students understand that the primary function of the stomata is to allow for the exchange of gases by the plant.

Resource Manager

Chapter Resources Booklet
  Transparency Activity, p. 40
  Directed Reading for Content Mastery, pp. 17, 18
  Note-taking Worksheets, pp. 29–31

Taking in Raw Materials, continued

IDENTIFYING
Misconceptions

Many students will think that all plant cells contain chlorophyll. Explain that cells deep within the plant where light does not penetrate and cells in underground plant parts lack this pigment and are not directly involved in photosynthesis. Ask: **What parts of a tree probably do not contain chlorophyll?** Woody parts that are not green, such as the stem (trunk), roots, and branches, do not contain chlorophyll.

Extension

Some students might investigate which plant pigments cause specific plant colors. Suggest that students study trees or other plants that turn particular colors in your area of the country. Anthocyanins are red; carotenoids are yellow. Leaves change color in fall because declining temperatures and short days lead to a breakdown of chlorophyll which allows other pigments to become visible. L2

✔ Reading Check

Answer They contain a green pigment called chlorophyll.

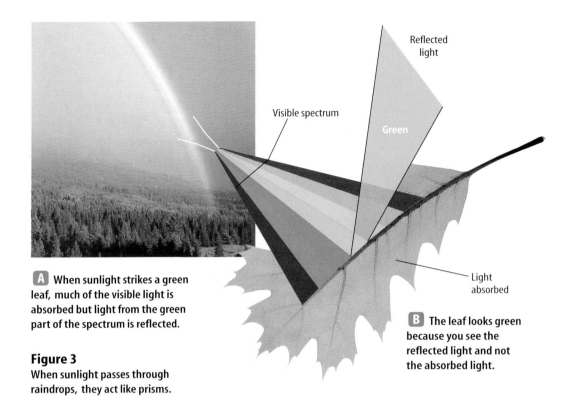

A When sunlight strikes a green leaf, much of the visible light is absorbed but light from the green part of the spectrum is reflected.

Figure 3
When sunlight passes through raindrops, they act like prisms. Light separates into the colors of the visible spectrum. You see a rainbow when this happens.

B The leaf looks green because you see the reflected light and not the absorbed light.

Chloroplasts and Plant Pigments If you look closely at the leaf in **Figure 2,** you'll see that some of the cells contain small, green structures called chloroplasts. Most leaves look green because their cells contain so many chloroplasts. Chloroplasts are green because they contain a green pigment called **chlorophyll** (KLOR uh fihl).

✔ Reading Check   *Why are chloroplasts green?*

As shown in **Figure 3,** light from the Sun contains all colors of the visible spectrum. A pigment is a substance that reflects a particular part of the visible spectrum and absorbs the rest. When you see a green leaf, you are seeing green light energy reflected from chlorophyll. Most of the other colors of the spectrum, especially red and blue, are absorbed by chlorophyll. In the spring and summer, most leaves have so much chlorophyll that it hides all other pigments. In fall, the chlorophyll in some leaves breaks down and the leaves change color as other pigments become visible. Pigments, especially chlorophyll, are important to plants because the light energy that they absorb is used to make food. For plants, this food-making process—photosynthesis—happens in the chloroplasts.

LAB DEMONSTRATION

Purpose to show that the colors we see are the colors objects reflect

Materials prism, light source, objects of different colors

Preparation Collect materials and have them grouped together to save time.

Procedure Place a prism in a bright light source so that the colors of white light entering the prism separate. Place objects of different colors in the paths of the separated beams.

Expected Outcome Objects will absorb all colors except the color they reflect.

✔ Assessment

What would happen if you placed a red rose with green leaves in a red beam of light in a darkened room? The rose would appear red and the leaves would appear black.

The Food-Making Process

Photosynthesis (foh toh SIHN thuh suhs) is the process during which a plant's chlorophyll traps light energy and sugars are produced. In plants, photosynthesis occurs only in cells with chloroplasts. For example, photosynthesis occurs only in a carrot plant's lacy green leaves, shown in **Figure 4.** Because a carrot's root cells lack chlorophyll and normally do not receive light, they can't perform photosynthesis. But excess sugar produced in the leaves is stored in the familiar orange root that you and many animals eat.

Besides light, plants also need the raw materials carbon dioxide and water for photosynthesis. The overall chemical equation for photosynthesis is shown below. What happens to each of the raw materials in the process?

$$6CO_2 + 6H_2O + \text{light energy} \xrightarrow{\text{chlorophyll}} C_6H_{12}O_6 + 6O_2$$

carbon dioxide · water · glucose · oxygen

Light-Dependent Reactions Some of the chemical reactions that take place during photosynthesis need light but others do not. Those that need light can be called the light-dependent reactions of photosynthesis. During light-dependent reactions, chlorophyll and other pigments trap light energy that eventually will be stored in sugar molecules. Light energy causes water molecules, which were taken up by the roots, to split into oxygen and hydrogen. The oxygen leaves the plant through the stomata. This is the oxygen that you breathe. Leftover hydrogen is used in photosynthesis reactions that occur when there is no light.

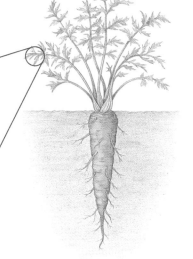

Figure 4
Because they contain chloroplasts, cells in the leaf of the carrot plant are the sites for photosynthesis.

Mini LAB

Inferring What Plants Need to Produce Chlorophyll

Procedure

1. Cut two pieces of **black construction paper** large enough so that each one completely covers one leaf on a **plant.**
2. Cut a square out of the center of each piece of paper.
3. Sandwich the leaf between the two paper pieces and **tape** the pieces together along their edges.
4. Place the plant in a sunny area. Wash your hands.
5. After seven days, carefully remove the paper and observe the leaf.

Analysis
In your **Science Journal,** describe how the color of the areas covered by paper compare to the areas not covered. Infer why this happened.

The Food-Making Process

Mini LAB

Purpose to determine if plants require light to produce and maintain chlorophyll L2

IS Kinesthetic

Materials black construction paper, plant, tape, scissors

Teaching Strategy Record results immediately upon removing the construction paper.

Analysis
The covered area should be less green than the uncovered area. Light is needed in the production and maintenance of chlorophyll.

✔Assessment

Process Have students suggest a way in which they could determine why they got their results. Use **PASC,** p. 99.

Science Journal

Carbon Dioxide Have students research how the buildup of carbon dioxide in the atmosphere might affect photosynthesis. Have them summarize their findings in their Science Journals. Increased carbon dioxide may correlate with increased photosynthesis in certain localities such as rain forests and marine environments with large amounts of plankton. L2 P

Resource Manager

Chapter Resources Booklet
  MiniLAB, p. 3
  Lab Activity, pp. 9–10
Science Inquiry Labs, p. 35

The Food-Making Process, continued

Quick Demo

Place a sprig of *Elodea* in a test tube with 5 mL of water and 1 mL of bromothymol blue indicator. Have students note the yellow color. Place the tube in strong light. The solution should turn blue as *Elodea* takes up carbon dioxide in light.

IDENTIFYING Misconceptions

Students may think that plants do not take in oxygen or give off carbon dioxide. Refer to page 122F for teaching strategies that address this misconception.

Fun Fact

A place where food is stored or used in a plant is called a sink. Depending on the plant, roots, stems, and leaves can be sinks.

Use Science Words

Word Meaning Have students look up the word *photosynthesis* and relate the meaning of its word parts to the process. *Photo* means light; *synthesis* means the combining of parts to make a whole. So photosynthesis is the process that uses light to combine carbon dioxide and water into a larger sugar molecule.

Research Besides glucose, what other sugars do plants produce? Visit the Glencoe Science Web site at **science.glencoe.com** for more information about plant sugars. In your Science Journal list three sugars produced by plants.

Light-Independent Reactions Reactions that don't need light are called the light-independent reactions of photosynthesis. Carbon dioxide, the raw material from the air, is used in these reactions. The light energy trapped during the light-dependent reactions is used to combine carbon dioxide and hydrogen to make sugars. One important sugar that is made is glucose. The chemical bonds that hold glucose and other sugars together are stored energy. **Figure 5** compares what happens during each stage of photosynthesis.

What happens to the oxygen and glucose that were made during photosynthesis? Most of the oxygen from photosynthesis is a waste product and is released through stomata. Glucose is the main form of food for plant cells. A plant usually produces more glucose than it can use. Excess glucose is stored in plants as other sugars and starches. When you eat carrots, as well as beets, potatoes, or onions, you are eating the stored product of photosynthesis.

Glucose also is the basis of a plant's structure. You don't grow larger by breathing in and using carbon dioxide. However, that's exactly what plants do as they take in carbon dioxide gas and convert it into glucose. Cellulose, an important part of plant cell walls, is made from glucose. Leaves, stems, and roots are made of cellulose and other substances produced using glucose. The products of photosynthesis are used by plants to grow.

Figure 5
Photosynthesis includes two sets of reactions, the light-dependent reactions and the light-independent reactions.

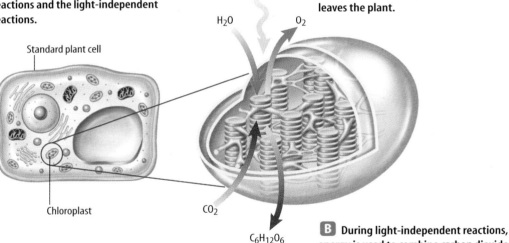

Sunlight

Standard plant cell

Chloroplast

H_2O O_2

CO_2

$C_6H_{12}O_6$

A During light-dependent reactions, light energy is trapped and water is split into hydrogen and oxygen. Oxygen leaves the plant.

B During light-independent reactions, energy is used to combine carbon dioxide and hydrogen to make glucose and other sugars.

Inclusion Strategies

Gifted Have students form an acrostic using the letters of the word *photosynthesis* to describe the process. L3

Internet Addresses

_____
_____
_____
_____
Explore the Glencoe Science Web site at **science.glencoe.com** to find out more about topics in this section.

Figure 6
Tropical rain forests
contain large numbers of
photosynthetic plants.

Importance of Photosynthesis Why is photosynthesis important to living things? First, photosynthesis produces food. Organisms that carry on photosynthesis provide food directly or indirectly for nearly all the other organisms on Earth. Second, photosynthetic organisms, like the plants in **Figure 6,** use carbon dioxide and release oxygen. This removes carbon dioxide from the atmosphere and adds oxygen to it. Most organisms, including humans, need oxygen to stay alive. As much as 90 percent of the oxygen entering the atmosphere today is a result of photosynthesis.

The Breakdown of Food

Look at the photograph in **Figure 7.** Do the fox and the plants in the photograph have anything in common? They don't look alike, but the fox and the plants are made of cells that break down food, and release energy in a process called respiration. How does this happen?

Respiration is a series of chemical reactions that breaks down food molecules and releases energy. Respiration occurs in cells of most organisms. The breakdown of food might or might not require oxygen. Respiration that uses oxygen to break down food chemically is called aerobic respiration. In plants and many organisms that have one or more cells, a nucleus, and other organelles, aerobic respiration occurs in the mitochondria (singular, *mitochondrion*). The overall chemical equation for aerobic respiration is shown below.

$$C_6H_{12}O_6 + 6O_2 \longrightarrow 6CO_2 + 6H_2O + \text{energy}$$

glucose   oxygen   carbon   water
                           dioxide

Figure 7
You know that animals such as this red fox carry on respiration, but so do all the plants that surround the fox.

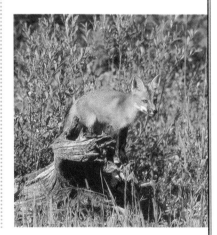

Discussion

Write the general equation for photosynthesis on the board. Use one color of chalk for the raw materials and another for the products. During the discussion, guide students to an understanding of what the equation means in terms of energy capture and conversion. ⌐L2⌐
IS **Visual-Spatial and Interpersonal**

The Breakdown of Food

Quick Demo

Demonstrate respiration in yeast by adding 1 mL of bromothymol blue to a mixture of 1 mL sugar syrup (0.5 g of granulated sugar in 100 mL water), 5 mL water, and 2 mL yeast suspension. The color will change from blue to green and eventually to yellow as the yeasts respire and give off carbon dioxide.

Use an Analogy

Use these analogies to help clarify the processes of photosynthesis and respiration. A chloroplast where photosynthesis occurs is like a factory in which small parts are used to assemble a larger whole. A mitochondrion, in which respiration occurs, is like a powerhouse that uses fuel as an energy source for the production of goods.

Resource Manager

Chapter Resources Booklet
Transparency Activity, pp. 43–44

Life Science Critical Thinking/Problem Solving, p. 8

Cultural **Diversity**

Severo Ochoa Have students research the efforts of Spanish-American biochemist Severo Ochoa (1905–1993). He received the Nobel prize with Arthur Kornberg in 1959 for his work on RNA. Much of his scientific work was on describing the mechanisms of the citric acid cycle and identifying the functions of key enzymes. Have them present their findings in a short report to the class.

The Breakdown of Food, continued

IDENTIFYING Misconceptions

Some students may think that plant cells contain chloroplasts, but not mitochondria. Be sure that students understand that plant cells do include mitochondria in which the breakdown of glucose produced through photosynthesis provides energy for the cell.

✔ Reading Check

Answer all living things

Teacher FYI

Fermentation is a type of anaerobic respiration. Anaerobic means "without oxygen." It results in increased waste products that build up in cells. Also, it is a less efficient method of respiration and cannot produce as much energy as aerobic respiration. To perform the same amount of work, a cell using fermentation must consume up to 20 times more glucose per second than a cell using aerobic respiration. In the human body, if the amount of oxygen delivered to muscle cells during strenuous activity is inadequate, the cells temporarily use fermentation. The waste products that build up in the cells add to muscle fatigue.

Figure 8
Aerobic respiration takes place in the mitochondria of plant cells.

B Oxygen is used in the mitochondrion to break down these two molecules.

A In the cytoplasm, each glucose molecule is broken down into two smaller molecules.

C Water and carbon dioxide are waste products of respiration.

Figure 9
Plants use the energy released from the respiration of food to carry out many functions.

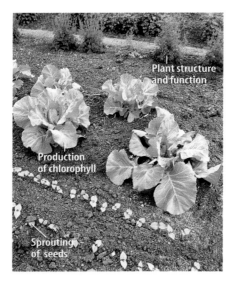

Plant structure and function

Production of chlorophyll

Sprouting of seeds

130 ◆ B CHAPTER 5 Plant Processes

Aerobic Respiration Before aerobic respiration begins, glucose molecules are broken down into two smaller molecules. This happens in the cytoplasm. The smaller molecules then enter a mitochondrion, where aerobic respiration takes place. Oxygen is used in the reactions that break the small molecules into the waste products water and carbon dioxide. The reactions also release energy. Every cell in the organism needs this energy. **Figure 8** shows aerobic respiration in a plant cell.

Importance of Respiration Although food contains energy, it is not in a form that can be used by cells. Respiration changes food energy into a form all cells can use. This energy drives the life processes of almost all organisms on Earth.

✔ Reading Check *What organisms use respiration?*

Plants use energy produced by respiration to transport sugars and open and close stomata. Some of the energy is used to produce substances needed for photosynthesis, such as chlorophyll. When seeds sprout, they use energy from the respiration of stored food in the seed. **Figure 9** shows uses of energy in plants.

The waste product carbon dioxide is also important. Aerobic respiration returns carbon dioxide to the atmosphere, where it can be used again by plants and some other organisms for photosynthesis.

Resource Manager

Chapter Resources Booklet
Enrichment, p. 27
Reinforcement, p. 25
Performance Assessment in the Science Classroom, p. 59

Visual Learning

Figure 8 Have students trace the pathways of the reactants and products of respiration in the mitochondrion. Help them understand that the arrows indicate materials moving in and out of the organelle.

Table 1 Comparing Photosynthesis and Aerobic Respiration

	Energy	Raw Materials	End Products	Where
Photosynthesis	stored	water and carbon dioxide	glucose and oxygen	cells with chlorophyll
Aerobic Respiration	released	glucose and oxygen	water and carbon dioxide	cells with mitochondria

Comparison of Photosynthesis and Respiration

Look back in the chapter to find the equations for photosynthesis and aerobic respiration. Do they resemble each other? If you look closely, you can see that overall, aerobic respiration is almost the reverse of photosynthesis. Photosynthesis combines carbon dioxide and water by using light energy. The end products are glucose (food) and oxygen. During photosynthesis, energy is stored in food. Photosynthesis occurs only in cells that contain chlorophyll, such as those in the leaves of plants. Aerobic respiration combines oxygen and food to release the energy in the chemical bonds of the food. The end products of aerobic respiration are energy, carbon dioxide, and water. Because all plant cells contain mitochondria, all plant cells and any cell with mitochondria can use the process of aerobic respiration. **Table 1** compares photosynthesis and aerobic respiration.

Section Assessment

1. Explain how a leaf exchanges carbon dioxide and water vapor.
2. Why are photosynthesis and respiration important?
3. What must happen to glucose molecules before respiration begins?
4. Compare the number of organisms that respire to those that photosynthesize.
5. **Think Critically** Humidity is water vapor in the air. How do plants contribute to the amount of humidity in the air?

Skill Builder Activities

6. **Forming Hypotheses** White potatoes sometimes have green areas on their skins. Hypothesize what process can take place in the green part but not in the white part of the potato. **For more help, refer to the** Science Skill Handbook.
7. **Solving One-Step Equations** How many CO_2 molecules result from the aerobic respiration of a glucose molecule ($C_6H_{12}O_6$)? Refer to the equation in this section. **For more help, refer to the** Math Skill Handbook.

Comparison of Photosynthesis and Respiration

Activity

Have students make up songs that include the equations for photosynthesis and respiration. Then have them sing their songs to the class.

③ Assess

Reteach

Have students place one plant in the light and another in a dark area while keeping all other variables constant. Have them observe the plants once each day for a week. Then have students explain any changes that occur.

Challenge

How many atoms of oxygen are needed to produce six molecules of glucose? 6 atoms of oxygen × 6 molecules = 36 atoms

✔ Assessment

Performance Using molecular model kits, have groups of students make the reactants of either photosynthesis or aerobic respiration. Exchange reactants between opposite groups and have them make the products of those reactants. Students should find that the reactants of one are the products of the other. Use **Performance Assessment in the Science Classroom**, p. 123.

Answers to Section Assessment

1. Carbon dioxide and water vapor are exchanged by diffusion through the stomata on leaf surfaces.
2. Photosynthesis provides the basic food source used by most organisms on Earth, either directly or indirectly. Respiration releases the energy stored in the product of photosynthesis (glucose) for use in cells.
3. Glucose molecules must be broken down into simpler molecules in the cytoplasm before respiration can begin.
4. Only organisms that contain chlorophyll photosynthesize, but all organisms respire.
5. Plants transpire water from their leaves, contributing water vapor to the air.
6. Photosynthesis can occur in the green areas of a potato but not in the white areas.
7. For every sugar molecule respired, six carbon dioxide molecules are produced.

Activity

Purpose
Students observe the activity of stomata in green plants. L2 ELL COOP LEARN
IS Visual-Spatial

Process Skills observing and inferring, recognizing cause and effect

Time Required 45 minutes

Alternate Materials Celery or onion epidermis may be substituted for lettuce.

Safety Precaution Emphasize that students should be careful when using microscopes.

Teaching Strategy Remind students that osmosis is diffusion of water through a semipermeable membrane.

Troubleshooting If an alternative tissue is used, try the activity beforehand to make sure observations will be appropriate.

Answers to Questions
1. the wet mount with plain water
2. Salt water causes water to leave the guard cells, causing them to become limp and close.
3. Stomata provide an entry and exit site in the leaf for gases such as carbon dioxide.

✔Assessment

Performance To further assess students' understanding of stomata, have them repeat the activity using one of the alternate materials and describe the outcome. Use **Performance Assessment in the Science Classroom**, p. 97.

Activity

Stomata in Leaves

Stomata open and close, which allows gases into and out of a leaf. These openings are usually invisible without the use of a microscope. Do this activity to see some stomata.

What You'll Investigate
Where are stomata in lettuce leaves?

Materials
lettuce in dish of water   microscope slide
coverslip   salt solution
microscope   forceps

Goals
■ **Describe** guard cells and stomata.
■ **Infer** the conditions that make stomata open and close.

Safety Precautions

WARNING: *Do not eat or taste any of the materials in the activity.*

Procedure
1. Copy the Stomata Data table into your Science Journal.
2. From a head of lettuce, tear off a piece of an outer, crisp, green leaf.
3. Bend the piece of leaf in half and carefully use a pair of forceps to peel off some of the epidermis, the transparent tissue that covers a leaf. Prepare a wet mount of this tissue.
4. **Examine** your prepared slide under low and high power on the microscope.
5. **Count** the total number of stomata in your field of view and then count the number of open stomata. Enter these numbers in the data table.

Communicating Your Data

Data should be similar throughout the class. Differences might occur if students don't all use the same side of the leaf tissue. Upper and lower leaf surfaces often have different numbers of stomata.

Stomata Data		
	Wet Mount	**Salt-Solution Mount**
Total Number of Stomata	50	60
Number of Open Stomata	40	5
Percent Open	80	8

6. Make a second slide of the lettuce leaf epidermis. This time place a few drops of salt solution on the leaf instead of water.
7. Repeat steps 4 and 5.
8. **Calculate** the percent of open stomata using the following equation:

$$\frac{\text{number of open stomata}}{\text{total number of stomata}} \times 100 = \text{percent open}$$

Conclude and Apply
1. Determine which slide preparation had a greater percentage of open stomata.
2. **Infer** why fewer stomata were open in the salt-solution mount.
3. What can you infer about the function of stomata in a leaf?

Communicating Your Data

Collect data from other students in your class. Compare your data to the class data. Discuss any differences you find and why these differences occurred. **For more help, refer to the** Science Skill Handbook.

Resource Manager

Chapter Resources Booklet
Activity Worksheet, pp. 5–6

2 Plant Responses

What are plant responses?

It's dark. You're alone in a room watching a horror film on television. Suddenly, the telephone near you rings. You jump, and your heart begins to beat faster. You've just responded to a stimulus. A stimulus is anything in the environment that causes a response in an organism. The response often involves movement either toward the stimulus or away from the stimulus. A stimulus may come from outside (external) or inside (internal) the organism. The ringing telephone is an example of an external stimulus. It caused you to jump, which is a response. Your beating heart is a response to an internal stimulus. Internal stimuli are usually chemicals produced by organisms. Many of these chemicals are hormones. Hormones are substances made in one part of an organism for use somewhere else in the organism.

All living organisms, including plants, respond to stimuli. Many different chemicals are known to act as hormones in plants. These internal stimuli have a variety of effects on plant growth and function. Plants respond to external stimuli such as touch, light, and gravity. Some responses, such as the response of the Venus's-flytrap plant in **Figure 10,** are rapid. Other plant responses are slower because they involve changes in growth.

As You Read

What **You'll Learn**

- **Identify** the relationship between a stimulus and a tropism in plants.
- **Compare and contrast** long-day and short-day plants.
- **Explain** how plant hormones and responses are related.

Vocabulary

tropism
auxin
photoperiodism
long-day plant
short-day plant
day-neutral plant

Why **It's Important**

You will be able to grow healthier plants if you understand how they respond to certain stimuli.

Figure 10
A Venus's-flytrap has three small trigger hairs on the surface of its toothed leaves. When two hairs are touched at the same time, the plant responds by closing its trap in less than 1 second.

SECTION 2 Plant Responses **B ◆ 133**

SECTION

Plant Responses

1 Motivate

Bellringer Transparency

Display the Section Focus Transparency for Section 2. Use the accompanying Transparency Activity Master. L2 ELL

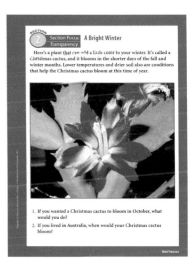

Tie to Prior Knowledge

Draw on the board a simple sketch of a flowering plant. Have students identify as many parts of the plant as they can and name the functions of those parts.

Section ✓*Assessment* Planner

PORTFOLIO
Curriculum Connection, p. 138
Reteach, p. 139

PERFORMANCE ASSESSMENT
Try at Home MiniLAB, p. 136
Skill Builder Activities, p. 139
See page 146 for more options.

CONTENT ASSESSMENT
Section, p. 139
Challenge, p. 139
Chapter, pp. 146–147

Plant Responses

Discussion

Have students brainstorm a list of possible ways to determine the cause of various plant responses. Lead them to understand the difference between external and internal stimuli. External stimuli include touch, light, and gravity. Internal stimuli include hormones.

Tropisms

Activity

Small groups of students can grow a pea plant from seed. As the plant begins to grow, they place a stick in the pot. The stem and tendrils will respond by growing around the stick. Have students identify the type of response this illustrates. thigmatropism Challenge students to record and graph the growth of the pea plant. L3

Quick Demo

Bring a Venus's-flytrap to class to demonstrate nastic movements. The trap of the Venus's-flytrap is triggered when three or more of the sensitive hairs on the upper surfaces of the hinged leaves are touched. Use the fine tip of a needle or pencil to manipulate the hairs.

Physics
INTEGRATION

Students may propose various experiments. Look for those that include a control and a method that would include a true test of the effects of gravity.

Figure 11
Tropisms are responses to external stimuli.

A The pea plant's tendrils respond to touch by coiling around things.

B This plant is growing toward the light, an example of positive phototropism.

C This plant was turned on its side. With the roots visible, you can see that they are showing positive gravitropism.

Physics
INTEGRATION

Gravity is a stimulus that affects how plants grow. Can plants grow without gravity? In space the force of gravity is low. Write a paragraph in your Science Journal that describes your idea for an experiment aboard a space shuttle to test how low gravity affects plant growth.

Tropisms

Some responses of a plant to an external stimuli are called tropisms. A **tropism** (TROH pih zum) can be seen as movement caused by a change in growth and can be positive or negative. For example, plants might grow toward a stimulus—a positive tropism—or away from a stimulus—a negative tropism.

Touch One stimulus that can result in a change in a plant's growth is touch. When the pea plant, shown in **Figure 11A,** touches a solid object, it responds by growing faster on one side of its stem than on the other side. As a result the stem bends and twists around any object it touches.

Light Did you ever see a plant leaning toward a window? Light is an important stimulus to plants. When a plant responds to light, the cells on the side of the plant opposite the light get longer than the cells facing the light. Because of this uneven growth, the plant bends toward the light. This response causes the leaves to turn in such a way that they can absorb more light. When a plant grows toward light it is called a positive response to light, as shown in **Figure 11B.**

Gravity Plants respond to gravity. The downward growth of plant roots is a positive response to gravity, as shown in **Figure 11C.** A stem growing upward is a negative response to gravity. Plants also may respond to electricity, temperature, and darkness.

Visual Learning

Figure 11 Use these photographs to launch a discussion on plant responses caused by various external stimuli. **Where have you seen responses such as these? How might they help a plant meet its needs?** Answers will vary. Many of these responses help a plant grow toward the light, their source of energy.

Teacher FYI

Unlike tropisms, nastic movements are independent of the direction of the stimulus. The most common are "sleep" or nyctinastic movements. These movements position leaves of some plants horizontally during the daylight and vertically at night. This response results from turgor pressure changes in cells.

Plant Hormones

Hormones control the changes in growth that result from tropisms and affect other plant growth. Plants often need only millionths of a gram of a hormone to stimulate a response.

Ethylene Many plants produce the hormone ethylene (EH thuh leen) gas and release it into the air around them. This means that ethylene produced by one plant can cause a response in a nearby plant. One plant response to ethylene causes a layer of cells to form between a leaf and the stem. That's why most leaves fall from plants.

Ethylene is produced in cells of ripening fruit, which stimulates the ripening process. Commercially, fruits such as oranges and bananas are picked when they are still green. During shipping the green fruits are exposed to ethylene and they ripen.

Math Skills Activity

Calculating Averages

Example Problem

What is the average height of control bean seedlings after 14 days?

Solution

1 *This is what you know:*
height of control seedlings after 14 days
number of control seedlings

2 *This is what you need to find:*
average height of control seedlings after14 days

3 *This is what you must do:*
total the heights of all control seedlings
$15 + 12 + 14 + 13 + 10 + 11 = 75$ cm

4 *Divide the total height by the total number of control seedlings:*
75 cm/6
average height of control seedlings = 12.5 cm

Practice Problem

Calculate the average height of seedlings treated with gibberellin.

For more help, refer to the Math Skill Handbook.

Control seedlings

Gibberellin-treated seedlings

SECTION 2   Plant Responses   **B** ◆ **135**

Resource Manager

Chapter Resources Booklet

Transparency Activity, p. 41

Directed Reading for Content Mastery, pp. 19, 20

Mathematics Skill Activities, p. 25

✔ Active Reading

Quickwrites This strategy, sometimes called freewrites, lets students use spontaneous writing to discover what they already know. Have students write a list of ideas about a topic, then share these ideas with the class. Next, have students write their ideas freely in a paragraph without worrying about punctuation, spelling, and grammar. Have students use a Quickwrite to share ideas about plant responses.

Plant Hormones

Activity

Use an activity kit for rapidly growing plants of the genus *Brassica*, available from biological supply houses, to demonstrate plant responses to hormones. These plants can grow from seed to flower in about 15 days.

Discussion

Review the names of the parts of flowering plants with students. Ask if they think every structure responds equally to every stimulus. Possible answer: different parts of a flowering plant respond to different stimuli.

Math Skills Activity

National Math Standards
Correlation to Mathematics Objectives
1, 2, 4, 6, 8, 9

Teaching Suggestion:

Students may be asked to provide the following information from the graph:

a. range of heights for control seedlings

b. range of heights for gibberellin-treated seedlings

c. percent difference in height of gibberellin-treated seedlings compared to control seedlings

It may be necessary to help students interpolate the height values on the graph.

Answer to Practice Problem

135 cm ÷ 6 = 22.5 cm

Note: Students' answers may differ slightly from the answer provided. Accept answers that are reasonably close. Variation in answers may be caused by differing interpolations of seedling heights as read from the graph.

Plant Hormones, continued

✔ Reading Check

Answer Auxin is the hormone that causes stems and leaves to exhibit positive phototropism.

Quick Demo

Obtain two coleus cuttings. Apply a rooting hormone to one cutting before planting both stems. After several days, have students observe the roots of both stems and explain the results. The cutting with the hormone should show greater root growth due to the presence of the chemical.

TRY AT HOME
Mini LAB

Purpose to observe the effects of ethylene on ripening fruit

L1 ELL **Kinesthetic**

Materials two green bananas, paper bag

Teaching Strategies
• Tell students to choose two green bananas that are at the same stage of ripeness.
• Students may eat the bananas after use.

Analysis

The green banana in the bag; the ethylene produced by the ripening banana was trapped in the bag, causing the fruit to ripen more quickly.

✔ Assessment

Oral Have students explain their results to the class. Use **Performance Assessment in the Science Classroom**, p. 143.

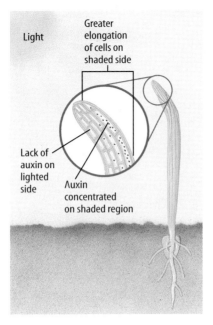

Figure 12

The concentration of auxin on the shaded side of a plant causes cells to lengthen on that side.

TRY AT HOME
Mini LAB

Observing Ripening

Procedure
1. Place a **green banana** in a **paper bag**. Roll the top shut.
2. Place another green banana on a counter or table.
3. After two days check the bananas to see how they have ripened. **WARNING:** *Do not eat the materials used in the lab.*

Analysis
Which banana ripened more quickly? Why?

Auxin Scientists identified the plant hormone, **auxin** (AWK sun) more than 100 years ago. Auxin is a type of plant hormone that causes plant stems and leaves to exhibit positive response to light. When light shines on a plant from one side, the auxin moves to the shaded side of the stem where it causes a change in growth, as shown in **Figure 12**. Auxins also control the production of other plant hormones, including ethylene.

✔ Reading Check   *How are auxins and positive response to light related?*

Development of many parts of the plant, including flowers, roots, and fruit, is stimulated by auxins. Because auxins are so important in plant development, synthetic auxins have been developed for use in agriculture. Some of these synthetic auxins are used in orchards so that all plants produce flowers and fruit at the same time. Other synthetic auxins damage plants when they are applied in high doses and are used as weed killers.

Gibberellins and Cytokinins Two other groups of plant hormones that also cause changes in plant growth are gibberellins and cytokinins. Gibberellins (jih buh REH lunz) are chemical substances that were isolated first from a fungus. The fungus caused a disease in rice plants called "foolish seedling" disease. The fungus infects the stems of plants and causes them to grow too tall. Gibberellins can be mixed with water and sprayed on plants and seeds to stimulate plant stems to grow and seeds to germinate.

Like gibberellins, cytokinins (si tuh KI nunz) also cause rapid growth. Cytokinins promote growth by causing faster cell divisions. Like ethylene, the effect of cytokinins on the plant also is controlled by auxin. Interestingly, cytokinins can be sprayed on stored vegetables to keep them fresh longer.

Abscisic Acid Because hormones that cause growth in plants were known to exist, biologists suspected that substances that have the reverse effect also must exist. Abscisic (ab SIH zihk) acid is one such substance. Many plants grow in areas that have cold winters. Normally, if seeds germinate, or buds develop on plants during the winter, they will die. Abscisic acid is the substance that keeps seeds from sprouting and buds from developing during the winter. This plant hormone also causes stomata to close and helps plants respond to water loss on hot summer days. **Figure 13** summarizes how plant hormones affect plants and how hormones are used.

🧑‍🤝‍🧑 Cultural **Diversity**

Ewiti Kurosawa Japanese scientist Ewiti Kurosawa discovered gibberellin while investigating the cause of "foolish seedling disease." He discovered that rice plants grew so tall that they fell over (thus, "foolish seedlings") after being infected with a fungus that secreted the substance. He named gibberellin after the genus of the fungus, *Gibberella fujikuroi.*

Figure 13

Chemical compounds called plant hormones help determine how a plant grows. There are five main types of hormones. They coordinate a plant's growth and development, as well as its responses to environmental stimuli, such as light, gravity, and changing seasons. Most changes in plant growth are a result of plant hormones working together, but exactly how hormones cause these changes is not completely understood.

◀ **GIBBERELLINS** The larger mustard plant in the photo at left was sprayed with gibberellins, plant hormones that stimulate stem elongation and fruit development.

▲ **ETHYLENE** By controlling the exposure of these tomatoes to ethylene, a hormone that stimulates fruit ripening, farmers are able to harvest unripe fruit and make it ripen just before it arrives at the supermarket.

◀ **CYTOKININS** Lateral buds do not usually develop into branches. However, if a plant's main stem is cut, as in this bean plant, naturally occurring cytokinins will stimulate the growth of lateral branches, causing the plant to grow "bushy."

Lateral buds

Lateral branches

▼ **AUXINS** Powerful growth hormones called auxins regulate responses to light and gravity, stem elongation, and root growth. The root growth on the plant cuttings, center and right, is the result of auxin treatment.

Bag Bag Bag

Leaf Leaf Leaf

0.4% IBA 0.3% 0.8% IBA

▶ **ABA (ABSCISIC ACID)** In plants such as the American basswood, right, abscisic acid causes buds to remain dormant for the winter. When spring arrives, ABA stops working and the buds sprout.

SECTION 2 Plant Responses **B** ◆ **137**

Visualizing Plant Hormones

Have students examine the pictures and read the captions. Then ask the following questions.

Which of the hormones here do not stimulate plant growth? What functions do these hormones serve? ABA causes dormancy instead of growth, and ethylene stimulates fruit ripening instead of growth.

How could farmers use plant hormones to enhance their profits? By controlling plant growth, budding, dormancy periods and ripening of fruits, farmers can deliver more product to the market.

What plant hormone has most likely been studied by researchers working in space? Auxins, which control a plant's response to gravity would be of great interest to those studying a plant's response to the reduced gravity in space.

Activity

Have students work in teams to write a poem with five verses. Each verse should name a type of plant hormone, and tell the function of the hormone and the particular parts of the plant the hormone acts on.

Extension

Evidence exists that a plant hormone called florigen controls flowering in plants, but scientists haven't isolated it yet. Have students research some of the experiments scientists have done in their search for florigen. Students should report their findings to the class.

Resource Manager

Chapter Resources Booklet
MiniLAB, p. 4
Lab Activity, pp. 11–14
Home and Community Involvement, p. 45

Photoperiods

Extension

Take the class on a field trip to a commercial greenhouse. Have students interview the staff to find out how they encourage plants to flower at times other than their normal flowering seasons. Growers often plan six to twelve months ahead in order to supply plants that are blooming out of season.

✔ Reading Check

Answer A specific amount of darkness is needed, which varies depending on the species of plant.

Figure 14
When short-day plants receive less darkness than required to produce flowers, they produce larger leaves instead.

Photoperiods

Earth Science
INTEGRATION

Sunflowers bloom in the summer, and cherry trees flower in the spring. Some plant species produce flowers at specific times during the year. A plant's response to the number of hours of daylight and darkness it receives daily is **photoperiodism** (foh toh PIHR ee uh dih zum).

Earth revolves around the Sun once each year. As Earth moves in its orbit, it also rotates. One rotation takes about 24 h. Because Earth is tilted about 23.5° from a line perpendicular to its orbit, the hours of daylight and darkness vary with the seasons. As you probably have noticed, the Sun sets later in summer than in winter. These changes in lengths of daylight and darkness affect plant growth.

Darkness and Flowers Many plants require a specific length of darkness to begin the flowering process. Generally, plants that require less than 10 h to 12 h of darkness to flower are called **long-day plants.** You may be familiar with some long-day plants such as spinach, lettuce, and beets. Plants that need 12 or more hours of darkness to flower are called **short-day plants.** Some short-day plants are poinsettias, strawberries, and ragweed. **Figure 14** shows what happens when a short-day plant receives less darkness than it needs to flower.

✔ Reading Check *What is needed to begin the flowering process?*

Day-Neutral Plants Plants like dandelions and roses are **day-neutral plants.** They have no specific photoperiod, and the flowering process can begin within a range of hours of darkness.

In nature, photoperiodism affects where flowering plants can grow and produce flowers and fruit. Even if a particular environment has the proper temperature and other growing conditions for a plant, it will not flower and produce fruit without the correct photoperiod. **Table 2** shows how day length affects flowering in all three types of plants.

Sometimes the photoperiod of a plant has a narrow range. For example, some soybeans will flower with 9.5 h of darkness but will not flower with 10 h of darkness. Farmers must choose the variety of soybeans with a photoperiod that matches the hours of darkness in the section of the country where they plant their crop.

Curriculum Connection

Geography Have students research the place of origin for different plants and plot the locations on a world map. Challenge students to determine whether location of origin correlates with the length of darkness a plant needs to flower.

Table 2 Photoperiodism

	Long-Day Plants	Short-Day Plants	Day-Neutral Plants
Early Summer Noon / 6 AM / 6 PM / Midnight			
Late Fall Noon / 6 AM / 6 PM / Midnight			
	An iris is a long-day plant that is stimulated by short nights to flower in the early summer.	Goldenrod is a short-day plant that is stimulated by long nights to flower in the fall.	Roses are day-neutral plants and have no specific photoperiod.

Today, greenhouse growers are able to provide any length of artificial daylight or darkness. This means that you can buy short-day flowering plants during the summer and long-day flowering plants during the winter.

Section 2 Assessment

1. Give an example of an internal stimulus and an external stimulus in plants.

2. Compare and contrast photoperiodism and phototropism.

3. Some red raspberries produce fruit in late spring, then again in the fall. What term describes their photoperiod?

4. How do the effects of abscisic acid differ from those of gibberellins?

5. **Think Critically** What is the relationship between plant hormones and tropisms?

Skill Builder Activities

6. **Comparing and Contrasting** Different plant parts exhibit positive and negative tropisms. Compare and contrast the responses of roots and stems to gravity. **For more help, refer to the Science Skill Handbook.**

7. **Communicating** For three years a farmer in Costa Rica grew healthy strawberry plants. But the plants never produced fruit. In your Science Journal, explain why this happened. **For more help, refer to the Science Skill Handbook.**

Reteach

Have students make a chart describing the various tropisms. For each tropism, they should include the stimulus, the response, and the effect on the plant. P

Challenge

Some roses bloom more in the spring and fall than during the summer. **What type of photoperiod is this?** short-day

Assessment

Oral Use question 6 to assess students' abilities to compare and contrast the responses of roots, stems, and leaves to light by having students explain their answers to you. Use **Performance Assessment in the Science Classroom,** p. 143.

Answers to Section Assessment

1. Possible answers: Internal stimuli include hormones; external stimuli include environmental factors such as gravity and light.

2. Photoperiodism is plant responses to the length of the period of darkness; phototropism is any growth response to light.

3. short-day

4. Abscisic acid slows growth; gibberellins speed growth in plants.

5. Plant hormones are responsible for some tropisms.

6. Roots show positive gravitropism and grow downward. Stems show negative gravitropism and grow upward.

7. Strawberries are short-day plants. Because Costa Rica is near the equator, the days are about the same length as the nights, so there are too few hours of darkness to produce flowering in strawberries.

Activity

What You'll Investigate

Purpose

Students experiment to observe plant responses to gravity. L2

ELL   Logical-Mathematical

Process Skills

observing and inferring, communicating, making and using tables, comparing and contrasting, recognizing cause and effect, separating and controlling variables, interpreting data, using numbers

Time Required

1 class period to set up; 20 minutes one day each week for up to two weeks

Materials

clear jar, marking pen, mustard seeds, aluminum foil, paper towel, water

Alternate Materials

Bean seeds can be substituted for mustard seeds.

Safety Precautions

Some kinds of seeds are poisonous. Do not allow students to put seeds in their mouths.

Activity

Tropism in Plants

Grapevines can climb on trees, fences, or other nearby structures. This growth is a response to the stimulus of touch. Tropisms are specific plant responses to stimuli outside of the plant. One part of a plant can respond positively while another part of the same plant can respond negatively to the same stimulus. Gravitropism is a response to gravity. Why might it be important for some plant parts to have a positive response to gravity while other plant parts have a negative response? You can design an experiment to test how some plant parts respond to the stimulus of gravity.

What You'll Investigate

Do stems and roots respond to gravity in the same way?

Materials

paper towel
30 cm × 30 cm sheet of aluminum foil
water
mustard seeds
marking pen
1-L clear glass or plastic jar

Goals

- Describe how roots and stems respond to gravity.
- Observe how changing the stimulus changes the growth of plants.

Safety Precautions

WARNING: *Some kinds of seeds are poisonous. Do not put any seed in your mouth. Wash your hands after handling the seeds.*

Inclusion Strategies

Learning Disabled Provide clear directions both orally and in writing. Assign a buddy to each student to help him or her assemble the seed packets.

Science Journal

Old Seeds Ask students if they think the age of the seeds used would make a difference in the results. Have them write their hypotheses and possible investigations in their Science Journals.

Procedure

1. Copy the following data table in your Science Journal.

2. Moisten the paper towel with water so that it's damp but not dripping. Fold it in half twice.

3. In the center of the foil, place the folded paper towel and sprinkle mustard seeds in a line across the center of the towel.

4. Fold the foil around the towel and seal each end by folding the foil over. Make sure the paper towel is completely covered by the foil.

5. Use a marking pen to draw an arrow on the foil, and place the foil package in the jar with the arrow pointing upward.

6. After five days carefully open the package and record your observations in the data table. (Note: *If no stems or roots are growing yet, reseal the package and place it back in the jar, making sure that the arrow points upward. Reopen the package in two days.*)

Response to Gravity

Position of Arrow on Foil Package	Observations of Seedling Roots	Observations of Seedling Stems
Arrow Up	Growing away from arrow	Growing toward arrow
Arrow Down	Growing toward arrow	Growing away from arrow

7. Reseal the foil package, being careful not to disturb the seedlings. Place it in the jar so that the arrow points downward instead of upward.

8. After five more days reopen the package and observe any new growth of the seedlings' roots and stems. Record your observations in your data table.

Conclude and Apply

1. **Classify** the responses you observed as positive or negative tropisms.

2. **Explain** why the plants' growth changed when you placed them upside down.

3. Why was it important that no light reach the seedlings during your experiment?

4. What are some other ways you could have changed the position of the foil package to test the seedlings' response?

*C*ommunicating Your Data

Use drawings to **compare** the growth of the seedlings before and after you turned the package. **Compare** your drawing with those of other students in your class. **For more help, refer to the** Science Skill Handbook.

ACTIVITY B ◆ 141

Procedure

Teaching Strategy Explain to students that there may be more than one variable at work and that stems and roots may be responding differently to these stimuli.

Troubleshooting Be sure that students always place the seeds back in the dish with the arrow pointing up.

Expected Outcome

Roots will grow downward and shoots will grow upward.

Conclude and Apply

1. Stem growth upward is negative gravitropism; root growth downward is positive gravitropism.

2. The plants' growth continued to respond to the stimulus provided by gravity, even though the direction of this stimuli had changed.

3. If light reached the seedlings, they could have responded to it (phototropism), and results due to gravitropism would be uncertain.

4. Possible answers: The packages could have been laid flat or put on a spinning turntable.

Error Analysis

Have students compare their data with that of others and explain any differences they encounter.

✔ Assessment

Portfolio Have students make a labeled poster of their experimental results and share it with the class. Use **Performance Assessment in the Science Classroom,** p. 145.

Resource Manager

Chapter Resources Booklet
  Activity Worksheet, pp. 7–8
Lab Management and Safety, p. 58

*C*ommunicating Your Data

Drawings will indicate that roots grow downward and shoots grow upward, notwithstanding the orientation of the seed.

✔ Pre-Reading Activity

Ask students what they know about the Sun before they read the retelling of this fable by the De La Fuentes. Encourage all kinds of responses, from what the Sun looks like throughout the day, to more scientific facts about the Sun such as how it helps support life on Earth. Write down student responses on the board as they are being called out.

Respond to the Reading

Active Reading Strategies

Visualize Keep the events and setting in your mind's eye as you read. Form pictures in your mind. The fable goes to great lengths to describe the natural setting of the story. **Is the setting a fictional place?**

Review Review what you have read. By looking back over several paragraphs, you can see how the information fits together. **Why do they characterize the flower as a human, or in this case, a girl?**

Answers to Questions

1. The plants need the Sun to survive and grow.
2. The flowers need water to survive and grow.
3. Student answers will vary. Some students might suggest that it does not give enough detail about photosynthesis. Others might suggest that the visual imagery of the story is enough to convey the message.

Sunkissed: An Indian Legend
as told by Alberto and Patricia De La Fuente

Respond to the Reading

1. What does this passage tell you about the relationship between the Sun and plants?
2. What does this passage tell you about the relationship between water and the growth of flowers?
3. Do you think this passage is effective in making the reader understand the importance of light and darkness to a growing plant? Why or why not?

A long time ago, deep down in the very heart of the old Mexican forests, so far away from the sea that not even the largest birds ever had time to fly that far, there was a small, beautiful valley. A long chain of snow-covered mountains stood between the valley and the sea.... Each day the mountains were the first ones to tell everybody that Tonatiuh, the King of Light, was coming to the valley. The meadows would see the shining white tops of the mountains and spread out their flowery skirts for the Sun.

"Good morning, Tonatiuh!" cried a little meadow.

"Hurry up and bring us warmth and light!" sang all the wild roses along the river bank together as an opening line....

The wild flowers always started their fresh new day with a kiss of golden sunlight from Tonatiuh, but it was necessary to first wash their sleepy baby faces with the dew that Metztli, the Moon, sprinkled for them out of her bucket onto the nearby leaves during the night....

...All night long, then, Metztli Moon would walk her night-field making sure that by sun-up all flowers had the magic dew that made them feel beautiful all day long.

However, much as flowers love to be beautiful as long as possible, they want to be happy too. So every morning Tonatiuh himself would give each one a single golden kiss of such power that it was possible to be happy all day long after it. As you can see, then, a flower needs to feel beautiful in the first place, but if she does not feel beautiful, she will not be ready for her morning sun-kiss. If she cannot wash her little face with the magic dew, the whole day is lost.

Reading Further

American Indian Myths and Legends by Richard Erdoes (Editor) and Alfonso Ortiz (Editor), Pantheon Books, 1985.

Old Indian Legends by Zitkala-Sa, Sa Zitkala, and Angela Decora (Illustrator), University of Nebraska Press, 1985.

Understanding Literature

Legends and Oral Traditions   A legend is a traditional story often told orally and believed to be based on actual people and events. Legends are believed to be true even if they cannot be proved. Sunkissed: An Indian Legend is a legend about a little flower that is changed forever by the Sun. What in this story indicates that it is a legend? This legend also is an example of an oral tradition. Oral traditions are stories or skills that are handed down by word of mouth. They can be stories about real people and events, fictional stories, recipes, or crafts.

Science Connection   In this chapter, you learned about the processes of photosynthesis and respiration. The passage from Sunkissed: An Indian Legend does not teach us the details about photosynthesis or respiration. However, it does show how sunshine and water are important to plant life. The difference between the legend and the information contained in your textbook is this— photosynthesis and respiration can be proved scientifically, and the legend, although fun to read, cannot.

Linking Science and Writing

Creating Oral Traditions
Create an idea for a fictional story that explains why the sky becomes so colorful during a sunset. Write a few short notes about your story on a piece of paper. Then retell your story to your classmates using only your short notes and your imagination. When you retell your story, remember that good storytellers are enthusiastic and entertaining. An oral tradition is started because listeners want to pass the story along.

Career Connection

Horticulturist/Landscape Designer

Jill Nokes is a horticulturist who studies plants and how to grow them. Many horticulturists work in large nurseries as managers or plant breeders. Nokes works as a landscape designer, a person who creates gardens for homes and businesses. There are two important parts to a landscape designer's job. Designers must first create attractive landscapes for their clients. They also have to be plant experts so they can choose plants that will thrive in the local climate and with other plants in the design.

SCIENCE*Online*   To learn more about careers in horticulture, visit the Glencoe Science Web site at **science.glencoe.com.**

SCIENCE AND LANGUAGE ARTS   B ◆ 143

Understanding Literature

Answer to Question

Answers will vary but should include that a legend is usually a fictional story relaying information about a specific culture, in this case Mexican.

Science Connection

The study of photosynthesis began in 1771, with observations made by the English chemist Joseph Priestley. Priestly had burned a candle in a closed container until the air within the container could no longer support combustion. He then placed a sprig of mint plant in the container and discovered that after several days the mint had produced some substance (later recognized as oxygen) that enabled the confined air to again support combustion. In 1779 the Dutch physician Jan Ingenhouz showed that the plant must be exposed to light if oxygen is to be restored.

Linking Science and Writing

Teaching Strategies

Lead students in brainstorming to come up with reasons that sunsets are colorful. Let them know that causes of pigment in the sky are not always natural. For example, some sky color can be caused by pollution. This exercise will give them a start on the writing activity.

Career Connection

While landscape designers design gardens, there is also the landscape architect. Landscape architecture is defined as "the art of arranging land and the objects upon it for human use and enjoyment." Landscape architecture includes site planning, land planning, master planning, urban design, and environmental planning.

SCIENCE *Online*
Internet Addresses

_____

_____

_____

_____

Explore the Glencoe Science Web site at **science.glencoe.com** to find out more about topics in this feature.

Chapter 5 Study Guide

Reviewing Main Ideas

Preview

Students can answer the questions in their Science Journals. Discuss the answers as you go through the chapter. **LS Linguistic**

Review

Students can write their answers, then compare them with those of other students. **LS Interpersonal**

Reteach

Students can look at the illustrations and describe details that support the main ideas of the chapter. **LS Visual-Spatial**

Answers to Chapter Review

SECTION 1

3. They produce food for themselves and consumers.
5. Respiration provides energy the sprouting seed needs for growth and development.

SECTION 2

2. Gravity; some students may say light.
3. They do not depend on length of dark periods to trigger flowering.

Reviewing Main Ideas

Section 1 Photosynthesis and Respiration

1. Carbon dioxide and water vapor gases enter and leave a plant through openings in the epidermis called stomata. Guard cells cause a stoma to open and close.

2. Photosynthesis takes place in the chloroplasts of plant cells. Light energy is used to produce glucose and oxygen from carbon dioxide and water.

3. Photosynthesis provides the food for most organisms on Earth. *Why are plants called producers?*

4. All organisms use respiration to release the energy stored in food molecules. Oxygen is used in the mitochondria to complete respiration in plant cells and many other types of cells. Energy, carbon dioxide, and water are produced.

5. The energy produced from respiration is needed by most living organisms including plants. *Why is respiration important to this sprouting seed?*

6. Photosynthesis and respiration are almost the reverse of each other. The end products of photosynthesis are the raw materials needed for aerobic respiration. The end products of aerobic respiration are the raw materials needed for photosynthesis.

Section 2 Plant Responses

1. Plants respond positively and negatively to stimuli. The response may be a movement, a change in growth, or the beginning of some process such as flowering.

2. A stimulus from outside the plant is called a tropism. Outside stimuli include such things as light, gravity, and touch. *What outside stimulus is affecting the growth of this plant?*

3. The length of darkness each day can affect flowering times of plants. *Why can day-neutral plants, such as this one, flower almost any time?*

4. Hormones control changes from inside plants. These chemicals affect plants in many ways. Some hormones cause plants to exhibit tropisms. Other hormones cause changes in plant growth.

FOLDABLES Reading & Study Skills

After You Read

Use the information in your Compare and Contrast Study Fold to compare and contrast aerobic respiration that occurs in plants and animals.

FOLDABLES Reading & Study Skills

After You Read

After students have read the chapter and completed the Foldable described in Before You Read, have them do the activity on the student page.

Dinah Zike

Visualizing Main Ideas

Complete the following cycle concept map that shows how photosynthesis and respiration are related.

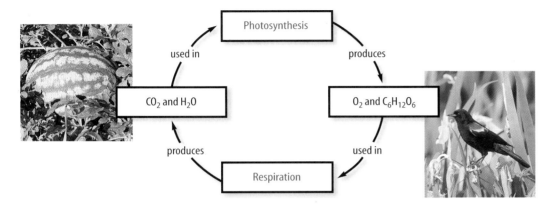

Photosynthesis

used in — produces

CO_2 and H_2O

O_2 and $C_6H_{12}O_6$

produces — used in

Respiration

Visualizing Main Ideas

See student page.

Vocabulary Review

Using Vocabulary

1. Auxin
2. photosynthesis
3. Chlorophyll
4. short-day plant
5. Respiration
6. long-day plant
7. Tropism
8. stomata
9. Photoperiodism
10. day neutral plants

Vocabulary Review

Vocabulary Words

a. auxin
b. chlorophyll
c. day-neutral plant
d. long-day plant
e. photoperiodism
f. photosynthesis
g. respiration
h. short-day plant
i. stomata
j. tropism

Using Vocabulary

Replace the underlined definition with the correct vocabulary word from the list above.

1. A plant hormone causes plant stems and leaves to exhibit positive phototropism.

THE PRINCETON REVIEW Study Tip

Outline the chapters to make sure that you understand the key ideas that are presented. Writing down the main points of the chapter will help you remember important details and understand larger themes.

2. An important process of green plants is using light to make glucose and oxygen.

3. A green pigment is important in the process of photosynthesis.

4. A poinsettia, often seen flowering during December holidays, is a plant that requires long nights to flower.

5. The process of energy release from food occurs in most living things.

6. Spinach is a plant that requires only ten hours of darkness at night to flower.

7. A response of a plant to an outside stimulus can cause the plant to bend toward light.

8. Plants usually take in carbon dioxide through tiny pores in their leaves.

9. A plant's response to the number of hours of darkness it receives daily determines many plant processes.

10. Marigolds are plants that flower without regard to the length of darkness.

IDENTIFYING Misconceptions

Assess

Use the assessment as follow-up to page 122F after students have completed the chapter.

Procedure Give the following statements, and ask students to respond with "plants," "animals," or "both plants and animals": takes in oxygen; gives off carbon dioxide; takes in carbon dioxide; gives off oxygen; make glucose; uses glucose.

Expected Outcome Students should know that both plants and animals take in oxygen, give off carbon dioxide, and use glucose. Only plants give off oxygen, take in carbon dioxide, and make glucose.

Checking Concepts

1. C
2. D
3. D
4. C
5. D
6. A
7. D
8. C
9. A
10. B

Thinking Critically

11. Put them in a brown paper bag to retain ethylene.
12. a. negative gravitropism; b. positive gravitropism; c. positive phototropism; d. positive thigmotropism
13. Oxygen is a by-product of photosynthesis. Until organisms that used carbon dioxide for photosynthesis evolved, little free oxygen was available.
14. Apple trees bloom in the spring when the days are short and nights are long. The number of dark hours in the summer is less than an apple tree's photoperiod.
15. Day-neutral plants will flower anywhere if they receive a minimum number of hours of darkness and if other environmental conditions are favorable. Long-day plants require the number of hours of darkness that occurs near the equator.

Chapter 5 Assessment

Checking Concepts

Choose the word or phrase that best answers the question.

1. What raw material needed by plants enters through open stomata?
   A) sugar
   C) carbon dioxide
   B) chlorophyll
   D) cellulose

2. What is a function of stomata?
   A) photosynthesis
   B) to guard the interior cells
   C) to allow sugar to escape
   D) to permit the release of oxygen

3. What plant process produces water, carbon dioxide, and energy?
   A) cell division
   C) growth
   B) photosynthesis
   D) respiration

4. What type of plant needs short nights in order to flower?
   A) day-neutral
   C) long-day
   B) short-day
   D) nonvascular

5. What do you call things such as light, touch, and gravity that cause plant growth responses?
   A) tropisms
   C) responses
   B) growth
   D) stimuli

6. What are the products of photosynthesis?
   A) glucose and oxygen
   B) carbon dioxide and water
   C) chlorophyll and glucose
   D) carbon dioxide and oxygen

7. What are plant substances that affect plant growth called?
   A) tropisms
   C) germination
   B) glucose
   D) hormones

8. Leaves change colors because what substance breaks down?
   A) hormone
   C) chlorophyll
   B) carotenoid
   D) cytoplasm

9. Which of these is a product of respiration?
   A) CO_2
   C) C_2H_4
   B) O_2
   D) H_2

10. What is a plant's response to gravity called?
   A) phototropism
   C) thigmotropism
   B) gravitropism
   D) hydrotropism

Thinking Critically

11. You buy pears at the store that are not completely ripe. What could you do to help them ripen more rapidly?

12. Name each tropism and state whether it is positive or negative.
   a. Stem grows up.
   b. Roots grow down.
   c. Plant grows toward light.
   d. A vine grows around a pole.

13. Scientists who study sedimentary rocks and fossils suggest that oxygen was not in Earth's atmosphere until plantlike, one-celled organisms appeared. Why?

14. Explain why apple trees bloom in the spring but not in the summer.

15. Why do day-neutral and long-day plants grow best in countries near the equator?

Developing Skills

16. **Forming Hypotheses** Make a hypothesis about when guard cells open and close in desert plants.

17. **Identifying and Manipulating Variables and Controls** Plan an experiment to test your hypothesis in question 16.

18. **Predicting** Make a prediction about how the number and location of stomata differ in land plants and water plants whose leaves float on the water's surface.

Chapter ✓Assessment Planner

Portfolio Encourage students to place in their portfolios one or two items of what they consider to be their best work. Examples include:
- Science Journal, p. 127
- Curriculum Connection, p. 138
- Reteach, p. 139

Performance Additional performance assessments, Performance Task Assessment Lists, and rubrics for evaluating these activities can be found in Glencoe's **Performance Assessment in the Science Classroom.**

19. Concept Mapping Complete the following concept map about photoperiodism using the following information: flower year-round—*corn, dandelion, tomato;* flower in the spring, fall, or winter—*chrysanthemum, rice, poinsettia;* flower in summer—*spinach, lettuce, petunia.*

corn
dandelion — Day-neutral plants — tomato

Long-day plants — spinach, lettuce, petunia

Photoperiodism

Short-day plants — chrysanthemum, rice, poinsettia

20. Comparing and Contrasting Compare and contrast the action of auxin and the action of ethylene on a plant.

Performance Assessment

21. Coloring Book Create a coloring book of day-neutral plants, long-day plants, and short-day plants. Use pictures from magazines and seed catalogs to get your ideas. Label the drawings with the plant's name and how it responds to darkness. Let a younger student color the flowers in your book.

TECHNOLOGY

Go to the Glencoe Science Web site at **science.glencoe.com** or use the **Glencoe Science CD-ROM** for additional chapter assessment.

THE PRINCETON REVIEW **Test Practice**

Eileen and Logan wanted to learn more about the materials that plants use during photosynthesis. They designed the following data table to record the results of their investigation.

Resources Used During Photosynthesis

Plant	Water Used	Carbon Dioxide Used	Light Absorbed	Oxygen Produced
Plant X				
Plant Y				
Plant Z				

Study the table and answer the following questions.

1. Using your knowledge of photosynthesis, which of the data columns would not be needed for recording results from the investigation?
   A) water used
   B) carbon dioxide used
   C) light absorbed
   D) oxygen produced

2. The most likely source of energy for the plants during this investigation is _____.
   F) water
   G) carbon dioxide
   H) light
   J) oxygen

THE PRINCETON REVIEW **Test Practice**

The Test-Taking Tip was written by The Princeton Review, the nation's leader in test preparation.
1. D
2. H

Developing Skills

16. Desert plants' stomata might open at night and close during the day in order to conserve moisture. This is opposite to most other plants.
17. Experimental designs will differ but should include a comparison of several species of plants from deserts and other environments.
18. Floating water plants have stomata on the upper leaf surfaces, whereas land plants usually have more stomata on lower leaf surfaces.
19. See student page.
20. Both are hormones. Auxin makes stems grow toward light; ethylene makes fruit ripen.

Performance Assessment

21. At a minimum each plant's drawing should include its name and photoperiod. Use **Performance Assessment in the Science Classroom,** p. 133.

✓Assessment **Resources**

📁 **Reproducible Masters**
Chapter Resources Booklet
Chapter Review, pp. 33–34
Chapter Tests, pp. 35–38
Assessment Transparency Activity, p. 45

Glencoe Science Web site
Interactive Tutor
Chapter Quizzes

Glencoe Technology
🖌 Assessment Transparency
💿 Interactive CD-ROM Chapter Quizzes
💿 ExamView Pro Test Bank
💿 Vocabulary PuzzleMaker Software
📺 MindJogger Videoquiz

QUESTION 1: A

Students must read carefully the context surrounding the underlined word. The fact that *there are fewer than twenty living specimens of these plants now* implies that the species is in danger of dying out. Therefore, choice A, *death of species*, is the correct answer.

Teaching Tip

Suggest that students number the paragraphs as they go through a reading passage.

QUESTION 2: H

Students must identify the main idea of the second paragraph.

- **Choice F** No; this is a detail from the third paragraph.
- **Choice G** No; this is a detail from the second paragraph.
- **Choice H** Yes; this is the main idea of the second paragraph.
- **Choice J** No; this is a detail from the second paragraph.

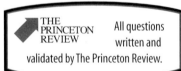

Read the passage carefully. Then read the questions that follow the passage. Decide which is the best answer to each question.

Medicine Plants

As part of his job, Paul Alan Cox, the director of the National Tropical Botanical Garden in Hawaii, leads teams of brave young people as they rappel down steep cliffs, hang from helicopters, and perform other daring feats. Are these people competing in an extreme sport? No, they are botanists, and they perform these daring acts with Cox in order to collect seeds from the nearly ninety Hawaiian plant species that are threatened with <u>extinction</u>. There are fewer than twenty living specimens of each of these plants now.

Why is Cox interested in saving plants from extinction? He knows that many plants contain medicinal, or healing, properties. For the past fifteen years, Cox has traveled all over the world to learn about the unique ways that people have been using plants to treat illnesses and to survive harsh environments. When Cox started this research, some of his colleagues thought he was throwing away his career as a scientist. Why, they wanted to know, would he be interested in what they considered nonscientific knowledge and folklore? Cox soon proved the value of his research.

Cox went to Western Samoa to record the practices of a 73-year-old woman, Epenesa Mauigoa. Epenesa gave him a detailed account of 121 herbal remedies she made from 90 different species of plants. One of those remedies she described especially caught Cox's attention. It was a preparation to fight hepatitis made from the mamala tree, or, as botanists call it, *Homolanthus nutans*.

The herbal remedy has since become the basis for an antiviral drug, prostratin. It is being studied as a drug to treat type 1 HIV.

In 1994, a study found that there are at least 119 plant-derived substances in use worldwide as medicines. Cox is on the hunt to find more.

Test-Taking Tip
Consider the actions of the people in the passage.

Dr. Cox holds a branch of the mamala tree from which the antiviral drug, prostratin, is obtained.

1. What is the meaning of <u>extinction</u> in the context of this passage?
   A) death of a species
   B) survival
   C) ethnobotany
   D) herbal medicine

2. What is the main idea of the second paragraph?
   F) Cox discovered a preparation that could be used to fight hepatitis.
   G) Cox's colleagues thought he was throwing his career away.
   H) Cox decided to research how people use plants to treat illnesses and to survive harsh environments.
   J) Cox's colleagues thought Cox was interested in nonscientific knowledge.

Standardized Test Practice

Reasoning and Skills

Read each question and choose the best answer.

1. Which of the following chemical compounds does not influence the growth of plants?
   A) cytokinins
   B) gibberellins
   C) auxins
   D) pheromones

Test-Taking Tip Think about the roles of hormones in plants and animals.

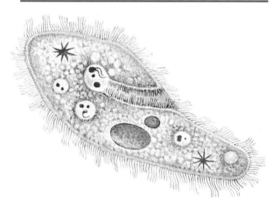

2. Protozoans are complex one-celled organisms that feed on other organisms. The four major groups of protozoans are classified primarily according to _____.
   F) the presence of chlorophyll
   G) their method of locomotion
   H) the presence of food vacuoles
   J) the types of human disease they cause

Test-Taking Tip Consider what you know about protozoans.

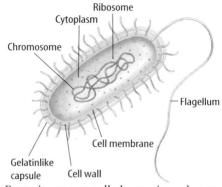

Ribosome
Cytoplasm
Chromosome
Flagellum
Cell membrane
Gelatinlike capsule
Cell wall

3. Bacteria are one-celled organisms that are found almost everywhere. In general, the presence of bacteria in the human body could benefit human health the most by _____.
   A) decreasing the body's absorption of vitamins
   B) decreasing the growth of other bacteria
   C) increasing the production of vitamins
   D) increasing the rate of cell division

Test-Taking Tip Consider what you know about the role of bacteria in human intestines.

Consider this question carefully before writing your answer on a separate sheet of paper.

4. Consider what you have learned about the evolution of plants. Explain how the similarities and differences between plants and algae suggest that plants originally came from the sea. You might wish to begin by making a table that summarizes characteristics of plants and algae.

Test-Taking Tip Consider the important characteristics of plants and algae before you begin writing.

Reasoning and Skills

QUESTION 1: D

Students must understand that choices F, G, and H are different kinds of plant hormones that affect growth.

QUESTION 2: G

Students must understand that protozoans are classified as flagellates, amoeboids, and ciliates according to how they move.

QUESTION 3: C

Students should read the question carefully and remember that they are looking for an answer choice that shows how bacteria *benefit* human health.

- **Choice A** No; this does not benefit human health.
- **Choice B** No; this is not supported by what students should know about bacteria.
- **Choice C** Yes; this is a beneficial effect of the presence of bacteria in the human system.
- **Choice D** No; this is not supported by what students should know about bacteria.

QUESTION 4: Answers will vary.

Students should mention that plants and algae have some pigments in common and carry on photosynthesis. Adaptations that allowed plants to survive on land were the result of random mutations and natural selection.

Student Resources

CONTENTS

About the Field Guide

- This field guide contains representative descriptions and photos of the cones of twelve types of conifers that enable the user to classify some cones.

- In using a field guide, students will apply steps of a scientific method as they observe, investigate, and draw conclusions.

- This field guide applies nationally; local and regional field guides are usually available. Remind students that plants vary and cones may not match exactly.

- Encourage students to use the field guide outside the classroom.

Tie to Prior Knowledge

Students may have seen cones on different needled trees and referred to all of them as pinecones. After using this field guide, they will be aware of the different needled plants and the uniqueness of their cones.

Field Activity

Student responses to this activity will vary. If students use cones from craft items, they may need help in identifying the species from which they came. Be sure they research each cone's plant in order to include a description of it. Student sketches of cones should reflect one of the shapes shown in the field guide.

When you hear the word *cone*, you might think of a tasty, edible holder for your favorite ice cream. Maybe you think of the orange cones used on highways and in public places to direct vehicular or pedestrian traffic. However, there's another type of cone in the environment that plays an important role for some plants. These cones are the reproductive organs of a large plant group called the conifers, or cone bearers. The seeds of pines, firs, spruces, redwoods, and other conifers are formed in cones.

Types of Cones

Conifers have two types of cones, male and female. The male cones produce pollen grains and break apart soon after they release pollen. Depending on the species of conifer, the female cones can stay on plants for up to three years. Female cones can be woody or berrylike. Woody cones consist of scales growing from a central stalk and vary in shape and size. Berrylike cones are round and either hard or soft. Each genus of conifers has a different type of female cone. They are so different from one another that you can use them to identify a conifer's genus.

Cones

Cone Characteristics

Cylindrical
This cone is shaped like a cylinder and is nearly uniform in size from the base to the tip.

Ovoid
Although this cone is shaped like a cylinder, it is smaller at the ends than in the middle.

Globose
This cone is rounded like a globe.

Conic
Shaped like a cone, it decreases in diameter from the base to the tip.

Cone scale
Umbo
(end view)

Umbo
A raised, triangular area at the tip of a cone scale varies in size and thickness.

Field Activity

Find three different cones in your neighborhood, a park, around your school, or as part of a craft item. Using this guide, identify the genus of each cone. Go to the Glencoe Science Web site at **science. glencoe.com** if you don't have cones in your neighborhood. Here you can link to different sites about cones. In your Science Journal, sketch each cone and write a description of the plant it came from.

 Resources for Teachers and Students

Trees: An Explore your World Handbook, by Jon Arno, Discovery Books, 2000.

Conifers: The Illustrated Encyclopedia, by D.M. van Gelderen, Timber Press, 1996.

Cone Identification

This field guide contains some of the conifers. Plant features might differ in appearance because of environmental conditions.

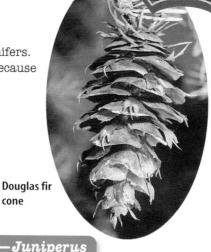

Douglas fir cone

Douglas Fir—*Psuedotsuga*

These ovoid cones on short stalks have a three-pointed, papery structure that extends from below each cone scale. The cones range from 5 cm to 10 cm in length.

Juniper berries

Juniper—*Juniperus*

These cones are hard, berrylike structures that stay on the tree or shrub for two to three years. They measure about 1.3 cm in diameter. They are bluish, pale green, reddish, or brown and covered with a white, waxy coating called a bloom.

Spruce—*Picea*

These cones are cylindrical and brown with thin cone scales and tips that usually are pointed. They can be 6 cm to 15 cm long. They stay on the plant for two years and hang from branches on the upper third of the tree. As they mature, they become brittle.

Spruce cones

Redwood—*Sequoia*

Ovoid and reddish brown, these cones hang from the tips of needled twigs. They develop in one year and are small in comparison to the size of the tree—only 1.2 cm to 3 cm. The cone scales are flattened on their ends.

Redwood cones

FIELD GUIDE   B   153

Discussion

What are some of the characteristics of cones that scientists could use to classify a newly discovered species of tree? Possible answers: size, shape, color, and texture of the cone; its location on the tree; the length of time it stays on the tree

Quick Demo

Bring in branches from several different pines. Show students that pines have their needles in groups of two or three to five. Use enlarged pictures if pines are not available in your area. **IS** **Visual-Spatial**

Visual Learning

Junipers The female cones of the juniper plant are often referred to as "juniper berries." These cones have fleshy scales that are fused together, giving a berrylike appearance. The "berries" of some species of juniper are used to flavor food and beverages.

Fun Fact

The Giant Sequoias are the largest of the conifers. The largest Giant Sequoia tree is about 80 meters high and weighs about 2,500 metric tons.

Curriculum Connection

Geography Have students choose a type of conifer and research where it grows. Have students plot on a large world map the locations of the conifers they have researched. Discuss these locations, and have students draw conclusions based on their knowledge of climates in various locations around the world.

L2 **IS** **Logical-Mathematical**

SCIENCE Online
Internet Addresses

_____
_____
_____

Explore the Glencoe Science Web site at **science.glencoe.com** to find out more about topics in this field guide.

Content Background

In 1994 a park ranger in an Australian National Park discovered a species of coniferous tree thought to have been extinct for thousands of years. The trees were growing in a deep cavern about 150 km outside Sidney, Australia. Fossil evidence shows that this ancient form of conifer was plentiful during the Jurassic and Cretaceous periods. There currently are fewer than 100 trees of this species known to exist. Botanists and conservationists are working to ensure the species' survival.

Fun Fact

The seeds of nearly all pines are edible. They contain mostly oils, but the protein content ranges from 15 percent to 30 percent.

Activity

Have each student bring in an item or a picture of an item made from the wood of a conifer. Make a list of all of the uses of conifer wood represented by the items.

Extension

Have interested students research amber, the fossilized resin of pines. Amber sometimes contains fossilized insects and provides valuable information to paleontologists and other scientists. Have students report their findings to the class. **IS Linguistic**

Field GUIDE

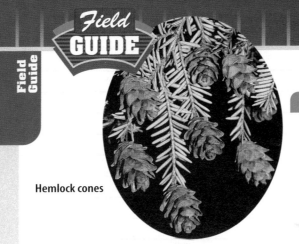

Hemlock cones

Hemlock—*Tsuga*

These cones hang from twigs and are small, ovoid to cylindrical, and 2 cm to 7 cm long. The few cone scales have rounded tips. Although they develop in one year, they usually stay on the tree for more than one year.

Pine—*Pinus*

Each cone has a thick, woody scale tipped with an umbo. The umbo can have a small spine, or prickle. Most pine cones are cylindrical or conic and grow on a small stalk. They vary in length from about 4 cm (scrub pine) to 45 cm (sugar pine) and remain on the tree or shrub for two to three years.

Pine cone

Arborvitae—*Thuja*

These egg-shaped cones are 1.2 cm to 1.5 cm long. They have paired cone scales, usually from six to 12, that are straplike and end in a sharp point. The cones remain attached to the shrub after opening and releasing their seeds.

Arborvitae cones

Cypress—*Cupressus*

These globose cones, which are usually 2 cm to 2.5 cm in diameter, have only six to eight scales. The cone scales have a raised point in the center. They develop in about 18 months and stay closed and attached to the tree.

Cypress cones

Inclusion Strategies

Visually Impaired Help visually impaired students develop a key for several cones using sensory characteristics such as texture, size, and smell. **IS Kinesthetic**

SCIENCE Online
Internet Addresses

_____

_____

_____

Explore the Glencoe Science Web site at **science.glencoe.com** to find out more about topics in this field guide.

False Cypress—*Chamaecyparis*

These small globose cones are only 0.5 cm to 4 cm in diameter with four to ten cone scales. Unlike the cones of the *Cupressus* trees, they open after they are fully developed.

False cypress cones

Swamp or Bald Cypress—*Taxodium*

This globose cone is about 2.5 cm across and develops in one year. The tips of the cone scales are four sided, forming an irregular pattern on the surface of the cone. Trees in this genus are recognized by the projections, called knees, that grow upward from around the base of the tree trunk.

Swamp cypress cones

Fir—*Abies*

Fir cones grow upright on branches and range from 5 cm to 20 cm in length. They are seldom used for identification because the scales drop off when they are developed, leaving only the bare central stalk.

Fir cones

Cedar—*Cedrus*

These barrel-shaped cones with flattened tips grow upright on branches. They are 5 cm to 10 cm in length and nearly half as wide. After two years, the scales drop off. Cedar trees do not produce these cones until they are 40 to 50 years old.

Cedar cones

FIELD GUIDE B 155

Discussion

How might your life be different if all species of conifer trees were extinct? Possible answers: Some students may mention that if there were no conifers, they would have to use something different for a Christmas tree. Other students may mention that much of their furniture would not exist without conifers. Students may also point out the value of conifers as a beautiful part of nature that couldn't be enjoyed if they were extinct.

Make a Model

Have students use available materials to make a model of one of the types of cones discussed in this field guide. Students should label their model to indicate the shape and characteristics of the cone, as well as the type of tree on which it is found. Students should share their model with the class. L1 LS **Kinesthetic**

Visual Learning

Bald Cypress Show students additional pictures of bald cypress trees. Point out the knees that form around the base of the trunk. Some scientists think the knees provide stability in loose soil.

Science Journal

More on Cones Provide students with pictures of cones of genera not described in this guide. Have them use other field guides to identify the cones. Encourage students to write descriptions of these cones and their genera in their Science Journals. They should also explain the steps they used to identify the cones. LS **Logical-Mathematical**

As you study science, you will make many observations and conduct investigations and experiments. You will also research information that is available from many sources. These activities will involve organizing and recording data. The quality of the data you collect and the way you organize it will determine how well others can understand and use it. In **Figure 1,** the student is obtaining and recording information using a microscope.

Putting your observations in writing is an important way of communicating to others the information you have found and the results of your investigations and experiments.

Researching Information

Scientists work to build on and add to human knowledge of the world. Before moving in a new direction, it is important to gather the information that already is known about a subject. You will look for such information in various reference sources. Follow these steps to research information on a scientific subject:

Step 1 Determine exactly what you need to know about the subject. For instance, you might want to find out what happened to local plant life when Mount St. Helens erupted in 1980.

Step 2 Make a list of questions, such as: When did the eruption begin? How long did it last? How large was the area in which plant life was affected?

Step 3 Use multiple sources such as textbooks, encyclopedias, government documents, professional journals, science magazines, and the Internet.

Step 4 List where you found the sources. Make sure the sources you use are reliable and the most current available.

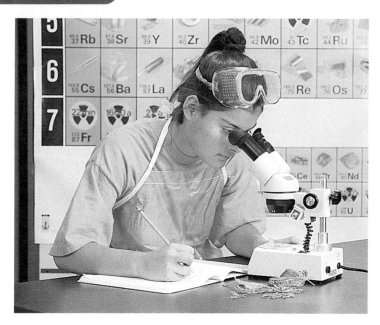

Figure 1
Making an observation is one way to gather information directly.

Evaluating Print and Nonprint Sources

Not all sources of information are reliable. Evaluate the sources you use for information, and use only those you know to be dependable. For example, suppose you want information about the digestion of fats and proteins. You might find two Websites on digestion. One Web site contains "Fat Zapping Tips" written by a company that sells expensive, high-protein supplements to help your body eliminate excess fat. The other is a Web page on "Digestion and Metabolism" written by a well-respected medical school. You would choose the second Web site as the more reliable source of information.

In science, information can change rapidly. Always consult the most current sources. A 1985 source about the human genome would not reflect the most recent research and findings.

Interpreting Scientific Illustrations

As you research a science topic, you will see drawings, diagrams, and photographs. Illustrations help you understand what you read. Some illustrations are included to help you understand an idea that you can't see easily by yourself. For instance, you can't see the bones of a blue whale, but you can look at a diagram of a whale skeleton as labeled in **Figure 2** that helps you understand them. Visualizing a drawing helps many people remember details more easily. Illustrations also provide examples that clarify difficult concepts or give additional information about the topic you are studying.

Most illustrations have a label or a caption. A label or caption identifies the illustration or provides additional information to better explain it. Can you find the caption or labels in **Figure 2?**

Figure 2
A labeled diagram of the skeletal structure of a blue whale

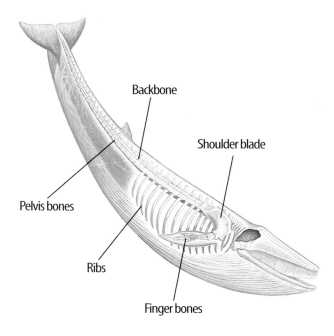

Backbone

Shoulder blade

Pelvis bones

Ribs

Finger bones

Venn Diagram

Although it is not a concept map, a Venn diagram illustrates how two subjects compare and contrast. In other words, you can see the characteristics that the subjects have in common and those that they do not.

The Venn diagram in **Figure 3** shows the relationship between two categories of organisms, plants and animals. Both share some basic characteristics as living organisms. However, there are differences in the ways they carry out various life processes, such as obtaining nourishment, that distinguish one from the other.

Concept Mapping

If you were taking a car trip, you might take some sort of road map. By using a map, you begin to learn where you are in relation to other places on the map.

A concept map is similar to a road map, but a concept map shows relationships among ideas (or concepts) rather than places. It is a diagram that visually shows how concepts are related. Because a concept map shows relationships among ideas, it can make the meanings of ideas and terms clear and help you understand what you are studying.

Overall, concept maps are useful for breaking large concepts down into smaller parts, making learning easier.

Figure 3
A Venn diagram shows how objects or concepts are alike and how they are different.

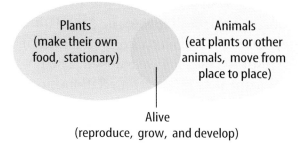

Plants
(make their own
food, stationary)

Animals
(eat plants or other
animals, move from
place to place)

Alive
(reproduce, grow, and develop)

Science Skill Handbook

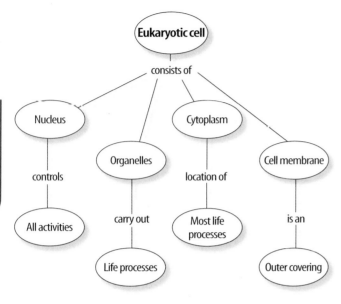

Figure 4
A network tree shows how concepts or objects are related.

Network Tree Look at the network tree in **Figure 4,** that shows details about a eukaryotic cell. A network tree is a type of concept map. Notice how some words are in ovals while others are written across connecting lines. The words inside the ovals are science terms or concepts. The words written on the connecting lines describe the relationships between the concepts.

When constructing a network tree, write the topic on a note card or piece of paper. Write the major concepts related to that topic on separate note cards or pieces of paper. Then arrange them in order from general to specific. Branch the related concepts from the major concept and describe the relationships on the connecting lines. Continue branching to more specific concepts. Write the relationships between the concepts on the connecting lines until all concepts are mapped. Then examine the network tree for relationships that cross branches, and add them to the network tree.

Events Chain An events chain is another type of concept map. It models the order of items or their sequence. In science, an events chain can be used to describe a sequence of events, the steps in a procedure, or the stages of a process.

When making an events chain, first find the one event that starts the chain. This event is called the *initiating event.* Then, find the next event in the chain and continue until you reach an outcome. Suppose you are asked to describe the main stages in the growth of a plant from a seed. You might draw an events chain such as the one in **Figure 5.** Notice that connecting words are not necessary in an events chain.

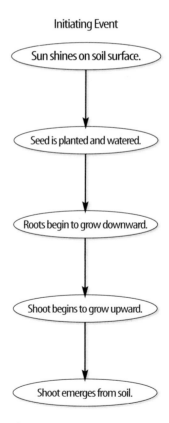

Figure 5
Events chains show the order of steps in a process or event.

Cycle Map A cycle concept map is a specific type of events chain map. In a cycle concept map, the series of events does not produce a final outcome. Instead, the last event in the chain relates back to the beginning event.

You first decide what event will be used as the beginning event. Once that is decided, you list events in order that occur after it. Words are written between events that describe what happens from one event to the next. The last event in a cycle concept map relates back to the beginning event. The number of events in a cycle concept varies but is usually three or more. Look at the cycle map in **Figure 6.**

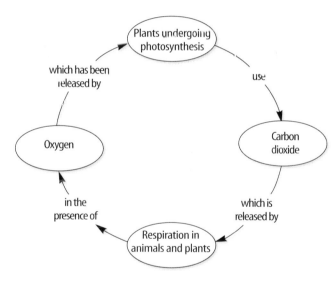

Figure 6
A cycle map shows events that occur in a cycle.

Spider Map A type of concept map that you can use for brainstorming is the spider map. When you have a central idea, you might find you have a jumble of ideas that relate to it but might not clearly relate to each other. The circulatory system spider map in **Figure 7** shows that if you write these ideas outside the main concept, then you can begin to separate and group unrelated terms so they become more useful.

Figure 7
A spider map allows you to list ideas that relate to a central topic but not necessarily to one another.

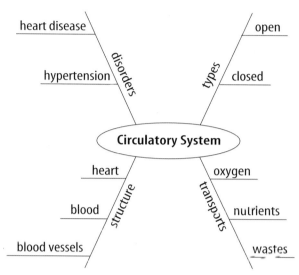

Writing a Paper

You will write papers often when researching science topics or reporting the results of investigations or experiments. Scientists frequently write papers to share their data and conclusions with other scientists and the public. When writing a paper, use these steps.

Step 1 Assemble your data by using graphs, tables, or a concept map. Create an outline.

Step 2 Start with an introduction that contains a clear statement of purpose and what you intend to discuss or prove.

Step 3 Organize the body into paragraphs. Each paragraph should start with a topic sentence, and the remaining sentences in that paragraph should support your point.

Step 4 Position data to help support your points.

Step 5 Summarize the main points and finish with a conclusion statement.

Step 6 Use tables, graphs, charts, and illustrations whenever possible.

You might say the work of a scientist is to solve problems. When you decide to find out why one corner of your yard is always soggy, you are problem solving, too. You might observe that the corner is lower than the surrounding area and has less vegetation growing in it. You might decide to see if planting some grass will keep the corner drier.

Scientists use orderly approaches to solve problems. The methods scientists use include identifying a question, making observations, forming a hypothesis, testing a hypothesis, analyzing results, and drawing conclusions.

Scientific investigations involve careful observation under controlled conditions. Such observation of an object or a process can suggest new and interesting questions about it. These questions sometimes lead to the formation of a hypothesis. Scientific investigations are designed to test a hypothesis.

Identifying a Question

The first step in a scientific investigation or experiment is to identify a question to be answered or a problem to be solved. You might be interested in knowing why an animal like the one in **Figure 8** looks the way it does.

Figure 8
When you see a bird, you might ask yourself, "How does the shape of this bird's beak help it feed?"

Forming Hypotheses

Hypotheses are based on observations that have been made. A hypothesis is a possible explanation based on previous knowledge and observations.

Perhaps a scientist has observed that bean plants grow larger if they are fertilized than if they are not. Based on these observations, the scientist can make a statement that he or she can test. The statement is a hypothesis. The hypothesis could be: *Fertilizer makes bean plants grow larger.* A hypothesis has to be something you can test by using an investigation. A testable hypothesis is a valid hypothesis.

Predicting

When you apply a hypothesis to a specific situation, you predict something about that situation. First, you must identify which hypothesis fits the situation you are considering. People use predictions to make everyday decisions. Based on previous observations and experiences, you might form a prediction that if fertilizer makes bean plants grow larger, then fertilized plants will yield more beans than plants not fertilized. Someone could use this prediction to plan to grow fewer plants.

Testing a Hypothesis

To test a hypothesis, you need a procedure. A procedure is the plan you follow in your experiment. A procedure tells you what materials to use, as well as how and in what order to use them. When you follow a procedure, data are generated that support or do not support the original hypothesis statement.

For example, suppose you notice that your guppies don't seem as active as usual when your aquarium heater is not working. You wonder how water temperature affects guppy activity level. You decide to test the hypothesis, "If water temperature increases, then guppy activity should increase." Then you write the procedure shown in **Figure 9** for your experiment and generate the data presented in the table below.

Procedure

1. Fill five identical glass containers with equal amounts of aquarium water.
2. Measure and record the temperature of the water in the first container.
3. Heat and cool the other containers so that two have higher and two have lower water temperatures.
4. Place a guppy in each container; count and record the number of movements each guppy makes in 5 minutes.

Figure 9
A procedure tells you what to do step by step.

Number of Guppy Movements		
Container	Temperature (°C)	Movements
1	38	56
2	40	61
3	42	70
4	36	46
5	34	42

Are all investigations alike? Keep in mind as you perform investigations in science that a hypothesis can be tested in many ways. Not every investigation makes use of all the ways that are described on these pages, and not all hypotheses are tested by investigations. Scientists encounter many variations in the methods that are used when they perform experiments. The skills in this handbook are here for you to use and practice.

Identifying and Manipulating Variables and Controls

In any experiment, it is important to keep everything the same except for the item you are testing. The one factor you change is called the independent variable. The factor that changes as a result of the independent variable is called the dependent variable. Always make sure you have only one independent variable. If you allow more than one, you will not know what causes the changes you observe in the dependent variable. Many experiments also have controls—individual instances or experimental subjects for which the independent variable is not changed. You can then compare the test results to the control results.

For example, in the guppy experiment, you made everything the same except the temperature of the water. The glass containers were identical. The volume of aquarium water in each container and beginning water temperature were the same. Each guppy was like the others, as much as possible. In this way, you could be sure that any difference in the number of guppy movements was caused by the temperature change—the independent variable. The activity level of the guppy was measured as the number of guppy movements—the dependent variable. The guppy in the container in which the water temperature was not changed was the control.

Skill Handbooks

Collecting Data

Whether you are carrying out an investigation or a short observational experiment, you will collect data, or information. Scientists collect data accurately as numbers and descriptions and organize it in specific ways.

Observing Scientists observe items and events, then record what they see. When they use only words to describe an observation, it is called qualitative data. For example, a scientist might describe the color of a bird or the shape of a bird's beak as seen through binoculars. Scientists' observations also can describe how much there is of something. These observations use numbers, as well as words, in the description and are called quantitative data. For example, if a particular dog is described as being "furry, yellow, and short-haired," the data are clearly qualitative. Quantitative data for this dog might include "a mass of 14 kg, a height of 46 cm, and an age of 150 days." Quantitative data often are organized into tables. Then, from information in the table, a graph can be drawn. Graphs can reveal relationships that exist in experimental data.

When you make observations in science, you should examine the entire object or situation first, then look carefully for details. If you're looking at a plant, for instance, check general characteristics such as size and overall structure before using a hand lens to examine the leaves and other smaller structures such as flowers or fruits. Remember to record accurately everything you see.

Scientists try to make careful and accurate observations. When possible, they use instruments such as microscopes, metric rulers, graduated cylinders, thermometers, and balances. Measurements provide numerical data that can be repeated and checked.

Sampling When working with large numbers of objects or a large population, scientists usually cannot observe or study every one of them. Instead, they use a sample or a portion of the total number. To *sample* is to take a small, representative portion of the objects or organisms of a population for research. By making careful observations or manipulating variables within a portion of a group, information is discovered and conclusions are drawn that might apply to the whole population.

Estimating Scientific work also involves estimating. To *estimate* is to make a judgment about the size or the number of something without measuring or counting every object or member of a population. Scientists first count the number of objects in a small sample. Looking through a microscope lens, for example, a scientist can count the number of bacterial colonies in the 1-cm^2 frame shown in **Figure 10.** Then the scientist can multiply that number by the number of cm^2 in the petri dish to get an estimate of the total number of bacterial colonies present.

Figure 10
To estimate the total number of bacterial colonies that are present on a petri dish, count the number of bacterial colonies within a 1-cm^2 frame and multiply that number by the number of frames on the dish.

Measuring in SI

The metric system of measurement was developed in 1795. A modern form of the metric system, called the International System, or SI, was adopted in 1960. SI provides standard measurements that all scientists around the world can understand.

The metric system is convenient because unit sizes vary by multiples of 10. When changing from smaller units to larger units, divide by a multiple of 10. When changing from larger units to smaller, multiply by a multiple of 10. To convert millimeters to centimeters, divide the millimeters by 10. To convert 30 mm to centimeters, divide 30 by 10 (30 mm equal 3 cm).

Prefixes are used to name units. Look at the table below for some common metric prefixes and their meanings. Do you see how the prefix *kilo-* attached to the unit *gram* is *kilogram*, or 1,000 g?

Metric Prefixes			
Prefix	**Symbol**	**Meaning**	
kilo-	k	1,000	thousand
hecto-	h	100	hundred
deka-	da	10	ten
deci-	d	0.1	tenth
centi-	c	0.01	hundredth
milli-	m	0.001	thousandth

Now look at the metric ruler shown in **Figure 11.** The centimeter lines are the long, numbered lines, and the shorter lines are millimeter lines.

When using a metric ruler, line up the 0-cm mark with the end of the object being measured, and read the number of the unit where the object ends. In this instance it would be 4.5 cm.

Figure 11
This metric ruler shows centimeter and millimeter divisions.

Liquid Volume In some science activities, you will measure liquids. The unit that is used to measure liquids is the liter. A liter has the volume of 1,000 cm³. The prefix *milli-* means "thousandth (0.001)." A milliliter is one thousandth of 1 L and 1 L has the volume of 1,000 mL. One milliliter of liquid completely fills a cube measuring 1 cm on each side. Therefore, 1 mL equals 1 cm³.

You will use beakers and graduated cylinders to measure liquid volume. A graduated cylinder, as illustrated in **Figure 12,** is marked from bottom to top in milliliters. This graduated cylinder contains 79 mL of a liquid.

Figure 12
Graduated cylinders measure liquid volume.

Mass Scientists measure mass in grams. You might use a beam balance similar to the one shown in **Figure 13.** The balance has a pan on one side and a set of beams on the other side. Each beam has a rider that slides on the beam.

Before you find the mass of an object, slide all the riders back to the zero point. Check the pointer on the right to make sure it swings an equal distance above and below the zero point. If the swing is unequal, find and turn the adjusting screw until you have an equal swing.

Place an object on the pan. Slide the largest rider along its beam until the pointer drops below zero. Then move it back one notch. Repeat the process on each beam until the pointer swings an equal distance above and below the zero point. Sum the masses on each beam to find the mass of the object. Move all riders back to zero when finished.

Figure 13
A triple beam balance is used to determine the mass of an object.

You should never place a hot object on the pan or pour chemicals directly onto the pan. Instead, find the mass of a clean container. Remove the container from the pan, then place the chemicals in the container. Find the mass of the container with the chemicals in it. To find the mass of the chemicals, subtract the mass of the empty container from the mass of the filled container.

Making and Using Tables

Browse through your textbook and you will see tables in the text and in the activities. In a table, data, or information, are arranged so that they are easier to understand. Activity tables help organize the data you collect during an activity so results can be interpreted.

Making Tables To make a table, list the items to be compared in the first column and the characteristics to be compared in the first row. The title should clearly indicate the content of the table, and the column or row heads should tell the reader what information is found in there. The table below lists materials collected for recycling on three weekly pick-up days. The inclusion of kilograms in parentheses also identifies for the reader that the figures are mass units.

Recyclable Materials Collected During Week			
Day of Week	Paper (kg)	Aluminum (kg)	Glass (kg)
Monday	5.0	4.0	12.0
Wednesday	4.0	1.0	10.0
Friday	2.5	2.0	10.0

Using Tables How much paper, in kilograms, is being recycled on Wednesday? Locate the column labeled "Paper (kg)" and the row "Wednesday." The information in the box where the column and row intersect is the answer. Did you answer "4.0"? How much aluminum, in kilograms, is being recycled on Friday? If you answered "2.0," you understand how to read the table. How much glass is collected for recycling each week? Locate the column labeled "Glass (kg)" and add the figures for all three rows. If you answered "32.0," then you know how to locate and use the data provided in the table.

Recording Data

To be useful, the data you collect must be recorded carefully. Accuracy is key. A well-thought-out experiment includes a way to record procedures, observations, and results accurately. Data tables are one way to organize and record results. Set up the tables you will need ahead of time so you can record the data right away.

Record information properly and neatly. Never put unidentified data on scraps of paper. Instead, data should be written in a notebook like the one in **Figure 14.** Write in pencil so information isn't lost if your data gets wet. At each point in the experiment, record your data and label it. That way, your information will be accurate and you will not have to determine what the figures mean when you look at your notes later.

Figure 14
Record data neatly and clearly so it is easy to understand.

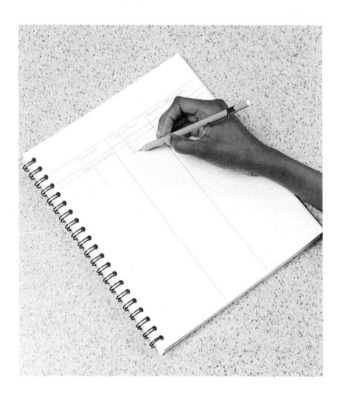

Recording Observations

It is important to record observations accurately and completely. That is why you always should record observations in your notes immediately as you make them. It is easy to miss details or make mistakes when recording results from memory. Do not include your personal thoughts when you record your data. Record only what you observe to eliminate bias. For example, when you record that a plant grew 12 cm in one day, you would note that this was the largest daily growth for the week. However, you would not refer to the data as "the best growth spurt of the week."

Making Models

You can organize the observations and other data you collect and record in many ways. Making models is one way to help you better understand the parts of a structure you have been observing or the way a process for which you have been taking various measurements works.

Models often show things that are very large or small or otherwise would be difficult to see and understand. You can study blood vessels and know that they are hollow tubes. The size and proportional differences among arteries, veins, and capillaries can be explained in words. However, you can better visualize the relative sizes and proportions of blood vessels by making models of them. Gluing different kinds of pasta to thick paper so the openings can be seen can help you see how the differences in size, wall thickness, and shape among types of blood vessels affect their functions.

Other models can be devised on a computer. Some models, such as disease control models used by doctors to predict the spread of the flu, are mathematical and are represented by equations.

Making and Using Graphs

After scientists organize data in tables, they might display the data in a graph that shows the relationship of one variable to another. A graph makes interpretation and analysis of data easier. Three types of graphs are the line graph, the bar graph, and the circle graph.

Line Graphs A line graph like in **Figure 15** is used to show the relationship between two variables. The variables being compared go on two axes of the graph. For data from an experiment, the independent variable always goes on the horizontal axis, called the *x*-axis. The dependent variable always goes on the vertical axis, called the *y*-axis. After drawing your axes, label each with a scale. Next, plot the data points.

A data point is the intersection of the recorded value of the dependent variable for each tested value of the independent variable. After all the points are plotted, connect them.

Bar Graphs Bar graphs compare data that do not change continuously. Vertical bars show the relationships among data.

To make a bar graph, set up the *y*-axis as you did for the line graph. Draw vertical bars of equal size from the *x*-axis up to the point on the *y*-axis that represents the value of *x*.

Figure 16

The number of wing vibrations per second for different insects can be shown as a bar graph or circle graph.

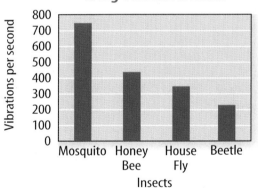

Circle Graphs A circle graph uses a circle divided into sections to display data as parts (fractions or percentages) of a whole. The size of each section corresponds to the fraction or percentage of the data that the section represents. So, the entire circle represents 100 percent, one-half represents 50 percent, one-fifth represents 20 percent, and so on.

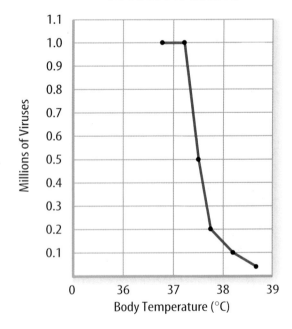

Figure 15

This line graph shows the relationship between body temperature and the millions of infecting viruses present in a human body.

Analyzing Results

To determine the meaning of your observations and investigation results, you will need to look for patterns in the data. You can organize your information in several of the ways that are discussed in this handbook. Then you must think critically to determine what the data mean. Scientists use several approaches when they analyze the data they have collected and recorded. Each approach is useful for identifying specific patterns in the data.

Forming Operational Definitions

An operational definition defines an object by showing how it functions, works, or behaves. Such definitions are written in terms of how an object works or how it can be used; that is, they describe its job or purpose.

For example, a ruler can be defined as a tool that measures the length of an object (how it can be used). A ruler also can be defined as something that contains a series of marks that can be used as a standard when measuring (how it works).

Classifying

Classifying is the process of sorting objects or events into groups based on common features. When classifying, first observe the objects or events to be classified. Then select one feature that is shared by some members in the group but not by all. Place those members that share that feature into a subgroup. You can classify members into smaller and smaller subgroups based on characteristics.

How might you classify a group of animals? You might first classify them by putting all of the dogs, cats, lizards, snakes, and birds into separate groups. Within each group,

you could then look for another common feature by which to further classify members of the group, such as size or color.

Remember that when you classify, you are grouping objects or events for a purpose. For example, classifying animals can be the first step in identifying them. You might know that a cardinal is a red bird. To find it in a large group of animals, you might start with the classification scheme mentioned here. You'll locate a cardinal within the red grouping of the birds that you separate from the rest of the animals. A male ruby-throated hummingbird could be located within the birds by its tiny size and the bright red color of its throat. Keep your purpose in mind as you select the features to form groups and subgroups.

Figure 17
Color is one of many characteristics that are used to classify animals.

Science Skill Handbook

Skill Handbooks

Comparing and Contrasting

Observations can be analyzed by noting the similarities and differences between two or more objects or events that you observe. When you look at objects or events to see how they are similar, you are comparing them. Contrasting is looking for differences in objects or events. The table below compares and contrasts the nutritional value of two cereals.

Nutritional Values		
	Cereal A	Cereal B
Calories	220	160
Fat	10 g	10 g
Protein	2.5 g	2.6 g
Carbohydrate	30 g	15 g

Recognizing Cause and Effect

Have you ever gotten a cold and then suggested that you probably caught it from a classmate who had one recently? If so, you have observed an effect and inferred a cause. The event is the effect, and the reason for the event is the cause.

When scientists are unsure of the cause of a certain event, they design controlled experiments to determine what caused it.

Interpreting Data

The word *interpret* means "to explain the meaning of something." Look at the problem originally being explored in an experiment and figure out what the data show. Identify the control group and the test group so you can see whether or not changes in the independent variable have had an effect. Look for differences in the dependent variable between the control and test groups.

These differences you observe can be qualitative or quantitative. You would be able to describe a qualitative difference using only words, whereas you would measure a quantitative difference and describe it using numbers. If there are qualitative or quantitative differences, the independent variable that is being tested could have had an effect. If no qualitative or quantitative differences are found between the control and test groups, the variable that is being tested apparently had no effect.

For example, suppose that three pepper plants are placed in a garden and two of the plants are fertilized, but the third is left to grow without fertilizer. Suppose you are then asked to describe any differences in the plants after two weeks. A qualitative difference might be the appearance of brighter green leaves on fertilized plants but not on the unfertilized plant. A quantitative difference might be a difference in the height of the plants or the number of flowers on them.

Inferring Scientists often make inferences based on their observations. An inference is an attempt to explain, or interpret, observations or to indicate what caused what you observed. An inference is a type of conclusion.

When making an inference, be certain to use accurate data and accurately described observations. Analyze all of the data that you've collected. Then, based on everything you know, explain or interpret what you've observed.

Drawing Conclusions

When scientists have analyzed the data they collected, they proceed to draw conclusions about what the data mean. These conclusions are sometimes stated using words similar to those found in the hypothesis formed earlier in the process.

Conclusions To analyze your data, you must review all of the observations and measurements that you made and recorded. Recheck all data for accuracy. After your data are rechecked and organized, you are almost ready to draw a conclusion such as "Plants need sunlight in order to grow."

Before you can draw a conclusion, however, you must determine whether the data allow you to come to a conclusion that supports a hypothesis. Sometimes that will be the case; other times it will not.

If your data do not support a hypothesis, it does not mean that the hypothesis is wrong. It means only that the results of the investigation did not support the hypothesis. Maybe the experiment needs to be redesigned, but very likely, some of the initial observations on which the hypothesis was based were incomplete or biased. Perhaps more observation or research is needed to refine the hypothesis.

Avoiding Bias Sometimes drawing a conclusion involves making judgments. When you make a judgment, you form an opinion about what your data mean. It is important to be honest and to avoid reaching a conclusion if no supporting evidence for it exists or if it is based on a small sample. It also is important not to allow any expectations of results to bias your judgments. If possible, it is a good idea to collect additional data. Scientists do this all the time.

For example, animal behaviorist Katharine Payne made an important observation about elephant communication. While visiting a zoo, Payne felt the air vibrating around her. At the same time, she also noticed that the skin on an elephant's forehead was fluttering. She suspected that the elephants were generating the vibrations and that they might be using the low-frequency sounds to communicate.

Payne conducted an experiment to record these sounds and simultaneously observe the behavior of the elephants in the zoo. She later conducted a similar experiment in Namibia in southwest Africa, where elephant herds roam. The additional data she collected supported the judgment Payne had made, which was that these low-frequency sounds were a form of communication between elephants.

Evaluating Others' Data and Conclusions

Sometimes scientists have to use data that they did not collect themselves, or they have to rely on observations and conclusions drawn by other researchers. In cases such as these, the data must be evaluated carefully.

How were the data obtained? How was the investigation done? Has it been duplicated by other researchers? Did they come up with the same results? Look at the conclusion, as well. Would you reach the same conclusion from these results? Only when you have confidence in the data of others can you believe it is true and feel comfortable using it.

Communicating

The communication of ideas is an important part of the work of scientists. A discovery that is not reported will not advance the scientific community's understanding or knowledge. Communication among scientists also is important as a way of improving their investigations.

Scientists communicate in many ways, from writing articles in journals and magazines that explain their investigations and experiments, to announcing important discoveries on television and radio, to sharing ideas with colleagues on the Internet or presenting them as lectures.

People who study science rely on computers to record and store data and to analyze results from investigations. Whether you work in a laboratory or just need to write a lab report with tables, good computer skills are a necessity.

Using a Word Processor

Suppose your teacher has assigned a written report. After you've completed your research and decided how you want to write the information, you need to put all that information on paper. The easiest way to do this is with a word processing application on a computer.

A computer application that allows you to type your information, change it as many times as you need to, and then print it out so that it looks neat and clean is called a word processing application. You also can use this type of application to create tables and columns, add bullets or cartoon art to your page, include page numbers, and even check your spelling.

Helpful Hints

- If you aren't sure how to do something using your word processing program, look in the help menu. You will find a list of topics there to click on for help. After you locate the help topic you need, just follow the step-by-step instructions you see on your screen.
- Just because you've spell checked your report doesn't mean that the spelling is perfect. The spell check feature can't catch misspelled words that look like other words. If you've accidentally typed *wind* instead of *wing*, the spell checker won't know the difference. Always reread your report to make sure you didn't miss any mistakes.

Figure 18
You can use computer programs to make graphs and tables.

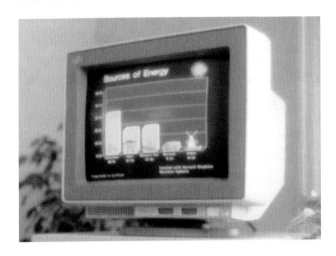

Using a Database

Imagine you're in the middle of a research project busily gathering facts and information. You soon realize that it's becoming more difficult to organize and keep track of all the information. The tool to use to solve information overload is a database. Just as a file cabinet organizes paper records, a database organizes computer records. However, a database is more powerful than a simple file cabinet because at the click of a mouse, the contents can be reshuffled and reorganized. At computer-quick speeds, databases can sort information by any characteristics and filter data into multiple categories.

Helpful Hints

- Before setting up a database, take some time to learn the features of your database software by practicing with established database software.
- Periodically save your database as you enter data. That way, if something happens such as your computer malfunctions or the power goes off, you won't lose all of your work.

Doing a Database Search

When searching for information in a database, use the following search strategies to get the best results. These are the same search methods used for searching Internet databases.

- Place the word *and* between two words in your search if you want the database to look for any entries that have both words. For example, "fox *and* mink" would give you information that mentions both fox and mink.
- Place the word *or* between two words if you want the database to show entries that have at least one of the words. For example "fox *or* mink" would show you information that mentions either fox or mink.
- Place the word *not* between two words if you want the database to look for entries that have the first word but do not have the second word. For example, "canine *not* fox" would show you information that mentions the term *canine* but does not mention the fox.

In summary, databases can be used to store large amounts of information about a particular subject. Databases allow biologists, Earth scientists, and physical scientists to search for information quickly and accurately.

Using an Electronic Spreadsheet

Your science fair experiment has produced lots of numbers. How do you keep track of all the data, and how can you easily work out all the calculations needed? You can use a computer program called a spreadsheet to record data that involve numbers. A spreadsheet is an electronic mathematical worksheet.

Type in your data in rows and columns, just as in a data table on a sheet of paper. A spreadsheet uses simple math to do data calculations. For example, you could add, subtract, divide, or multiply any of the values in the spreadsheet by another number. You also could set up a series of math steps you want to apply to the data. If you want to add 12 to all the numbers and then multiply all the numbers by 10, the computer does all the calculations for you in the spreadsheet. Below is an example of a spreadsheet that records data from an experiment with mice in a maze.

Helpful Hints

- Before you set up the spreadsheet, identify how you want to organize the data. Include any formulas you will need to use.
- Make sure you have entered the correct data into the correct rows and columns.
- You also can display your results in a graph. Pick the style of graph that best represents the data with which you are working.

Figure 19
A spreadsheet allows you to display large amounts of data and do calculations automatically.

Technology Skill Handbook

Using a Computerized Card Catalog

When you have a report or paper to research, you probably go to the library. To find the information you need in the library, you might have to use a computerized card catalog. This type of card catalog allows you to search for information by subject, by title, or by author. The computer then will display all the holdings the library has on the subject, title, or author requested.

A library's holdings can include books, magazines, databases, videos, and audio materials. When you have chosen something from this list, the computer will show whether an item is available and where in the library to find it.

Helpful Hints

- Remember that you can use the computer to search by subject, author, or title. If you know a book's author but not the title, you can search for all the books the library has by that author.

- When searching by subject, it's often most helpful to narrow your search by using specific search terms, such as *and*, *or*, and *not*. If you don't find enough sources, you can broaden your search.

- Pay attention to the type of materials found in your search. If you need a book, you can eliminate any videos or other resources that come up in your search.

- Knowing how your library is arranged can save you a lot of time. The librarian will show you where certain types of materials are kept and how to find specific holdings.

Using Graphics Software

Are you having trouble finding that exact piece of art you're looking for? Do you have a picture in your mind of what you want but can't seem to find the right graphic to represent your ideas? To solve these problems, you can use graphics software. Graphics software allows you to create and change images and diagrams in almost unlimited ways. Typical uses for graphics software include arranging clip art, changing scanned images, and constructing pictures from scratch. Most graphics software applications work in similar ways. They use the same basic tools and functions. Once you master one graphics application, you can use any other graphics application relatively easily.

Figure 20
Graphics software can use your data to draw bar graphs.

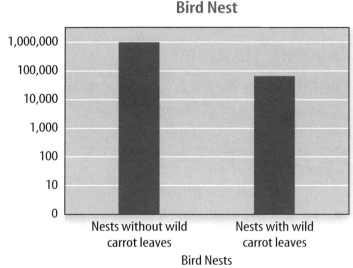

Number of Mites per Bird Nest

Bird Nests: Nests without wild carrot leaves, Nests with wild carrot leaves

Skill Handbooks

Figure 21

Graphics software can use your data to draw circle graphs.

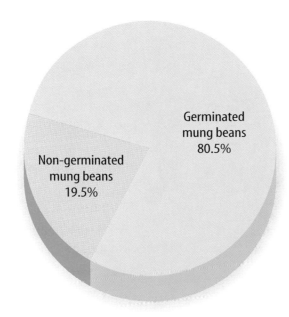

Helpful Hints

■ As with any method of drawing, the more you practice using the graphics software, the better your results will be.

■ Start by using the software to manipulate existing drawings. Once you master this, making your own illustrations will be easier.

■ Clip art is available on CD-ROMs and the Internet. With these resources, finding a piece of clip art to suit your purposes is simple.

■ As you work on a drawing, save it often.

Developing Multimedia Presentations

It's your turn—you have to present your science report to the entire class. How do you do it? You can use many different sources of information to get the class excited about your presentation. Posters, videos, photographs, sound, computers, and the Internet can help show your ideas.

First, determine what important points you want to make in your presentation. Then, write an outline of what materials and types of media would best illustrate those points. Maybe you could start with an outline on an overhead projector, then show a video, followed by something from the Internet or a slide show accompanied by music or recorded voices. You might choose to use a presentation builder computer application that can combine all these elements into one presentation. Make sure the presentation is well constructed to make the most impact on the audience.

Figure 22

Multimedia presentations use many types of print and electronic materials.

Helpful Hints

■ Carefully consider what media will best communicate the point you are trying to make.

■ Make sure you know how to use any equipment you will be using in your presentation.

■ Practice the presentation several times.

■ If possible, set up all of the equipment ahead of time. Make sure everything is working correctly.

*Use this Math Skill Handbook to help solve problems you are given in this
text. You might find it useful to review topics in this Math Skill Handbook first.*

Converting Units

In science, quantities such as length, mass, and time sometimes are measured using different units. Suppose you want to know how many miles are in 12.7 km.

Conversion factors are used to change from one unit of measure to another. A conversion factor is a ratio that is equal to one. For example, there are 1,000 mL in 1 L, so 1,000 mL equals 1 L, or:

$$1,000 \text{ mL} = 1 \text{ L}$$

If both sides are divided by 1 L, this equation becomes:

$$\frac{1,000 \text{ mL}}{1 \text{ L}} = 1$$

The **ratio** on the left side of this equation is equal to 1 and is a conversion factor. You can make another conversion factor by dividing both sides of the top equation by 1,000 mL:

$$1 = \frac{1 \text{ L}}{1,000 \text{ mL}}$$

To **convert units,** you multiply by the appropriate conversion factor. For example, how many milliliters are in 1.255 L? To convert 1.255 L to milliliters, multiply 1.255 L by a conversion factor.

Use the **conversion factor** with new units (mL) in the numerator and the old units (L) in the denominator.

$$1.255 \text{ L} \times \frac{1,000 \text{ mL}}{1 \text{ L}} = 1,255 \text{ mL}$$

The unit L divides in this equation, just as if it were a number.

Example 1 There are 2.54 cm in 1 inch. If a meterstick has a length of 100 cm, how long is the meterstick in inches?

Step 1 Decide which conversion factor to use. You know the length of the meterstick in centimeters, so centimeters are the old units. You want to find the length in inches, so inch is the new unit.

Step 2 Form the conversion factor. Start with the relationship between the old and new units.

$$2.54 \text{ cm} = 1 \text{ inch}$$

Step 3 Form the conversion factor with the old unit (centimeter) on the bottom by dividing both sides by 2.54 cm.

$$1 = \frac{2.54 \text{ cm}}{2.54 \text{ cm}} = \frac{1 \text{ inch}}{2.54 \text{ cm}}$$

Step 4 Multiply the old measurement by the conversion factor.

$$100 \text{ cm} \times \frac{1 \text{ inch}}{2.54 \text{ cm}} = 39.37 \text{ inches}$$

The meterstick is 39.37 inches long.

Example 2 There are 365 days in one year. If a person is 14 years old, what is his or her age in days? (Ignore leap years)

Step 1 Decide which conversion factor to use. You want to convert years to days.

Step 2 Form the conversion factor. Start with the relation between the old and new units.

$$1 \text{ year} = 365 \text{ days}$$

Step 3 Form the conversion factor with the old unit (year) on the bottom by dividing both sides by 1 year.

$$1 = \frac{1 \text{ year}}{1 \text{ year}} = \frac{365 \text{ days}}{1 \text{ year}}$$

Step 4 Multiply the old measurement by the conversion factor:

$$14 \text{ years} \times \frac{365 \text{ days}}{1 \text{ year}} = 5,110 \text{ days}$$

The person's age is 5,110 days.

Practice Problem A cat has a mass of 2.31 kg. If there are 1,000 g in 1 kg, what is the mass of the cat in grams? 2310 g

Using Fractions

A **fraction** is a number that compares a part to the whole. For example, in the fraction $\frac{2}{3}$, the 2 represents the part and the 3 represents the whole. In the fraction $\frac{2}{3}$, the top number, 2, is called the numerator. The bottom number, 3, is called the denominator.

Sometimes fractions are not written in their simplest form. To determine a fraction's **simplest form,** you must find the greatest common factor (GCF) of the numerator and denominator. The greatest common factor is the largest common factor of all the factors the two numbers have in common.

For example, because the number 3 divides into 12 and 30 evenly, it is a common factor of 12 and 30. However, because the number 6 is the largest number that evenly divides into 12 and 30, it is the **greatest common factor.**

After you find the greatest common factor, you can write a fraction in its simplest form. Divide both the numerator and the denominator by the greatest common factor. The number that results is the fraction in its **simplest form.**

Example Twelve of the 20 corn plants in a field are more than 1.5 m tall. What fraction of the corn plants in the field is 1.5 m tall?

Step 1 Write the fraction.

$$\frac{part}{whole} = \frac{12}{20}$$

Step 2 To find the GCF of the numerator and denominator, list all of the factors of each number.

Factors of 12: 1, 2, 3, 4, 6, 12 (the numbers that divide evenly into 12)

Factors of 20: 1, 2, 4, 5, 10, 20 (the numbers that divide evenly into 20)

Step 3 List the common factors.

1, 2, 4.

Step 4 Choose the greatest factor in the list of common factors.

The GCF of 12 and 20 is 4.

Step 5 Divide the numerator and denominator by the GCF.

$$\frac{12 \div 4}{20 \div 4} = \frac{3}{5}$$

In the field, $\frac{3}{5}$ of the corn plants are more than 1.5 m tall.

Practice Problem There are 90 duck eggs in a population. Of those eggs, 66 hatch over a one-week period. What fraction of the eggs hatch over a one-week period? Write the fraction in simplest form. $\frac{11}{15}$

Math Skill Handbook

Skill Handbooks

Calculating Ratios

A **ratio** is a comparison of two numbers by division.

Ratios can be written 3 to 5 or 3:5. Ratios also can be written as fractions, such as $\frac{3}{5}$. Ratios, like fractions, can be written in simplest form. Recall that a fraction is in **simplest form** when the greatest common factor (GCF) of the numerator and denominator is 1.

Example From a package of sunflower seeds, 40 seeds germinated and 64 did not. What is the ratio of germinated to not germinated seeds as a fraction in simplest form?

Step 1 Write the ratio as a fraction.

$$\frac{\text{germinated}}{\text{not germinated}} = \frac{40}{64}$$

Step 2 Express the fraction in simplest form. The GCF of 40 and 64 is 8.

$$\frac{40}{64} = \frac{40 \div 8}{64 \div 8} = \frac{5}{8}$$

The ratio of germinated to not germinated seeds is $\frac{5}{8}$.

Practice Problem Two children measure 100 cm and 144 cm in height. What is the ratio of their heights in simplest fraction form? $\frac{25}{36}$

Using Decimals

A **decimal** is a fraction with a denominator of 10, 100, 1,000, or another power of 10. For example, 0.854 is the same as the fraction $\frac{854}{1,000}$.

In a decimal, the decimal point separates the ones place and the tenths place. For example, 0.27 means twenty-seven hundredths, or $\frac{27}{100}$, where 27 is the **number of units** out of 100 units. Any fraction can be written as a decimal using division.

Example Write $\frac{5}{8}$ as a decimal.

Step 1 Write a division problem with the numerator, 5, as the dividend and the denominator, 8, as the divisor. Write 5 as 5.000.

Step 2 Solve the problem.

```
      0.625
  8)5.000
    48
    ──
     20
     16
     ──
      40
      40
      ──
       0
```

Therefore, $\frac{5}{8} = 0.625$.

Practice Problem Write $\frac{19}{25}$ as a decimal. 0.76

Using Percentages

The word *percent* means "out of one hundred." A **percent** is a ratio that compares a number to 100. Suppose you read that 77 percent of all fish on Earth live in the Pacific Ocean. That is the same as reading that the ratio of Earth's fish that live in the Pacific Ocean is $\frac{77}{100}$. To express a fraction as a percent, first find an equivalent decimal for the fraction. Then, multiply the decimal by 100 and add the percent symbol. For example, $\frac{1}{2} = 1 \div 2 = 0.5$. Then $0.5 \cdot 100 = 50 = 50\%$.

Example Express $\frac{13}{20}$ as a percent.

Step 1 Find the equivalent decimal for the fraction.

$$
\begin{array}{r}
0.65 \\
20)\overline{13.00} \\
\underline{120} \\
100 \\
\underline{100} \\
0
\end{array}
$$

Step 2 Rewrite the fraction $\frac{13}{20}$ as 0.65.

Step 3 Multiply 0.65 by 100 and add the % sign.

$0.65 \cdot 100 = 65 = 65\%$

So, $\frac{13}{20} = 65\%$.

Practice Problem In an experimental population of 365 sheep, 73 were brown. What percent of the sheep were brown? 20%

Using Precision and Significant Digits

When you make a **measurement,** the value you record depends on the precision of the measuring instrument. When adding or subtracting numbers with different precision, the answer is rounded to the smallest number of decimal places of any number in the sum or difference. When multiplying or dividing, the answer is rounded to the smallest number of significant figures of any number being multiplied or divided. When counting the number of **significant figures,** all digits are counted except zeros at the end of a number with no decimal such as 2,500, and zeros at the beginning of a decimal such as 0.03020.

Example The lengths 5.28 and 5.2 are measured in meters. Find the sum of these lengths and report the sum using the least precise measurement.

Step 1 Find the sum.

$$
\begin{array}{ll}
5.28 \text{ m} & 2 \text{ digits after the decimal} \\
+5.2 \text{ m} & 1 \text{ digit after the decimal} \\
\hline
10.48 \text{ m} &
\end{array}
$$

Step 2 Round to one digit after the decimal because the least number of digits after the decimal of the numbers being added is 1.

The sum is 10.5 m.

Practice Problem Multiply the numbers in the example using the rule for multiplying and dividing. Report the answer with the correct number of significant figures. 27m^2

Math Skill Handbook

Solving One-Step Equations

An **equation** is a statement that two things are equal. For example, $A = B$ is an equation that states that A is equal to B.

Sometimes one side of the equation will contain a **variable** whose value is not known. In the equation $3x = 12$, the variable is x.

The equation is solved when the variable is replaced with a value that makes both sides of the equation equal to each other. For example, the solution of the equation $3x = 12$ is $x = 4$. If the x is replaced with 4, then the equation becomes $3 \cdot 4 = 12$, or $12 = 12$.

To solve an equation such as $8x = 40$, divide both sides of the equation by the number that multiplies the variable.

$$8x = 40$$
$$\frac{8x}{8} = \frac{40}{8}$$
$$x = 5$$

You can check your answer by replacing the variable with your solution and seeing if both sides of the equation are the same.

$$8x = 8 \cdot 5 = 40$$

The left and right sides of the equation are the same, so $x = 5$ is the solution.

Sometimes an equation is written in this way: $a = bc$. This also is called a **formula.** The letters can be replaced by numbers, but the numbers must still make both sides of the equation the same.

Example 1 Solve the equation $10x = 35$.

Step 1 Find the solution by dividing each side of the equation by 10.

$$10x = 35 \qquad \frac{10x}{10} = \frac{35}{10} \qquad x = 3.5$$

Step 2 Check the solution.

$$10x = 35 \qquad 10 \times 3.5 = 35 \qquad 35 = 35$$

Both sides of the equation are equal, so $x = 3.5$ is the solution to the equation.

Example 2 In the formula $a = bc$, find the value of c if $a = 20$ and $b = 2$.

Step 1 Rearrange the formula so the unknown value is by itself on one side of the equation by dividing both sides by b.

$$a = bc$$
$$\frac{a}{b} = \frac{bc}{b}$$
$$\frac{a}{b} = c$$

Step 2 Replace the variables a and b with the values that are given.

$$\frac{a}{b} = c$$
$$\frac{20}{2} = c$$
$$10 = c$$

Step 3 Check the solution.

$$a = bc$$
$$20 = 2 \times 10$$
$$20 = 20$$

Both sides of the equation are equal, so $c = 10$ is the solution when $a = 20$ and $b = 2$.

Practice Problem In the formula $h = gd$, find the value of d if $g = 12.3$ and $h = 17.4$. 1.41

Using Proportions

A **proportion** is an equation that shows that two ratios are equivalent. The ratios $\frac{2}{4}$ and $\frac{5}{10}$ are equivalent, so they can be written as $\frac{2}{4} = \frac{5}{10}$. This equation is an example of a proportion.

When two ratios form a proportion, the **cross products** are equal. To find the cross products in the proportion $\frac{2}{4} = \frac{5}{10}$, multiply the 2 and the 10, and the 4 and the 5. Therefore $2 \cdot 10 = 4 \cdot 5$, **or 20 = 20.**

Because you know that both proportions are equal, you can use cross products to find a missing term in a proportion. This is known as **solving the proportion.** Solving a proportion is similar to solving an equation.

Example The heights of a tree and a pole are proportional to the lengths of their shadows. The tree casts a shadow of 24 m at the same time that a 6-m pole casts a shadow of 4 m. What is the height of the tree?

Step 1 Write a proportion.

$$\frac{\text{height of tree}}{\text{height of pole}} = \frac{\text{length of tree's shadow}}{\text{length of pole's shadow}}$$

Step 2 Substitute the known values into the proportion. Let h represent the unknown value, the height of the tree.

$$\frac{h}{6} = \frac{24}{4}$$

Step 3 Find the cross products.

$$h \cdot 4 = 6 \cdot 24$$

Step 4 Simplify the equation.

$$4h = 144$$

Step 5 Divide each side by 4.

$$\frac{4h}{4} = \frac{144}{4}$$

$$h = 36$$

The height of the tree is 36 m.

Practice Problem The proportions of bluefish are stable by the time they reach a length of 30 cm. The distance from the tip of the mouth to the back edge of the gill cover in a 35-cm bluefish is 15 cm. What is the distance from the tip of the mouth to the back edge of the gill cover in a 59-cm bluefish? 25 cm

Using Statistics

Statistics is the branch of mathematics that deals with collecting, analyzing, and presenting data. In statistics, there are three common ways to summarize the data with a single number—the mean, the median, and the mode.

The **mean** of a set of data is the arithmetic average. It is found by adding the numbers in the data set and dividing by the number of items in the set.

The **median** is the middle number in a set of data when the data are arranged in numerical order. If there were an even number of data points, the median would be the mean of the two middle numbers.

The **mode** of a set of data is the number or item that appears most often.

Another number that often is used to describe a set of data is the range. The **range** is the difference between the largest number and the smallest number in a set of data.

A **frequency table** shows how many times each piece of data occurs, usually in a survey. The frequency table below shows the results of a student survey on favorite color.

Color	Tally	Frequency
red	||||	4
blue	⊦⊦⊦⊦	5
black	||	2
green	|||	3
purple	⊦⊦⊦⊦ ||	7
yellow	⊦⊦⊦⊦ |	6

Based on the frequency table data, which color is the favorite?

Example The high temperatures (in °C) on five consecutive days in a desert habitat under study are 39°, 37°, 44°, 36°, and 44°. Find the mean, median, mode, and range of this set.

To find the mean:
Step 1 Find the sum of the numbers.

$$39 + 37 + 44 + 36 + 44 = 200$$

Step 2 Divide the sum by the number of items, which is 5.

$$200 \div 5 = 40$$

The mean high temperature is 40°C.

To find the median:
Step 1 Arrange the temperatures from least to greatest.

$$36, \ 37, \ \underline{39}, \ 44, \ 44$$

Step 2 Determine the middle temperature.

The median high temperature is 39°C.

To find the mode:
Step 1 Group the numbers that are the same together.

$$44, 44, 36, 37, 39$$

Step 2 Determine the number that occurs most in the set.

$$\underline{44, 44}, 36, 37, 39$$

The mode measure is 44°C.

To find the range:
Step 1 Arrange the temperatures from largest to smallest.

$$44, 44, 39, 37, 36$$

Step 2 Determine the largest and smallest temperature in the set.

$$\underline{44}, 44, 39, 37, \underline{36}$$

Step 3 Find the difference between the largest and smallest temperatures.

$$44 - 36 = 8$$

The range is 8°C.

Practice Problem Find the mean, median, mode, and range for the data set 8, 4, 12, 8, 11, 14, 16.

mean, 10; median, 11; mode, 8; range, 12

REFERENCE HANDBOOK A

Safety in the Science Classroom

1. Always obtain your teacher's permission to begin an investigation.

2. Study the procedure. If you have questions, ask your teacher. Be sure you understand any safety symbols shown on the page.

3. Use the safety equipment provided for you. Goggles and a safety apron should be worn during most investigations.

4. Always slant test tubes away from yourself and others when heating them or adding substances to them.

5. Never eat or drink in the lab, and never use lab glassware as food or drink containers. Never inhale chemicals. Do not taste any substances or draw any material into a tube with your mouth.

6. Report any spill, accident, or injury, no matter how small, immediately to your teacher, then follow his or her instructions.

7. Know the location and proper use of the fire extinguisher, safety shower, fire blanket, first aid kit, and fire alarm.

8. Keep all materials away from open flames. Tie back long hair and tie down loose clothing.

9. If your clothing should catch fire, smother it with the fire blanket, or get under a safety shower. NEVER RUN.

10. If a fire should occur, turn off the gas; then leave the room according to established procedures.

Follow these procedures as you clean up your work area

1. Turn off the water and gas. Disconnect electrical devices.

2. Clean all pieces of equipment and return all materials to their proper places.

3. Dispose of chemicals and other materials as directed by your teacher. Place broken glass and solid substances in the proper containers. Make sure never to discard materials in the sink.

4. Clean your work area. Wash your hands thoroughly after working in the laboratory.

First Aid	
Injury	Safe Response ALWAYS NOTIFY YOUR TEACHER IMMEDIATELY
Burns	Apply cold water.
Cuts and Bruises	Stop any bleeding by applying direct pressure. Cover cuts with a clean dressing. Apply ice packs or cold compresses to bruises.
Fainting	Leave the person lying down. Loosen any tight clothing and keep crowds away.
Foreign Matter in Eye	Flush with plenty of water. Use eyewash bottle or fountain.
Poisoning	Note the suspected poisoning agent.
Any Spills on Skin	Flush with large amounts of water or use safety shower.

REFERENCE HANDBOOK B

Reference Handbook

SI—Metric/English, English/Metric Conversions

	When you want to convert:	To:	Multiply by:
Length	inches	centimeters	2.54
	centimeters	inches	0.39
	yards	meters	0.91
	meters	yards	1.09
	miles	kilometers	1.61
	kilometers	miles	0.62
Mass and Weight*	ounces	grams	28.35
	grams	ounces	0.04
	pounds	kilograms	0.45
	kilograms	pounds	2.2
	tons (short)	tonnes (metric tons)	0.91
	tonnes (metric tons)	tons (short)	1.10
	pounds	newtons	4.45
	newtons	pounds	0.22
Volume	cubic inches	cubic centimeters	16.39
	cubic centimeters	cubic inches	0.06
	liters	quarts	1.06
	quarts	liters	0.95
	gallons	liters	3.78
Area	square inches	square centimeters	6.45
	square centimeters	square inches	0.16
	square yards	square meters	0.83
	square meters	square yards	1.19
	square miles	square kilometers	2.59
	square kilometers	square miles	0.39
	hectares	acres	2.47
	acres	hectares	0.40
Temperature	To convert °Celsius to °Fahrenheit	°C $\times$ 9/5 + 32	
	To convert °Fahrenheit to °Celsius	5/9 (°F − 32)	

*Weight is measured in standard Earth gravity.

Care and Use of a Microscope

Eyepiece Contains magnifying lenses you look through.

Arm Supports the body tube.

Low-power objective Contains the lens with the lowest power magnification.

Stage clips Hold the microscope slide in place.

Fine adjustment Sharpens the image under high magnification.

Coarse adjustment Focuses the image under low power.

Body tube Connects the eyepiece to the revolving nosepiece.

Revolving nosepiece Holds and turns the objectives into viewing position.

High-power objective Contains the lens with the highest magnification.

Stage Supports the microscope slide.

Light source Provides light that passes upward through the diaphragm, the specimen, and the lenses.

Base Provides support for the microscope.

Caring for a Microscope

1. Always carry the microscope holding the arm with one hand and supporting the base with the other hand.

2. Don't touch the lenses with your fingers.

3. The coarse adjustment knob is used only when looking through the lowest-power objective lens. The fine adjustment knob is used when the high-power objective is in place.

4. Cover the microscope when you store it.

Using a Microscope

1. Place the microscope on a flat surface that is clear of objects. The arm should be toward you.

2. Look through the eyepiece. Adjust the diaphragm so light comes through the opening in the stage.

3. Place a slide on the stage so the specimen is in the field of view. Hold it firmly in place by using the stage clips.

4. Always focus with the coarse adjustment and the low-power objective lens first. After the object is in focus on low power, turn the nosepiece until the high-power objective is in place. Use ONLY the fine adjustment to focus with the high-power objective lens.

Making a Wet-Mount Slide

1. Carefully place the item you want to look at in the center of a clean, glass slide. Make sure the sample is thin enough for light to pass through.

2. Use a dropper to place one or two drops of water on the sample.

3. Hold a clean coverslip by the edges and place it at one edge of the water. Slowly lower the coverslip onto the water until it lies flat.

4. If you have too much water or a lot of air bubbles, touch the edge of a paper towel to the edge of the coverslip to draw off extra water and draw out unwanted air.

Diversity of Life: Classification of Living Organisms

A six-kingdom system of classification of organisms is used today. Two kingdoms—Kingdom Archaebacteria and Kingdom Eubacteria—contain organisms that do not have a nucleus and that lack membrane-bound structures in the cytoplasm of their cells. The members of the other four kingdoms have a cell or cells that contain a nucleus and structures in the cytoplasm, some of which are surrounded by membranes. These kingdoms are Kingdom Protista, Kingdom Fungi, Kingdom Plantae, and Kingdom Animalia.

Kingdom Archaebacteria

one-celled; some absorb food from their surroundings; some are photosynthetic; some are chemosynthetic; many are found in extremely harsh environments including salt ponds, hot springs, swamps, and deep-sea hydrothermal vents

Kingdom Eubacteria

one-celled; most absorb food from their surroundings; some are photosynthetic; some are chemosynthetic; many are parasites; many are round, spiral, or rod-shaped; some form colonies

Kingdom Protista

Phylum Euglenophyta one-celled; photosynthetic or take in food; most have one flagellum; euglenoids

Phylum Bacillariophyta one-celled; photosynthetic; have unique double shells made of silica; diatoms

Phylum Dinoflagellata one-celled; photosynthetic; contain red pigments; have two flagella; dinoflagellates

Phylum Chlorophyta one-celled, many-celled, or colonies; photosynthetic; contain chlorophyll; live on land, in freshwater, or salt water; green algae

Phylum Rhodophyta most are many-celled; photosynthetic; contain red pigments; most live in deep, saltwater environments; red algae

Phylum Phaeophyta most are many-celled; photosynthetic; contain brown pigments; most live in saltwater environments; brown algae

Phylum Rhizopoda one-celled; take in food; are free-living or parasitic; move by means of pseudopods; amoebas

Kingdom Eubacteria
Bacillus anthracis

Phylum Chlorophyta
Desmids

Amoeba

Phylum Zoomastigina one-celled; take in food; free-living or parasitic; have one or more flagella; zoomastigotes

Phylum Ciliophora one-celled; take in food; have large numbers of cilia; ciliates

Phylum Sporozoa one-celled; take in food; have no means of movement; are parasites in animals; sporozoans

Phylum Myxomycota
Slime mold

Phylum Oomycota
Phytophthora infestans

Phyla Myxomycota and Acrasiomycota one- or many-celled; absorb food; change form during life cycle; cellular and plasmodial slime molds

Phylum Oomycota many-celled; are either parasites or decomposers; live in freshwater or salt water; water molds, rusts and downy mildews

Kingdom Fungi

Phylum Zygomycota many-celled; absorb food; spores are produced in sporangia; zygote fungi; bread mold

Phylum Ascomycota one- and many-celled; absorb food; spores produced in asci; sac fungi; yeast

Phylum Basidiomycota many-celled; absorb food; spores produced in basidia; club fungi; mushrooms

Phylum Deuteromycota members with unknown reproductive structures; imperfect fungi; *Penicillium*

Mycophycota organisms formed by symbiotic relationship between an ascomycote or a basidiomycote and green alga or cyanobacterium; lichens

Lichens

Kingdom Plantae

Divisions Bryophyta (mosses), **Anthocerophyta** (hornworts), **Hepatophytal** (liverworts), **Psilophytal** (whisk ferns) many-celled nonvascular plants; reproduce by spores produced in capsules; green; grow in moist, land environments

Division Lycophyta many-celled vascular plants; spores are produced in conelike structures; live on land; are photosynthetic; club mosses

Division Sphenophyta vascular plants; ribbed and jointed stems; scalelike leaves; spores produced in conelike structures; horsetails

Division Pterophyta vascular plants; leaves called fronds; spores produced in clusters of sporangia called sori; live on land or in water; ferns

Division Ginkgophyta deciduous trees; only one living species; have fan-shaped leaves with branching veins and fleshy cones with seeds; ginkgoes

Division Cycadophyta palmlike plants; have large, featherlike leaves; produces seeds in cones; cycads

Division Coniferophyta deciduous or evergreen; trees or shrubs; have needlelike or scalelike leaves; seeds produced in cones; conifers

Division Anthophyta
Tomato plant

Division Gnetophyta shrubs or woody vines; seeds are produced in cones; division contains only three genera; gnetum

Division Anthophyta dominant group of plants; flowering plants; have fruits with seeds

Kingdom Animalia

Phylum Porifera aquatic organisms that lack true tissues and organs; are asymmetrical and sessile; sponges

Phylum Cnidaria radially symmetrical organisms; have a digestive cavity with one opening; most have tentacles armed with stinging cells; live in aquatic environments singly or in colonies; includes jellyfish, corals, hydra, and sea anemones

Phylum Platyhelminthes bilaterally symmetrical worms; have flattened bodies; digestive system has one opening; parasitic and free-living species; flatworms

Division Bryophyta
Liverwort

Phylum Platyhelminthes
Flatworm

Reference Handbook

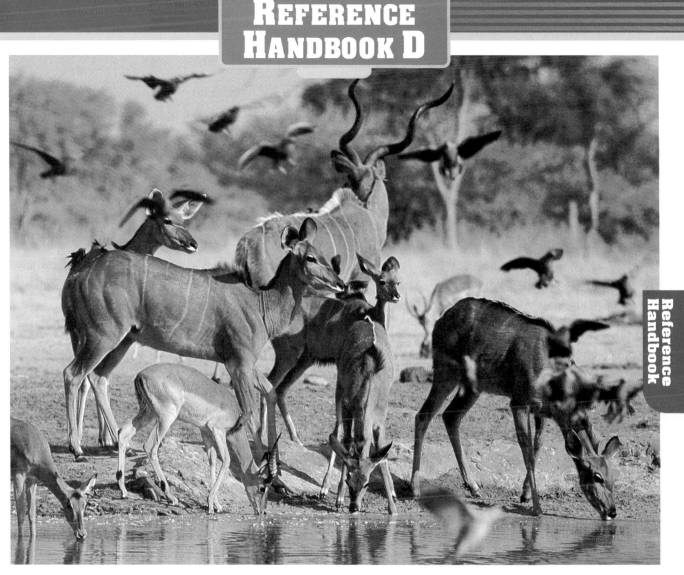

Phylum Chordata

Phylum Nematoda round, bilaterally symmetrical body; have digestive system with two openings; free-living forms and parasitic forms; roundworms

Phylum Mollusca soft-bodied animals, many with a hard shell and soft foot or footlike appendage; a mantle covers the soft body; aquatic and terrestrial species; includes clams, snails, squid, and octopuses

Phylum Annelida bilaterally symmetrical worms; have round, segmented bodies; terrestrial and aquatic species; includes earthworms, leeches, and marine polychaetes

Phylum Arthropoda largest animal group; have hard exoskeletons, segmented bodies, and pairs of jointed appendages; land and aquatic species; includes insects, crustaceans, and spiders

Phylum Echinodermata marine organisms; have spiny or leathery skin and a water-vascular system with tube feet; are radially symmetrical; includes sea stars, sand dollars, and sea urchins

Phylum Chordata organisms with internal skeletons and specialized body systems; most have paired appendages; all at some time have a notochord, nerve cord, gill slits, and a postanal tail; include fish, amphibians, reptiles, birds, and mammals

English Glossary

This glossary defines each key term that appears in bold type in the text. It also shows the chapter, section, and page number where you can find the word used.

A

aerobe (AY rohb): any organism that uses oxygen for respiration. (Chap. 1, Sec. 1, p. 10)

algae (AL jee): chlorophyll-containing, plantlike protists that produce oxygen as a result of photosynthesis. (Chap. 2, Sec. 1, p. 33)

anaerobe (AN uh rohb): any organism that is able live without oxygen. (Chap. 1, Sec. 1, p. 10)

angiosperms: flowering vascular plants that produce a fruit containing one or more seeds; monocots and dicots. (Chap. 3, Sec. 3, p. 79)

antibiotics: chemicals produced by some bacteria that are used to limit the growth of other bacteria. (Chap. 1, Sec. 2, p. 15)

ascus (AS kus): saclike, spore-producing structure of sac fungi. (Chap. 2, Sec. 2, p. 46)

auxin (AWK sun): plant hormone that causes plant leaves and stems to exhibit positive phototropisms. (Chap. 5, Sec. 2, p. 136)

B

basidium (buh SIHD ee uhm): club-shaped, reproductive structure in which club fungi produce spores. (Chap. 2, Sec. 2, p. 46)

budding: form of asexual reproduction in which a new, genetically identical organism forms on the side of its parent. (Chap. 2, Sec. 2, p. 46)

C

cambium (KAM bee um): vascular tissue that produces xylem and phloem cells as a plant grows. (Chap. 3, Sec. 3, p. 77)

cellulose (SEL yuh lohs): chemical compound made out of sugar; forms tangled fibers in the cell walls of many plants and provides structure and support. (Chap. 3, Sec. 1, p. 64)

chlorophyll (KLOR uh fihl): green, light-trapping pigment in plant chloroplasts that is important in photosynthesis. (Chap. 5, Sec. 1, p. 126)

cilia (SIHL ee uh): short, threadlike structures that extend from the cell membrane of a ciliate and allow the organism to move quickly. (Chap. 2, Sec. 1, p. 37)

cuticle (KYEWT ih kul): waxy, protective layer that covers the stems, leaves, and flowers of many plants and helps prevent water loss. (Chap. 3, Sec. 1, p. 64)

D

day-neutral plant: plant that doesn't require a specific photoperiod and can begin the flowering process over a range of night lengths. (Chap. 5, Sec. 2, p. 138)

dicot: angiosperm with two cotyledons inside its seed, flower parts in multiples of four or five, and vascular bundles in rings. (Chap. 3, Sec. 3, p. 80)

E

endospore: thick-walled, protective structure produced by a pathogen when conditions are unfavorable for survival. (Chap. 1, Sec. 2, p. 19)

F

fission: simplest form of asexual reproduction in which two new cells are produced with genetic material identical to each other and identical to the previous cell. (Chap. 1, Sec. 1, p. 10)

flagella: whiplike tails of many bacteria that help them move around in moist conditions. (Chap. 1, Sec. 1, p. 9)

flagellum: long, thin, whiplike structure of some protists that helps them move through moist or wet surroundings. (Chap. 2, Sec. 1, p. 34)

frond: leaf of a fern that grows from the rhizome. (Chap. 4, Sec. 2, p. 100)

G

gametophyte (guh MEE tuh fite) **stage:** plant life cycle stage that begins when cells in reproductive organs undergo meiosis and produce haploid cells (spores). (Chap. 4, Sec. 1, p. 97)

germination: series of events that results in the growth of a plant from a seed. (Chap. 4, Sec. 3, p. 112)

guard cells: pairs of cells that surround stomata and control their opening and closing. (Chap. 3, Sec. 3, p. 75)

gymnosperms: vascular plants that do not flower, generally have needlelike or scalelike leaves, and produce seeds that are not protected by fruit; conifers, cycads, ginkgoes, and gnetophytes. (Chap. 3, Sec. 3, p. 78)

H

hyphae (HI fee): mass of many-celled, threadlike tubes forming the body of a fungus. (Chap. 2, Sec. 2, p. 44)

L

lichen (LI kun): organism made up of a fungus and a green alga or a cyanobacterium. (Chap. 2, Sec. 2, p. 48)

long-day plant: plant that generally requires short nights—less than ten to 12 hours of darkness—to begin the flowering process. (Chap. 5, Sec. 2, p. 138)

M

monocot: angiosperm with one cotyledon inside its seed, flower parts arranged in multiples of three, and vascular tissues in bundles scattered throughout the stem. (Chap. 3, Sec. 3, p. 80)

mycorrhizae (mi kuh RI zee): network of hyphae and plant roots that helps plants absorb water and minerals from soil. (Chap. 2, Sec. 2, p. 48)

N

nitrogen-fixing bacteria: bacteria that convert nitrogen in the air into forms that can be used by plants and animals. (Chap. 1, Sec. 2, p. 16)

nonvascular plant: plant that absorbs water and other substances directly through its cell walls instead of through tubelike structures. (Chap. 3, Sec. 1, p. 67)

English Glossary

---O---

ovary: swollen base of an angiosperm's pistil, where egg-producing ovules are found. (Chap. 4, Sec. 3, p. 107)

ovule: in gymnosperms, the female reproductive part that produces eggs and food-storage tissues. (Chap. 4, Sec. 3, p. 105)

---P---

pathogen: disease-producing organism. (Chap. 1, Sec. 2, p. 19)

phloem (FLOH em): vascular tissue that forms tubes that transport dissolved sugar throughout a plant. (Chap. 3, Sec. 3, p. 77)

photoperiodism: a plant's response to the lengths of daylight and darkness each day. (Chap. 5, Sec. 2, p. 138)

photosynthesis (foh toh SIHN thuh suhs): food-making process that takes place in the chloroplasts of plant cells, where light energy is used to produce glucose and oxygen from carbon dioxide and water. (Chap. 5, Sec. 1, p. 127)

pioneer species: first organisms to grow in new or disturbed areas; break down rock and build up decaying plant material so that other plants can grow. (Chap. 3, Sec. 2, p. 69)

pistil: female reproductive organ inside the flower of an angiosperm; consists of a sticky stigma, where pollen grains land, and an ovary. (Chap. 4, Sec. 3, p. 107)

pollen grain: small structure produced by the male reproductive organs of a seed plant; has a water-resistant coat, can develop from a spore, and contains gametophyte parts that will produce sperm. (Chap. 4, Sec. 3, p. 103)

pollination: transfer of pollen grains to the female part of a seed plant by agents such as gravity, water, wind, and animals. (Chap. 4, Sec. 3, p. 103)

prothallus (proh THA lus): small, green, heart-shaped gametophyte plant form of a fern that can make its own food and absorb water and nutrients from the soil. (Chap. 4, Sec. 2, p. 100)

protist: one- or many-celled eukaryotic organism that can be plantlike, animal-like, or funguslike. (Chap. 2, Sec. 1, p. 32)

protozoan: one-celled, animal-like protist that can live in water, soil, and living and dead organisms. (Chap. 2, Sec. 1, p. 37)

pseudopods (SEWD uh pahdz): temporary cytoplasmic extensions used by some protists to move about and trap food. (Chap. 2, Sec. 1, p. 38)

---R---

respiration: series of chemical reactions used to release energy stored in food molecules. (Chap. 5, Sec. 1, p. 129)

rhizoids (RI zoydz): threadlike structures that anchor nonvascular plants to the ground. (Chap. 3, Sec. 2, p. 68)

rhizome: underground stem of a fern. (Chap. 4, Sec. 2, p. 100)

---S---

saprophyte: organism that feeds on dead or decaying tissues of other organisms. (Chap. 1, Sec. 2, p. 16) (Chap. 2, Sec. 2, p. 44)

short-day plant: plant that generally requires long nights—12 or more hours of darkness—to begin the flowering process. (Chap. 5, Sec. 2, p. 138)

sori: fern structures in which spores are produced. (Chap. 4, Sec. 2, p. 100)

sporangium (spuh RAN jee uhm): round spore case of a zygote fungus. (Chap. 2, Sec. 2, p. 47)

spores: haploid cells produced in the gametophyte stage that can divide by mitosis and form plant structures or an entire new plant or can develop into sex cells. (Chap. 2, Sec. 2, p. 45)(Chap. 4, Sec. 1, p. 97)

sporophyte (SPOR uh fite) **stage:** plant life cycle stage that begins when an egg is fertilized by a sperm. (Chap. 4, Sec. 1, p. 97)

stamen: male reproductive organ inside the flower of an angiosperm; consists of an anther, where pollen grains form, and a filament. (Chap. 4, Sec. 3, p. 107)

stomata (STOH muh tuh): small openings in the surface of most plant leaves that allow carbon dioxide, water, and oxygen to enter and exit. (Chap. 3, Sec. 3, p. 75)(Chap. 5, Sec, 1, p. 125)

T

toxin: poisonous substance produced by some pathogens. (Chap. 1, Sec. 2, p. 19)

tropism: positive or negative plant response to an external stimulus such as touch, light, or gravity. (Chap. 5, Sec. 2, p. 134)

V

vaccine: preparation made from killed bacteria or damaged particles from bacterial cell walls that can prevent some bacterial diseases. (Chap. 1, Sec. 2, p. 21)

vascular plant: plant with tubelike structures that move minerals, water, and other substances throughout the plant. (Chap. 3, Sec. 1, p. 67)

X

xylem (ZI lum): vascular tissue that forms hollow vessels that transport substances, other than sugar, throughout a plant. (Chap. 3, Sec. 3, p. 77)

Spanish Glossary

Este glossario define cada término clave que aparece en negrillas en el texto. También muestra el capítulo, la sección y el número de página en donde se usa dicho término.

A

aerobe / aerobio: cualquier organismo que usa oxígeno para la respiración. (Cap. 1, Sec. 1, pág. 10)

algae / algas: protistas que parecen plantas que producen oxígeno mediante la fotosíntesis. (Cap. 2, Sec. 1, pág. 33)

anaerobe / anaerobio: cualquier organismo que puede vivir sin oxígeno. (Cap. 1, Sec. 1, pág. 10)

angiosperms / angiospermas: plantas vasculares con flores que produce un fruto que contiene una o más semillas; monocotiledóneas y dicotiledóneas. (Cap. 3, Sec. 3, pág. 79)

antibiotics / antibióticos: sustancias químicas producidas por algunas bacterias que se usan para limitar el crecimiento de otras bacterias. (Cap. 1, Sec. 2, pág. 15)

ascus / asco: estructura productora de esporas, en forma de saco, en los hongos ascomicetos. (Cap. 2, Sec. 2, pág. 46)

auxin / auxina: hormona vegetal gracias a la cual las hojas y tallos de las plantas exhiben fototropismos positivos. (Cap. 5, Sec. 2, pág. 136)

B

basidium / basidio: estructura reproductora en forma de bastón, en la cual los hongos producen esporas. (Cap. 2, Sec. 2, pág. 46)

budding / gemación: forma de reproducción asexual en que un organismo nuevo y genéticamente idéntico crece de un lado del organismo progenitor . (Cap. 2, Sec. 2, pág. 46)

C

cambium / cámbium: tejido vascular que produce las células del xilema y del floema a medida que crece la planta. (Cap. 3, Sec. 3, pág. 77)

cellulose / celulosa: compuesto químico hecho de azúcares; este compuesto forma fibras enredadas en las paredes celulares de muchas plantas y les provee estructura y apoyo. (Cap. 3, Sec. 1, pág. 64)

chlorophyll / clorofila: pigmento verde y absorbente de luz, fijado a los cloroplastos de las plantas, el cual es importante en el proceso de la fotosíntesis. (Cap. 5, Sec. 1, pág. 126)

cilia / cilios: estructuras cortas filamentosas que se extienden de la membrana celular de un ciliado y las cuales permiten que el organismo se mueva rápidamente. (Cap. 2, Sec. 1, pág. 37)

cuticle / cutícula: capa protectora y ceresa que cubre los tallos, hojas y flores de muchas plantas y que les ayuda a prevenir la pérdida de agua. (Cap. 3, Sec. 1, pág. 64)

Spanish
Glossary

D

day-neutral plant / planta de día neutro: planta que no necesita un fotoperíodo específico y que puede comenzar el proceso de floración a lo largo de un rango de períodos nocturnos. (Cap. 5, Sec.2, pág. 138)

dicot / dicotinedónea: angiosperma con dos cotiledóneos dentro de la semilla, partes florales en múltiples de cuatro u cinco y bultos vasculares en forma de anillos. (Cap. 3, Sec. 3, pág. 80)

E

endospore / endósporas: estructuras protectoras de paredes gruesas que producen los patógenos cuando las condiciones son desfavorables para la sobrevivencia. (Cap. 1, Sec. 2, pág. 19)

F

fission / fisión: la forma más sencilla de reproducción asexual en la cual se producen dos células nuevas con material genético idéntico al de la célula original. (Cap. 1, Sec. 1, pág. 10)

flagella / flagelos: filamentos móviles de muchas bacterias que les facilitan la locomoción en condiciones húmedas. (Cap. 1, Sec. 1, pág. 9)

flagellum / flagelo: estructura larga y delgada en forma de látigo de algunos protistas, la cual les facilita el movimiento a través de medios mojados o húmedos. (Cap. 2, Sec. 1, pág. 34)

frond / fronda: hoja de helecho que crece desde el rizoma. (Cap. 4, Sec. 2, pág. 100)

G

gametophyte stage / etapa gametofita: etapa del ciclo de vida vegetal que comienza cuando las células de los órganos reproductores pasan por la meiosis y producen células haploides. (Cap. 4, Sec. 1, pág. 97)

germination / germinación: serie de procesos que dan como resultado el crecimiento de una planta a partir de una semilla. (Cap. 4, Sec. 3, pág. 112)

guard cells / células guardianas: pares de células que rodean los estomas y controlan su apertura y cierre. (Cap. 3, Sec. 3, pág. 75)

gymnosperms / angiospermas: plantas vasculares que no florecen; generalmente tienen hojas en forma de agujas o de escamas y producen semillas que no están protegidas por el fruto; algunos ejemplos son las coníferas las cicadáceas, los ginkgoes y las gnetofitas. (Cap. 3, Sec. 3, pág. 78)

H

hyphae / hifa: masa de tubos multicelulares filamentosas que forman el cuerpo de un hongo. (Cap. 2, Sec. 2, pág. 44)

Spanish Glossary

L

lichen / liquen: organismo compuesto de un hongo y un alga verde o una cianobacteria. (Cap. 2, Sec. 2, pág. 48)

long-day plant / planta de día largo: planta que necesita, por lo general, noches cortas (menos de diez a 12 horas de oscuridad) para comenzar el proceso de floración. (Cap. 5, Sec. 2, pág. 138)

M

monocot / monocotiledónea: angiosperma con un cotiledón dentro de la semilla; las partes de la flor están arregladas en múltiplos de tres y los tejidos vasculares se encuentran esparciados a lo largo del tallo formando bultos. (Cap. 3, Sec. 3, pág. 80)

mycorrhizae / micorriza: red de hifas y raíces vegetales que ayudan a las plantas a absorber agua y minerales del suelo. (Cap. 2, Sec. 2, pág. 48)

N

nitrogen-fixing bacteria / bacterias nitrificantes: bacteria que convierte el nitrógeno del aire en formas que pueden usar las plantas y los animales. (Cap. 1, Sec. 2, pág. 16)

nonvascular plant / plantas no vasculares: planta que absorbe el agua y otras sustancias directamente a través de sus paredes celulares en lugar de a través de estructuras en forma de tubo. (Cap. 3, Sec. 1, pág. 67)

O

ovary / ovario: base hinchada del pistilo de una angiosperma donde se hallan los óvulos productores de huevos. (Cap. 4, Sec. 3, pág. 107)

ovule / óvulo: en las gimnospermas, la parte reproductora femenina que produce huevos y tejidos almacenadores de alimento. (Cap. 4, Sec. 3, pág. 105)

P

pathogen / patógeno: organismo que causa enfermedad. (Cap. 1, Sec. 2, pág. 19)

phloem / floema: tejido vascular que forma tubos que transportan azúcares disueltos por toda la planta. (Cap. 3, Sec. 3, pág. 77)

photoperiodism / fotoperiodismo: reacción de una planta a la duración de horas de luz y oscuridad cada día. (Cap. 5, Sec. 2, pág. 138)

photosynthesis / fotosíntesis: proceso de elaboración de alimento que se efectúa en los cloroplastos de las células vegetales, donde la energía luminosa se usa para producir glucosa y oxígeno a partir de dióxido de carbono y agua. (Cap. 5, Sec. 1, pág. 127)

pioneer species / especie pionera: primeros organismos que crecen en áreas nuevas o que han sido perturbadas; desintegran las rocas y acumulan material en descomposición para que otras plantas puedan crecer en el lugar. (Cap. 3, Sec. 2, pág. 69)

pistil / pistilo: órgano reproductor femenino que se encuentra dentro de la flor de las angiospermas; consta de un estigma pegajoso (donde aterrizan los granos de polen) y de un ovario. (Cap. 4, Sec. 3, pág. 107)

pollen grain / grano de polen: estructura pequeña producida por los órganos reproductores masculinos de una planta de semilla; posee un revestimiento resistente al agua, se puede desarrollar a partir de una espora y contiene partes gametofitas que producen espermatozoides. (Cap. 4, Sec. 3, pág. 103)

pollination / polinización: traspaso de los granos de polen a la parte femenina de una planta de semilla efectuado por agentes como la gravedad, el agua, el viento y los animales. (Cap. 4 Sec. 3, pág. 103)

prothallus / protalo: forma vegetal gametofita de un helecho, pequeña, verde y en forma de corazón, capaz de producir su propio alimento y absorber agua y nutrientes del suelo. (Cap. 4, Sec. 2, pág. 100)

protist / protista: organismo eucariota unicelular o multicelular que puede parecerse a las plantas, a los animales o a los hongos. (Cap. 2, Sec. 1, pág. 32)

protozoan / protozoario: protista unicelular que parece un animal y que puede vivir en el agua, en la tierra y en organismos vivos o muertos. (Cap. 2, Sec. 1, pág. 37)

pseudopods / seudópodos: extensión citoplásmica temporal que usan algunos protistas para la locomoción y para atrapar alimentos. (Cap. 2, Sec. 1, pág. 38)

R

respiration / respiración celular: serie de reacciones químicas utilizadas para liberar la energía almacenada en las moléculas de los alimentos. (Cap. 5, Sec. 1, pág. 129)

rhizoids / rizoides: estructuras parecidas a hilos que anclan las plantas no vasculares al suelo. (Cap. 3, Sec. 2, pág. 68)

rhizome / rizoma: tallo subterráneo de un helecho. (Cap. 4, Sec. 2, pág. 100)

S

saprophyte / saprofito: organismo que se alimenta de los tejidos de otros organismos muertos o en proceso de descomposición. (Cap. 1, Sec. 2, pág. 16; Cap. 2, Sec. 2, pág. 44)

short-day plant / planta de día corto: tipo de planta que necesita, por lo general, noches largas (12 ó más horas de oscuridad) para comenzar el proceso de floración. (Cap. 5, Sec. 2, pág. 138)

sori / soros: estructuras de los helechos en los cuales se producen las esporas. (Cap. 4, Sec. 2, pág. 100)

sporangium / esporangio: cápsula de espora redonda de un hongo cigote. (Cap. 2, Sec. 2, pág. 47)

spores / esporas: células haploides producidas en la etapa gametofita que se puede dividir por mitosis y formar estructuras vegetales o una planta nueva completa o que se puede desarrollar en células sexuales. (Cap. 2, Sec. 2, pág. 45; Cap. 4, Sec. 1, pág. 97)

sporophyte stage / etapa esporofita: etapa del ciclo de vida vegetal que comienza cuando un espermatozoide fecunda un huevo. (Cap. 4, Sec. 1, pág. 97)

stamen / estambre: órgano reproductor masculino que se encuentra dentro de la flor de las angiospermas; consta de una antera (donde se forman los granos de polen) y de un filamento. (Cap. 4, Sec. 3, pág. 107)

stomata / estomata: pequeñas aperturas en la superficie de la mayoría de las hojas de las plantas que permiten la entrada y salida del dióxido de carbono, del agua y del oxígeno. (Cap. 3, Sec. 3, pág. 75; Cap. 5, Sec. 1 pág. 125)

vascular plant / planta vascular: planta con estructuras en forma de tubo por donde se mueven los minerales, el agua y otras sustancias por toda la planta. (Cap. 3, Sec. 1, pág. 67)

T

toxin / toxina: sustancia venenosa que producen algunos patógenos. (Cap. 1, Sec. 2, pág. 19)

tropism / tropismo: reacción positiva o negativa a un estímulo externo como el tacto, la luz o la gravedad. (Cap. 5, Sec. 2, pág. 134)

X

xylem / xilema: tejido vascular que forma vasos huecos que transportan sustancias, excluyendo los azúcares, por toda la planta. (Cap. 3, Sec. 3, pág. 77)

V

vaccine / vacuna: preparación que se elabora a partir de bacterias muertas o partículas dañadas de las paredes celulares de bacterias; se usa para prevenir algunas enfermedades. (Cap. 1, Sec. 2, pág. 21)

The index for *From Bacteria to Plants* will help you locate major topics in the book quickly and easily. Each entry in the index is followed by the number of the pages on which the entry is discussed. A page number given in boldfaced type indicates the page on which that entry is defined. A page number given in italic type indicates a page on which the entry is used in an illustration or photograph. The abbreviation *act.* indicates a page on which the entry is used in an activity.

A

Abscisic acid, 136

Activities, 14, 22–23, 43, 52–53, 83, 84–85, 102, 114–115, 132, 140–141

Aerobe, 10, *10*

Aerobic respiration, 129, 130, *130,* 131

Agriculture: fungi in, 50, *50*

Algae, 33–36, *33, 34, 35, 36, act.* 43; green, 64

Amoeba, 38, *38,* 40

Anaerobe, 10, *10,* 13

Angiosperms, 79–82, *79, 80, 81, 82,* 106–110, *107, 108, 109, 110*

Animal-like protists, 33, 37–40, *37, 38, 39, act.* 43

Annuals, 81, *81*

Antibiotics, 15, 21, *21,* 51

Appendices. *see* Reference Handbooks

Archaebacteria, 13, *13*

Ascus, 46

Asexual reproduction, 39, *39,* 94, *94,* 95, *95,* 100, *100*

Auxin, 136, *136*

B

Bacilli, 8

Bacteria, 6–11, *6;* aerobic, 10, *10;* anaerobic, 10, *10,* 13; archaebacteria, 13, *13;* beneficial, *15–18, 15, 16, 17, 18, act.* 22–23; characteristics of, 8–10, *8, 9, 10;* as consumers, 10, 12; cyanobacteria, 11–12, *12, act.* 14; diseases and, 15, 19, 21, *21;* eubacteria, 11–12, *11, 12;* growth of, 16, 20; harmful, 19–21, *20, 21;* methane-producing, 13, *13, 18, 19;* nitrogen-fixing, **16,** *17;* as producers, 10, 13, *13;* reproduction of, 10, *10;* saprophytic, 16, *16;* shapes of, 8, *8;* size of, 9; on surfaces, *act.* 7

Bacterial cells: structure and function of, 9, *9*

Basidium, 46, *46*

Before You Read, 7, 31, 61, 93, 123

Biennials, 81, *81*

Binomial nomenclature, 67, *67*

Bioreactor, 18

Bioremediation, 16

Blue-green bacteria, 11–12

Bog, 73, *73*

Botulism, 19

Brown algae, 35, *35*

Budding, 46, *46*

C

Cactus, 75

Cambium, 77, *77*

Carbon dioxide, and plants, 124, 125, 127, 128, *128,* 130

Career, 2–3, 87, 116–117, 143

Carrageenan, 36, *36*

Cell(s): bacterial, 9, *9;* guard, **75,** 125, *125*

Cellulose, 64, 65, *65,* 128

Cell walls, 34, 63, 64, 65

Cheese: and bacteria, 18, *18*

Chemistry Integration, 18, 64,

Chlorophyll, 10, 11, 33, 35, 45, 63, **126,** *126,* 127

Chloroplasts, 63, 126, *126,* 127

Cilia, 37, *37*

Ciliates, 37, *37*

Classification of plants, 66, 67, *67:* of protists, *32, 33:* scientific names in, 67, *67*

Club fungi, 46, *46*

Club mosses, 72, *72*

Cocci, 8, *8*

Composting: *act.* 22–23

Cone-bearing plants, 63, 78, *78*

Cones, 104–106, *105, 106*

Conifers, 78, *78, 82, act.* 83

Consumers, 10, 12

Contractile vacuole, 37, *37*

Cuticle, 64, 65

Cuttings, 94

Cyanobacteria, 11–12, *12, act.* 14

Cycads, 78, *78*

Cycles: life cycles of plants, 96–97, *97,* 99, *99,* 100, *101*

Cytokinins, 136

Cytoplasm, *130*

Index

Index

Art Credits

Glencoe would like to acknowledge the artists and agencies who participated in illustrating this program: Absolute Science Illustration; Andrew Evansen; Argosy; Articulate Graphics; Craig Attebery represented by Frank & Jeff Lavaty; CHK America; Gagliano Graphics; Pedro Julio Gonzalez represented by Melissa Turk & The Artist Network; Robert Hynes represented by Mendola Ltd.; Morgan Cain & Associates; JTH Illustration; Laurie O'Keefe; Matthew Pippin represented by Beranbaum Artist's Representative; Precision Graphics; Publisher's Art; Rolin Graphics, Inc.; Wendy Smith represented by Melissa Turk & The Artist Network; Kevin Torline represented by Berendsen and Associates, Inc.; WILDlife ART; Phil Wilson represented by Cliff Knecht Artist Representative; Zoo Botanica.

Photo Credits

Abbreviation Key: AA=Animals Animals; AH=Aaron Haupt; AMP=Amanita Pictures; BC=Bruce Coleman, Inc.; CB=CORBIS; DM=Doug Martin; DRK=DRK Photo; ES=Earth Scenes; FP=Fundamental Photographs; GH=Grant Heilman Photography; IC=Icon Images; KS=KS Studios; LA=Liaison Agency; MB=Mark Burnett; MM=Matt Meadows; PE=PhotoEdit; PD=PhotoDisc; PQ=PictureQuest; PR=Photo Researchers; SB=Stock Boston; TSA=Tom Stack & Associates; TSM=The Stock Market; VU=Visuals Unlimited.

Cover PD; **v** Farrell Grehan/PR; **vi** Dan Suzio/PR; **vii** DM; **2** GH; **3** (t) Dr. Jeremy Burgess/Science Photo Library/PR, (b)Jack M. Bostracr; **4** Kevin Fitzsimons; **5** (t)Dwayne Newton/PE, (b)Jim Strawser/GH; **6** M. Cobos/M. Yokoyama; **6-7** David Matherly/VU; **7** AH; **8** (l)Oliver Meckes/PR, (c)CNRI/Science Photo Library/PR, (r)CNRI/Science Photo Library/PR; **10** Dr. L. Caro/Science Photo Library/PR; **11** (tl) Dr. Dennis Kunkel/PhotoTake NYC, (tc)David M. Phillips/VU, (tr) Dr. Kessel- G. Shih/VU, (bl)Ann Siegleman/VU, (br)SCIMAT/PR; **12** (t)T.E. Adams/VU, (b)Manfred Kage/Peter Arnold, Inc.; **13** R. Kessel/ G. Shih/VU; **14** T.E. Adams/VU; **15** (tl)M. Abbey Photo/PR, (tc)Oliver Meckes/Eye of Science/PR, (tr)S. Lowry/University of Ulster/Stone, (bl)Richard J. Green/PR, (br)A.B. Dowsett/Science Photo Library/PR; **16** Ray Pfortner/Peter Arnold, Inc.; **17** (tl)Jeremy Burgess/Science Photo Library/PR, (tr)Ann M. Hirsch/UCLA, (c)Jeremy Burgess/Science Photo Library/PR, (bl)John D. Cunningham/VU, (br)Astrid & Hanns-Frieder Michler/Science Photo Library/PR; **18** (l)Paul Almasy/ CB, (r)Joe Munroe/PR; **19** (t)Terry Wild Studio, (b)J.R. Adams/VU; **20** AMP; **21** John Durham/Science Photo Library/PR; **22** (t)KS, (b)John Evans; **23** John Evans; **24** (tl)P. Canumette/VU, (tr)John Evans, (b)Ken Graham/BC; **24-25** Dr. Philippa Uwins, The University of Queensland; **25** (t)Heide Schulx/Max Planck Institute of Science, (b)West Chester University; **26** (tl)David M. Phillips/VU, (tr)David Woodfall/DRK, (bl)George J. Wilder/VU, (br)Argus Fotoarchiv/Peter Arnold, Inc.; **27** (l)Edward Webber/VU, (r)Phillip Slattery/VU; **30** Volker Steger/Peter Arnold, Inc.; **30-31** Art Wolfe; **31** (t)AMP, (b)Jana R. Jirak/VU; **33** (l)Jean Claude Revy/PhotoTake NYC, (r)Anne Hubbard/PR; **34** (tl)NHMPL/Stone, (tr)Microfield Scienctific Ltd./Science Photo Library/PR, (bl)David M. Phillips/PR, (br)M.I. Walker/Science Source/PR; **35** (l)Pat & Tom Leeson/PR, (r)Jeffrey L. Rotman/Peter Arnold, Inc.; **36** Walter H. Hodge/Peter Arnold, Inc.; **37** Eric V. Grave/PR; **38** (t)Kerry B. Clark, (b)Astrid & Hanns-Frieder Michler/ Science Photo Library/PR; **39** Lennart Nilsson/Albert Bonniers Forlag AB; **40** (l)Ray Simons/PR, (c)MM/Peter Arnold, Inc., (r)Gregory G. Dimijian/PR; **41** (t)Dwight Kuhn, (b)AMP; **42** Richard Calentine/ VU; **43** Biophoto Associates/Science Source/PR; **44** (l)Joe McDonald/ BC, (r)James W. Richardson/VU; **45** Carolina Biological Supply/PhotoTake NYC; **46** (tl)file photo, (tr)Ken Wagner/VU, (b)Dennis Kunkel; **47** (l)Science VU/VU, (r)J.W. Richardson/VU; **48** (tl)Frank Orel/Stone, (tc)Charles Kingery/PhotoTake NYC, (tr)Bill Bachman/PR, (b)Nancy Rotenberg/ES; **49** (tl)Stephen Sharnoff, (tr)Biophoto Associates/PR, (c)Stephen Sharnoff, (bl)L. West/PR, (br)Larry Lee Photography/CB; **50** (l)Nigel Cattlin/Holt Studios International/PR, (r)Michael Fogden/ES; **51** Ray Elliott/Stone; **52** (t)Ken Wagner/VU, (b)AMP; **53** AMP; **54** (l)Walter Sanders/Time Pix, (r)Alvarode Leiva/LA; **55** Courtesy Beltsville Agricultural Research Center-West/USDA; **56** (t)Andrew J. Martinez/PR, (c)Dennis Kunkel, (b)Nigel Cattlin/Holt Studios/PR; **57** (l)Michael Delaney/VU, (r)AMP; **58** Nigel Cattlin/Holt Studios/PR; **60** Harry N. Darrow/BC; **60-61** Tom Bean/DRK; **61** MB; **62** TSA; **63** Laat-Siluur; **64** (t)Kim Taylor/BC, (b)William E. Ferguson; **65** (tl)AMP, (tr)Ken Eward/PR, (bl)PR, (br)AMP; **66** (tl)Douglas Peebles/CB, (tc)Gerald & Buff Corsi/VU, (tr)Dan McCoy from Rainbow, (c, l to r)Edward S. Ross, Martha McBride/Unicorn Stock Photos, David Sieren/VU, Philip Dowell/DK Images, (bl)Gerald & Buff Corsi/VU, (blc)Mack Henley/VU, (brc)Steve Callaham/VU, (br)Kevin & Betty Collins/VU; **67** (l)Gail Jankus/PR, (b)Michael P. Fogden/BC; **68** (l)Larry West/BC, (c)Scott Camazine/PR, (r)Kathy Merrifield/PR; **69** Michael P. Gadomski/PR; **71** (t)Farrell Grehan/PR, (c)R. Van Nostrand, (bl)Steve Solum/BC, (br)Inga Spence/VU; **72** (t)Joy Spurr/BC, (b)W.H. Black/BC; **73** Farrell Grehan/PR; **74** AMP; **75** (l)Nigel Cattlin/PR, (c)Doug Sokel/TSA, (r)Charles D. Winters/PR; **76** Bill Beatty/VU; **78** (tl)Robert C. Hermes, (tr)Bill Beatty/VU, (c)Doug Sokell/TSA, (b)David M. Schleser/PR; **79** (t)E. Valentin/PR, (c)Dia Lein/PR, (bl)Wardene Weisser/BC, (blc)Joy Spurr/PR, (brc br)Eva Wallander; **81** (l)Dwight Kuhn, (c)Joy Spurr/BC, (r)John D. Cunningham/VU; **82** (l)J. Lotter/TSA, (r)J.C. Carton/BC; **84** (l)Inga Spence/VU, (r)Jim Steinberg/PR; **85** David Sieren/VU; **86** Michael Rose/Frank Lane Picture Agency/CB; **87** (t)Dr. Jeremy Burgess/Science Photo Library/PR, (b)Ron Levy/PR; **88** (t)Robert Hitchman/BC, (c)Stephen P. Parker/PR, (b)Milton Rand/TSA; **89** (l)Adam Jones/PR, (r)William J. Weber; **92** Noble Proctor/PR; **92-93** Layne Kennedy/CB; **93** DM; **94** (l)Stephen Dalton/PR, (r)MM; **95** (l)Holt Studios/Nigel Cattlin/PR, (r)Inga Spence/VU; **96** (l)H. Reinhard/ OKAPIA/PR, (c)John W. Bova/PR, (r)John D. Cunningham/VU; **98** (l)Biology Media/PR, (c)Andrew Syred/Science Photo Library/PR, (r)Runk/Schoenberger from Grant Heilman; **100 101** Kathy Merrifield 2000/PR; **102** MM; **103** (l)John Kaprielian/PR, (r)Scott Camazine/Sue Trainor/PR; **104** Dr. Wm. H. Harlow/PR; **105** Christian Grzimek/ OKAPIA/PR; **106** (l)M. J. Griffith/PR, (c)Stephen P. Parker/PR, (r)Dan Suzio/PR; **107** (t)Rob Simpson/VU, (c)Gustav Verderber/VU, (b)Alvin E. Staffan/PR; **108** (tl) C. Nuridsany & M. Perennou/Science Photo Library/PR, (tr)Merlin D. Tuttle/PR, (bl)Anthony Mercreca Photo/PR, (bc)Kjell B. Sandved/PR, (br)Holt Studios /PR; **109** William J. Weber/VU; **111** (tl)Kevin Shafer/CB, (tr)Dwight Kuhn, (c)Darryl Torckler/Stone, (bl)Dwight Kuhn, (bc)Tom & Pat Leeson, (br)Dwight Kuhn; **112 114** DM; **115** MM; **116** Michael Black/BC; **117** (t)courtesy NIGMS OCPL, (b)Kevin Laubacher/FPG; **118** (t)Zig Leszczynski/ES, (c)Tim Davis/PR, (b)MM/Peter Arnold, Inc.; **119** (l)Nils Reinhard/ OKAPIA/PR, (c)Adrienne T. Gibson/ES, (r)Oliver Meckes/PR; **120** Marcia Griffen/ES; **122** AMP; **122-123** Terry Thompson/Panoramic Images; **123** MM; **125** Dr. Jeremy Burgess/Science Photo Library/PR; **126** (l)John Kieffer/Peter Arnold, Inc., (r)Runk/Schoenberger from Grant Heilman; **127** M. Eichelberger/VU; **129** (t)Jacques Jangoux/Peter Arnold, Inc., (b)Jeff Lepore/PR; **130** Michael P. Gadomski/PR; **133** Howard Miller/PR; **134** (l)Scott Camazine/PR, (c r)MM; **137** (tl tr)Artville, (cl)Runk/Schoenberger from Grant Heilman, (c cr)Prof. Malcolm B. Wilkins/University of Glasgow, (bl)Eric Brennan, (br)John Sohlden/VU; **138** Jim Metzger; **140** (t)Ed Reschke/Peter Arnold, Inc., (b)MM; **141** MM; **142** Stone; **143** Kennedy Colombo; **144** (tl)Ed Reschke/Peter Arnold, Inc., (tr)Runk/Schoenberger from Grant Heilman, (bl)Holt Studios International/Nigel Cattlin/PR, (br)Laura Dwight/Peter Arnold, Inc.; **145** (l)Norm Thomas/PR, (r)S.R. Maglione/PR; **148** Christopher Hallowell; **150-151** PD; **153** (tl)ES, (tr)Patti Murray/ES, (bl)Larry Ulrich/DRK, (br)Doug Sokell/TSA; **154** (tl)Bill Beatty/ES, (tr)Tom Bean/DRK, (bl)R. Calentine/VU, (br)Gerald and Buff Corsi/VU; **155** (tl)C.C. Lockwood/DRK, (tr)Joseph G. Strauch Jr., (bl)John Frett, (br)Gerald and Buff Corsi/VU; **156** Timothy Fuller; **160** First Image; **163** Dominic Oldershaw; **164** StudiOhio; **165** First Image; **167** Richard Day/AA; **170** Paul Barton/TSM; **183** Charles Gupton/TSM; **184** (t)NIBSC/Science Photo Library/PR, (bl)Dr. Richard Kessel, (br)David John/VU; **185** (t)Runk/Schoenberger from Grant Heilman, (bl)Andrew Syred/ Science Photo Library/PR, (br)Rich Brommer; **186** (t)G.R. Roberts, (bl)Ralph Reinhold/ES, (br)Scott Johnson/AA; **187** Martin Harvey/DRK.

Acknowledgements

The excerpt from "Sunkissed: An Indian Legend" is reprinted with permission from the publisher of *Tun-ta-ca-tun* (Houston: Arte Publico Press—University of Houston, 1986)

Credits

PERIODIC TABLE OF THE ELEMENTS

Columns of elements are called groups. Elements in the same group have similar chemical properties.

Gas
Liquid
Solid
Synthetic

Element — Hydrogen
Atomic number — 1
Symbol — H
Atomic mass — 1.008
State of matter

The first three symbols tell you the state of matter of the element at room temperature. The fourth symbol identifies human-made, or synthetic, elements.

1

1		
Hydrogen 1 H 1.008	**2**	
Lithium 3 Li 6.941	Beryllium 4 Be 9.012	
Sodium 11 Na 22.990	Magnesium 12 Mg 24.305	

3	**4**	**5**	**6**	**7**	**8**	**9**
Scandium 21 Sc 44.956	Titanium 22 Ti 47.867	Vanadium 23 V 50.942	Chromium 24 Cr 51.996	Manganese 25 Mn 54.938	Iron 26 Fe 55.845	Cobalt 27 Co 58.933
Yttrium 39 Y 88.906	Zirconium 40 Zr 91.224	Niobium 41 Nb 92.906	Molybdenum 42 Mo 95.94	Technetium 43 Tc (98)	Ruthenium 44 Ru 101.07	Rhodium 45 Rh 102.906
Lanthanum 57 La 138.906	Hafnium 72 Hf 178.49	Tantalum 73 Ta 180.948	Tungsten 74 W 183.84	Rhenium 75 Re 186.207	Osmium 76 Os 190.23	Iridium 77 Ir 192.217
Actinium 89 Ac (227)	Rutherfordium 104 Rf (261)	Dubnium 105 Db (262)	Seaborgium 106 Sg (266)	Bohrium 107 Bh (264)	Hassium 108 Hs (277)	Meitnerium 109 Mt (268)

Period 4: Potassium 19 K 39.098 | Calcium 20 Ca 40.078
Period 5: Rubidium 37 Rb 85.468 | Strontium 38 Sr 87.62
Period 6: Cesium 55 Cs 132.905 | Barium 56 Ba 137.327
Period 7: Francium 87 Fr (223) | Radium 88 Ra (226)

The number in parentheses is the mass number of the longest lived isotope for that element.

Rows of elements are called periods. Atomic number increases across a period.

The arrow shows where these elements would fit into the periodic table. They are moved to the bottom of the page to save space.

Lanthanide series

Cerium 58 Ce 140.116	Praseodymium 59 Pr 140.908	Neodymium 60 Nd 144.24	Promethium 61 Pm (145)	Samarium 62 Sm 150.36

Actinide series

Thorium 90 Th 232.038	Protactinium 91 Pa 231.036	Uranium 92 U 238.029	Neptunium 93 Np (237)	Plutonium 94 Pu (244)